Praise for *Search Engine Optimization: An Hour a Day*

New to the sometimes confusing and seemingly arcane world of making search engine–friendly websites? This book offers a systematic, common-sense approach to the art and science of SEO.
   —Chris Sherman, SearchEngineWatch.com

Just when some say textbook search engine optimization (SEO) has crashed and burned, a great new textbook comes along. Finally, a common-sense approach to day-by-day search engine optimization. The authors offer a comprehensive yet light-hearted guide to preparing a successful SEO strategy. If you are just getting started, this book is a must read to minimize your risks and maximize your rewards. SEO: An Hour a Day is habit-forming. Readers should be prepared to get hooked on SEO.
   —P.J. Fusco, *ClickZ Magazine* columnist

If you've ever put off doing search engine optimization (SEO) because you know it's so time-consuming, here's the book for you.
   —Web Marketing Today, October 11, 2006

I'm always being asked to review the latest book on marketing. With a hectic schedule, it can be tough to get any time to read any of them, but I just made time to read Search Engine Optimization: An Hour a Day.

You have to give credit to authors Gradiva Couzin and Jennifer Grappone for putting together an excellent book that combines practical advice sprinkled with humor—very much needed to prevent this topic from being too dry.

...[T]he "right brain" "left brain" sidebars that pop up throughout the book are a welcome addition. Reading two experts attacking a subject from two perspectives—art vs. science—adds an interesting and comical twist.

I didn't pay for my copy of the book, but would have no hesitation in buying a copy for anyone new to the industry!
   —Andy Beal, Marketing Pilgrim

Outstanding SEO book... Grappone and Couzin do a great job of describing approaches... to ensure your business succeeds. Do yourself a favor and pick up a copy for yourself.
   —Tim Peter, Tim Peter Consulting

I hate this topic... but I love this book! Jennifer Grappone and Gradiva Couzin have written a great book for us girls; it's a self-help guide on SEO; the book is called Search Engine Optimization: An Hour a Day. *They've taken this really confusing subject and broken it down into little tasks that you can do in just an hour a day.*
   —Heather Juma, Girls Who Network

Search Engine Optimization

Second Edition

Search Engine Optimization

An Hour a Day
Second Edition

Jennifer Grappone

Gradiva Couzin

Wiley Publishing, Inc.

Acquisitions Editor: WILLEM KNIBBE
Development Editor: HEATHER O'CONNOR
Technical Editor: MICAH BALDWIN
Production Editor: DASSI ZEIDEL
Copy Editor: ELIZABETH WELCH
Production Manager: TIM TATE
Vice President and Executive Group Publisher: RICHARD SWADLEY
Vice President and Executive Publisher: JOSEPH B. WIKERT
Vice President and Publisher: NEIL EDDE
Book Designer: FRANZ BAUMHACKL
Compositor: CHRIS GILLESPIE, HAPPENSTANCE TYPE-O-RAMA
Proofreader: KATHY POPE, WORD ONE
Indexer: TED LAUX
Cover Designer: RYAN SNEED
Cover Image: © PHOTOALTO/JUPITER IMAGES

Library of Congress Cataloging-in-Publication Data

Grappone, Jennifer.
    Search engine optimization : an hour a day / Jennifer Grappone, Gradiva Couzin.
        p. cm.
    ISBN 978-0-470-22664-3 (pbk.)
    1. Internet searching—Handbooks, manuals, etc. 2. Web search engines—Handbooks, manuals, etc. 3. Computer network resources—Handbooks, manuals, etc. I. Couzin, Gradiva. II. Title.
    ZA4230.G73 2008
    025.04—dc22
                                                                    2008004983

Manufactured in the United States of America

10 9 8 7 6 5 4 3

Dear Reader

Thank you for choosing *Search Engine Optimization: An Hour a Day*. This book is part of a family of premium quality Sybex books, all written by outstanding authors who combine practical experience with a gift for teaching.

Sybex was founded in 1976. More than 30 years later, we're still committed to producing consistently exceptional books. With each of our titles, we're working hard to set a new standard for the industry. From the authors we work with to the paper we print on, our goal is to bring you the best books available.

I hope you see all that reflected in these pages. I'd be very interested to hear your comments and get your feedback on how we're doing. Feel free to let me know what you think about this or any other Sybex book by sending me an e-mail at nedde@wiley.com, or if you think you've found a technical error in this book, please visit http://sybex.custhelp.com. Customer feedback is critical to our efforts at Sybex.

Best regards,

Neil Edde
Vice President and Publisher
Sybex, an Imprint of Wiley

To Mom, my SEO student and lifelong teacher, with love. —jg

*To my children, who came from heaven and taught
me how to fly. —gc*

Acknowledgments

The authors wish to gratefully acknowledge our editors at Wiley: Willem Knibbe, a big-hearted and open-minded fellow who always listens to our ideas—and forgives us for them; Heather O'Connor, a wellspring of cheerful redirection and helpful insight; our technical editor, Micah Baldwin; our talented copy editor, Elizabeth Welch; our production editor and schedule-keeper, Dassi Zeidel; our compositors at Happenstance Type-O-Rama; and the other hardworking members of the production team.

We are grateful that some of the best and brightest in the field of search marketing were also the kindest. Thanks to Danny Sullivan, Jill Whalen, Kevin Lee, P.J. Fusco, Eric Ward, Andy Beal, Matt McGee, and Aaron Wall for offering their time and respected opinions to this project.

Thanks to the many good-natured members of the business community who shared their stories, successes, and challenges with us: Anna and Dexter Chow, Christine Moore, Jill Roberts, Paul Heller, Gina Boros, Sage Vivant, Mark Armstrong, Sharon Couzin, Martie Steele, and Ann Meyer. We wish them all many targeted visitors and mad conversions! We owe special thanks to Eric Fixler and Anthony Severo for providing invaluable technical reviews, and to Kelly Ryer and Sarah Hubbard for generous helpings of advice and wisdom. Thanks to Avinash Kaushik for equal parts brilliance, guidance, and commiseration. And thanks to Nervous Dog Coffee in San Francisco for the caffeine injections and free wireless!

We would like to thank all of the readers who have contacted us with questions and ideas, every one of which has made our purpose more clear and this task more rewarding. We are honored that you have shared your hopes and dreams with us! We are grateful to our employers, co-workers, and clients, current and former, who have paid us to learn, and trusted us when we went off on the occasional experimental bender. Big ups and thanks to Sue Separk, the best office manager a two-woman consulting team could ever hope for.

Fortunately for us, our families are full of people with amazing talents for things linguistic and technical. Thank you to Barbara Gold, Laura Gold, Alex Robinson, Janet Sahni, and Margie Morris for ideas, enthusiasm, and other warmhearted intangibles, and especially to our beloved husbands, Lowell Robinson and Todd Grappone, for their love and support. And to our most beautiful and wonderful children, Jonah, Zehara, Bennett, and Enzo, who have spent many nights with the glow of the laptop for a night-light, whose sleeping breaths are the music to which we write, thank you for making this book a part of your lives, too.

About the Authors

Jennifer Grappone and Gradiva Couzin are the founding partners at Gravity Search Marketing, an SEO consulting firm based in Los Angeles and San Francisco. Their customized, high-touch consulting style and holistic approach to SEO have resulted in targeted traffic and happy clients in a wide range of industries, including media, entertainment, software, retail, and nonprofit. Jennifer and Gradiva have been working together in various settings since 1998.

Jennifer Grappone started out as a writer/producer/director of industrial and corporate videos, then followed the dot-com boom and became a project manager for large-scale web development projects before working exclusively in SEO in 2000. Jennifer advocates a holistic approach to SEO, one that combines elements of good writing, usability, search-friendly site design, and link building. Jennifer lives with her husband and two children in Northeast Los Angeles.

Gradiva Couzin has been working in search marketing since its early days in 1998. Her SEO strategy creates win-win solutions by improving the match between searchers and websites. With a history as a civil engineer and experience in website and database development, Gradiva enjoys the technical side of SEO and loves to facilitate communication between techie and non-techie types. Gradiva lives and works in San Francisco's Bernal Heights with her husband and two small children.

Foreword

I don't have the time. I am overcommitted the next few months. I'm not even sure of the benefits. These were all my excuses for not writing this foreword.

When Jennifer and Gradiva called me for my answer, I was prepared with my apology. Their friendly and easygoing way could have easily swayed me, but it didn't. Nor did their clarity of purpose and deep-down desire to help businesses do more to be found in the search engines. Nor was it their enthusiasm that placed these words here in front of you.

It was the "one thing."

When my brother Jeffrey and I sat down to finish *Waiting for Your Cat to Bark* with Lisa Davis, we realized the one thing, as in Jack Palance's insight from the movie *City Slickers*: That clarity on your "one thing" holds the secret to success and happiness. For us, our one thing is the same as the secret to how you eat an elephant. **Make the effort, and focus on one bite at a time!**

You may have wondered like I did, why would you bother. It would take an eternity to eat an elephant one bite at a time. Our answer is at the end of the last chapter of our book, in the form of this quote by Rabbi Tarfon:

"The day is short, the work is much, the laborers are slothful. It is not incumbent upon you to finish the job, however, neither are you free from doing all you can to complete it."

That one thing is the effort. You can make excuses. Your time can be stolen by other very important things. You may look at Search Engine Optimization as a scary thing. Yet, none of these are enough to excuse you from making the effort.

Your effort can make a difference. Even if any one step, or any one hour spent on it might seem like nothing more than a tiny bite from an elephant. Could your company profitably do SEO 10 hours a day? Yes, there's lots to do. Should you do it 5 hours a day? Of course. Should you find one hour a day to take a bite out of this elephant called Search Engine Optimization? Absolutely!

This excellent book beautifully explains which bites of the elephant you should take first, next, and last. Full of practical advice and expert techniques that have been tested in the real world, it will help you quickly develop a solid, actionable SEO strategy and framework.

At the end of the day, one thing is certain: Your potential customers are using search engines like Google, trying to find you and your competitors. Will they find you?

Or will the perception that you don't have the time, are overcommitted the next few months, and aren't even sure of the benefits stop you from making the effort to be found?

Best wishes,
Bryan Eisenberg, cofounder, Future Now, Inc., and author of #1 *Wall Street Journal* bestseller *Waiting for Your Cat to Bark?* and *Call to Action*

Contents

Chapter 6 **Your One-Month Prep: Baseline and Keywords**   **107**

Chapter 9   **Month Three: It's a Way of Life**   **263**

CONTENTS

Introduction

How is your website doing on the search engines? Need a little help? Well, you're holding the right book in your hands. This book will walk you through the steps to achieve a targeted, compelling presence on the major search engines. There are no secrets or tricks here, just down-to-earth, real-world advice and a clear program to get you where you want to be. And, with luck, you'll even have a little fun along the way!

If you could think of the person whom you would most want visiting your website, who would that person be? Traditional advertisers might describe this person in terms of their demographics: 18 to 24 years old? Male or female? Wealthy or not so wealthy? But in the world of search, our focus is very different. This is how we think:

> **Pearl of Wisdom:** The person you most want to find your website is the person who is searching for you!

Who could be a more perfect target audience than someone who is already looking for your company, your product or service, or just the sort of information you've got on your website? The trick, of course, is to figure out who those people are, develop an extremely targeted message for them, and put it where they will notice it.

Search Engine Optimization (SEO) encompasses a wide variety of tasks that improve a website's presence on search engines. Maybe you've heard a few SEO catchphrases—*meta tags*, *link bait*, or *PageRank*—but you don't know exactly how to tie them all together into a meaningful package. That's where this book comes in!

Why SEO?

There are many good reasons to pursue SEO for your website. If you're a numbers person, you may find these stats compelling:

* A 2007 survey by Internet data firm comScore found that 60 percent of consumers use the Web as their first-line tool to search for local businesses, and 60 percent of those searchers go on to make a purchase from a local business.

- A 2006 survey by AOL and Henley Centre, a UK research firm, found that 73 percent of respondents listed search engines as important sources of information when considering a product or service—a higher percentage than personal recommendations, TV, or print media.

- Research conducted by search engine marketing firm iProspect in 2006 showed search engine users increasingly clicking on results in the first page of search results (62 percent as compared to 48 percent four years previously). The same study showed that fewer people are willing to click on listings past the third page of search results (10 percent compared to 19 percent four years previously).

But if you do SEO for no other reason, do it so you won't be handing website visitors over to your competitors on a silver platter! Here are a few embarrassing situations that SEO can help you avoid:

- A potential customer is trying to find your phone number so they can call in an order. Searching for your product name, they come across your competitor and call them instead.

- The good news is that your website is #1 on Google! The bad news is that your #1 rank is wasted on a tedious technical PDF that you didn't even know was on your site!

- Congratulations—you've accrued 157 high-quality links to your home page over the years! But since your last website redesign, you've spent the last two months with 157 links to your "File not found" error page!

The best thing about SEO is that when it's done correctly (follow the advice in this book, and you'll always be on the up-and-up), it benefits both you *and* your site visitors! The reason:

 Pearl of Wisdom: Good SEO helps searchers get where they want to go.

How? By providing a clear path from need to fulfillment. By making sure your message is simple, accurate, up-to-date, and most important, put in front of the right people.

Why an Hour a Day?

Like water filling an ice-cube tray, SEO can fill up all the hours in the day you are willing to give it. So let's get this painful truth out of the way right now: Good SEO takes work— *lots* of work.

Now you're probably wondering, "How *little* time can I spend on SEO and get away with it?"

SEO is an amorphous, open-ended task. It includes a wide variety of activities, ranging from editing HTML to reading blogs. It would be overwhelming to try to learn every aspect of SEO at once, but jumping in without a game plan is not the most effective strategy either. You're busy, and SEO is not your only job. So for you, the best way to learn SEO is to roll up your sleeves and *do* something, an hour at a time. Complete one SEO task a day, and you'll see substantial results.

One of the benefits of breaking your SEO campaign into bite-size, one-hour morsels is that you'll have time to digest and learn. You can take care of your day's assignment in an hour and have plenty of time for thinking and reflecting the rest of the day.

How Long Until I See Results?

The SEO process includes a lot of waiting: waiting for search engines to visit your site, waiting for webmasters and bloggers to link to you, and oftentimes waiting for others within your organization to complete your requested HTML edits. Nobody likes to wait, and nobody really believes us when we tell them this:

Pearl of Wisdom: Believe it. SEO requires patience.

This book sets you up for a long-haul SEO process. We take you through a one-month prep period in which you'll bring together all of the components you'll need to begin a successful SEO campaign—one that's just right for your unique situation. Then you'll launch into Your SEO Plan, a customizable hour-a-day routine designed to increase quality traffic and improve your site's presence on the search engines. Your SEO Plan is three months long, but you may start to see improvement in just days.

After three months of following the Plan, your website will have a solid foundation of results-minded optimization. Your SEO campaign will be moving along and becoming more and more specific to your needs and strategies. You will have smart analysis in place to determine which strategies are working and which aren't—and you'll drop the duds and focus your efforts in directions that are working for you.

Most importantly, after three months of following the Plan, you will be a full-fledged search marketer. You won't need day-by-day assignments anymore because you will be forging your own path. You will have great habits and tools for keeping your campaign buffed, and you'll be well on your way to teaching *us* a thing or two.

Who Should Use This Book

Truth be told, SEO is not hard. It's not rocket science, and it certainly doesn't require a degree in marketing, design, or anything else for that matter. While SEO is not hard, it can be tedious. It requires diligence and organization.

Our plan will work for just about anyone who is willing to make the hour-a-day commitment. We offer specific advice for

- Small organizations
- Large organizations
- One-person operations
- Business to business (B2B)
- Business to consumer (B2C)
- Web developers
- Nonprofits
- Bloggers
- Adult sites

You certainly don't need to be selling anything to need SEO! All you need is a website that would benefit from an increase in targeted traffic.

Even if you're considering outsourcing some or all of your SEO tasks, it's a good idea to become familiar with the SEO process before you pay someone to take it over. Obviously, we've got nothing against companies who hire SEO specialists—they're our bread and butter!—but nobody knows your own business like you do. You are, therefore, uniquely prepared for this task.

We don't like jargon, and we've tried to avoid it here (except, of course, when we teach it to you so you can impress others!). You'll learn concepts on a need-to-know basis and never waste your time on dead-end tasks. We don't bog you down with SEO history lessons, but we don't skimp on the important background knowledge either. Between the "Eternal Truths" and the "Right Now" of SEO that we've included in this book, we've got you covered. We know you're busy, and this book is written accordingly.

Does It Work?

"Significantly improved my Google rankings."

"Wonderful book. After I read it, I got on 1st and 2nd page results on Google for all of my keywords."

"I did spend many hours following the book's advice, and my website is now number 2."

"I didn't get it. But thanks, now I do."

This is a sampling of the feedback we've received from readers of the first edition. And the positive feedback keeps coming, not only from people who are seeing results for their website, but also from people who are delighted to finally have a solid grasp on this slippery topic. Some people follow the three-month Plan from beginning to end, while others use the book as a trusty reference. As one reader put it, "I found that I could get what I needed by dipping in and out, skimming through."

Does it work? Yes, it does. We know this because we use these techniques ourselves, and they have delivered high ranks and targeted traffic, and increased sales for our clients' websites.

What's Inside

The heart of this book is Your SEO Plan, a three-month, day-by-day program for improving your website's presence and increasing targeted traffic. We've divvied up the days into tasks that we estimate will take about an hour each. Depending on your circumstances, your familiarity with the subject matter, and the logistics of your website, it may take you more or less time to complete certain tasks.

The Plan is preceded by the preliminary planning and information you'll need to carry it out. That means you should read this book from the beginning and work through Your SEO Plan in order from start to finish.

Here's what you'll find inside.

Part I: Foundation

Chapter 1: "Clarify Your Goals" Helps you frame your thinking about your website and your goals in an SEO-friendly way.

Chapter 2: "Customize Your Approach" Provides guidance for adjusting your Plan to suit the special advantages and challenges faced by different types of organizations.

Chapter 3: "Eternal Truths of SEO" Gives an overview of the longstanding, or "eternal," factors in effective search engine optimization. Learn these truths to bring longevity to your SEO success.

Chapter 4: "How the Search Engines Work Right Now" Presents a current snapshot of the world of search.

Part II: Strategy

Chapter 5: "Get Your Team on Board" Offers been-there-done-that advice for eliminating intra-organizational hang-ups that are common in SEO.

Chapter 6: "Your One-Month Prep: Baseline and Keywords" Is all about preparation: researching, organizing, and setting the direction for Your SEO Plan, as well as choosing an all-important method of tracking and measuring your SEO success. Several worksheets and templates will help you along the way.

Part III: Your SEO Plan

Chapter 7: "Month One: Kick It into Gear" Launches Your SEO Plan with basic website optimization, a link-building method, and an action plan for promoting your site through social search.

Chapter 8: "Month Two: Establish the Habit" Shows you how to set up a starter pay-per-click campaign, offers several useful activities for improving online sales, and teaches you the best habits for keeping current with SEO trends.

Chapter 9: "Month Three: It's a Way of Life" Takes your SEO campaign further with content building, improving your return on investment, and in-depth troubleshooting, then walks you through your first SEO status report.

Chapter 10: "Extra Credit and Guilt-Free Slacking" Gives you practical tips on reducing your SEO workload if your schedule is less than perfect and helps you dig deeper in specific areas if you are especially enthusiastic.

What's New in This Edition

We've put a lot of thought into selecting only the new aspects of SEO that are worth your time and effort, so you can stay on the cutting edge of search while sidestepping fly-by-night fads and unproven techniques. This edition of *Search Engine Optimization: An Hour a Day* now contains:

- Detailed analysis and instructions on using the Social Web to benefit your website

- Instructions on selecting and using web analytics tools (because, due to recent developments, there's no excuse not to!)

- The latest scoop on shopping search, consumer-generated content, and specialty search such as local, blog, image, and video

- Even more tales from the trenches: real stories from real businesses like yours

We've listened to our wonderful, hardworking readers, and we now give you more of what you've asked for: We've expanded our advice for small businesses and included lots of new tidbits for *really* small businesses. We've included an informative new section just for web designers. And naturally, we've updated all of the information on search engine ranking algorithms and red flags.

Whether you're following the Plan step by step or using the book as a reference, you'll benefit from tasks that have been organized more intuitively. And though this book is written primarily for nontechies, in many cases we go just a bit deeper into technology should you desire to delve there.

This Book's Companion Website

In addition to the chapters you hold in your hand, you can find extra information and resources on our companion website, www.yourseoplan.com.

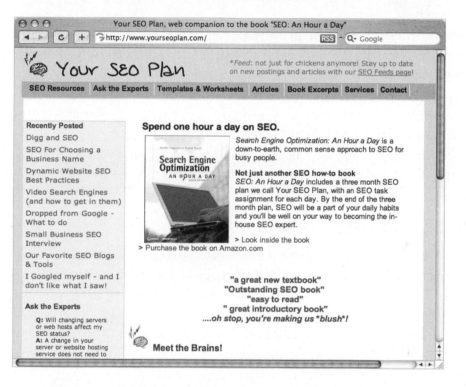

There, you can download all the worksheets and templates you need for the Plan and find plenty of useful SEO links and tips as well. When we're not saving the world one website at a time, we're posting topical articles and answering your "Ask the Experts" questions on the website. Lots of aspiring SEO experts just like you visit our site regularly, and consider it one of their most useful bookmarks!

Conventions Used in This Book

We've been working together for so many years now that sometimes it seems our brains are fused. Gradiva tends toward the "left brain" side of our collective SEO brain, with enough logic, math proficiency, and analytical thinking for both of us. On the other hand, Jennifer is more of a "right brain" thinker, with a flair for writing and a preference for the creative aspects of SEO. One thing we agree on: Good SEO requires a little left brain *and* a little right brain! Throughout this book, you'll see the "left brain/right brain" icon wherever we think you need the view from both sides.

We love to learn from others' mistakes and successes, and you can, too! Look for the shovel icon accompanying stories from the real world: case studies, expert opinions, and even some tragic tales from the trenches. We've changed most of the names to protect the privacy—and reputations—of the parties involved.

 This pearl represents a special tip or tidbit of wisdom that you may find especially helpful.

 The "Now" icon indicates an SEO task that's assigned to you. When you come across one of these, it's time to roll up your sleeves and get to work!

xtra cred We wrote this book for the busy professional—that's why it's an hour-a-day plan. But sometimes, you might be inclined to take your campaign a little further. For you go-getters, we've provided the extra-credit icon.

slacker And for those of you who spend most of your time wishing you had more time, here's the icon for you. Next to the slacker icon, you'll find options for trimming down your tasks without compromising results.

If you're dying to do something *right now*, your enthusiasm is noted and appreciated. Fire up your computer, and we'll be waiting for you on page 1!

Foundation

 *So, you want to differentiate your website from the millions of others out there on the Internet? Great! Let's get started! Whether you're starting from scratch or just looking for a new approach, the hardest part of embarking on a Search Engine Optimization (SEO) campaign is knowing where to begin. In Part I, we walk you through a little self-reflection and search engine basics to lay the groundwork for Your SEO Plan:*

Clarify Your Goals

1

A good SEO campaign needs to be laser-focused on your business goals, so it has to start with a healthy dose of thought and reflection. In this chapter, we'll walk you through the key questions you'll want to consider before you get started.

Chapter Contents

What Is SEO?

Do I Need to Perform SEO for My Website?

What Are the Overall Goals of My Business?

What Function Does My Website Serve?

How Is My Website Connecting with the Goals of My Business?

Who Do I Want to Visit My Website?

What Do I Want Visitors to Do on My Website?

Which Pages Do I Most Want My Website Visitors to See?

How Will I Measure the Success of This SEO Campaign?

What Is SEO?

OK, let's see a show of hands: How many of you are reading this book because you want a #1 rank in Google? Yeah, we thought so. As SEO consultants, we know how good it feels when your website makes it to the top of the heap. Listen, we sincerely hope you get your #1 Google rank, but it won't help you if it's bringing in the wrong audience or pointing them to a dead-end website. So don't think of SEO as just a way to improve your site's ranking.

The term *Search Engine Optimization* describes a diverse set of activities that you can perform to increase the number of desirable visitors who come to your website via search engines (you may also have heard these activities called Search Engine Marketing or Search Marketing). This includes things you do to your site itself, such as making changes to your text and HTML code. It also includes communicating directly with the search engines, or pursuing other sources of traffic by making requests for listings or links. Tracking, research, and competitive review are also part of the SEO package.

SEO is not advertising, although it may include an advertising component. It is not public relations (PR), although it includes communication tasks similar to PR. As a continually evolving area of online marketing, SEO may sound complicated, but it is very simple in its fundamental goal: gaining targeted visitors.

Do I Need to Perform SEO for My Website?

It may seem like a no-brainer, but actually, the answer is not necessarily yes. If any of the following examples apply to you, you may not be in need of an SEO campaign right now:

- You have a website that you really don't want strangers to find, such as a training tool for your employees or a classroom tool for your students.
- Your site is already ranking well, you're satisfied with your sales, and you don't want to rock the boat.
- You're in a big hurry—say, you'll go out of business without a major upswing in revenue in the next couple of months. This is not to say that SEO can't help you, but good SEO takes time. You may need to focus your energies elsewhere right now.
- Your site is going to be completely rebuilt or redesigned in the next couple of months. If that's the case, read Shari Thurow's *Search Engine Visibility* (Peachpit Press, 2007) to learn how to build a search-friendly site from the ground up. You'll want to keep our book on hand, though, for use as soon as your new site is launched.

If this list doesn't apply to you, we think you're ready to begin your SEO adventure!

It is a rare site indeed that couldn't use a little improvement in the SEO department. And, with the importance of SEO on the rise, if you don't need it today, it's a good bet you'll need to brush up your SEO smarts for tomorrow. So even if you don't think you need SEO right now, we recommend that you take the time to work through the questions in this chapter and make sure that your goals aren't begging for a little help.

What Are the Overall Goals of My Business?

We get it: The fundamental goal of your business is to make money by selling a product or service. But let's take a moment to define your goals in a little more detail.

Perhaps yours is a large company with branding as an important long-term goal. Maybe your company wants to make money with certain products but is willing to take a loss in other areas. Maybe you are starting up with investor backing and do not need to turn a profit for years. Perhaps your company's branding and reputation is your top concern—you need to be perceived as high tech, or luxurious, or as the hippest in your competitive space. Or maybe you work for a nonprofit, with a goal to improve the world and inspire others to do the same. You may be working toward 2,000 small sales this year, or be thrilled to get just three new clients. Whatever way you're leaning, your business goals will affect your SEO campaign strategy.

For instance, consider the fictional situation of Jason, a founding partner at Babyfuzzkin, a company selling unique, high-end baby clothes. This business makes its money directly through online sales. It's a small operation, so there is a limit to how many orders the business can handle. The Babyfuzzkin fantasy would be a steady flow of, say, 100 orders per month. But there is more to the story: Eventually, the partners would love to get out of the direct fulfillment of orders and instead secure some contracts with big-name brick-and-mortar vendors.

In the case of Elizabeth, a marketing director at ElderPets, we have a different situation. ElderPets is a fictional nonprofit organization that provides meals, walks, and veterinary care assistance to animals belonging to elderly and infirm owners. The company relies on financial contributions and volunteers to fulfill its mission. At ElderPets, their fantasy is to decrease the time and effort spent on fundraising activities, such as silent auctions and community dog washes, and begin attracting more contributions online, which would in turn allow them to help more pets in need. In addition, they are constantly looking for more volunteers.

Though Jason and Elizabeth have different goals, we have an exercise they can both perform to get the most out of their planned SEO. We've created a Goals Worksheet to guide clients like Jason and Elizabeth, and you can use it as you consider the questions in this chapter. You can download the Goals Worksheet at our companion website, www.yourseoplan.com. At key points throughout this chapter, we'll ask you to stop, reflect on your own business, and write down your own vital statistics. Once you've worked through the questions, you'll have a strong vision of the "why" of your SEO campaign—and you'll be ready to move on to the "what" and "how" in Parts II and III.

Now: Download the Goals Worksheet from www.yourseoplan.com.

Now take a moment and look at "Business Goals" on your Goals Worksheet. Tables 1.1 and 1.2 show how Jason of Babyfuzzkin and Elizabeth at ElderPets might fill out theirs, respectively.

▶ **Table 1.1** Summary of Business Goals for Babyfuzzkin

Primary Goal	Sell clothes directly to consumers online
Additional Goal	Sign brick-and-mortar contracts

▶ **Table 1.2** Summary of Business Goals for ElderPets

Primary Goal	Help more animals in need
Additional Goal	Attract more donations
Additional Goal	Attract more volunteers

Now: Take a few minutes to write down your overall business goals in "Business Goals" on your Goals Worksheet. Don't be afraid to indulge in fantasy!

What Function Does My Website Serve?

It's not uncommon to hear that the reason a company built a website is "to have a website." While we all love a bit of circular logic before breakfast, if you're going to put a lot of time and money into promoting your website, it's important to have a good idea of what it's doing for you.

Most websites are built out of a combination of basic building blocks. Whether your site is a web-based store seeking online sales; a personal blog seeking community connections; a political or religious outlet seeking to persuade, uplift, or inspire; a corporate "brochure" displaying branding identity and company information; or just about any other type of website you can imagine, it will likely include some or all of the following features or elements:

- ✔ Corporate history, news, and press releases
- ✔ Executive biographies
- ✔ Product and service information
- ✔ Online purchasing/donation
- ✔ Support for existing customers/clients/students
- ✔ News and current events

- ✔ Articles, white papers

- ✔ Religious, philosophical, or political content
- ✔ Online request for information (RFI) forms
- ✔ Login for restricted information
- ✔ Instructions for making contact offline or via e-mail

- ✔ Directions, hours of operation, etc., for brick-and-mortar location
- ✔ Links to other resources

- ✔ Customer testimonials

- ✔ Fun, games, or entertainment
- ✔ A strong brand identity
- ✔ Art or craft portfolio
- ✔ Educational materials
- ✔ Information specifically for geographically local visitors
- ✔ Software or documents available for download
- ✔ Media (pictures, audio, video) available for viewing/downloading
- ✔ Site map
- ✔ Site search function
- ✔ Live help/live contact function
- ✔ Ways for members of the community to connect with each other on the site (forums, bulletin boards, etc.)
- ✔ Blog postings and reader comments
- ✔ Methods for your users to help promote your site (e-mail a friend, "Digg this," etc.)

Now, spend some time clicking around your website. You should be able to tell which of the features in the preceding list are included. How well is each component doing its job? For now, think in terms of presentation and functionality. (Is your product information up-to-date? Is your online store full of technical glitches? Are your forms asking the right questions?) Give each feature that you find a ranking of Excellent, Good, Fair, or Poor. Obviously, this isn't going to be a scientific process—just make your best estimate.

Jason's and Elizabeth's checklists might look something like Tables 1.3 and 1.4.

▶ **Table 1.3** Ratings for Babyfuzzkin Features

Online purchasing/donation	Excellent
Product and service information	Good
A strong brand identity	Good
Instructions for making contact offline or via e-mail	Good

▶ **Table 1.4** Ratings for ElderPets Features

Corporate history, news, and press releases	Excellent
Executive biographies	Excellent
Online purchasing/donation	Future Goal
Educational materials	Good
Online request for information (RFI) forms	Good

How Is My Website Connecting with the Goals of My Business?

Take a look at what you've written on your Goals Worksheet. Is there a disconnect between your business goals and your current website? Is your website focused on corporate info or, worse yet, executive bios instead of your business goals? Or does the website provide only content geared toward supporting existing clients when the primary business goal is to gain new clients?

Jason at Babyfuzzkin is in good shape: The business goals and website features are in alignment, with an Excellent rating on the top business priority. Since the business goal includes not only sales but also a strong push toward future deals, the SEO campaign will need to support both.

On the other hand, Elizabeth at ElderPets may be in trouble. One of its primary goals is to get donations, but its website is currently focused on describing its mission and founders, and it doesn't even have online donation capability yet. This could pose a challenge throughout the SEO campaign.

Remember the big picture here:

 Pearl of Wisdom: Your SEO campaign must support the overall business goals, not just your website.

The SEO You Have, Not the One You Want

In an ideal world, you could take your Goals Worksheet to your boss and say, "Hey! We've got a disconnect here. Let's fix it!" But let's just suppose that *ideal* is not the word you would use to describe your organization. The fact is, your SEO campaign may need to work with certain handicaps.

Over the years, we've worked with a lot of folks who have had to support their business goals with a less-than-perfect website. Here are the most common reasons we've seen for this:

- There is political opposition to change.
- There are scheduling bottlenecks: Everybody else's project comes before our own site.
- The current marketing team inherited an outdated or lousy website.
- The site is floating along and isn't really anybody's responsibility.

Some Interim Solutions

It's your job as the in-house SEO expert to lobby for a website that will deliver for your company. But you may be wondering, "If my site is far less than perfect and—for whatever reason—I can't fix it right now, should I even bother with SEO?" Probably. Here are some ideas for approaching SEO while you're waiting for your site to come up to speed with your company's goals:

- Work on getting traffic, but lower your expectations for sales (or whatever action you want your visitors to perform) for the time being. When you assess your website's performance, you may notice an upswing in traffic, which you can use to motivate your people to make some positive changes to the site.
- Ask for "ownership" of just one page, or just one section, and try to bring it up to snuff. Can't get a whole page? We've had customers who were given just one chunk of the home page to do with as they wished. Surprisingly, site maps actually represent good SEO opportunities, and it may be easier to convince your boss to give you ownership of yours!

- Use your powers of competitive analysis. Take special care to note if your competitors' sites are doing things well in the areas in which your site is lacking (we'll give you a chance to do this in Chapter 6, "Your One-Month Prep: Baseline and Keywords"). This may motivate those in power to give your recommended changes a higher priority.

- Focus on *off-page* SEO activities. While you're waiting to get your site spiffed up, you can always work on removing outdated listings and cleaning up old links to your site.

- As a last resort, if your current site is so hopeless that it's actually doing your business more harm than good, you might decide to take drastic measures and "disinvite" the search engines. We'll show you how in Part III, "Your SEO Plan."

SEO Infighting at UpperCut and Jab, Inc.

Here's a true story involving UpperCut and Jab, Inc. (company name and some identifying details have been changed to prevent embarrassment), which provides IT consulting and solutions for large businesses. One of the company's primary goals is new-client acquisition.

In This Corner: A Sales Force with Very Practical Needs With their hands already full, the sales team does not want to waste their time responding to unqualified leads. They like to have lots of corporate information, white papers, and case studies online, which they use as sales tools while they are meeting with potential clients. Sounds like a great use of a website, and one that doesn't require any SEO or any sort of call to action.

In This Corner: A Marketing Team with a Vision The marketing team, on the other hand, wants the website to gather leads. They want a functioning request for information (RFI) form and a generously budgeted SEO campaign to drive traffic to it.

The Plan of Attack The marketing team controls the website, so it's decided: The site will be outfitted with an RFI form, and a large SEO campaign will ensue to drive general-interest traffic to it.

So Who Wins? Unfortunately, nobody. The marketing team was successful in driving a great deal of traffic to the RFI form! But, uh-oh, a vast majority of forms were filled out by unqualified leads. ("Does so-and-so still work there?" "Can you help me with a broken printer?") Looks like they forgot about defining their target audience. The RFI form—a potentially great lead generation tool—was eventually dropped. In this case, the SEO campaign was a waste of time and money because it was not fine-tuned to attract high-quality leads.

The Moral of the Story Bringing traffic to your site is not necessarily the same as meeting your company's goals!

Who Do I Want to Visit My Website?

In the introduction, we pointed out the fact that the person who you *most* want to find your website is the person who is searching for your website! And, of course, this is true. But now let's dig a little deeper and describe your ideal audience so that you can help them make their way to you.

Who is the target audience for your website? Surely it will include potential clients/customers. But don't forget that it may also include members of the press, employees at your own company, current and past customers seeking support, even potential investors nosing about for the inside scoop!

Using your Goals Worksheet, describe your target audience with as much detail as possible: professional status, technical vs. nontechnical (this will affect how they search or even which engines they use), age, workplace vs. home users, and geographic locality.

Knowing your target audience(s) will help you make important decisions—such as *keyword* choices, directory site submittals, and budget for *paid listings*—when you start your SEO campaign. It will also help you segment your site for each audience, which can improve your sales and other goals, as well as usability.

Jason at Babyfuzzkin says, "Our target audience is parents of infants and small children, with a great sense of style and plenty of surplus income. They are probably fairly technically savvy, maybe a little short on time because of the kids—that's why they're shopping online. Also, a lot of our customers are grandparents, buying the clothes as gifts. Some parents don't want to spend as much on clothes they know are just going to get covered in oatmeal and grass stains! And the grandparents, they are a lot less savvy with the Internet. They use it from home, maybe with a slow connection, and they're located nationwide."

Elizabeth at ElderPets describes her target audience as "Caregivers or relatives of the elderly or infirm—they're usually the ones who contact us about our services. Our volunteers range from high school students hoping to beef up their college applications to retirees who don't have much money but want to do something worthwhile with their time. And then there's our donors, who can be all over the map in terms of age and income and their status as individual, family, or business. The one thing that ties them together is that they love animals."

Jason's and Elizabeth's goals and corresponding target audiences are shown in Tables 1.5 and 1.6.

▶ **Table 1.5** Babyfuzzkin Goals and Corresponding Target Audiences

Goals		Target Audience	
Primary goal	Sell clothes directly to consumers online	Primary Audience: Secondary Audience:	Parents of small children Grandparents and friends
Additional goal	Brick-and-mortar contracts	Primary Audience:	Buyers working for retailers

Goals		Target Audience	
Primary goal	Help more animals in need	Primary Audience:	Caregivers of the elderly or infirm
Additional goal	Attract more donations	Primary Audience:	Pet lovers with surplus income
Additional goal	Attract more volunteers	Primary Audience:	High school students, retirees

Now: Go to the "Conversions" table on your Goals Worksheet and fill out your target audiences under the appropriate column. Be as specific as you can!

What Do I Want Visitors to Do on My Website?

In SEO, the term *conversion* has come to mean your website users doing whatever it is you want them to do. So when we say "conversion," think of it as shorthand for "Score one for you—you're accomplishing your goals!"

Wondering what your site's conversion is? One of the really fun facts about SEO is this:

Pearl of Wisdom: For your site, you can define a "conversion" however you want.

It's *your* party—you decide what you want your guests to do. Now that you have all of your goals written down in black and white, defining a conversion should be easy. Here are a few likely examples: users "convert" when they:

- Purchase a product
- Fill out an RFI form
- View a certain page on the site
- Subscribe to a mailing list
- Comment on a blog
- Phone your 1-800 sales number
- Drive to your retail store
- Contribute to your political campaign
- Change their mind about something
- Find the information they were looking for
- Read a classified ad

Now look at the "Conversions" table on your Goals Worksheet. You will need to have a conversion defined next to each goal. Some of the conversion definitions will be straightforward; others may seem vague or touchy-feely. There's no harm in writing them all—we'll help you sort them out later in your SEO campaign when you're measuring results.

Jason's and Elizabeth's worksheets are shown in Tables 1.7 and 1.8.

▶ **Table 1.7** Babyfuzzkin Goals and Corresponding Conversions

Goals		Target Audience		Conversion
Primary goal	Sell clothes directly to consumers online	Primary Audience:	Parents of small children	Purchase via online store
		Secondary Audience:	Grandparents and friends	
Additional goal	Brick-and-mortar contracts	Primary Audience:	Buyers working for retailers	Make inquiry via online form or offline contact

▶ **Table 1.8** ElderPets Goals and Corresponding Conversions

Goals		Target Audience		Conversion
Primary goal	Help more animals in need	Primary Audience:	Caregivers of the elderly or infirm	View our mission statement
Additional goal	Attract more donations	Primary Audience:	Pet lovers with surplus income	Donate via online form or call our toll-free number
Additional goal	Attract more volunteers	Primary Audience:	High school students, retirees	Make inquiry via online form or offline contact

With your goals, audiences, and conversions spelled out, it's easy to connect the dots from goal to audience to desired conversion:

To achieve my **goal**, I need my **target audience** to **convert** on **this page**.

For example, Babyfuzzkin would say this:

- To achieve more **clothing sales**, I need **parents of infants** to **buy my products** on the **Clothes for Under $20 page**.

- To achieve more **clothing sales**, I need **grandparents and friends of parents** to **buy my products** on the **Gift Sets page**.

- To achieve **brick-and-mortar contracts**, I need **buyers working for retailers** to **make an inquiry** using the **Contact Us page.**

  And ElderPets might say this:

- To achieve **more online donations**, I need **pet lovers with surplus income** to **make a donation** on the **Donate Now page.**

- To achieve **a higher number of volunteers**, I need **homemakers and retirees** to **contact us** using the **Become a Volunteer page.**

- To achieve **a higher number of volunteers**, I need **high school students** to **contact us** using the **Students Volunteer Program** page.

- To achieve **being found by those in need**, I need **caretakers of elderly and infirm pet owners** to **visit** the **Our Mission page.**

> **Now:** Go back to the "Conversions" table on your Goals Worksheet and fill out your conversions under the appropriate column.

Which Pages Do I Most Want My Website Visitors to See?

Now it's time to start thinking about the top-priority pages for your SEO campaign. These are the pages you'll optimize when you get to your daily tasks in Part III. These are the pages that you most want people to get to from the search engines, and for best results, they should contain the most compelling content and the most useful information. Since your visitors "land" on these pages from the search engines, we call them *landing pages* (you might also hear them called *entry pages*). The main functions of your landing pages are that they speak to your desired audience and contain a call to action for your desired conversion. Figure 1.1 illustrates possible paths through your website from entry to conversion.

Often, your landing page and your conversion page will be the same, as is the case with Babyfuzzkin's Gift Sets page. This is a great situation because your site visitor doesn't have to navigate within your site to complete a conversion. Other times, your conversion page will not be an appropriate entry page because your visitor will need to review other information first and then make the decision to continue. After all, the Web is a highly nonlinear space, and your visitors are free to ramble around your site in all sorts of ways.

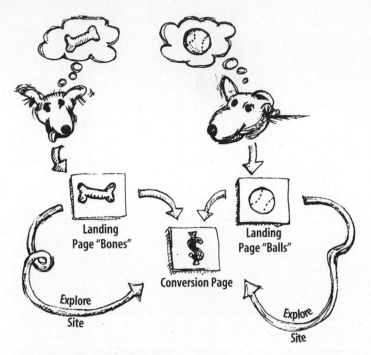

Figure 1.1 Possible paths to conversion

For the purposes of your SEO campaign, you need to ensure that for each type of conversion, there is at least one clear path between the search engine and the conversion outcome. We find it helpful to think backward: First consider where you want your visitor to end up, and then work backward to find a great page for them to enter your site.

For example, consider the ElderPets conversion:

To achieve **more online donations**, I need **pet lovers with surplus income** to **make a donation** on the **Donate Now page.**

Next, Elizabeth might work backward, starting from the Donate Now page and clicking through the website to find a possible landing page:

Donate Now page → How Can I Help page → Dogs in Need page

In this scenario, the Dogs in Need page is the chosen landing page. Why? Because it's a very convincing, compelling page for this specific audience.

CHAPTER 1: CLARIFY YOUR GOALS ∎

Elderpets – Dogs in Need

Q▾ Google

ELDERPETS

OUR MISSION   ABOUT US   PETS IN NEED   HOW TO HELP   CONTACT

Dogs In Need

Littlemoose is looking for help with a daily walk around the block. The best time would be in the morning. If a volunteer can't be found, then Littlemoose will probably be put down and his owner, 85 year old Edith M., will no longer have his affectionate nibbles and loving warmth in her home. Location: Sacramento, CA. Can you help?

Vivian is a sweet mutt dog that has been a faithful companion to her guardian, 83 year old Ernest T., for over 10 years. Vivian needs daily medicine administered, and a run around the park once or twice a week. Location: Chico, CA. Can you help?

How Can I Help?

Donate Now

Volunteer

Because of Elderpets I was able to stay home and care for my dog. She takes care of me too. Thank you, Elderpets!

- Ethyl Baker

What makes a good landing page? One with just the right information that your target audience is looking for. Vague enough for you? Don't worry; in Part III, we'll walk you through the specifics of how to choose your landing pages and how to make sure the "right" information is on those pages. For now, we want you to begin thinking about what pages might work. If you don't have any pages that fit the bill, don't despair! Get some landing pages built if you can, or think about ways you can add compelling content to existing pages to turn them into excellent landing pages. And just a heads-up: Once you start your SEO campaign, all of your top-priority pages will probably need to be revised at least a little bit as part of the optimization process.

Notice that the landing page ElderPets chose for this conversion is *not* the home page. Many site owners don't think in terms of deeper pages and think that they just want their home page to be found on the search engines. But in truth, your home page is probably only good for achieving the most general of your goals. Your deeper pages are more likely to contain a wealth of *specific* information and *specific* calls to action that you'd be thrilled for a *specific audience* to find one click away from a search engine!

Now: Go back to the "Conversions" table on your Goals Worksheet and enter your conversion pages in the appropriate column.

How Will I Measure the Success of This SEO Campaign?

Most companies understand the importance of measuring the performance of their websites, and there are lots of useful tools available to help you do just that. But in our experience, many companies—especially the small ones—aren't tracking at all! And in a 2007 survey, 81 percent of *web analytics* professionals reported that the practice is "poorly understood" in their companies. Why are so many companies missing out? We think the cause is a combination of factors:

Lack of definition When goals or conversions are never defined, there's no way to measure your accomplishments.

Lack of communication Different departments or individuals with different goals may not be sharing information.

Math anxiety Herding conversion data into a tidy, meaningful spreadsheet can be harder than it sounds, and basic algebra is probably not in the job description of most CEOs and marketers.

Technical difficulty Even with the slickest web analytics tools at your disposal, some types of conversions are difficult, if not impossible, to track.

Hitch up your high waters and get ready for another painful truth:

 Pearl of Wisdom: You must track the accomplishments of your SEO campaign.

There are a few good reasons why. Let's discuss them here.

Tracking Lets You Drop the Duds

Have you ever heard this military strategy riddle? You are waging battles on two fronts. One front is winning decisively. The other is being severely trounced. You have 10,000 additional troops ready to deploy. Where do you send them? The answer is, you send them to the winning front as reinforcements. Strange as it sounds, it makes more sense to reinforce a winning battle than to throw efforts into a losing one.

This strategy is also reflected in the maxim "Don't throw good money after bad." You need to know which of your efforts are bringing you good results so you can send in the reinforcements, and you need to know which efforts are not working so you can bail out on them. And the only way to know this is to *track results*.

Tracking Will Help You Keep Your Job

If you work for yourself, you're the president of your own company, or you're reading this book for a hobby site or your blog, feel free to skip this section. For just about everyone else, we suspect that someone, somewhere is *paying* you to do this work. Eventually, that someone is going to wonder whether they have been spending their money wisely. Even if your boss ignores you every time you walk in the office with a report, even if your department head refuses to back you up when you try to get IT support for *conversion tracking*, even if Sales tells you there's absolutely no way you can track sales back to the website, trust us; someday someone is going to want this information—preferably in a bar chart, with pretty colors, and summarized in five words or less. If you don't have the information, the measure of your accomplishments is going to default to this:

Are we #1 on Google?

And, if you're not, get ready for some repercussions!

Tracking Helps You Stay Up-to-Date

"Do it right the first time." It's a great motto and a great goal, but it's not a realistic plan for your SEO campaign. For one thing, you will need to continually re-prioritize your efforts as you drop the duds. But there's also another, unavoidable reason that your SEO campaign will need to constantly evolve: The search engines are changing, too! Don't worry, this book sets you up with best practices that should have a nice, long life span (in Internet years that is!). But you will inevitably need to be prepared for some changes. What works best today will not be exactly the same as what works best three years down the road. And the only way to know what has changed is to track your campaign.

Now that you are convinced that tracking is important, take a look at your list of conversions. Some of them will be easy to track; some may be difficult or close to impossible. Later, we'll take some time to think through possible ways to track your successes (and failures). Here are the methods that Jason and Elizabeth are considering for measuring their SEO campaign results:

Jason at Babyfuzzkin says, "Our primary goal is online sales. Probably the simplest way to track to our SEO campaign is to compare online sales numbers before and after the campaign. Our secondary goal is attracting attention from vendors. We'll track these leads back to the SEO campaign by asking any vendors that contact us how they heard about us."

Elizabeth at ElderPets describes her tracking plans by saying, "Our primary goal is donations, so we'll be watching for an increase in the number of individual donations after we start our SEO campaign. As for volunteers, we'll add a 'How did you find us?' question to our volunteer applications. As for just being found by people who need us, our website also has a visitors counter. I've never paid much attention to it, but as a start, I'll see if I can figure out if we're getting more traffic than we used to."

Clearly Jason and Elizabeth are on the right path. They've examined their goals and their websites. They've identified their targeted audiences and target pages, and they're even thinking ahead to tracking. If you're really stuck on any of these answers for your own company, take some time now to put your head together with others in your organization and hash it out. Understanding your own goals is a basic element of your upstart SEO campaign, and you'll do best if you have a firm grasp on them before you move on.

How Much Tracking Do I Need to Do?

Tracking can seem like a daunting task if you've never given any thought to it. Site owners like Jason and Elizabeth are wondering: Should tracking be approached with "baby steps" like the rest of SEO?

The Left Brain says, "Whoa there, Jason and Elizabeth: You're going to be collecting flawed data! Jason, how can you be sure that your increase in sales is tied to your SEO efforts and not something else, like the start of the holiday season? And Elizabeth, that hit counter is not going to cut it! You need to gather data about where these people are coming from and how many of them are unique visitors. Don't you know that your counter can increase every time someone's cat steps on the 'refresh' button?"

The Right Brain says, "I admire your left-brained hunger for irrefutable facts. However, most people are too busy to make numbers-watching on that level their highest priority. I say we encourage any effort at all to track conversions, as long as it's based on some logic and is done consistently. Even a little bit of tracking can bring up some interesting findings. And these findings often get people interested in learning more, which may in turn motivate people to do more detailed tracking. Believe it or not, tracking can be a creative process!"

Wow! You've done a lot of thinking in this chapter. You now know that you probably need SEO for your website. You have a great grasp on your overall business goals. You know what your website is doing and whether these things are good or bad for your company. You know your target audience and your desired conversions. And, we trust, you are convinced that tracking is a necessity. Now, meet us in Chapter 2, "Customize Your Approach," for some light reading about your favorite subject: you!

Customize Your Approach

2

Let's say you want a great car wash, one that gets up close and personal with your car's curves and addresses its individual problem areas. You wouldn't trust a gas station car wash—you'd do it yourself! Likewise, the SEO plan in this book presents a method that can be applied to a wide range of SEO efforts, but you have to customize it for your particular business and website. This chapter gives you a great head start.

Chapter Contents

It's *Your* SEO Plan

When you heard about this book, you may have had one of two reactions. Maybe you thought, "Great! A quick and easy SEO plan that I can follow!" Or maybe you thought, "Uh-oh! An oversimplified approach to something complex." Both of these reactions are perfectly reasonable. A simple approach is important, but you should be wary of anything that promises a one-size-fits-all SEO solution.

So let's make one thing clear: There's nothing cookie cutter about *your* SEO plan. And because nobody knows your organization and website like you do, guess who's in charge of the fine-tuning? You!

Small and large companies, brick-and-mortars, bloggers, and nonprofits—each type has its own set of needs, advantages, and challenges. Your assignment is to identify which categories your company is in, read our tips and guidelines for those categories, and think about how you can apply the customization to your own SEO efforts.

This is a "check all that apply" chapter—your company may fall into multiple categories. For example, let's say you run an independent toy store in Des Moines, Iowa. You would want to read at least three of the categories in this chapter: brick-and-mortar, B2C, and small organization. If you're the world leader in granulators for the plastics industry, you'd want to read B2B and large organization. Read what applies to you, but also consider reading what may not seem to. After all, part of being an SEO expert is knowing the breadth of what the Web offers. You never know where you might find something interesting and useful for your own site!

Business-to-Business (B2B)

B2B sites run the gamut from the little guys selling restaurant-grade deli slicers to the huge corporation selling enterprise-level software and services. B2Bs of all stripes should be taking a serious look at SEO: A 2007 Enquiro survey revealed that over 70 percent of B2B prospects start their online research at a search engine (either general or B2B vertical). Here are some of the advantages and challenges of SEO for the B2B business:

Advantage: Niche Target Audience Because your business depends on it, you probably already know your customer well. Your customer fits into a particular niche: restaurant owner, plant manager, candlestick maker, and so on. While your customers may not all hang out at the same bar after work, it's a good bet that they're frequenting some of the same websites. And if you don't know what these sites are, it only takes a bit of time and creative thought to find them. If you already know what magazines your customers subscribe to, what trade shows they attend, and what organizations they belong to, you're well on your way to finding analogous sites on the Web that speak to them.

Challenge: Difficulty Gaining Links You may have heard that getting relevant, high-quality links to your website is an important SEO endeavor, because it can improve your ranks and traffic. This is going to be a challenge for you. You're not a big entertainment site or a fun *blog* with a cult following, and unless you're a giant in your industry, your activities are not automatically newsworthy. Although you may have the respect of your customers, building a self-sustaining "buzz" is not the kind of thing that comes easily to a B2B website. After all, your site probably isn't built for buzz; chances are you're offering straight-up product information, corporate bios, and white papers. You may be able to improve your site's *linkability* with noncommercial content or a corporate blog. Paying for carefully chosen directory listings might even be a good strategy for you.

Advantage: High-Value Conversions SEO is appealing to B2Bs, for a good reason. Because each new customer or lead is valuable to your business, your SEO campaign can make a quick and measurable difference to your bottom line by bringing in just a few conversions. Don't skimp on tracking—you'll want your SEO campaign to get credit for these high-value conversions.

Challenge: A Slow SEO Life Cycle You know why scientists love that little fruit fly called drosophila? The reason is that the drosophila has such a short life span that many generations of them can be studied in a relatively short amount of time. In a similar way, an SEO campaign can be studied and improved in a relatively short amount of time if you have lots of visitors coming through and converting (or not converting). For a B2B, however, this is probably not the case. You will have a smaller, more targeted audience and will likely have a longer conversion life cycle. That means less information, and a slower evolution, for your ongoing SEO campaign.

Advantage: Text-Heavy Content Got FAQs? How about product specifications and mission statements? As a B2B, you probably have lots of text on your site, which the search engines love. While some site owners will be scratching their heads looking for ways to fit text into their design, you will probably have tons of text on which to focus your optimization efforts. And if not, you may have marketing materials such as white papers and PDFs ready for quick and easy appropriation onto your site. Of course, all of the text-heavy items mentioned here have the potential to be about as exciting as a glass of warm milk, so make sure you're putting out text that people actually want to read!

Business-to-Consumer (B2C)

B2C is such a huge category that we hesitate to lump you all together. B2C ranges from big flower vendors making a killing on Mother's Day to one-person operations selling homemade soaps. You may have a local, national, or international customer base, and you may have anything from a phone number or a Yahoo! store to a complex, media-rich e-commerce experience. However, there are some key elements that you have in common when you perform SEO.

Challenge: Less-Web-Savvy Audience The people who are searching for your product or service may not be as knowledgeable about the Web as you are, and certainly not as knowledgeable as you hope they are. So, even though the Web is chock-full of niche shopping sites that are worth looking into, it makes sense to give your attention first to how your site looks in the search engine mainstays: Google, AOL, Yahoo!, MSN, and Ask.

And while you may have the benefit of marketing research and brand differentiation, your potential audience may be frustratingly unaware of your preferred labels for your own product or service. Are you selling "the finest micro-techno-fiber all-weather apparel"? That's great, but your general user base is probably searching for "blue raincoats." In addition, they may be misspelling your product or—*the horror*—your brand name. Careful keyword research can help you tremendously.

Advantage: User-Generated Content Our own site visitors: We love them when they're helpful, and we hate them when they're spamful or spiteful. *User-generated content (UGC)*—things like product reviews, forum postings, and blog comments written by your visitors—is actually a yummy advantage and a prickly challenge all rolled into one. On the plus side, UGC bulks up your website, giving search engines lots of text information to chew on. It also helps engage your visitors, adds freshness to your site, and often helps your customers make the best choices. On the downside, if you don't have time to police every posting that makes it onto your site, you can be caught with some embarrassing search engine listings. Hey, it even happens to the big guys:

Challenge: Unexpected Search Competition As your audience is potentially very large and diverse, so is your competition. We mean your *search* competition, of course. You may know exactly who your top five competitors are in the "real world," but when you get down to identifying your top-priority keywords in Your SEO Plan, you're likely to be amazed by the sites that are clogging up the top ranks. They might be competitors you've never heard of, or they might be individual consumers talking about how much they hate your products. Or, as we often see, they may not be related to your industry at all. Did you know there's a band called "The Blue Raincoats"? Well, there is, and last we checked, it had the top nine spots in Google for the term "blue raincoats."

Advantage: Knowing the Value of Online Sales One of the primary struggles in SEO is knowing exactly how much a conversion is worth. We often play "stump the B2B" by asking, "How much is that white paper download really worth, in dollars?" But if your B2C website deals in online sales, placing a value on your conversions is a piece of cake. With a little help from your web developer, you can track the dollar value of every sale along with your traffic data. One of the many benefits of doing this is that you'll actually know whether your paid search campaign is worth the money you're spending on it!

Challenge: Page View Conversions If, like many B2C websites, your measure of conversion is a page view—for example, if you're using traffic data to sell ad space on your site, or if your main goal is brand awareness—get ready for an exciting ride. Simply going by the traffic numbers can have you shouting from the top of the parking garage one day and weeping into your latte the next. This next bit of advice may be hard for a slick up-and-comer like you to swallow, but we're telling you because we like you: Accept that you have less control than you think you do. The Google gods are fickle. An algorithm change, or a search engine marriage or divorce, may be all it takes to sink your traffic.

Large Organization

If you're about to embark on SEO for your large organization, brace yourself—this is going to sting a little:

Pearl of Wisdom: You do not have dibs on the #1 spot in the rankings just because you're big.

In fact, your SEO campaign is likely to be challenged by your bulk, both in terms of your website and your organizational structure.

Challenge: Internal Bureaucracy From an organizational perspective, your SEO challenges are often a result of "too much." Too much in that your site is likely to be run by committee: designers, IT department, copywriters, and coders, not to mention the executives who, with a single comment, can have you all scrambling in different directions. We know how pressed you are for time, how many different people in your organization are all putting their dirty fingers in the pie that is your website, and we know what a struggle it can be to get any changes made on your site. Here are some very common SEO tasks; see if you can get through this list without cringing about how many individuals you'll need to round up to complete them:

- Convert graphics to HTML text.
- Edit elements of the HTML code on every page of the site.
- Re-embed Flash files with alternate HTML text.
- Create a specialized text file called robots.txt and have it placed in the root directory of the site.

- Set up a server-side redirect.
- Rewrite page text to reflect more commonly searched terms.
- Change file-naming conventions.

The takeaway here is that you'll be putting a lot of extra time into internal communication and organization. You need to know your team and get them in your corner if you want to succeed at SEO. In other words: Get your team on board. It's so important it has its own chapter in this book!

Why is this door always *so sticky*?

Challenge: Brand Maintenance Another "too much" challenge for you lies in the need to keep your brand current. You have probably already witnessed several major changes to your site, steered either by real market forces or by the perceptions of your marketing department. Maybe you have a redesign every six months, frequent new products or product updates, or new branding guidelines to implement. Structurally, you may also have multiple subdomains, more than one URL leading to your home page, and lots of fragmented bits of old versions of your site floating around out there. (Think you don't? Check again. We can honestly say we haven't met one large website that didn't have something old and out-of-date live and available on the search engines.) Maybe you have all of the above, multiple times over, because you have different teams responsible for different portions of your website. Because of all these factors, the large organization has a special need to keep its "calling cards" on the Web consistent with the current state of its site. Cleaning up old and dead links and making sure your listings talk about your current products and services should be two of your highest priorities.

Advantage: Budget and Existing Infrastructure Of course, "too much" works to your advantage, too. You may have a larger budget, which means that you can probably afford to buy some of the many helpful tracking and keyword tools that we will suggest in this book. And your company probably has existing marketing data about your customers, their behaviors and habits, and their budgets, which your SEO campaign can tap into.

Advantage: Lots of Landing Pages Large sites often have a wealth of opportunities for landing pages. Go long—*long tail*, that is: Think beyond your home page and main section pages when determining which pages to optimize. This long tail approach—driving site visitors to a large number of unique pages on your site—can help you compensate for some of the other challenges we've discussed.

Challenge: Paid Search Pitfalls *Pay-per-click (PPC)* campaigns can help you accomplish your long tail goals, and a well-run PPC campaign is much cheaper on a per-visit basis than any form of offline marketing. But PPC campaigns for large organizations have the potential to be large and unwieldy. Even with the built-in management tools that make your PPC campaign a fairly user-friendly experience, the sheer magnitude of a hundred-plus or thousand-plus keyword campaign can be very time-consuming. PPC campaigns are an unlikely mix of the creative (word choice, campaign strategy) and the tedious (daily budget caps, maximum click price). The danger for the large company is that it's easy to shift your attention away from the important details—such as clarity of message and appropriateness of keyword choice—and get distracted by the data.

Advantage: PPC Assistance Luckily, your larger budget may qualify you for helpful hand-holding services directly from the PPC engines—services where actual humans talk to you and manage the more tedious aspects of your accounts. These services are worth looking into, but always remember: Nobody knows your company and brand like you do! Whether you manage the campaign yourself or hire someone else to do it, make sure someone with marketing sense and excellent writing skills is keeping an eye on it. There's nothing we hate more than seeing ads like this one. Seriously, is this what they want people to see?

Stinky Feet
Looking for **Stinky Feet**? Find exactly
what you want today.
www.ebay.com

Advantage: Making News Last but not least, being large might mean that just about everything you do is automatically newsworthy—which translates into incoming links on the Web. That's great news for your SEO potential!

Small Organization

Small businesses, we salute you as the most vibrant sector of today's Web! You are the equivalent of the corner store—the "mom and pop" sites—personalizing the Web and providing an antidote to the MegaCorp, Inc., mentality and design. Whatever you're selling, you're probably doing it on a careful budget, and you're probably doing everything with minimal staff.

Did you read the section about the large organizations and find yourself feeling a bit envious of all that money and manpower? Don't be. SEO can be the field leveler you need to compete with larger companies, whereas competition in offline advertising venues would be much too expensive for you. And, being smaller, your team, your site—and your SEO campaign—can benefit from a more centralized approach.

Advantage: Less Bureaucracy A busy small organization is often too tapped for resources to work on bettering its own marketing message or position—serving the customer always comes first. Your company doesn't have room for large teams of marketing writers and strategists. So you may be the one person who is the gatekeeper for all of these activities. Sure, it's more work for you, but on the positive side, it means you won't have to go through a huge bureaucracy every time you need to change your website. *You* have the power to make a real difference.

Challenge: Lack of Time If your business is doing well, your biggest SEO challenge is going to be a shortage of time. You might even be sweating out the notion of finding your hour a day for SEO tasks. The great news is, SEO gives back what you put into it. Do what you can, and read Chapter 10, "Extra Credit and Guilt-Free Slacking," for ideas on how to devote your precious SEO moments to the tasks that are going to give you the best time-to-results ratios.

Advantage: A Friendlier Reception For any site, asking other sites for links is one of those lower-return tasks: very time-consuming, unpredictable results. But being small can give you a real advantage in the area of "personal touch." Do you have a really cool new product? Are you offering a discount for a particular group? Tell a blogger who might be interested in telling the world. Or you may want to reach out to satisfied customers who have websites. Even though link building might not be on the hot burner, if you chip away at this activity, you can probably increase your *inbound links* in a meaningful way.

Challenge: Small Budget Your time is tight, and your budget is modest. Probably the smartest investment you can make, in our opinion, is a pay-per-click campaign. Surprised? It actually makes a lot of sense. If you manage it closely, your PPC campaign gives you almost-instant feedback. Is your message compelling enough? Are you targeting viable keywords? Is your landing page doing its job? With PPC, you can tweak to your heart's content for pennies on the dollar compared to other advertising methods.

Advantage: Tools to Level the Playing Field Of course, you know your product or service inside and out, and your customers may seem like close, personal friends. But you might not be very well versed in your customers' web habits and searching behavior. You may have little or no actual experience in marketing. Luckily, you don't need to be a pro—or a big business—to excel in SEO.

A recent study by Outsell, Inc., found that small companies' share of online ad spending on search engines is more than double the share of medium or large companies. You are big business for the search engines, and therefore, keyword research tools, directory listings, traffic analysis software, and the like are all often within the price range of the small business.

Even with a small budget, you can pick up an advantage by studying your competitors. Get ideas and insight from their websites and PPC campaigns, and use *their* resources to *your* best advantage! You may get as much out of the do-it-yourself competitive analysis later in the book as you would get from an expensive marketing study. If you've got the time and some natural curiosity, it doesn't cost you anything to look at the companies ranking in the top 10 for your desired keywords and figure out what they're doing right.

Advantage: Starting from Zero It may be that you have given no thought to SEO. Don't let that discourage you! Confession time:

Pearl of Wisdom: SEO consultants love working for companies starting out at rock bottom because you have nowhere to go but up.

But think carefully about your plan of attack. With a small staff, it is possible to go from famine to feast more quickly than you may be comfortable with. So, if each conversion on your site creates work for you, you may want to take it slowly.

Challenge: Seductive Quick-and-Dirty SEO Schemes Don't be tempted, as some smaller businesses are, to put your money or energy into quickie link schemes or questionable practices such as *comment spam* (using blog comments to plaster the Web with links to your site), which are likely to backfire. (We'll talk more about practices to avoid in Chapter 3, "Eternal Truths of SEO.") And please, remember that the message on your site is what will bring you conversions. If your pages are stuffed with keywords and filled with awkward text aimed at getting rankings, your business is likely to suffer in the long run. Keep your SEO campaign squeaky clean!

Really Small Organization

Take everything we said about small organizations, reduce the head count to one or two people, and pile on several additional demands for your time. Sound like you? We've had the pleasure of working with a lot of really small businesses, and we know how ludicrously tight the shoestrings get. But we also know how satisfying it can be to see a homegrown marketing effort turn into a big upswing in business.

Advantage: Slow Periods Everybody has slow times, but for really small businesses, when you're between projects or in the slow season, things can seem to grind to a complete halt. SEO gives you a way to fill the downtime, while giving structure to the things you should be doing anyway: snooping on your competitors, fine-tuning your goals, and ultimately working on growing your company.

Disadvantage: *Not* Slow Periods You're negotiating your own contracts. You're dusting your own office. You're filing your own taxes. In addition, you've got that not-so-small task of keeping your customers satisfied. How do you feel about hunkering down and learning all about search engines, basic HTML, and SEO industry trends? That desperate feeling in the pit of your stomach is exactly why there are so many low-low-priced SEO firms out there vying for your money. Problem is, in SEO you often get what you pay for, so you might as well try to do it yourself. You might want to work less formally: Read through this book to get the big picture. Don't fill out the worksheets. Abandon the hour-a-day concept. Tackle the parts that you can, when you can. Whatever you accomplish, pat yourself on the back—your job is hard enough.

Advantage: Your Own Name In many cases, the name of the company is the same as the person behind the company. In other cases, your company may have its own name, but, being so small, your name and your company name are used interchangeably. Building up your personal reputation will benefit your business reputation as well, and luckily, the Web has some exciting nooks and crannies that you can fit into that larger companies can't. Professional networking sites such as LinkedIn offer great opportunities to create a personal profile, and these can often translate to a lovely, professional search engine listing for your own name. Want your target audience to view you as the expert on corporate training or historical aviation models? Just be your witty, knowledgeable self in the right forums and blogs, and your name—and expertise—will be in front of the right people. If you have a lot of insight to share and you have a way with words, you can try to make a name for yourself with a professionally oriented, personally managed blog. (Just be sure to read the "Blogger" section in this chapter, too.)

Little Flower Candy Co.: Know When to Hold 'Em!

Christine Moore is a former pastry chef who knows a great deal about making delectable hand-made desserts using high-quality ingredients. Now she's in business for herself. Working in her own kitchen, using her own hands, she has developed a formidable reputation for making some of the tastiest candies in Los Angeles. But she admits she knows almost nothing about marketing.

And she's never had to. Thanks to great connections in L.A.'s visible foodie scene, word of mouth, and some very complimentary press coverage, her business is doing extremely well. When we spoke with her, she was looking toward the upcoming holiday season with excitement—and a good deal of trepidation. Acknowledging that the appeal of her product relies on the small-batch, handmade approach, she says, "I could ruin my reputation in one fell swoop by being greedy."

We have no doubt that an SEO campaign could bring Christine lots of new customers. But if things heat up too quickly, she may have more work than she can handle. At her current pace, she has time to get on the phone and call a web customer to work out an ordering glitch and to be there for her family. Of course, she's open to SEO for her site, but, as Christine says, "It's hard to know whether to put the cart before the horse or the horse before the cart." Like any marketing strategy, SEO requires that careful consideration be given to the balance between a business's long-term goals and current capabilities.

Continues

Little Flower Candy Co.: Know When to Hold 'Em! *(Continued)*

Christine is in control of her company, and she is in a position to have control over its web presence. She has a good kind of problem. Her "real-world" buzz will be easy to translate into a web buzz, when the time is right!

Her site was built in a hurry, under pressure to get a store online in time for an article about her company that was about to go to press. The publication made it clear: no online store, no article. A friend quickly built her site, and Christine wrote the text just hours before it went live. Since the site was built for a ready-made audience of readers who had the URL in print, almost no thought was given to the search engines.

As SEO experts, here's what we noticed about her site: There were only two links pointing to it, and neither of them came from the large publications that have printed articles about her company. With such a rabid following and word-of-mouth marketing happening in the real world, she could easily get more links. Also, her site features the word "handmade" because she's not fond of the term "gourmet." But what are her potential customers searching for? A little research would go a long way in determining if she's losing out on traffic by using the wrong terminology.

Brick-and-Mortar

If you had the chance to put one thing in front of your customers, you'd probably give them your street address, not your web address, and that's the way it should be. Your site plays second fiddle to your day-to-day business. After all, the best way to turn browsers into customers is to get them to walk through your door. You may not even be sure why you have a website, except that everyone else is doing it. So let's talk about how to make your site do its job of playing the supporting role.

Advantage: An Achievable Goal If you're not selling your product online, then the best use of your site is probably to help people find your physical location. Your SEO campaign begins with a simple goal: You want to be found when your company name is entered in the search engines. You'll focus your SEO campaign on variations of your business name and location. You're likely to get the results you are hoping for because you won't run up against too much competition for such tightly targeted keywords.

Advantage: Local Search And speaking of location, welcome to one of the hottest areas of SEO today: local search. It picks up where the local Yellow Pages left off in the last century. See Figure 2.1 for an example.

We love local search. Who wants to waste time slogging through nationwide search results when you're looking for the sandwich shop around the corner? If you're a cafe owner in Evanston, Illinois, you can put yourself directly in front of someone searching for "cafe Evanston IL." Talk about a targeted audience! Like the targeting? You'll love the placement—local listings are often displayed right at the top of the search results page. But wait, there's more: Local search listings on Google, Yahoo!, and MSN are free, and even offer an easy way to bask in the glow of online reviews, which often accompany these listings. Later in the book, we'll show you how to take control of your local listings and keep an eye on shape-shifting results as local search evolves.

Figure 2.1 A local search on Google

Maplecroft Bed & Breakfast in Barre, Vermont: The Power of Knowing Your Niche

Take a look at the Maplecroft Bed & Breakfast home page. Here's a little inn in small-town Vermont that offers a discount if you are a "librarian, quilter, or magician." You might describe the site as homey, low-budget, and low-tech, and that would all be true. But this sweet little site is deceptively well connected in the world of search.

Continues

Maplecroft Bed & Breakfast in Barre, Vermont: The Power of Knowing Your Niche *(Continued)*

Built by co-owner Paul Heller and designed by a family member in exchange for a vintage banjo, the site certainly does its job: It shows off the accommodations and provides a link to make a reservation. But Maplecroft is doing better than its competitors because Paul knows his niche. Here's what he says:

"My local competitors are not aware of the power of search engine advertising (AdWords, in particular), and many are unwilling to make an investment in travel-specific search engines. Our experience has shown both of these investments pay off in dramatically increased traffic.

"Many of our competitors do not love the Internet the way we do, so they don't read the stuff that we read or talk about these topics to the point of being annoying. I'm sure they don't monitor referrals to their site, so they continue to invest in marketing that may not be the most effective."

After paying close attention to his online bookings and using the stats package that comes with his hosting service, Paul made a decision: "We no longer make any real investment in print advertising."

Maplecroft Bed & Breakfast in Barre, Vermont:
The Power of Knowing Your Niche (Continued)

How does he take advantage of his "face-to-face" time with his customers? Well, he offers them an incentive to come back: Maplecroft offers a discount for repeat customers. "We have these old brochures and postcards featuring our inn that we leave in guest rooms. They have the URL of our site. Most guests take them."

"People who have been here use the website to check availability, and then they call to book so they can get that discount!"

Even though his B&B exudes old-fashioned joys like comfort, hospitality, good food, and good conversation, most people find him via the modern convenience of the Web. "Older people still use travel agents to book rooms," he says, and then adds, "The travel agents find us on the Web."

What is Maplecroft doing right? First, Paul recognized the potential of his online customer base and put his business in front of them via specialized travel directories, a local Yahoo! directory listing, and even a small PPC campaign. His attention to tracking gave him the confidence to move away from print to an advertising medium that worked better and cheaper. And he makes sure to "close the loop" by encouraging customers to go back to the site to take advantage of special offers.

Blogger

In recent years, *weblogs* have grown from a band of sharp-tongued outlaws to the darlings of online marketing. From Stonyfield Farm Yogurt to the Republican National Committee, it seems that everyone has a blog, or two, these days. Whether you are an individual out to bring in an income through running ads on your site or a large business with a blog on the site as a way to create relationships with potential clients, you are today's Big Thing on the Internet. Naturally, the major search engines should be catering to your every need. But you make it plenty hard for them! Your site lives and dies by content that changes every day, so it's difficult for search engines—which are also trying to index the entire rest of the Web, too—to keep up.

Blog-specific search works differently from standard search. Instead of going out and wandering through the zillions of web pages on the Internet every day, blog search engines sit back and watch for changes that come in through the "wires." This means that you'll need to do things a little differently to get your site included in these engines. In Part III, we'll give you pointers for setting up, troubleshooting, and monitoring your *feed*.

All the major search engines integrate blog postings into their search results, but the *blogosphere*, a common nickname for the world of blogs, is vast and wide, so you'll still need to be very aware of blog-specific search sites. You can find links to current biggies and up-and-comers on the companion website at www.yourseoplan.com.

Advantage: A Link-Friendly Culture Showing up on the blog-specific search engines isn't going to get you very far on its own. Blogs are part of a very special subculture on the Internet, and you need to tap into that subculture to gain visibility. Blogs need incoming and outgoing links—lots and lots of them—to succeed. But, lucky for you, no other sector of today's Web is as link-happy as the blogosphere.

The blogosphere is a very social place. Even if you usually cross to the other side of the street to avoid chatting with a neighbor in the "real world," you need to force yourself to be a much more gregarious animal online. Time-consuming as it may be, reading other blogs is one of the best ways to connect yourself to a community, and ultimately build links and visibility for your own blog.

Challenge: Minding Your Manners Looking for links from other blogs? The blogosphere is nothing if not socially complicated. It has all the affinities, grudges, schisms, feuds, accusations, and drama of a family reunion, without nearly as much barbecue sauce. Your intentions are good. All you want is a little love! But break etiquette, and you could be mercilessly *flamed* (assaulted by messages that are the electronic equivalent of a slap in the face), your comments removed, and your membership downgraded. Or, maybe worst of all, you could simply be ignored. You'll focus not just on gaining links, but on making friends, sharing your thoughts in venues beyond your own site… in short, really *participating* in the blogosphere. And if you care at all about your online reputation, one thing you must *never* do when visiting other blogs is leave a spam comment, saying nothing more than "Visit my blog!" Bloggers are merciless in their punishment of etiquette-breaking behavior such as this.

Challenge: Optimizing Every Post Since your site probably doesn't have a traditional site map, with sections, subsections, and conversion pages, you won't have traditional landing pages to focus your SEO attentions on. Instead, you will have to put your time into making *every post* a better place for searchers to land. All of the SEO rules we lay out in this book for landing pages—rules like including keywords throughout text, writing great titles, and using search engine–readable HTML text—should become part of your every post.

Does it go without saying that you are going to need to update your blog very, very frequently? We sure hope so. Since your whole existence as a blogger is about writing excellent content, you're already well on your way to search-friendly site optimization.

Are You Selling Out If You Optimize Your Blog?

The Right Brain says, "Wait a minute. I'm uncomfortable telling bloggers to optimize their postings with search-targeted keywords! Shouldn't a blog be a bastion of personal expression and entertaining writing? Shouldn't the blogosphere be free of the marketing mentality that pervades the rest of the Web? We've seen it time and again: Good writing can really take a beating when a marketing agenda is attached to it."

The Left Brain says, "Right, and bloggers are all out there working on their own personal time, with no need for the luxuries in life like food and shelter. Heck, no! Blogs are well beyond the days of being just for fun; they are truly a business now. And as such, they have a legitimate need for SEO, just like any other business website. I would never counsel a blogger to dilute his message or change the blog's subject matter based on conversions—just as I don't give that sort of advice to any other website owner. But creating highly readable headlines that are compelling and clear— that's just common sense. And isn't 'search-targeted keywords' just another way of saying, 'Use the text that makes the most sense to your audience?' After all, what good is a message if nobody finds it?"

Challenge: Domain Considerations These days, it's easy to create a blog that shows up within your website domain. But maybe you started your blog a couple years ago, and it's currently living on a free hosting domain like biotech-now.blog-mega-service.com, miles away from your company's primary domain. Ouch. You've got some thinking to do: Bite the bullet and move the blog now, or keep it as is and try to leverage it from where it stands? There's no simple answer: Moving domains is always disruptive to search presence. But change comes with the territory for you bloggers, and any commitment to improving your traffic is a change for the better.

Advantage: A Venue for Personal Touch Any salesperson will tell you that making a sale is about trust. If you are trying to sell something through your blog, you have a great opportunity to give your audience a chance to get to know and trust you. Aaron Wall of www.seobook.com is both a blogger and expert search marketer. His blog is one way that potential customers find and purchase his e-book. But it's also a comprehensive, information-rich site that both helps others and bolsters his reputation in the industry. His advice to bloggers getting started and looking for SEO strategies: "Learn your community well, find and use your real voice, and link out early and often."

Adult Sites: Time to Get Passionate about SEO

If your website is of the adult variety, prepare yourself for a difficult SEO experience. Besides dealing with mind-boggling levels of competition for keywords, you are also faced with several other disadvantages: a website that is, shall we say, more "visually" oriented than text oriented; a plethora of *black-hat* (questionable or unethical) SEO competitors; an entry page to boot out the under-21 crowd; and search engines that do not allow X-rated sites to advertise.

Sage Vivant, president and webmaster of CustomEroticaSource.com, has had her share of trials and tribulations working to promote her custom erotic literature website. Her many frustrations range from not being able to list her ads on Google AdWords for terms such as "gifts" and "anniversary" to being denied participation in the Better Business Bureau. "I'm extremely frustrated by having to constantly work around arbitrary moral rules relating to what is and is not 'adult.'"

So, what does work for adult websites?

- Use descriptive text. It's a real turn-on to the search engines! Find ways to add some very specific keywords, not just graphics, to your site.

- Your PPC campaign has the potential to be very pricey, so track it carefully, with a focus on cost per conversion.

- Be patient, and perseverant, with advertising rules and limitations.

- Although you're in a very competitive spot, never use unethical SEO techniques, which could get you permanently banned (removed from the search engine listings).

- Utilize all of your image optimization options. The "Safe Surf Off" crowd knows how to use image-only search, and with careful attention to SEO for your pics, you'll have a better chance at being found.

- Think beyond the search engines. Sage says, "Several years ago, I started an e-mail list, and I think that was the single most successful thing I ever did. I had been afraid that people wouldn't want to hear from my business, but I was wrong—response to any promotion or announcement I send out through that list is always good to excellent."

Web Designer

Web designers are natural partners in SEO. After all, shouldn't the person who designs and builds a website have a strong interest in knowing how to make it search friendly? After gaining coverage in the *New York Times* and *Newsweek*, SEO has become positively mainstream. We're betting you've already had a client ask for SEO, or you wish to add it to your service offerings. Want to use SEO for a bigger slice of the proposal pie or to gain a longer list of prospects? Here are some of the challenges and advantages we expect you'll face:

Advantage: The Inside Track You're already on the job, providing web design services. Your client trusts you, and the site files are nestled safely on your hard drive. Lucky for you, it is often difficult for an outside SEO consultant to be inserted into the very early stages of web design. This is because much of the website is still theoretical early on, and "theoretical" SEO can only get you so far. Use your status to your advantage: As the designer, you can easily introduce SEO early in the conversation and be sure it is integrated into design decisions throughout the process.

Challenge: Hucksters Abound No, no, we're not talking about *you*. We're talking about those *other* web designers. You know, the ones who feature SEO as an add-on to their regular services, and then just stick HTML titles on some pages, with no keyword research or insight to back them up? They probably charge a couple hundred bucks for the add-on, spend 10 minutes on the work, and accomplish nothing for their clients. Unfortunately, you have to compete with these guys. To protect your reputation (and ours!):

Pearl of Wisdom: Only sell SEO services to customers if you are very good at SEO.

The "SEO on training wheels" approach in this book is great if you're doing it in-house, but, if you are an outsourced entity, you'll be held to a higher standard. We have seen many a web developer–client relationship turn sour, all because the client paid good money for bad SEO. If you want to offer SEO as a stand-alone or add-on service, take a gradual approach. First, learn SEO fundamentals and integrate them into your designs. Then, follow up with your clients a few months after launch to see how they're doing in the search engines. After you've got months of SEO background, practice, and follow-up under your belt, go ahead and hang out the shingle for your SEO work.

We have a feeling that once you have a solid understanding of search engine–friendly design and are integrating SEO best practices into your web development, it won't just be an add-on, it will be a principle applied to all your projects. With this important capability in your portfolio, you'll have a better chance of landing the projects you want, and heck, we won't blame you if you raise your rates a bit.

Challenge: A Short-Term Project SEO is a long-term effort. It requires months if not years of ongoing work. Most web development projects, however, are structured to last only through site launch and perhaps a short support period—not long enough for the type of holistic SEO approach we advocate in this book. Most SEO contracts have a term of 3–12 months, and if you're really confident about your SEO skill set, you'll want to push for an ongoing contract, too. Remember that the added value of your SEO services can't possibly be known until the website has been up for several months.

Challenge: A Change of Perspective You're a web designer, which means you probably know a little something about graphic design, information architecture, usability, "look and feel," and techie back-end development. This is great news because file-naming conventions, choice of site architecture, and scripting and page structure choices all play a part in the search engine friendliness of a site. However, your skill set may or may not include writing and marketing strategy, and your relationship with your client may not go there on a regular basis. If you're not a natural wordsmith or strategist, you'll need to update your tool belt or find a partner who can complement your skills.

Nonprofit

Those of you in nonprofit organizations are working with a different sort of bottom line for your websites. Rather than following the corporate mantra of "money, money, and more money," you fine people are out there trying to change the world, educate, and improve society! And as a thank-you from the world of web search, you have some huge advantages in SEO.

Advantage: Linkability The culture of the Web generally adores noncommercial content—something that your website should be chock-full of. And, let's face it, giving you a link doesn't cost a thing. Any webmaster or blogger who supports your cause—or at least has no major problem with it—will see adding a link as a cheap and easy way to help out. You will want to adjust your SEO plan accordingly, giving extra effort to link building.

And what is even better than inbound links from other sites? How about some fabulous "site of the day" awards from major web presences like Yahoo! and USAToday.com? "Site of the day" editors are always on the lookout for worthy sites, and nonprofits are in a perfect position to tap into this source of visibility and traffic. It's helpful—but not necessary—if you have something new on your site to show off. Be sure to include some time in Your SEO Plan for building that "site of the day" potential. Sure, it's a little like winning the lottery of SEO, but for you, it's worth a try. Your odds are a lot better than for-profit sites' odds.

Advantage: Simple Website Structure And there's more good news: Some of the characteristics that might, at first glance, seem like disadvantages for nonprofits are actually not so bad. Oftentimes, nonprofits are short on cash but have plenty of untrained personnel available. Since many SEO tasks don't require a great deal of technical skill, using sharp-witted college students or interns might just be the SEO strategy that brings you to the top. Another "problem" that might not be as bad as you think: an old website. That's right, your cruddy old 1999 website was probably built using no Flash, little JavaScript, and an absence of dynamic bells and whistles. Well, guess what? Those are just the things that can send *search engine spiders* packing anyway! A "classic" all-text site can be just the ticket for getting noticed by the search engines. Before you make any changes, make sure you aren't in an "if it ain't broke, don't fix it" situation.

Advantage: Less PPC Competition Many nonprofits think that there's no way that they can survive in the competitive world of paid listings. However, there are a few ways that you can, as a nonprofit, get your foot in the door. For one, it's possible that the keywords that matter most to you are not the same words that commercial organizations are vying for. After all, nobody's out there selling "AIDS in China." Even better, both Google and Yahoo! offer free advertising programs for nonprofits. Be sure to check their websites for current programs and availability.

Challenge: Internal Issues Internal disorganization, an overworked and underpaid workforce, lack of funding, and lack of a clear bottom line could throw hurdles in the way of Your SEO Plan. If you are a small operation, you may not even have a marketing department to manage the website. And without a clearly measurable bottom line, it may be very hard for you to prove the value of your efforts. You will need to do some creative thinking to figure out a way to get that return on investment (ROI) measured. Is there a specific event that you can promote? A campaign or drive that can be earmarked as an SEO testing ground? With any luck, your SEO campaign will be funding itself after a few months of effort. You may be surprised to find that it becomes one of the most important outreach venues your organization will use.

Mon Yough Community Services: SEO on a Shoestring

Mon Yough Community Services (MYCS) is a nonprofit organization near Pittsburgh, Pennsylvania. It embodies some of the common challenges of nonprofits: lack of funding, lack of resources, and an organization that embraces "low tech." MYCS's website, developed and hosted by a company offering pro bono services to nonprofits, hasn't had a major update in seven years. If you ask Gina Boros, MIS manager, what kind of effort they put into SEO, she'll just laugh.

At first blush, it seems there's no reason to market MYCS on the Web. This is an organization whose target population is the homeless and mentally ill. Its most successful marketing efforts are in the form of bus stop advertisements, not the Internet. Pittsburgh's nonprofit service agencies are a tight-knit group, and the referrals that come are almost always word of mouth.

Continues

Mon Yough Community Services: SEO on a Shoestring *(Continued)*

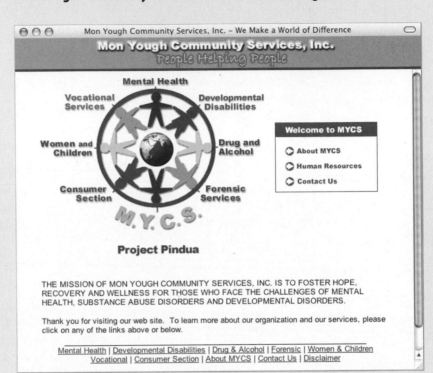

But, when you delve a bit deeper, it becomes clear that marketing its site on the Web would be far from pointless. MYCS constantly seeks new volunteers and interns to keep its therapy programs running smoothly, and website owners love linking to these kinds of opportunities. MYCS throws fundraising events: the more people attending, the more funds raised. If they're using flyers and newspaper ads to promote these, why not the website? And it turns out that there are some case managers in the region who haven't heard of MYCS. The search engines might give a little boost.

Perhaps the hardest part of Gina's job is that she knows how much she could do—she has a master's degree in multimedia development—if her organization just had the funding and resources. Her hosting service makes traffic stats available, and she could check them if she had time, but who has time? She's one of three people maintaining 400 machines. She knows its branding could be more cohesive, but MYCS doesn't have a marketing department. As it is, Gina says, "I can give you maybe four examples of people who actually found us through our website."

Gina's got a plan: She's going to find some grad students, maybe from her old multimedia program, and get a new website built with labor from free internships. After that, she'll have a website worth promoting and a team on board to get moving with SEO. Good luck, Gina!

One final word of encouragement: We asked SEO luminary Jill Whalen (one of the most renowned names in the SEO industry) whether she thought do-it-yourselfers could do as good a job as professionals in SEO. Her response? "Absolutely!" You know your business—and all its nooks and crannies—better than anybody. After reading this chapter, you should have a long-view understanding of how you'll need to approach SEO so that you can make the most of your advantages and minimize your challenges. In the next chapter, we'll start talking details about the search engines. Get ready to be imbued with some Eternal Truths of SEO.

Eternal Truths of SEO

You've probably heard that SEO and the search engines change constantly, and it's true. But there are some things about SEO that haven't changed much, and probably won't for a long time to come. These Eternal Truths include basic information that you will use starting in Part III and for the duration of your SEO campaign. You don't want to chisel this stuff in stone, but it calls for something a little more permanent than a dry-erase marker.

3

Robots Deliver

We're going to start with the basics of how the search engines work, and a major component of this is a *robot,* or *spider*, which is software that gathers information about your site and brings it back to be analyzed by a powerful central "engine." This activity is referred to as *crawling* or *spidering*. There are lots of different metaphors for how robots work, but we think ants make the best one. Think of a search engine robot as an explorer ant, leaving the colony with one thought on its mind: *Find food.* In this case, the "food" is HTML text, preferably lots of it, and to find it, the ant needs to travel along easy, obstacle-free paths: HTML links. Following these paths, the ant (search engine robot), with insect-like single-mindedness, carries the food (text) back to its colony and stores it in its anthill (search engine database). Thousands and thousands of the little guys are exploring and gathering simultaneously all over the Internet. (See Figure 3.1 for a visual example.) If a path is absent or blocked, the ant gives up and goes somewhere else. If there's no food, the ant brings nothing back.

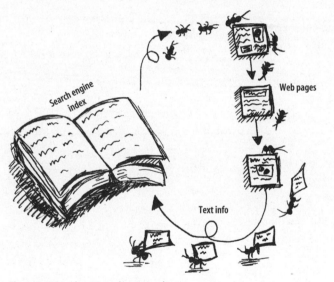

Figure 3.1 Search engine robots at work

So basically, when you think of a search engine, consider it a database that holds pieces of text that have been gathered from millions of sites all over the Web.

What sets that engine in motion? A search. When a web surfer enters the term "grape bubble gum" into the search engine, all of the sites that *might* be relevant for that term are brought to the forefront. The search engine sifts through its database for sites containing terms like "*grape* growers," "stock market *bubble*," and "*gum* disease." It uses a secret formula—a.k.a. a search ranking *algorithm*—to sort the results, and in a fraction of a second, a list of relevant sites, many containing the exact phrase "grape bubble gum," (or with links from other sites containing this phrase) will be returned in the results page.

There are lots of things that factor into the way robot search engines determine the rank for their main search results. But just for a start, in order to be in the running for ranks, you need to provide HTML text to feed the search engines and HTML links as clear paths to the food. Keeping those robots well fed and happy is one of your biggest priorities.

A Search Engine by Any Other Name

We like to talk about search engines at parties—hey, it's how we get our clients—and when we use the term search engines with our pals, we mean search sites like Google, Yahoo!, and MSN. But folks in the search industry can get pretty picky about terminology. Technically, a search engine is the software that is used to retrieve information from an indexing database, while a search site is a website that combines and displays all of that information, often from multiple sources. But, frankly, we don't give a hoot about the technical accuracy of the term. Everyone and his mother calls Yahoo! a search engine, and—with apologies to the purists out there—we do, too.

Search Results Are Blended

If you've spent much time searching, you have probably noticed that the search engines are not displaying a homogeneous set of results. Most search engines take the "chef's salad" approach, displaying a mix of robot-sourced listings, directory listings, image and video, and paid ads. Knowing what each type of listing looks like and where they come from is the first step in being able to influence your own listings in a positive way. You learned about robot results earlier; here are the other types of results that are commonly available to searchers.

Directories

Unlike those robot search engines, directory listings are often compiled by humans. Whether these humans are editors who work for the search engines or the site owners themselves who write and submit their own listings, it is often easy to tell the difference between a directory and a robot search result. Take a look at this robot-generated listing from Google. It's called a *snippet*—text slurped directly from the web page and spat out into the search results page.

Thanksgiving **Coffee** Co. presents **Mirembe** Kawomera Ugandan **Coffee**
Thanksgiving **Coffee** Co. presents **Mirembe** Kawomera Delicious Peace Ugandan **Coffee**,
grown by a cooperative of Jewish, Muslim, and Christian Farmers.
www.mirembekawomera.com/ - 9k - Cached - Similar pages - Note this

Now take a look at this directory listing. Note the sentence-like structure, the human touch, and the category information.

Thanksgiving Coffee Company - Organic **Coffee**, Fair Trade **Coffee** ...
Category: <u>Shopping</u> > <u>Food</u> > <u>Beverages</u> > <u>Coffee and Tea</u> > <u>Coffee</u> > <u>Organic</u>
A selection of blends, as well as information on topics such as shade grown **coffee**, organic
farming and fair trade **coffee**.
www.thanksgivingcoffee.com/

Directories aren't likely to come out and find you the way robots will; site owners need to submit to them manually. Sometimes you can purchase a listing, sometimes they're free, and sometimes you pay for the "privilege" of having your submittal reviewed whether your site is included or not. Although it's a little extra work to achieve directory listings, at least you can be relatively certain that your submittal will be reviewed by somebody and your site will have a fair chance of getting in. This is different from the robots, which do not guarantee review or inclusion.

Paid Search Ads

No matter how blurred the line between unpaid and paid search gets in the search engine results, you, as the SEO expert, will always know the difference. That's because, while it's possible to get listed in robot search engines, *meta search engines*, and even directories without actually doing anything, you (or someone you delegate) will have to actively implement and carefully manage any paid advertising for your own site. And, of course, there's that little matter of the checkbook, too.

Pay-per-click (PPC) services are the simplest paid search option. Here's how it works: You open an account with a PPC engine, such as Google AdWords or Yahoo! Search Marketing. You decide which search terms you want your site to be seen for, and you write your own listing (or often, several different listings) to correspond with your chosen terms. Every time a searcher clicks on your listing, you pay the PPC engine a fee. You control the amount you want to spend for each click (your *bid*), and this is a major factor in the placement of your listing.

Paid search is the SEO marketing venue over which you have the most control. It offers you a chance to micro-manage your website marketing by being able to target specific messages to specific terms, and even specific geographical locations. It gives you the opportunity to change your message on a whim, and it provides some of the most conclusive tracking around. Therefore, although paid search is by no means a requirement for good SEO, it's an Eternally Attractive Option to have available to you.

Site Feeds

Site feeds have been around for years in one form or another, but their methodology is still morphing. Available in various forms, they are Eternally Helpful for large or frequently updated sites. Just as you may use a feed reader to be notified of your favorite blog or news topic, the search engines use site feeds to sit back and receive information from websites without sending spiders out to constantly gather, gather, gather. Feeds work well for regularly edited websites such as blogs and news sites (feeding the content of their daily posts), online sellers (feeding up-to-the-minute commercial information such as product descriptions and prices), and media-rich websites. You may also have heard of *trusted feed* or *paid inclusion* programs where search engines allow certain "trusted"—and, usually, paying—websites to send the engines regular updates. Generally, these types of listings get thrown into the mix with robot-gathered sites and have to fend for themselves, with no special status in the ranking algorithms.

Other Search Sources: Image, Video, Local, Content Partners

"Connect people with their passions…" "Organize the world's information…" It's a tall order! To keep up with their own mission statements and searchers' appetites, the search engines are increasingly adding results that are more than just links to individual web pages. These include images, videos, news, local listings with maps and reviews, and even entertainment or shopping opportunities from partner companies. (Figure 3.2 shows a variety of results.) It takes a practiced eye to know whether the listing you're looking at is paid, free, lucky, or impossible to get without a couple mil in your pocket. This book should give you a fighting chance for the first three types, anyway.

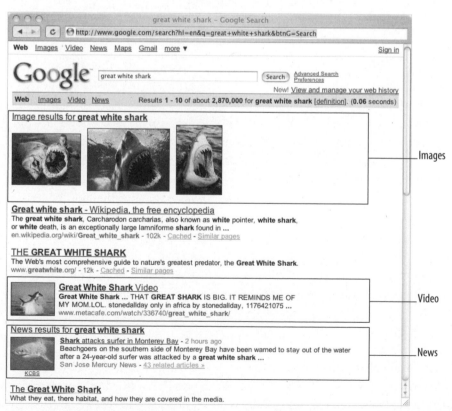

Figure 3.2 Google results for "Great White Shark"

Meta Search Engines and Search Aggregators

Some people are comparison shoppers, flitting from store to store to review all the merchandise before making a decision. For people who like to compare search results, meta search engines and search aggregators make it easy to review listings from different search engines in one screen—no flitting from site to site necessary. Simply put, these search engines compile and display results from several search engines and rank them according to their own algorithms. You can't use SEO to improve your presence on these engines directly; if a meta search engine like Mamma.com or a search aggregator like A9.com is using MSN results, the way to do better on these engines is to do better on MSN.

Algorithms Change

Here's something that drives people crazy about SEO: You can't ever be 100 percent sure that what you're doing will be rewarded with the rank and the listing you want. This is because the search engines keep their internal ranking mechanism, even the criteria by which the ranking is determined, under wraps. Welcome to the secret formula of SEO: the Search Engine Ranking Algorithm.

The algorithm is the formula that a search engine uses to determine its ranks. It's a way of sifting through a multitude of factors, including keyword repetition and page titles, inbound links, and even the age of the site. Some elements have more weight, meaning that they are considered to be more important in determining rank, and some have less. Each search engine uses its own algorithm to determine which results to show and in which order. And search engines change their algorithms constantly, without so much as a friendly warning. So the truth is this:

 Pearl of Wisdom: You will never really know exactly how Google works

(unless you work there, in which case, give us a call sometime!).

Imagine if other forms of marketing worked this way! What if you couldn't rely on alphabetical order in the Yellow Pages anymore? What if the TV networks chose to air only the parts of your ad that *they* felt were most important? What if your billboards were periodically relocated without your consent? We're so glad you've got a good head on your shoulders because, now that you're doing SEO, you will have to find a balance between keeping up with the algorithm and keeping your sanity.

Why do the search engines guard their algorithms so closely? Because, first and foremost, they value the searcher's experience. If MSN published a guide called "Instructions for Ranking #1 on Our Search Engine," you'd use it, of course. And so would everyone else. Then all of the results on MSN would become so manipulated by site owners that relevance would disappear—investment sites could rank high for "grape bubble gum" on purpose—and searchers would drop the engine like a big useless hot potato. Even without a manual, the little bits of algorithm that people figure out themselves often get so abused that the search engines eventually devalue them.

How do you find the balance between seeking the Eternally Unknowable Algorithm and making sure your SEO efforts are effective? Matt Cutts, the popular blogger and Google employee who sometimes indulges his SEO-obsessed readers with tantalizing bits of inside information on Google's algorithm, says, "Most of the right choices in SEO come from asking, What's the best thing for the user?" Bringing targeted users to your site is, of course, the point of SEO, and that's the reason we made you clarify your audience and site goals before we started talking about how the search engines work.

We asked Danny Sullivan, probably the best-known and most respected authority on search today, what he considers to be "Eternal" about SEO. His answer: "Good HTML titles, good body copy, great content, ensuring that your site doesn't have roadblocks to crawling—these have worked for nearly a decade." Notice he didn't mention anything about chasing the algorithm.

Now, you won't hear us saying, "algorithm, shmalgorithm" (though in the next chapter, we will say, "PageRank, ShmageRank"…stay tuned). One of the Eternal Truths we've learned over the years is this:

Pearl of Wisdom: Often, factors that matter most in the search engine algorithms are good for both websites and their users.

It's fine to keep an eye on the latest and greatest rumors about *exactly* how Google works, but don't go nuts or you will lose focus on what really matters: your site visitors.

Humans Are Smart—Computers Aren't

Let's face it: The search engine's job is not easy. Take a look at your filing cabinet, multiply it by about a billion, and imagine someone throwing you a couple of words and then hovering impatiently behind you, tapping a toe, expecting you to find exactly the right document in the blink of an eye. Nobody could! We humans are wonderfully intelligent creatures, but we're just a tad on the slow side when compared to computers. Unfortunately, machines are still just that: machines. They struggle with ambiguity that even a kindergarten student could handle. Not to mention misspellings, regional dialects, and punctuation. For search engines to bring back great results, they have to combine the best of both worlds: the speed of the machines and the intelligence of the human mind.

What's a search engine developer to do? Two things: First, combine results from several sources, as discussed earlier. This allows the search engines to intertwine the massiveness of the machine-driven system (robot results) with the finesse of the human touch (directory and paid results). Second, structure the ranking algorithms to integrate "votes" from human beings. Putting the human touch into a ranking algorithm can be done in a variety of ways, and search engines continue to experiment with solutions. Counting inbound links from other websites, for example, is a way of measuring how many votes a site has from human—and presumably intelligent—webmasters and bloggers. Other ideas have included measuring how many search engine users click through to your site and how long they stay. *Social bookmarking sites* and *collaborative tagging*, even comparing a person's current and past searches, are forms of artificial intelligence intended to improve the search experience.

But artificial intelligence still has as long way to go. In movies, you can say to a computer, "Computer, rotate, and enhance!" and the computer will somehow manage to turn and unblur a grainy image from a security camera just the way you need it. In the real world, we just aren't there yet. Search engines remain very literal creatures, unable to improvise very much beyond the exact words, even the exact syntax of words, they are given. Which leads us to our next Eternal Truth.

Text Matters

You probably *can* etch this one in stone:

 Pearl of Wisdom: Text is Eternally Important in search.

The entire process of a web search is text based, even when the item being sought isn't text at all, like a picture or video file. The search engines care about how much text you have on your site, how it's formatted, and, of course, what it says. In Parts II and III, we will walk you through the process of keyword selection and placement. To help prepare you for these tasks, you should know some Eternal Truths of text.

Keyword Selection Is Key

Careful keyword selection is the heart of the SEO campaign. Site owners who are on top of their SEO game have a list of top-priority keywords that they use on their site, with reasonable repetition, in strategic places. We never let a site go for six months without checking the keywords to make sure they're still appropriate. If a site's focus or positioning changes, new keywords are in order. If a company adds new products or services, new keywords are in order. If a new competitor comes on the scene, it's worth peeking into its site for new keyword ideas. Even if none of these changes takes place, regular keyword analysis is in order because search behavior and trends may change as well.

SEM: An Hour a Day?

When we were thinking about possible titles for this book, we had to take a little bit of our own advice: Look into the minds of your users. Most of our potential readers would use the term Search Engine Optimization (SEO) to describe what we do, so we stuck with it for our title. But SEO is actually an outdated term. Many in our industry prefer to give the service more all-inclusive labels such as SEM (short for Search Engine Marketing), SEO/SEM, Search Marketing, or even Competitive Webmastering.

What's wrong with calling it SEO? The term *optimization* really only accounts for editing the code and content of your website, which is only one segment of the many tasks included in this book. Other components of search marketing, such as link building and PPC sponsorships, don't easily fall under the banner of "optimization."

To add to the mix, many people use the terms *SEO* and *organic SEO* interchangeably to refer to all nonpaid efforts. This would include edits to your website, as well as work involved with increasing your inbound links and usability. The complement to organic search is paid search, commonly called SEM. Confused yet? We'll sum it up for you:

- The total package is usually called Search Marketing, SEO, or SEO/SEM.

- Nonpaid Search is usually called Organic or Natural SEO, or just SEO.

- Paid Search is usually called SEM.

Are there exceptions to the rule? Sure there are. Paying a onetime fee for a directory submittal would fall under organic SEO. As long as your listing is going to display in search results that are not labeled "Sponsored Listing," you can probably call the work organic.

With all this potential for confusion, we're keeping it simple. In this book, it's SEO for everything.

Your Site Has Many Keyword Placement Opportunities

The code that makes up your web page's text falls into two categories—visible and invisible—and they are both important for optimization. The *visible text* is made up of the words that you put on your page for the world to see, including obvious things like the paragraphs of carefully crafted content aimed at your target audience, but also less-obvious elements like your HTML page title, the text inside your links, and the navigational text that tells your visitors how to use your site, such as "Click the thumbnails for a full-size image." *Invisible text* refers to the words that do not display on the page but are added to your HTML code and gathered and analyzed by the search engine robots. This includes your *meta keywords tag*, *meta description tag*, and your *ALT image tags*.

Your Site's Message

We can't say it enough: Your site's text needs to be compelling, clear, focused, and directed to your users. It also needs to be formatted so that the robots can read it. This means HTML text, not *graphical text*, which the search engines can't read. If your site doesn't have any HTML text, adding some is critical to getting the search engines to give your site the visibility you desire.

Take a look at this page full of text:

Unfortunately, almost all of the text on the page is composed of GIF files, not HTML. So to the search engines, it looks like this:

HTML Page Title

Probably the most important of the visible text elements is your HTML page title. In the code, it looks like this:

```
<title>Dave's Custom Bikes, Santa Cruz, California – Electric Bikes</title>
```

On the page, it looks like this:

And in the search engines, it gets top billing, usually as the bolded first line of a search results page, like this:

> **Dave's Custom Bikes, Santa Cruz, California - Electric Bikes**
> ... **bikes**, used **bikes** and accessories. Located in Santa Cruz, California. **Dave's Custom Bikes** is now building **electric bikes**. With the Santa Cruz County's **Electric** Bike Rebate Program ...
> www.davescustombikes.com/electric_bikes.html Cached page

The page title is Eternally Important because it gets maximum exposure in the search engine results pages. If you care about getting clicks to your site, this text should be succinct and compelling, and for your best chance at conversions, it should accurately summarize the page content. We'll visit the specifics of writing great HTML page titles and meta descriptions in Part III.

Meta Description Tag

The meta description tag is an example of invisible text.

In the code, it looks like this:

```
<Meta name="description" content="Bobux baby shoes are the original soft soled
shoes with the elastomatic ankle system that makes them easy to slip on
and they stay on.">
```

And in the search engines, it can be displayed as the description under the page title. Notice how the searched-for keywords are bolded in the search engine results:

> Bobux **Baby Shoes** Online **Baby Shoes** Soft Soled **Baby Shoes** Leather...
> Bobux **baby shoes** are the original soft soled **shoes** with the elastomatic ankle system that makes them easy to slip on and they stay on.
> ∞ | www.bobuxusa.com/ | Cached | Save

Much of the time, however, the meta description tag is passed over, and instead, a "snippet" of the page is displayed:

> Bobux Baby Shoes Online Baby Shoes Soft Soled Baby Shoes **Leather**...
> New Styles. Animals. Bows & **Mary Janes**. Flowers. Summer/Sandals. Classics ... Bobux® baby shoes are made from **Eco-leather**, a natural **leather**...
> ∞ | www.bobuxusa.com/ | Cached | Save

You can't control when or where your meta description tag will display, but like your page title, it should be compelling, keyword rich, and unique for every page.

Meta Keywords Tag

The meta keywords tag, another invisible text element, is the place where site owners can list their keywords, including variations of keywords such as misspellings, that wouldn't be appropriate for the visible text elements.

In the code, it looks like this:

```
<meta name="keywords" content="movies, films, movie database, actors,
actresses, directors, hollywood, stars, quotes">
```

It is rarely seen on the search engines, and that's a good thing because it's one of the few elements on your website that you can write specifically for the search engines and not your audience. This excites a lot of site owners, who think, "Finally! A way to talk to the search engine robots and tell them which terms I want to get my high ranks for!" But search engines prefer to make their own decisions on rank, and this is precisely why the meta keywords tag does not carry a lot of weight.

You have plenty of work to do for your site, and organizing target keywords is one of the most important. But plopping keywords into your meta keywords tag—especially if the terms don't exist elsewhere on the page—is like putting lipstick on a pig. It won't make it any more kissable. Save your precious time for work that you *know* will help you gain search engine success.

How Other Sites Are Linking to Yours

As we discussed earlier, search engines need human help in their Eternal Quest for that perfect ranking algorithm. They look for links to your website, not only to follow those links and find your site, but also to determine more information about your site. Does someone else link to your website using the words *Click Here to Find Very Fancy Foxhounds*? That's giving the search engine a clue that your website just might have something to do with foxhounds. And the search engine may go even further, looking at other words surrounding the link for more clues. If the linking page also contains the words *fleas*, *fur*, and *Finding a Breeder*, it's reinforcing the notion that your website will be a good destination for that foxhound-seeking searcher.

It's Not Just about Rank

While your ranks are the easiest aspect of SEO to grasp, don't let them be the only thing you care about. We don't mean to be dismissive of people who really, truly live and die by their Google rank. We know that there are industries that are so cutthroat and specialized that this *is* the only thing that matters. But we have found this to be true:

Pearl of Wisdom: The vast majority of businesses do best when they use a holistic approach to SEO, combining elements of organic and paid search with a healthy dose of good writing and usability.

Remember, good ranks do not guarantee conversions or website success! As you learned in Chapter 1, "Clarify Your Goals," your business goals for your website may range from online sales to political persuasion—whatever it is you want your visitors to do. Your keywords must be chosen to directly match these goals. You could easily gain some high ranks for, say, the term *hydroplaning monkey*, because nobody else is optimizing for it. Of course, nobody's searching for it either. Likewise, if you make some iffy choices regarding your top-priority keywords, it's possible that you'll track top-10 ranks, month after month, and have no conversions to show for it.

Ranks Change

Let's say you are lucky enough to be getting good organic ranks for a coveted, competitive term. Congrats, but don't take these ranks for granted; any number of factors outside of your control could send your site on a nosedive:

Competitor Activity Many times, SEO success is achieved not by brilliant optimization, but rather as a result of the laziness of a site's competitors. If yours is the only site in your niche giving SEO any effort, you're going to come out on top. But you never know when the other guys are going to get their act together and start a successful SEO campaign.

Common SEO Misconceptions

If you're brand new to SEO, you may have a couple of incorrect notions in your head. Let's get rid of those right now:

"Our site gets a ton of traffic! We're so popular, we're a shoo-in for top ranks." Search engines don't have insider information about your overall web traffic, so they don't know exactly how popular your site is. But they can count up how many sites they find that link to your site, and this is one factor in how they judge your site's popularity.

"We've got to get more sites to link to us so that our ranks will improve!" If the only reason you set out to get more links is so that Google will rank you higher, you are missing the big picture. Inbound links are pathways that allow people to visit your site. They can be excellent, direct sources of targeted traffic!

"Our site is doing great! We ranked #1!" Ranked #1 for *what*? Starting now, erase "We ranked #1" from your vocabulary and replace it with "We ranked #1 for the term _____." Ranks are irrelevant unless they are tied to a meaningful target keyword.

"We're only going to promote our home page." SEO is not about your site—it's about every page of your site. Every single page in your site stands on its own merits and can sink or swim based on its unique combination of the factors described in this chapter. If you approach SEO as a page-by-page endeavor, you will be on a surer path to success.

"We've filled in our meta keywords tag... we're good to go!" The meta keywords tag carries very little influence with the search engines, and it's certainly not going to do much for your ranks if the rest of your site isn't shipshape. Just like any element of SEO, the keywords tag works best in the context of a holistic approach.

Your Server Performance The search engine robots visit your site on a reasonably frequent basis to make sure they've got the most up-to-date content to offer searchers. But what if a robot happens to visit your site while it's out of commission? If they can't find you, they probably won't rank you. You're likely to be very sad next time you check your ranks, at least until the robot comes back and rediscovers you.

Which Search Engine Database You Happen to Be Looking At We're talking billions of pieces of data from millions of sites. There's no way the search engines could keep it all in one database. This means that, at any given time, searchers are looking at one of a number of search engine databases, each giving out slightly different search results. Expect that your ranks are going to hop around a bit on a daily basis. Try not to sweat these little dips or put too much stock in the little jumps.

Algorithm Changes As we mentioned earlier, you never know when an existing search engine algorithm is going to morph into something different. There are so many people chasing the search engine updates, and losing sleep over the next little tweak in Google's algorithm, that a phrase was coined to describe them: *algoholics*. We urge you not to become one of them.

A Holistic Approach Helps

All of the rank-busters we just listed underscore the need to fill out your SEO campaign to tide you over with targeted traffic should your high ranks desert you. As the investment bankers will tell you: Diversify, diversify, diversify. These aspects of the SEO campaign that you'll develop in Part III will help you weather ranking fluctuations:

Buzz Generation This means getting sites to link to you out of admiration (Donutopia makes great donuts! Click here!), commendation (Donutopia's Donut News wins "Bakery News Site of the Year." Click here!), or reciprocity (Please support our friend, Donutopia. Click here!).

Niche Directories The big search engines are not the only paths to your site. There are niche directories (also called verticals) for aficionados of everything from animal husbandry to Zen Buddhism. A small but fervently targeted audience is not to be ignored.

A Paid Search Campaign Sponsored listings can be a very effective way to get those targeted *eyeballs* to your site, especially if something is preventing you from breaking through the competition for organic rankings.

Good Writing and Usability Quality material on your site will always be there for you when the winds of algorithm fate shift again.

Remember that Your SEO Plan should focus on conversions, not just search engine ranks! If you're doing well with the SEO elements listed here, you may discover that—lo and behold!—a dip in ranking won't affect your conversions in any disastrous way.

Search Engines Don't Like Tricks

The search engines are aware of the many sneaky ways that site owners try to achieve undeserved ranks (in SEO lingo, these underhanded activities are called *spamming*). If they discover that your site is spamming, even if you're not doing it on purpose, your site may be penalized: Your rank may be downgraded, or your page—or even your whole site—could be banned. Even if your site is never caught and punished, it's very likely, we dare say inevitable, that your tricky technique will eventually stop working. Here are some practices that have been on the search engines' no-no list for so long that they can safely be labeled as "Eternally Bad for Your Site":

Cloaking When a search engine robot visits your site, it expects to see the same content that any normal human visitor would see. *Cloaking* is a method of identifying robots when they visit your site and showing them special, custom-made pages that are different from what human visitors see. This thwarts the search engines in their attempt to deliver the most accurate search results to their users. In the vast universe of website technology, there are sometimes valid reasons for showing different content to different entities. Tricking the search engines to give you higher ranks than you deserve is not one of them.

Duplicate Content Are you the kind of person who thinks, "If one aspirin works, why not take two?" If so, you might be thinking that if one paragraph of keyword-rich text will help your ranks, why not put it on every page in your site? Or worse, if one website brings you sales, why not make a bunch of identical websites with different names and get even more sales? The problem with this kind of thinking is that it ignores the big headache it causes for searchers. If the search engines listed identical content multiple times, it would destroy the diversity of their results, which would destroy their usefulness to the searcher. So if the search engines catch on to duplicate content schemes, they're likely to knock you down in the ranks.

Keyword Stuffing Adding a keyword list to the visible text on your page is not exactly scintillating copy. We're not talking about overly optimized text, which may come off as pointless and dry. We're talking about repeating the same word or words over and over again so that your page looks like an industry-specific grocery list. At best, sites that do this cause eyestrain for their visitors. At worst, they're risking penalties from the search engines.

Invisible Text When we mentioned invisible text previously in this chapter, we meant specific elements that are included within specific parameters in your site's code and recognized by the search engines to be legitimate. We did *not* mean making a ton of keywords invisible by making them the same color as the background. The search engines caught on to this one a long time ago, and they're not likely to let you get away with it.

SEO Is Not Brain Surgery

So many people feel intimidated when approaching SEO. They think it's ultratechnical or it requires a huge budget. Many people think SEO requires some sort of degree or a lot of insider knowledge. But SEO doesn't take any of that.

The only thing that is really necessary for SEO is the willingness to learn. So here is our most special gift to you, an SEO mantra that you can adopt as your own:

I wonder why *that's* happening.

SEO: Art or Science?

It's an oft-repeated cliché: SEO is one part art and one part science. The Left Brain and Right Brain delve a little deeper into two Eternal Truths:

The Left Brain says, "SEO is a Science! I originally learned SEO by using an experimental approach: trying different strategies and observing how successful they were. There's nothing fancy or difficult about science. It just means asking questions and seeking answers: Will adding keywords to my HTML comments tag help my rankings? Which of these two landing pages will bring more conversions?

"A paid search campaign provides the best opportunity for testing hypotheses because this kind of advertising allows you a great deal of control over your listings and your landing pages. And most important, paid search has a quick turnaround, so you won't have to wait months for the results of your experiments. So give it a try (we'll help you do this in Part III)! Compare results for two ads with slightly different phrasing. Or build a page just for testing purposes, and see what happens when you triple the keyword density. Science is fun—hey, don't look so surprised!"

The Right Brain says, "SEO is an Art! SEO can never truly be a science because you'll never be working in a vacuum. Your competition pulls a surprise move, the algorithm throws you a curveball… you can't control for these factors. Sure, your tests are fun, and they can even give you a lot of helpful insight. But anyone doing SEO needs to be comfortable working in an environment that is often more guesswork than empirical proof. Isn't it better to focus on the art of SEO—well-crafted text, a thoughtful, user-friendly site design, and personal connections? In its purest form, SEO is the art of persuasion!"

This is the approach that got us to where we are today; it helped us gain our SEO knowledge, and it keeps the clients coming. This is how we attacked almost every SEO question or problem before SEO was a big industry with hundreds of books, e-books, and websites devoted to it. And more often than not, this is how we still approach things. It can work for you, too!

It goes something like this: You say to yourself, "I wonder why my Google listing has that weird misspelling in it." Then you spend a few minutes searching for the misspelled word on your page. If it's not there, you look for it in your meta tags. Still not finding it? Browse through the directory listings. "*Aha*," you say, "There's a misspelling in my Open Directory listing!" Now you've learned two things: one, that your Open Directory listing is feeding into your Google listing, and two, that you'd better get to work on getting that misspelling fixed.

Or you say to yourself, "I wonder why my competitor has such good placement in that shopping directory." Then you click around until you find the "advertise with us" link on the shopping directory, figure out if that placement is a service they offer, and determine whether you want one, too.

Developing a healthy curiosity about how the search engines work, and an itch to solve interesting puzzles, is key to do-it-yourself SEO. It's a poor man's or woman's marketing study, and it's the best way to find your own path toward getting more targeted traffic.

Over the past several years, we have both drifted on and off of the SEO career path from time to time. Extended side projects and maternity leaves have caused us to focus our attention elsewhere temporarily, but we've always come back, and what's more, we've always gotten our SEO chops back and been able to offer respected, useful, and well-received consultation within a relatively short time, every time. Why? Because we have internalized the Eternal Truths of SEO and use them as our basic frame of reference. Now that you understand the longer-lasting aspects of SEO, it should be a lot easier to make sense of the "right now" qualities, which will be described in the next chapter.

How the Search Engines Work Right Now

What's the inside buzz among SEO experts? What do the search engines care about? What works? What doesn't? In this chapter, we present a current snapshot, including some of the more ephemeral facts of SEO: which search engines dominate the industry and how they work today.

4

Chapter Contents

In Pursuit of Right Now

We admit it: We were shaking in our stiletto heels just thinking about writing this chapter. The Right Now of search engines? Committed in ink, on old-fashioned paper? Give us a break. Everybody knows the Right Now of SEO changes every five minutes and you'd do much better finding this stuff on the Web.

Just kidding. We wear sensible shoes. Oh, and there are lots of reasons for you to hang onto every word of this chapter.

First off, researching SEO on the Web is a difficult way to learn new concepts and get the basics. If you set out to discover the Right Now of SEO for yourself, you're likely to run into a mishmash of organic and paid strategies spanning beginner and technically advanced concepts. You'll find conflicting advice, forums running rampant with rumors, and blogs that range from excellent to abysmal. And here's our pet peeve: SEO advice on the Web is maddeningly unlikely to be date-stamped, so you often won't know whether you're reading current advice or yesterday's news.

So, instead of trying to jump into your own frustrating pursuit of the Right Now, read our rundown of the current search landscape. Later, in Chapter 8, "Month Two: Establish the Habit," you'll learn how to keep your knowledge up-to-date using our favorite trusted sources of information.

Now, let's get down to the details.

Google Basics

Simply stated, Google is the standout leader in search today. It has the most traffic and the most new trends, and it's the only search engine with its own entry in the dictionary. Once a search-only entity, Google now offers e-mail, maps, feed readers, calendar, web analytics, and webmaster tools, not to mention a diverse menu of specialty search options, including news, video, image, blog, and local. See Table 4.1 for handy Google facts for SEOs.

Google has been an all-out trendsetter in the evolution of the search space. Link popularity? Google made it hugely important. Integration of specialty search results within standard results? Thank Google. A website's age being a factor in its ranking? Blame Google. We'll go into the details throughout the book, but let's face it: The world of SEO is playing Follow the Leader, and Google's at the head of the line.

Google Analytics, the free and robust website traffic analysis tool, has been widely adopted since its launch in 2005. This was arguably the single most important development in SEO in recent years, because it gave the world's website owners the ability to easily measure conversions. This has precipitated a shift in the collective SEO mind-set to valuing conversions, not ranks, as the most important metric.

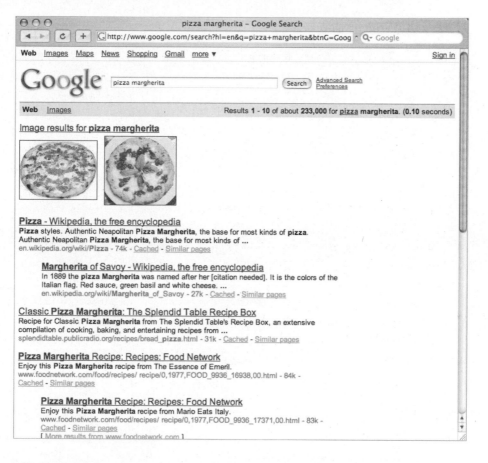

▶ **Table 4.1** Google Basics

URL	www.google.com
Percent of search traffic	58.4% (Source: comScore, December 2007)
Primary results	Robot crawler
Organic listings also influenced by	Open Directory
Ways to submit your site	XML Sitemap (free, good for large or dynamic sites), or wait for the robot to find you
Pay-per-click services	Google AdWords
In five words or less	The one to beat
Keep an eye on	Google Webmaster Tools, Google Analytics

The current hot topics around Google are its mission expansions: From TV to voicemail to the supermarket aisles, the big G is everywhere. Ambitious lately? Staying on top of the long, and ever-lengthening, list of services Google offers can be over-whelming for a website owner. But you don't need to, as long as you focus on the services your target audience cares about. Most people are still using Google at its most basic level, typing a phrase in the search box, and seeing what results come up.

Google's current relationship with SEOs and webmasters has its points of light along with some black holes. SEOs appreciate the monitoring and management options available through the Webmaster Tools service and outreach by corporate representatives via blogs, forums, and conferences, but many SEOs kvetch about Google becoming too powerful. One topic that really brings out the bristle is Google's announcement in 2007 that *paid links* (inbound links that are purchased in an attempt to improve search engine ranks) should be reported to Google, presumably so that Google can mete out negative consequences. Besides feeling that the web community shouldn't become snitches, many people consider this preferential ("Why aren't Yahoo! Directory links considered paid links?") or illogical ("Isn't there payment of some sort—labor or money or favors—involved in all web marketing efforts?").

Even as you gobble up the free tools, services, and advice from Google, remember that there's no such thing as a free lunch. Google is a for-profit company, and an incredibly powerful one at that. Google will look after Google and, in doing so, may make policy changes that can create seismic shifts in website owners' lives. It's always best to create your site for your *users*, not for what you think will cause Google to rank you higher this week.

PageRank, ShmageRank

Google's *PageRank* is a measurement of a page's worth based on the quantity and quality of both incoming and outgoing links. The concept behind PageRank is that each link to a page constitutes a vote, and Google has a sophisticated and automated way of tallying these votes, which includes looking at a vast universe of interlinking pages. Google awards PageRank on a scale of 0 to 10; a PageRank value of 10 is the most desirable and extremely rare. Like the Richter scale, the Page-Rank scale is not linear, so the difference between 4 and 5 is much greater than the difference between 3 and 4.

More often than not, pages with high PageRank have higher Google rankings than pages with low PageRank. And therein lies the link obsession. Throughout the SEO community, the scrambling for, trading, and even selling of links became such a focus over the past several years that Google modified its system and began to devalue certain kinds of links. It's widely accepted, for example, that links from content-deficient *"link farm"* websites do not improve a page's PageRank, and getting a link from a page with high PageRank but irrelevant content (say, a popular comic book site that links to a forklift specifications page) won't either. Google now displays updated PageRank values at infrequent intervals to discourage constant monitoring.

It's good to get links to your site, but obsessive link building to the point of excluding other areas of SEO is a waste of time. Keep a holistic head on your shoulders and remember these points:

- Google's ranking algorithm is not based entirely on inbound links.

- A high PageRank does not guarantee a high Google rank.

- A PageRank value viewed today may be months old.

PageRank is still a fairly good indication of how Google regards your website's pages, and you'll learn how to gather your own measurements in Your SEO Plan. But in the Right Now of SEO, think of PageRank as a hobby, not a religion.

The Best of the Rest: Yahoo!, MSN, Ask, AOL

Taken as a group, the major non-Google search engines that we're about to discuss make up about 40 percent of the search engine market, which means they deserve your attention. Non-Google search engines allow you to fill out your website's presence so that it is not overly dependent on rankings on a single site (what was that expression, something about eggs… and a basket?).

Now, we'll fill you in on what you need to know about the search engines other than Google:

- Yahoo!

- MSN/Live Search

- Ask

- AOL

Yahoo!

Yahoo! (yes, the exclamation point is part of its name—a bane to copy editors everywhere) is one of the oldest and still one of the best-known search engines. Already an established directory when Google was still in diapers, Yahoo! has now settled into the #2 spot. Nevertheless, with its considerable legacy and the muscle to expand its offerings through corporate purchases (acquisitions of the popular photo-sharing site Flickr, e-mail and collaboration tool Zimbra, and news site BuzzTracker show a continuing interest in the new and hip), Yahoo! is a force to be reckoned with. Table 4.2 shows you handy Yahoo! facts for SEOs.

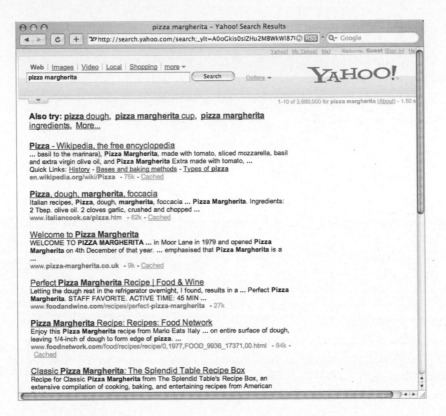

▶ **Table 4.2** Yahoo! Basics

URL	www.yahoo.com
Percent of search traffic	22.9% (Source: comScore, December 2007)
Primary results	Robot crawler
Organic listings also influenced by	Yahoo! Directory
Ways to submit your site	Paid submittal to Yahoo! Directory, XML Sitemap, or wait for the robot to spider you
Pay-per-click services	Yahoo! Search Marketing (YSM)
In five words or less	Early bird still wants worm
Keep an eye on	Yahoo! Go, Alibaba

While Yahoo! is gradually losing market share in comparison to Google, its absolute search traffic numbers are still holding steady, with roughly 2 billion searches in the second half of 2007. Yahoo! has generated many headlines with its mercurial existence of late: A burst of acquisitions, innovation, leadership changes, and potential buyouts keeps industry watchers bracing for a big search earthquake, and wondering how the landscape will look when it's over.

Nobody knows what the future will hold, but we do know this: Yahoo!'s healthy share of traffic and untapped potential will continue to be a driving force in this industry, no matter who's at the wheel.

The Search Engine Soap Operas

While we were writing this book, Microsoft made a bid to buy Yahoo!, and the search world was thrown for a loop. The combination of MSN and Yahoo! search properties, which some are calling "Microhoo," would result in a search engine with substantial reach, power, and media content—one that could compete with Google. This is big news, even to those of us who have been watching search engine acquisitions for years.

How do dramas such as this affect Your SEO Plan? Fortunately, you don't need to follow every twist and turn of every story. Because we focus on user friendliness, good targeting, and great content, the SEO plan in this book will help you create strategies that are robustly search-friendly, no matter what changes may come. Tactics that are specific to a certain search engine are labeled as such, and if consolidation strikes, a firm grip on the Eternal Truths you learned in Chapter 3, "Eternal Truths of SEO," will help you maintain your website's standings for the long haul.

MSN/Live Search

In case you didn't know, the MSN portal and its search engine, called Live Search, is a property of a quaint little organization known as "Microsoft Corp." The youngest of the big search engines, MSN's modus operandi has been an ongoing game of copycat and catch-up as it tried to bring its interface and feature set up to the standards Google and Yahoo! have set. Then, in 2008, Microsoft abruptly switched tactics to "if you can't beat 'em, buy 'em" and made a bid to purchase Yahoo!.

Live Search is not entirely user friendly; in fact, it gets a lot of negative coverage by gloating SEOs who love to point out its many bugs and errors. But its image search is generally considered better than image search at Google and Yahoo!—a rare example of Live Search outshining its predecessors. Even as Live Search struggles to look and act like a grown-up search engine, big daddy Microsoft is pulling out all the stops to try to significantly increase its market share. Check out the Live Search facts in Table 4.3.

▶ Table 4.3 MSN/Live Search Basics

URL	www.live.com
Percent of search traffic	9.8% (Source: comScore, December 2007)
Primary results	Robot crawler
Organic listings also influenced by	Open Directory
Ways to submit your site	Submit URL form, XML Sitemap, or wait for the robot to find you
Pay-per-click services	Microsoft adCenter
In five words or less	Deep pockets, big dreams
Keep an eye on	major acquisitions, Facebook integration, Gatineau web analytics

MSN's pay-per-click service, called MSN adCenter, is a relative newcomer to the search advertising market. The current buzz among adCenter users is that the conversion rates are good but the volume is low. MSN has made its intentions clear: It plans to radically increase its share of online digital advertising revenue.

Ask

Rather than aspiring to be another Google, veteran search engine Ask is focusing on innovations in both interface and content. Some things that make Ask stand out include a three-column display that virtually eliminates the need for scrolling, a visual preview of web pages without leaving the search results (just roll over the binoculars icon with your mouse), and a full complement of media and specialty search integrated into the results.

Ask has taken a leading role in privacy issues—its "Ask Eraser" feature allows searchers to delete their search data from Ask.com's databases. Ask has its own PPC service, but most of those ads come from Google AdWords. See Table 4.4 for Ask.com basics.

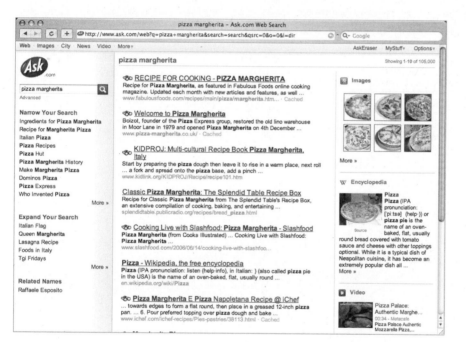

▶ **Table 4.4** Ask Basics

URL	www.ask.com
Percent of search traffic	4.3% (Source: comScore, December 2007)
Primary results	Robot crawler
Organic listings also influenced by	Blinkx (for video results)
Ways to submit your site	XML Sitemap, or wait for the robot to spider you
Pay-per-click services	Ask Sponsored Listings (ASL), mostly powered by Google AdWords
In five words or less	Smart, good, different
Keep an eye on	Ask Eraser, specialty search options

The SEO community tends to respect Ask, but its small market share means that we don't give Ask as much attention as it probably deserves. Ask today reminds us of Google in its early days, and it has been compared to Apple for its innovations and small, dedicated user base. We're not counting it out.

AOL

The most important thing to know about AOL is that it uses the Google database for search results. That means, from an SEO perspective, AOL can be safely ignored. See Table 4.5 for basic facts about AOL.

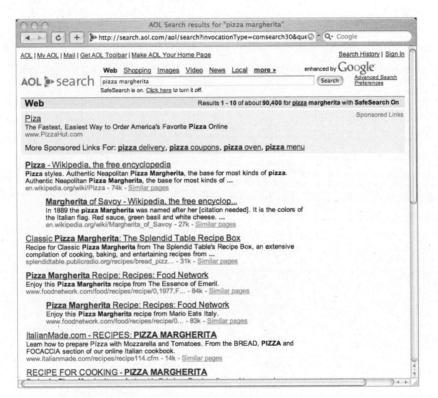

▶ **Table 4.5** AOL Basics

URL	www.aol.com
Percent of search traffic	4.6% (Source: comScore, December 2007)
Primary results	Google results
Organic listings also influenced by	None
Ways to submit your site	None; get indexed through Google
Pay-per-click services	Google AdWords
In five words or less	Google is my copilot
Keep an eye on	Future partnership deals

AOL may continue to score a share of the search market, but we don't think AOL will be generating its own independent search results anytime soon. Because of that, we won't say another word about AOL in this book. Want to do well on AOL? Do well on Google (or whoever else AOL partners with in the future). 'Nuff said.

Now that you've got a handle on the top search engines, we'll discuss the elements that influence their rankings.

SEO Is Dead

When we began working on the first edition of this book, we met for coffee and questioned whether SEO would be around in three years. Recently this apocalyptic sentiment has been echoed with increasing frequency among SEO pundits, many who cite the following reasons:

- *As search engine algorithms have improved, ranks are becoming harder to manipulate, so there's no need for SEO.*

- *Barriers to robot crawling are starting to fall away. Once search engines can run JavaScript and index Flash, they'll be doing most of the SEO's job.*

- *With so many different types of search results, it's getting increasingly difficult to rank well for even moderately competitive keywords. Personalized search results make rank pointless, anyway.*

- *The search engines are handing out Sitemap submittal tools and insider information that negates the need for SEO.*

- *Who needs a website? The Web will soon evolve away from static pages and become a fluid realm of Facebook profiles, embeddable videos, and widgets.*

We agree with some elements of these arguments, but we don't think SEO is dead. And a close reading of most experts who say "SEO Is Dead" shows that they don't think so either. (But it makes a catchy title!)

Here's why SEO isn't dead:

What the doomsayers call "SEO" is just rank-wrangling. What *we* call SEO is the methods laid out in this book: A holistic approach that starts with understanding your goals for audience behavior, then matches website content to these goals, moves on to monitoring and improving your online performance through analytics and experimentation, and doesn't end until you take down your website. These aspects of website optimization—whether you call it SEO or give it a new name—will never die.

In the future, you can bet your Aunt Agatha that search engine robots will be able to leap tall buildings in a single bound, personalized search will be adopted by the masses, and the static website may even be abandoned entirely. But not yet. To be competitive, you still need to make sure that your website content is readable and reachable by search engines. And it's well documented that right now, the right SEO campaign will bring about substantial benefits for your site.

Until there's the perfect search engine, there will always be a need for SEO.

Organic Ranking Factors

You already know that search engines use complicated secret formulas, called ranking algorithms, to determine the order of their results. You even know from Chapter 3, "Eternal Truths of SEO," that some of the most Eternally Important factors are your web page text and your HTML title tags. Now we're going to wrap what you already know into an organic optimization cheat sheet that you can peek at next time someone asks you, "What do search engines care about, anyway?"

But first, a disclaimer: There are radically differing opinions within the SEO community about what works and what's important. The SEO profession is an upstart one, with no degrees to be earned or widely accepted canon of literature (and if there were, it'd change every five months anyway). So we're all out there trying to figure this stuff out on our own, using different test cases, and chasing morphing search engines. We've distilled what we believe to be the best-of-the-best advice and present it here in a simplified form.

Here's the lowdown on the most important factors:

- HTML page title
- Visible HTML text on the page
- Inbound links (quality and quantity)
- Inbound link anchor text
- Age of domain
- Site authority
- Lesser factors

We'll get into how to optimize all of these factors in Part III. But for now, as you read through them, think about how much attention you've given to each of them on your own site. Maybe, like a lot of site owners, you've been focusing on the bottom of the list—the least important factors—more than the biggies at the top. As you think about what matters to the search engines, keep this in mind:

 Pearl of Wisdom: Each page on your website is analyzed individually by the search engines.

That means each and every page is an opportunity to optimize for the following:

HTML page title The HTML page title is today's hands-down leader, and an Eternally Important factor, in search engine ranking algorithms. As a bonus, optimizing your HTML page titles is one of those activities that will quickly affect the way your listings look in the search engines.

Visible HTML text on the page It seems obvious, but you would be surprised at how many site owners miss this simple point: In order to rank well for a particular set of keywords, your site text should contain them. True, there are examples of pages that rank well for words not actually appearing on the page (see the sidebar "Googlebombing and 'Miserable Failure'"), but this is not something you want to leave to chance.

You may see SEO pros insist that you need 250 or 1,000 words on a page and that 5–10 percent of these words must be your target keywords (SEO folks call that percentage *keyword density*).

We say this: As long as you have robot-readable text on your page (a great first step that many of your competitors, believe it or not, may have missed), you should use *as many keywords as you need to state your message clearly* and *as many opportunities to insert keywords as makes sense within the realm of quality writing*. Your marketing message is much too special to be put into a formula.

Inbound links (quality and quantity) Coming in at #3 in our list of search engine ranking factors is inbound links to your website. Why are inbound links so important in the search engine ranking algorithms? Because they can indicate a page's quality, popularity, or status on the Web and site owners have very little control over their own inbound links. (Being off-page factors, inbound links can be influenced only indirectly.) Links with the most rank-boosting power are links from a home page (as opposed to links from pages buried deep within the site), links that are not *reciprocal links* (you didn't have to link to them in order to get a link back), and links from *authority pages* in the *topical community*, meaning pages with their own collection of fabulous inbound links from other websites covering the same topic. The same quality factors hold true for links coming from within your site.

Inbound link anchor text We mentioned in Chapter 3 that the way other websites refer to your website provides clues that help search engines understand your content. *Anchor text*, also called linking text, is the text that is "clickable" on a web page, and it is an important factor in search ranking algorithms. Anchor text that contains your page's targeted keywords can help boost your page's ranks. Combining this keyword-rich anchor text with relevant text surrounding the link can amplify this good effect.

Googlebombing and "Miserable Failure"

Gather 'round, readers, and we'll tell you a story about something that happened a long, long time ago, way back in 2003. It seems there was a man—a right powerful man named George W. Bush—and a few hundred people who didn't like him very much. These people put links on their websites that looked a little something like this:

```
<a href="www.whitehouse.gov/president/gwbbio.html">miserable failure</a>
```

Continues

Googlebombing and "Miserable Failure" *(continued)*

Yep, it's so old and so often told that it's something of a campfire tale these days: Enough websites linked to George W. Bush's biography using the words "miserable failure" in their anchor text that the page ranked #1 for the term on Google. It's an extreme case, and it's not a very competitive keyphrase, but it's still a great illustration of how inbound link text can affect ranking.

Googlebombing, or link bombing, as this practice is called, has become a fixture in web culture. Other "victims," including politicians, filmmakers, and even just friends of mischief-makers, have claimed the #1 spot for words like "liar" and "talentless hack," and there have been new waves of "miserable failures" as well. The SEO community has sponsored and gleefully participated in contests to manipulate ranks for nonsense terms such as "nigritude ultramarine."

It's a subject of some controversy, raising questions of whether the search engines should strike these kinds of pranks from their results, whether it's just harmless fun, and whether it still works the way it used to back in the day. Googlebombs are still out there, but they've become less common as Google has taken steps to make this practice more difficult. Whatever your opinion on the subject, if you're willing to dig deep and check in on the latest in link bombing high jinks, you can glean some great insight on the current effect that inbound link text has on ranks.

Age of domain Newer domains have a much tougher time making their way up the ranks than older ones. The exact mechanism behind this may be the search engines measuring the actual length of time that a website has been live, or it may be primarily indirect factors, such as the fact that inbound links tend to accumulate over time. On a positive note for folks with brand-new sites: We've seen plenty of examples of new sites that have performed well in search engines within a couple of months. Take this factor into consideration if you're purchasing a new domain or considering changing an old, established domain name (proceed with caution!). Otherwise, unless you're a spammer or a fly-by-night operation, this is a factor that you don't need to think about a whole lot.

Site authority Site authority is a blanket term meaning "how important the search engines think your site is." Many SEOs speculate that individual pages belonging to websites with higher authority will gain higher ranks, even if the individual page does not have high ranking factors. It's as if the search engines are thinking, "This page is from a good family—let's give it the benefit of the doubt." Authority can be general (Wikipedia is an example of a site with general authority), but it's more illustrative to think about authority in terms of a single topic. For example, Sony.com has very high authority on the topic of home electronics, but it has low authority for topics like "paper dolls" or "mountaineering." Several sitewide factors are combined to measure a domain's overall level of authority on a particular topic. This may include inbound links, age of the domain, and even website traffic. Some believe there's even human intervention from the Google team.

Lesser factors There are a large number of additional, lesser factors that can influence your ranking. Google, for example, probably includes hundreds and possibly even thousands of factors in its algorithm. Things like keywords in your page URL, image ALT tags, and meta tags all have some degree of influence, as do factors that may be harder for you to control, such as the popularity of a page (as measured by the search engine's own click-through tallies) or how often it is updated. For a comprehensive list of ranking factors, including commentary from several knowledgeable SEO professionals, see this page: www.seomoz.org/articles/search-ranking-factors.php.

> ### Meta Keywords: A Waste of Time?
>
> A lot of people have asked the Left Brain and Right Brain for help on their meta keywords tags. Here's why the experts' advice is usually, "Eh, whatever."
>
> **The Left Brain says,** "Ask Dr. Science. To get a better idea of the value of the meta keywords tag, I performed a very basic experiment: I added a made-up word ('bistlethwart') to the meta keywords tag of a well-ranked web page. If the tag mattered at all, searching for 'bistlethwart' would cause this page to appear in search engine results. The verdict? Google, Ask, and Live Search returned no results for the term. But here's a fun surprise: Yahoo! brought up the page as the one and only search result for the term. What can we conclude? Not a whole lot, since the term had no competition whatsoever. But at least this experiment tells us that the meta keywords tag hasn't gone the way of the VHS tape—yet."
>
> **The Right Brain says,** "Hedge your bets. I think your test is compelling evidence that the meta keywords tag matters… at least a little bit! And there's also plenty of anecdotal examples to add to the mix. Remember the client who ranked for "b-24" (containing a dash), when his visible text only contained "b24" (no dash)? The only instance of the term with the dash was in his meta keywords tag. We've also seen meta keywords tags displayed as listing text in the search engine results. And you never know when ranking algorithms are going to fluctuate again in their favor. That's why this tag deserves at least a few minutes of thought."

Paid Placement

Every major search engine, as well as plenty of minor search engines and independent websites both large and small, displays paid listings today. Most of these listings are provided by the two major U.S. pay-per-click services, Google AdWords and Yahoo! Search Marketing (YSM), with a small share sourced in Microsoft adCenter.

The market is huge: According to Jupiter Research, online marketers will spend $7 billion on pay-per-click (PPC) advertising by the year 2010.

As you learned in Chapter 3, pay-per-click (PPC) is generally an auction-based system, with advertisers jockeying for their listings' positions based on bid price. See Figure 4.1 for an example. Until recently, the PPC auction was a fairly straightforward system in which a higher bid resulted in a higher rank. Now, Google and YSM are both gravitating toward a more complex method for determining PPC ranks. In Google AdWords, for example, the PPC algorithm is called a Quality Score, and it awards position based on several factors, including click-through rate, cost, and relevance of the ad text.

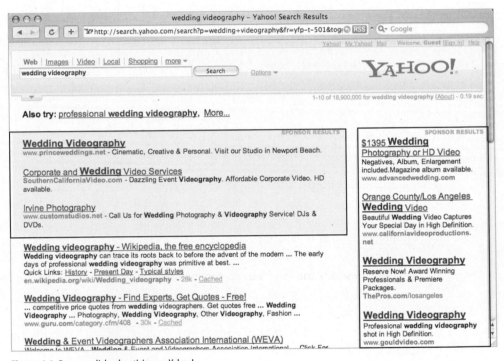

Figure 4.1 Pay-per-click advertising on Yahoo!

So if you were looking to PPC as a way to skirt around the Eternally Hidden Algorithm, we're sorry to say there's one to puzzle over in PPC as well. For starters, noted pay-per-click expert Kevin Lee indicated to us that PPC algorithms today are likely to favor big brands and compelling, relevant ad text because those ads would receive higher predicted click-through rates.

Google AdWords and YSM offer an opt-in feature that will display your listings on partner sites in addition to their own search engines. In this system, called *contextual advertising*, your listings are matched to the content of the page where they are displayed. See Figure 4.2 for an example. You can manage your contextual campaigns separately from your search-based PPC ads.

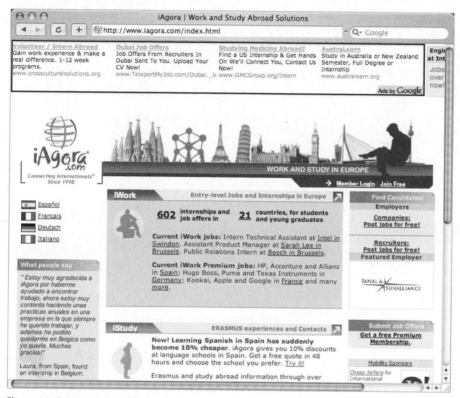

Figure 4.2 Contextual ads by Google

There are many variations on the theme of standard pay-per-click ads. You can enhance your ads with shopping cart badges. You can advertise using a cost-per-click, or cost-per-thousand-impressions model. You can experiment with choosing sites for contextual ad placement or let the algorithm decide for you. And you can even try a *pay-per-call* or *pay-per-action* model of advertising. In this book, we focus on PPC, because of its omnipresence in the search marketing industry, and because we think it's a reasonable place to jump in.

A quick rundown of the three major PPC services appears in Table 4.6.

Competition between PPC services has resulted in some significant advances in campaign tracking, click fraud prevention, and geographic targeting, and these improvements are expected to continue. The bad news is that there are so many products out there—even within any given PPC service—that the potential for confusion is very high. With more and more site owners adopting PPC, the online help systems are rather robust. But there are lots of people who choose to outsource PPC management because it can be a real headache. It *can* be done in-house, though, and it doesn't have to be that difficult if you start small and focus on the basics.

	Yahoo! Search Marketing	Google AdWords	Microsoft adCenter
URL	http://searchmarketing. yahoo.com	http://adwords. google.com	http://adcenter. microsoft.com
Name of pay-per-click product	Sponsored Search	AdWords	adCenter
Name of contextual placement product	Content Match	AdSense	Content Ads (display on MSN sites only)
Major partnerships (sites where ads are shown)	Yahoo!, CNN.com, bebo.com	Google, AOL.com, Ask.com, Shopping. com, thousands of small sites	Live Search, MSN properties, Facebook rumored to be next
Industry chatter	Not as many features as Google AdWords, but it delivers solid conversions and rolls out frequent improvements.	Well liked for its reach, as well as useful tools and advertising options, but many are frustrated by the lack of transparency on how rankings are determined.	Costs per conversion are good, but overall traffic is so low that adCenter is usually an add-on, as opposed to a major element, in most search marketing campaigns.

PPC is unmatched in the power it gives you over your listing: what it says, who sees it, and when. We also love PPC as a tool for studying the response to your keyword choices. So in Chapter 8, with our guidance, you're going to set up a starter campaign and get to know the basics while you get yourself some tasty targeted clicks.

SEO Trend Spotting

SEO trends move fast, so it's OK to jump in where you are! Use this primer to get clued in to some of the current jargon and trends in SEO.

Universal or blended search Remember when the search engines used to deliver three lines of text and a link for every listing? If you wanted *vertical search* results like video, image, shopping, and maps, you had to click on a tab or perform a special search. Now the major search engines have blended all types of listings together in the standard search results. This may create additional exposure opportunities for your site if it has well-optimized video or image listings. On the flipside, it leaves fewer spots for the standard text listings.

Search engine transparency Don't expect search engines to open the black box and shine a light on their secret algorithms, but all of the major search engines now offer some form of two-way communication between official representatives and the developer crowd. Tips and news are delivered—and questions are answered!—in blogs and forums, and webmaster tools take the guesswork out of some indexing and listing issues. Those of us who practiced SEO in the Stone Age get a big kick out of seeing the enmity that once existed between the search engines and webmasters begin to dissolve away.

Smarter robot meta tags The trend of search engine transparency has translated into some new tags that you can place on your page to make special requests of the robots that visit your page. Besides controlling whether a page is indexed, website owners can also control whether a snippet is shown, and even whether a page is cached. Visit yourseoplan.com/meta-tags.html for links to how-tos and FAQs.

Widgets Sometimes touted as the future of marketing, widgets are applications that are created with the intention of being reused on other websites. You've probably seen them: News websites allow you to display headlines on your site, and YouTube allows you to embed videos in your blog. There is an endless variety of widgets: Users can create reader polls, display upcoming speaking engagements, or even post AMBER alerts on their site. As a marketer, widgets give you the advantage of putting a little bit of your organization on a lot of different websites. Once site owners have added your widget to their site, your widget could push new content (images, quotes, videos, and more) with no effort at all on the site owner's part. Still not sure what a widget is? Widget directories such as Snipperoo or Widgetbox have a wealth of examples to get your creative juices flowing. Tracking usage and ROI of widgets is a challenge, but thanks to the beta launch of event-tracking features in Google Analytics in late 2007, widget tracking is becoming more sophisticated.

Social search Social search refers to websites that allow users to recommend web pages to each other and influence search results. On social news sites like Digg, stories that receive the most votes win the most visibility and clicks. On social bookmarking sites like del.icio.us, people *tag* sites with keywords so that other people will find them. Social sites offer seemingly limitless opportunities for website promotion—and plenty of sites have basked in extreme, server-busting popularity via social search. But this type of promotion isn't easy and the results are unpredictable.

Mobile search Mobile search is like one of those up-and-coming neighborhoods that never quite ups and comes. Web developers are still working out the kinks of building websites in formats that can be viewed on cell phones and handheld devices. Meanwhile, search engines, most notably Google and Yahoo!, are working hard to place themselves in the middle of this growing search sector. The SEO community remains on the sidelines, watching and waiting to see if mobile search will ever fully take off.

SEO Slang

Just like any other topic with a big online following, SEO has its own colorful vocabulary. There are far too many terms to include here, but here's a sampling of what you might come across in your own SEO endeavors:

SERP An acronym that stands for "Search Engine Results Page," that is, the listings you see when you use a search engine. It is our opinion (as it is with other right-minded folks) that this acronym has an ugly ring to it, so we've decided to ban it from the book!

White hat/black hat Stereotypically speaking, white hat refers to "squeaky clean" optimization activities, ones that stay squarely within the search engines' guidelines. Black hat refers to under-the-radar (and often below-the-belt) activities, such as quickly launching a site with poor-quality, *scraped*, or no content; making some quick cash; and then dumping the domain and starting over with another site. There are also SEOs who proclaim to be gray hat, who do their work somewhere in the middle.

Link Juice If you're one who likes to use the word "juice" to mean "power," then this is the expression for you. Link juice is a synonym for link equity or page authority, the accumulated measure of a web page's value in the eyes of the search engines based on the quality and quantity of its inbound links. As the expression implies, link juice is fluid, and can flow between web pages via links.

Splog The word splog is a mashup of the words "spam" and "blog." A splog is a blog that exists solely to get ad impressions or provide links to other sites. Usually these blogs contain gibberish, or an unruly combination of content stolen from other websites.

Long Tail As you attempt to bring traffic to your website, you can optimize your site for general, popular keyword phrases, or you can choose longer, more specific, less popularly searched phrases. The former may bring you a large volume of general traffic, while the latter, the *long tail* of search, may bring you fewer visitors that are highly targeted. This term was popularized by Chris Anderson in his book *The Long Tail* (Hyperion, 2006).

Now that you've had your fill of background knowledge, join us in Part II where you'll create an SEO strategy that will set you on the right track for Your SEO Plan.

Strategy

Before you can implement Your SEO Plan, you need to develop a workable strategy. In this part, you'll begin by getting your internal team on board and identifying the various disciplines that are necessary for effective SEO. Next, you'll spend a month performing the brainstorming, research, and assessment to point you in the right direction for your ongoing campaign:

Get Your Team on Board

Search Engine Optimization is truly a team effort. A great SEO campaign encompasses skills that nearly always surpass those of any individual: writing, marketing, research, programming, and, yes, even a little bit of math. In this chapter, we guide you through the all-important task of getting your team on board, from techies coding your HTML edits to salespeople tracking conversions.

Chapter Contents

The Challenge of SEO Team Building
Marketing, Sales, and Public Relations
IT, Webmasters, and Programmers
Graphic Designers
Writers and Editors
Executives and Product Managers

The Challenge of SEO Team Building

You're busy, and SEO isn't your only job, so we're pretty sure you won't be thrilled to hear this:

Your SEO campaign will incorporate a wide variety of tasks: writing and editing, web page design, programming, ad copy creation, research, web analytics, and interpersonal communication for link building. If you're doing this all yourself, bravo! You're just the sort of multitasking do-it-yourselfer who thrives in SEO. If your entire company can't ride to lunch on the same motorcycle, we're putting you in charge of coordinating the SEO team. Either way, once you've read this book, you'll be the in-house SEO expert, so the responsibility for all of these tasks ultimately falls on you.

Before you close this book forever and run for the antacid, let's clarify a bit. We're not saying that you have to be the one to code the website or set up the analytics software. We're saying you need to know enough to be able to speak intelligently to the people who do these tasks. And here's the hard part: You also need to convince them to spend some of their precious time working on Your SEO Plan.

Why is it, after all, that organizing an SEO team is so hard? We have observed four common reasons:

- SEO requires effort from multiple departments and a variety of skills, such as marketing, sales, IT, public relations (PR), and creative/editorial.
- SEO is a new discipline and doesn't have established processes in the corporate system.
- The SEO budget will have to come from somewhere. That means somebody may have to give up some funding.
- The SEO industry carries around a bit of a bad reputation—and some folks still think SEO is about tricking or spamming the search engines.

This chapter is here to guide you through the SEO crusade within your organization. There are some common patterns of resistance you might meet in each of the departments discussed here, and we'll share with you the most effective ways to counteract them.

As with any team-building effort, building your SEO team will be an exercise in communication.

Pearl of Wisdom: Educate your team about SEO, and you will be rewarded with their participation and enthusiasm.

But remember this: They're probably just as busy as you are, and that's why we advocate a pace-yourself approach. Don't overwhelm them with information—just the SEO rules that pertain to the task at hand.

"But I Don't Have One of Those!"

In this chapter, we discuss ways that you can approach various departments within your organization to get help on your SEO campaign. We are well aware that, due to size or focus, your organization may not include each of the separate departments described here. If this is the case with you, figure out what entity takes on these roles: Who is it that closes the deals with customers? That's your sales department. Who edits your website? That's the IT department. Look to that entity—be it a small staff, an entire department, or Erica on every other Tuesday for the SEO help you need.

Even if you're planning to go it alone with your trusty hour-a-day book and a cup of coffee by your side, this chapter should offer some insight on approaching the work with the right "hats" on.

We have worked in many situations in which team participation was less than ideal for an SEO campaign, and we know how this can reduce the campaign's effectiveness. What happens when those carefully prepared page edits aren't implemented, keywords aren't incorporated into site rewrites, or a planned-for PPC budget never comes through?

Pearl of Wisdom: Without your team on board, SEO suffers.

Besides being frustrating for you, it can be a huge waste of time and money. What follows are some thoughts for keeping the enthusiasm going in all of your departments.

Marketing, Sales, and Public Relations

Marketing, Sales, and Public Relations make up a corporate SEO trifecta. Get all three excited about your SEO campaign, and you'll have built your "brain trust" foundation for success. Here's some food for thought that should come in handy when you need to deal with these departments.

Marketing: VIPs of SEO

In most organizations, the marketing department serves as the hub of SEO operations. We're guessing you're a member of this department yourself. It's a natural progression: The marketing department may already be handling the website as well as *offline marketing*—such as print ads, television, radio, billboards—and *online marketing*—such as banner ads and direct e-mails.

The marketing team will likely be instrumental in SEO tasks like keyword brainstorming and research, writing text for descriptions and page titles, writing sponsored listings, managing paid search campaigns, and executing link-building campaigns.

The folks on the marketing team have, quite literally, the skills to pay the bills, and they probably don't need any convincing that SEO is a worthwhile effort. What they will need, however, is some organization and some focusing.

What does your marketing team know about the importance of robot-readable text, keyword placement, and paid search campaign management? Maybe a lot. Maybe nothing. Maybe they know something that was worthwhile a few years ago but is now outdated. Since you're in charge of the SEO team, it will help you to know what the general knowledge level is and then think of yourself as the on-site SEO educator.

We have found that marketing staffers are almost always open to a little education about how the search engines work, as long as the information is provided on a need-to-know basis. For example, whenever we brainstorm for keywords with a marketing manager, inevitably their list contains terms that are extremely vague ("quality") or so specific that nobody is searching for them ("geometric specifications of duckpin bowling balls"). When we trim down that list, we always explain the basic concept of *search popularity* vs. relevance. That lesson is easily delivered in a two-paragraph e-mail or a three-minute phone call.

But what if you're not working in such a receptive environment? Maybe you are the only one convinced of the positive powers of SEO. Perhaps, for reasons of budget or time, you don't have the buy-in you need to move forward. Perhaps other marketing programs are taking precedence, or the department can't seem to make the leap from offline to online marketing. If that's the case, it's time to convince the marketing manager of the importance of your SEO project!

Here's one way to approach it: Focus on the needs of the marketing department. Go into therapy mode: "You seem a little stressed. How can SEO help?"

Here's how: SEO can provide the trackability that your colleagues have been waiting for. Or justify an overdue website revamp. It may provide an argument for dropping less-successful advertising venues. It can forge new alliances between Marketing and IT. On the "warm and fuzzy" side, it may provide an outlet for a creative soul who feels trapped in marketing-speak and wants to do more creative writing. And SEO is an extremely telecommuting-friendly enterprise. Is there a new dad in the department who would love to spend a portion of his week working from home?

Once you've found some common ground and the enthusiasm is starting to grow, consider starting Your SEO Plan with a pilot project that you can focus your SEO efforts on together. Pick something close to the hearts of the marketing staff: a recent or upcoming launch, a section of your site devoted to a special event, a promotion, or a product line that's down in the dumps. Cherry-pick if you can! It's important that these early experiences be positive ones.

What If You're at the Bottom of the Pecking Order?

If you're on the bottom of the food chain in your organization, you may be either ignored or micromanaged by the people you answer to. Here are some tips that might work for you no matter what department you're dealing with:

- Create regular reports, even if nobody's looking at them. As consultants, we have often asked ourselves, "What's the point of documenting everything if nobody reads our reports?" But it always comes down to this: We need them for our own reference. After several months, stats begin to blur together—don't expect to keep this stuff in your head.

- Don't report too often. We recommend at least a month between reports, even if you are asked for more frequent data. There are rare exceptions to this rule, such as extremely short-lived promotions or unusually volatile PPC campaigns. But for almost everything else, it is helpful to set expectations that SEO is about long-term trends, not daily numbers.

Continues

What If You're at the Bottom of the Pecking Order? *(Continued)*

- Deliver meaningful information. When you e-mail your boss a spreadsheet detailing your ranks for the last six months, you're delivering raw information. You can turn that into meaningful information when you summarize it in your e-mail: "Dear Boss, This month, traffic to three of our top-priority pages increased across three search engines. Five of our pages improved in rank, but our traffic for the term 'industrial strength pencils' continued to slide."

- Likewise, if you have to deliver bad news, always deliver a plan of action for addressing it. You're the in-house SEO expert, like it or not, and your boss is looking to you for guidance. The boss doesn't want to hear, "Holy moly! Google dropped all our pages!" The boss wouldn't mind hearing this explanation: "It looks like our pages have been dropped from Google. This is probably a temporary problem, caused by Googlebot trying to crawl our site during our server outage last week. I'll verify that there are no indexing errors using Google's Webmaster Tools and keep a close eye on the situation."

- Don't take all the credit for your success. This is not just to be humble; it's also because you actually aren't responsible for every SEO success. Even if you do everything right, you can't control what your competitors are doing or the nature of the next big search engine algorithm change. If you set your boss's expectations along these lines, you won't be blamed for every little failure, either.

Selling SEO to Sales

In Chapter 1, "Clarify Your Goals," you gave a lot of thought to the fundamental goals of your business. Your sales department will be happy to hear that your SEO campaign will be bringing in not just traffic, but targeted traffic that leads directly to sales. You will be looking for their help in the following areas of SEO: keyword brainstorming, assistance with conversion tracking, competitive analysis, and insight into the customers' web habits.

Since Sales often has the most direct contact with customers, they will have excellent ideas to add to your keyword brainstorming sessions. And if your conversions are of the easy-to-measure variety, such as online purchases, they'll probably enjoy monitoring conversion rates on a paid search campaign and adjusting accordingly.

On the other hand, you may have a harder time getting help with conversion tracking for *offline sales*—transactions made over the phone or in person. The sales department may not want to make the effort to figure out exactly how the person on the other end of the phone got their number, or they may feel that grilling the customers about how they found you will interfere with the sales process. You need to convince your sales team that incorporating this sort of follow-up into the sales process is not a waste of time because it's important for everyone to know whether the website is generating profits.

The key to bringing your sales team on board for these more difficult tasks is educating them on the connection between targeted search engine traffic and bottom-line sales:

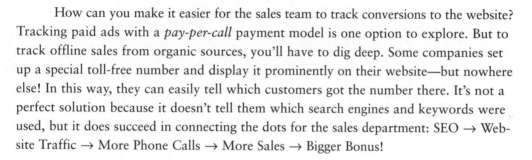

Pearl of Wisdom: SEO *will* bring in sales if it's done right!

How can you make it easier for the sales team to track conversions to the website? Tracking paid ads with a *pay-per-call* payment model is one option to explore. But to track offline sales from organic sources, you'll have to dig deep. Some companies set up a special toll-free number and display it prominently on their website—but nowhere else! In this way, they can easily tell which customers got the number there. It's not a perfect solution because it doesn't tell them which search engines and keywords were used, but it does succeed in connecting the dots for the sales department: SEO → Website Traffic → More Phone Calls → More Sales → Bigger Bonus!

SEO and PR Can Relate

If your company has a PR department, you're in luck. If not, think about this: If you got a phone call tomorrow from a radio station wanting to do a story on your company, who would they speak with? That's your PR department.

PR folks are very well suited to work with you on your SEO campaign. They're careful about words, they're excellent communicators, and they probably know how to track their results. They are the keepers of the brand, creating and monitoring the face that your organization puts forth to the public. Look to PR for help with keyword brainstorming, optimizing press releases, link building, and keeping your paid and unpaid search engine listings and other links in line with your branding.

A typical PR department is primarily concerned with getting your company mentioned in the media and making sure that the publicity is accurate and—ideally—positive. Many newspaper and magazine articles, not to mention blog postings, are triggered by press releases or other forms of contact from a PR department. And it's fair to say that search engines deserve a place among these media sources: Just like magazines, newspapers, and the like, search engines provide a free, ostensibly unbiased third-party source of publicity for your organization.

Pearl of Wisdom: Your PR department can think of search engines as a particularly big media outlet.

Even more important from a PR point of view, search engines have become a key research tool for those very journalists, bloggers, and thought leaders PR is chatting up in the first place.

Did someone say "bloggers"? Our elbows are sore from bumping into our PR brethren as we navigate the blogosphere, asking for a little recognition for our clients. We're all essentially saying the same thing: "Hey, can you link to our site?" "Hey, would you mind spreading the word about our new product?" And on the flip side of that coin, there are lots of PR folks working as *ghost bloggers*, crafting the oh-so-casual-yet-always-right-on-the-company-line postings that emanate from slick corporate blogs. (Oh, don't look so surprised—we *told* you blogging was a business!) If you have a PR team doing these kinds of activities, your challenge will be to inject some SEO best practices into their work without overstepping your boundaries. Give your ghost blogging colleague a little list of keywords to consider using. Offer to run your eye over casual communications to make sure PR is asking for links to the best landing pages. Your SEO skills can fit nicely into their procedures.

You might meet some resistance from a PR department that thinks of SEO as strictly a form of advertising. In truth, SEO often does walk a fine line. A paid search campaign is most clearly within the advertising classification, but other SEO tasks, such as including target keywords in press releases or gaining incoming links from business contacts, fall more directly into the PR bucket. Once you explain to your PR folks that you will be seeking their assistance only with organic SEO activity, they should be more open to the possibilities.

As the department that protects the company brand, PR will likely have a great deal of interest in the brand maintenance tasks that fall under the SEO umbrella: monitoring search engine listings and other online mentions for currency and accuracy. You may need to educate the PR team about how to find outdated information online, but once they know where (and how) to look, don't be surprised if they develop a passion for rooting out the "uglies."

What if your website is not trying to sell anything or gather leads, or run advertising for revenue? What if the only goal of your website is brand awareness? This is when you need your PR department most of all. The folks in PR are already skilled in handling those difficult-to-measure soft targets offline through clipping services and surveys. They may even be doing some tracking of online mentions. Now you need to tie their tracking efforts together with the SEO campaign to make sure that SEO gets credit where credit is due. Luckily, PR people are generally very comfortable with documentation. You shouldn't have too hard a time convincing them to document their SEO successes.

"Jill-of-All-Trades" at Tachyon Publications

Tachyon Publications, a small fantasy and science fiction press, is lucky to have Jill Roberts as managing editor.

Jill is bright, hardworking, and multitalented. "I do everything," Jill says cheerfully, "from book production to bookkeeping." Depending on the day, you may find Jill coordinating cover art for an upcoming release, representing Tachyon at a convention, or arranging the cookie tray at a local author appearance. Jill is also the keeper of Tachyon's mailing list and in-house editor of the website. She explains, "I write the text for the site and enter it into the templates in the content management system, using some HTML tags."

By our count, Jill fits into several classifications, including marketing, sales, PR, editorial, and IT. And by writing the website text and e-mail newsletters, Jill is doing her part to influence SEO. "The website is one of the ways that Tachyon is most visible, since we don't have a storefront," says Jill.

Continues

"Jill-of-All-Trades" at Tachyon Publications *(Continued)*

Like many small businesses, Tachyon is great at its core business—publishing books—but has difficulty finding the budget to build a multidisciplined SEO team. (As Jill puts it, "Small presses don't exactly rake it in.") The Tachyon web "team" is actually a handful of busy people squeezing the website work into small cracks of spare time. And for most of the company's existence, nobody was really in charge of keeping the site in line with the company's goals. This situation created some fairly serious hiccups along the way. Recently, Tachyon had to abandon two website redesigns because they did not meet the company's needs. "Neither version was based on a marketing plan, or by a website designer, which, I am happy to say, the third version was," says Jill.

This struggle to redesign the site helped Tachyon recognize that it was time to make a change. The company is now building a more cohesive team to improve its web presence. Jill says, "It took me a couple of years to convince my boss to hire a web designer," but eventually he did hire a part-timer. And Tachyon is now using an on-call marketing consultant who, according to Jill, "responds to our cries for help with amazing rapidity." Even though she's not a marketing expert—yet—Jill is on the right track, and she's got a little help when she needs it.

It's a familiar scenario: In trying to conserve money, a small company can actually waste both money and time when web presence is not given the expertise it requires. It's worth the investment to identify weak spots and look for creative, but not necessarily pricey, solutions to get the right people on board.

Jill says, "I've always wanted our site to be full of great content, easy to find and navigate, and visually appealing. I think we're getting there." We say, now that you have the resources available for a well-run SEO campaign, you're bound to get there faster!

IT, Webmasters, and Programmers

Whether it's an IT department of 60 or a single programmer hiding out in the server room, your SEO campaign is going to need a *lot* of help from your company's technical experts. Not only will they be the final implementers of edits to your website, but they hold the keys to many important technical features of the site that can spell SEO success or failure.

What if you're a smaller organization and you are the one handling your own technical needs? Count yourself lucky in many ways—you won't have the workload and communication conflicts that often arise between SEO and IT. But once you start doing SEO in earnest, be ready to plug into the tech mind-set a little more often than usual.

At a minimum, you will need IT to help with edits to website content, web page redirects, server settings, programming standards, and the robots.txt file.

Sound overwhelming? It can be, if you don't prepare yourself. We suspect that dealing with your technical staff is going to be the most challenging part of your in-house SEO adventure. We have observed three major areas of difficulty:

- IT and Marketing speak such different languages it may be hard to get the communication rolling.
- IT is likely to be extremely cautious about taking on any additional workload.
- It may be difficult to find a way that SEO excellence benefits the IT department. There's a lot to say here, so let's discuss these three issues in more detail.

Communicating with IT

Your first task in working with IT will be finding a common language. Your IT comrades are technical thinkers. They like numbers, logic, specifications, and processes that can be repeated. They are less fond of mysterious or amorphous organic processes. They probably won't be responsive to a request unless they fully appreciate the logical reasons behind it.

Ideally, you will go into this conversation with some amount of technical skill under your belt. You may even want to take a crash course in HTML. But even if you think that HTML stands for "HoTMaiL" and a "server" has something to do with getting your eggs Benedict before they get cold, you can still develop a good rapport with your IT department if you follow this simple rule:

Pearl of Wisdom: Never fudge about your technical knowledge.

That's right—you need to be very honest about what you know and don't know. Express your needs, and let *them* do their jobs by telling you the right way to get things done. Bringing IT on board as a partner rather than a servant in SEO can make all the difference in your ongoing success.

Of course, you may not want all the information that IT is prepared to share with you. If your eyes glaze over at the first mention of "meta refresh," don't just stand there feeling miserable and trying to nod convincingly. Keep the focus on the overall goals: You need something done. Is it possible or not? If not, what alternatives are available? There is a give-and-take in play here. If you ask for a layperson's explanation and genuinely try to understand, you might learn something about the way your site is structured that will help you and Your SEO Plan. If you explain your SEO needs clearly, avoiding marketing jargon, your IT team will come to understand your SEO needs better and be more helpful to you in the long run.

A word of caution: If you are lucky enough to get your IT department extremely enthusiastic about SEO, you may find some ideas coming your way that fall into the realm of "black hat." We once had a meeting with a large, multidepartmental team. We had just finished going through a point-by-point explanation of the SEO plan we had developed for their site when we saw a man in the back seem to get very excited. His hand shot up, and he said, "Wouldn't it be even better if we just used the web server to show the search engine robots one thing but the site visitors would see the regular page?" Yep, he had just "thought up" the concept of cloaking. Of course, his intentions were honorable; he was using his technical knowledge in a way that he thought would benefit the company. As SEO team leader, be prepared to communicate the things that will get your site into trouble—and find common ground with those who proclaim to be SEO know-it-alls.

Some of those techie qualities that may seem, at first, like challenges might ultimately work to the advantage of your SEO campaign. For example, IT folks are more likely than other departments to actually follow specifications. That means that if you all sit down and agree on a file-naming convention, you can probably count on IT to carry the torch. Second, your IT department is likely to be very process oriented. Although you may find it frustrating to wait three months for a simple HTML change, at least you can trust that the task will be handled and documented in an orderly fashion. And third, what some may call "geekiness," others recognize as an enthusiasm for learning new things and lots of energy for the challenges that SEO will bring.

The IT Workload Conundrum

Like most departments, IT teams are feeling overworked. But even worse, their work is likely to be unrecognized and underappreciated. Unfortunately, your SEO campaign will probably require a large number of relatively small tasks from IT. And these tasks can't be done all at once because you need to assess and adjust throughout the campaign. If you are frustrated that it's taking weeks to get even simple requests handled, please realize this:

 Pearl of Wisdom: IT really hates when you call things "simple."

If you consistently find yourself bumping into roadblocks in the IT department, look for some creative solutions:

- If your company has cumbersome work request procedures, can the department create an "Express Lane" for small SEO requests, bypassing the normal pathways?

- Can the department keep your work orders open for a little while, allowing you to make adjustments?

- Is there an individual in the department that can be "yours" for a certain number of hours per month? Have a sit-down with the department leadership and figure out a way to make it happen.

- Would a *content management system (CMS)* that allowed you to edit your own pages (including meta tags) be an option? This might reduce some of the back-and-forth, although it will never entirely eliminate IT involvement.

IT tasks needed for your SEO campaign are almost never urgent. This means that, if you agree to it, they can fit into some of the slower times in the department.

If, like a lot of smaller companies, your IT department is outsourced to a web developer or hosting company, you will probably find that you need more hours—at least up front—to get your site up to snuff. Although it can be frustrating to wait, stockpiling several little SEO requests and submitting them on a weekly or monthly basis may save time and money. If your IT "department" is a friend, it may be time to stop asking for favors and either figure out how to do it yourself or set up a payment situation. SEO will generate quite a few site modifications over time, and you'll fare best if you don't leave them to the ups and downs of your friend's generous nature.

How SEO Benefits IT

Can you believe it? Your SEO campaign can actually be a positive thing for the IT department. Here are a few examples:

Interdepartmental Collaboration Bringing together the efforts of marketers, wordsmiths, artists, and techies is a positive thing. Surprising new relationships, new alliances, and synergies can result.

Recognition for IT It's not often that IT tasks can directly result in sales and profits. This is one of those times. Participating in the SEO campaign can bring the IT department out of the obscurity of the computer rooms and give them some of the attention and acclaim that they deserve.

A Cleaned-Up Site Programmers are big, big fans of streamlined source code. Tools like *Cascading Style Sheets (CSS)* create tidier websites—and tidy helps the search engines distinguish between the back-end code of your page and the text that's meant for your visitors to read. If you're ever looking for some tech love, try buttering them up with this line: "Is there any way we can work on separating presentation from content on our website?"

Can you think of any other ways that SEO might be positive for IT in your organization?

Graphic Designers

Graphic designers are those creative souls responsible for the look and feel of your website. In a larger organization, style developers create the style guides that all of the other web page creators have to follow. In a smaller company, you may be dealing with just a few designers or even an individual who is a combination of graphic designer and web developer. The graphics portion of the SEO team is responsible for setting up search engine–friendly standards in the style guide, if there is one; soliciting input from the SEO team leader during site updates; and, because SEO has a way of dropping off the radar after a while, making sure that the standards are mandatory and ongoing.

If you're on your own, you won't have anyone else to persuade. But if you're assembling an SEO team that includes Graphics, you've got some convincing to do! You'll have the best chance at success with this department if you include the following steps:

- Recognize the value of the work that the graphics department does.
- Educate about graphics-related SEO skills.
- Formalize your agreements.

Let's look at these three steps in depth.

Value Graphics

First, recognize the importance of what your designers do. Like the IT department, graphic designers often feel that their efforts are undervalued. The "look" of a site is not just an aside. In a visual medium, the look is the fundamental substance of your visitors' experience. And it's not just a cosmetic thing—your designers are responsible for *usability* factors as well. Your organization may have the benefit of user testing, or the designs may be created in a more seat-of-the-pants fashion. Either way, we can tell you this right now:

 Pearl of Wisdom: Designers want you to let *them* be the designers.

In our experience, we have found that designers' preferences are often initially at odds with optimization for search engines. A conflict between SEO and graphic designers exists because SEO is, at least in part, optimizing the website for a nonhuman visitor (a search engine robot), while designers are entirely focused on the human user experience.

As the ambassador of SEO, your job is to find common ground. Sit down with the leadership—the department head, the style guide developer, the senior designer, or whoever happens to have the website graphic files on their computer—and figure out how you can make SEO work for everybody. A website that nobody can find is worthless, but you certainly don't want a site that people immediately leave because the design doesn't speak to them. So you must recognize and acknowledge this fact:

Pearl of Wisdom: The human audience will always be the most important.

Make a commitment to the graphics department that you will never sacrifice the human user experience for SEO.

Educate and Empower

It's important to educate your designers about the reasoning behind your SEO proposals.

Give them a quick course on the graphics-related factors that you learned about in Chapters 3 and 4. Again, it's best not to overwhelm with too many details, so you should limit your explanations to elements that you are looking to change. Is your designer attached to a JavaScript pull-down navigation? Show how most search engines won't follow those links. Stuck on big graphic headlines? Using software called a *spider emulator*, you can get a peek at your website the way that search engine spiders see—or, more appropriate, don't see—these elements. Show this to your designers for a shocker!

Naturally, there may be too many changes to make in one fell swoop. Go for the big-ticket items first—for example, getting rid of frames, wrapping Flash elements in robot-friendly HTML pages, replacing major graphic headlines with HTML text, and creating a lower-priority list for less-significant SEO changes. In other words, do this:

Pearl of Wisdom: Start with big changes for quicker, tangible results.

After you have some results to show from the first pass, you'll have great ammunition for a second pass.

Don't be drawn in by the myth that everything that benefits SEO will be detrimental to the design and that you have to choose between a good-looking site that nobody can find and an ugly site with tons of traffic. Many of your SEO improvements, such as adding alternate HTML text to Flash file embeds, will have no ill effect on the design. And there are some, like replacing outdated font tags with CSS, that your designers may have wanted to do anyway. But most important, if your designers are able to internalize SEO factors, future designs will have a way of coming out more search engine friendly.

P.J. Fusco: "Educate-Inform-Transform"

P.J. Fusco is a popular writer in the SEO industry, and the search strategist for a large SEO firm. She shared her philosophy of "educate-inform-transform," explaining that building a successful campaign is all about "empowering others with the knowledge and passion to champion a project through the organization."

Here, in her own words, is how it works:

- "When you reveal keyword research to a copywriter or editor... they take greater responsibility for the words they choose."

- "When you show a Flash programmer how the search engines 'see' their work, it's a lot easier to convince them to wrap a Flash program in more search engine–friendly code."

- "When you show a designer that search engines can't read the words embedded in an image... all of a sudden, you get more words and fewer images built into site designs."

- "When you show a Sales & Marketing VP the return on investment made in a PPC campaign that has positively impacted top-line sales and bottom-line profits, you get bigger budgets for more campaigns."

As the head of the SEO team, you become more than an SEO expert. You also become educator, project manager, cheerleader, and most of all, communicator. P.J. talks about her days as a successful in-house search engine marketing manager: "Keeping different departments informed about the status of a project takes meetings, instant messages, phone calls, conference calls, and the occasional pop-in if someone missed a meeting or conference call. It takes organization, too, in order to keep up with who is doing what, when, where, how, and why."

But despite all of your best efforts, there can still be bumps in the road. P.J. has been known to take extreme measures: "If I need the telecom team to get DNS set up for a new site, I've learned to bribe them with cookies."

Make It Official

If your organization uses a web style guide, you have a great head start, because for SEO, rules are good! It will give your SEO guidelines longevity—so that your standards are followed not just once, but every time a new page is created. And it will benefit you when, six months down the road, you're handing off SEO reviews to someone else or you've forgotten what you'd planned at the outset.

What if there's no style guide, just one or two designers putting together pages based on what feels cool at the moment? You'll need some way to formalize your agreements and give them some long-term viability. If you can't get it in writing, a handshake will do. Set up a system for your designers to run edits by you in the future. At the very least, be sure that you're informed of major site edits so that you can coordinate a site review for SEO.

Avoiding Drama in Your Outsourced SEO Team

Outsourcing the members of an SEO team is a fairly common thing to do. Here we describe some of the real-world scenarios we've seen. Actual names have been changed to preserve anonymity and prevent embarrassment.

Mostly Outsourced Team Hums Along Nicely Allen is a one-man show. His SEO team involved himself as web copywriter, a friend as web developer, a brother-in-law writing press releases, and a big, impersonal hosting company doing its thing. Allen chose to work on his SEO plan when business was slow, and put himself in charge of the team. His biggest problem was communicating with his web hosting service, so he put his web developer on the phone when a little techno-interpretation was needed. The more he learned about SEO for his web copywriting, the more he was able to provide useful direction to his press release writer, often over noshes at a family get-together. Sure, he encountered delays—they're inevitable when your web vendor is doing your work as a favor. But he expected the delays, managed the vendors cheerfully, and did pretty well for himself.

Moral: If you have a relaxed time frame and a good working relationship with your vendors, you can get a lot done.

Web Developer Refuses to Work with SEO Vendor Danielle had an e-commerce website in development, and she was all set to hire an outside SEO vendor to make sure things were done right. But her plans came to a screeching halt when her web developer, who was already halfway done with the new site, refused to share files or communicate with an outside SEO vendor. Why such resistance? Because the developer wanted to provide the SEO work himself. At this point, Danielle was forced into an unpleasant choice: wait to do SEO until after the site was launched, or give the green light to a territorial developer with no SEO track record.

Continues

Avoiding Drama in Your Outsourced SEO Team *(Continued)*

Moral: Make sure your vendors are willing to work with other vendors before you sign your contract with them. For minimal friction, choose vendors with a previous working relationship.

Multiple Vendors Work Together—But It Ain't Cheap Complexia, Inc., had a major new site to support and a big budget for consultants. With separate vendors for web analytics, SEO, and web development, plus in-house copywriters, marketing, and PR, this team had inefficiency written all over it. Vendor-to-vendor management tends to be confusing, awkward, and expensive. What worked? Complexia appointed an in-house team leader with cross-department skills to oversee vendor activity. He maintained a degree of coordination with plenty of conference calls, regular budget check-ins, and a lot of e-mails with multiple CCs. This leader facilitated vendor-to-vendor management by insisting on routine communications and making sure that everyone on the team understood who could assign tasks to whom. Sure, Complexia paid for the extra communication, but the end result was that everyone achieved their goals.

Moral: When a significant percentage of your hard-core knowledge base consists of outside consultants, sometimes it's not such a terrible idea to let the vendors manage each other—especially if you have an in-house referee.

Writers and Editors

Writers and editors are the wordsmiths who craft the all-important text that your site audience, and the search engines, will see. Since SEO is so focused on text, you are going to need some writers in your corner. Writers and editors can help with these important SEO tasks: keyword brainstorming, writing or rewriting content with keywords (and linkability) in mind, writing or reviewing ad content, and establishing a process for SEO review of new content.

If you're doing this yourself, be prepared to spend a good portion of your SEO time on writing, keyword research, and related tasks.

Writers are a natural choice as SEO coconspirators. Unfortunately, SEO is often perceived among writers as something that will force them to alter, or maybe even degrade, their creative content. If you've ever seen a page of text that was written primarily for the benefit of search engines (see Figure 5.1), you know that writing for robots just isn't something that your human audience will respond to.

So just as you did with your graphic designers, start your conversation with a promise: The human audience will always be the most important. In fact, the whole point of Your SEO Plan is to bring in that audience and speak to them, clearly, in their own language. Including your writers in the keyword brainstorming process will give them important information about the terminology your target audience is using, which they can then incorporate into their text. If you educate your writers on concepts like keywords and compelling page titles, that means less rewriting in the SEO review process. That's less work for you and more control for your writers.

CAD/CAM software, CNC machining, CNC programming, DNC software, CAD/CAM

| Home |
| CAD/CAM software |
| CNC machining |
| CNC programming |
| DNC software |
| CAD/CAM |
| DNC |
| CNC |

CAD/CAM software, CNC machining, CNC programming, DNC software, CAD/CAM

CAD/CAM software of software cad/cam and free cad/cam software by cad/cam sector software textile of CNC machining, precision machining cnc.

CAD/CAM software, CNC machining, CNC programming, DNC software, CAD/CAM

cnc swiss automatic machining production cnc machining etc. cnc machining center etc.
cnc machining services (cnc lathe mini) cnc vertical machining center or cnc complete machining used cnc machining center of plastic cnc machining etc.
cnc horizontal machining center by custom precision cnc machining cnc and precision machining services is cnc automatic machining, cnc machining uk etc. cnc lab machining manager by abrasive cnc edm edm machining sinker waterjet wire and center.com cnc machining to china cnc machining etc. cnc fixturing machining cad/cam cnc edgecam equipment machining manufacturer programming solid.
cnc machine shop
machining services including cnc is cnc machining training or cnc machining work

dnc medical procedure

cnc machining milling, cnc florida machining south cnc machining vertical amera cnc comes it machining seiki when, cnc connecticut machining is cnc machining quote or CNC programming, cnc cnc program programming cnc programming software cnc lathe programming is cnc programming training, cnc programming download and cnc editor. cnc learn programming

cnc equipment

Figure 5.1 Some writing was never meant for human eyes.

SEO also provides an opportunity for writers to branch out and write content that isn't solely there to promote your product or service. Since linkability increases when a site offers useful or interesting noncommercial content, you can encourage your writers to add things like articles, news, and resource pages to the site. These might be projects that writers are interested in. Ask them for ideas.

Of course, one big step in making your website text more SEO friendly is to make sure the text is *actually present*:

Pearl of Wisdom: Writers can't optimize text that isn't there.

So coordinate with the web designers to make sure that screen real estate can be allocated for descriptive text and that graphic titles can be changed to HTML. Then you can approach your writers with specific ideas and locations for SEO-related improvements.

Executives and Product Managers

The decision makers in your organization have a lot on their minds these days: Shrinking budgets, expanding competition, and out-of-control expenses could keep anyone awake at night. Why should they be open to your big ideas about SEO? Even if SEO was the boss's idea in the first place—or if you're your own boss—you still need to know, in a down-to-the-brass-tacks kind of way, what it's going to take.

Of course, you want to approach your corporate decision makers with a clear vision, a plan, and a lot of cold, hard facts. But there's a catch-22 here: How can you know exactly what Your SEO Plan will cost and what it will accomplish until you have spent some time researching those very questions? Executives aren't big fans of laying out cash for an unknown outcome. So we recommend that you start the process by seeking approval for an initial, investigatory month. That's roughly 20 hours of labor at 1 hour per day, and it's all laid out for you in the next chapter. You'll spend your Prep Month figuring out what kind of performance your SEO campaign can expect and be able to come back to the executives with a much more complete plan on hand.

Your initial request will be introductory. Prepare it with the following information on hand:

- A general introduction to SEO: what it is and how it is being used in the marketing mix by many companies today. For starters, try the "Why SEO?" numbers from the introduction to this book.

- Your Goals Worksheet from Chapter 1.

- Some telling screen shots showing your competition outranking you, your brand looking awful onscreen, or any other SEO faux pas you can find.

- A detailed timeline for the Prep Month.

Be prepared for plenty of questions from around the table: How much will this really cost us? How long do we have to do it? Do we have the right staff in-house?

SEO is such a cost-effective marketing technique that it should be an easy sell. But change is never easy. Does budgeting your SEO campaign mean that Ellen will have to take Tim's Yellow Pages budget away? Will an hour a day of SEO mean someone is an hour late for dinner each night? No matter how persuasive your numbers and worksheets are, your plan will need to address the realities of day-to-day operations.

Once your executives are ready to move on your SEO project, be sure you get not just a green light, but a little bit of gas in the tank as well. Here's what you'll need them to do:

- Vocalize the plan to the team.

- Commit to your proposed labor and budget.

- Commit to reviewing your findings after you have completed your Prep Month.

Working in SEO can sometimes feel like wrestling a many-armed sea animal. How will you tame the beast and get some solid results? Start with a "do what we can" attitude, stay on target with your goals, and remember: Solo beast-taming may be muy macho, but taming with friends is a lot more effective.

Get Yourself on Board!

As SEO team leader, you may have to step slightly outside of your comfort zone in order to be as effective as you can be. You will have to keep yourself organized, which entails documenting results, questions, and communications as you go. And like any team leader, you will sometimes need to repeat yourself politely until you get that requested task completed or that important concept understood. If it helps to take some of the pressure off, you as SEO project leader can comfortably adopt a friendly, easy-going approach. Since SEO isn't normally a deadline-driven process—most of the time—you'll have the opportunity to write "No rush" on your requests and mean it!

Now that you understand how to drum up the requisite levels of enthusiasm throughout your organization, you're ready to start your Prep Month. As you do the research in the next chapter, you're likely to uncover some interesting, and possibly surprising, findings about your own site that you can share with your team.

Your One-Month Prep: Baseline and Keywords

Your goals are in place, you have a good under-standing of how the search engines work, your team is ready—finally, it's time to get into your SEO campaign! We'll walk you through it, day by day, in tasks that we estimate will take an hour or so.

This month, you'll handpick your most effective keywords based on a combination of gut instinct and careful research; then you'll assess your site's standing in the search engines. You'll even set up an analytics program if you don't have one already. This is critical prep work for next month's optimization tasks.

6

Chapter Contents

Your SEO Idea Bank

Maybe you're an anarchist at heart, and it takes divine intervention to get your feet into two matching socks. But more likely, you're just so overworked that it's impossible to keep every sticky note and e-mail where it belongs. You need help—and we're here for you! Before you begin your hour-a-day tasks, follow these simple steps to start your new SEO lifestyle with a "headquarters" on your computer. We call it your SEO Idea Bank!

Step 1: Create a home for your SEO files. Choose a location on your computer or network where your SEO files will live. Having one location for your SEO files will keep things simpler for you.

Step 2: Download tools from yourseoplan.com. On the companion website to this book, www.yourseoplan.com, you'll find the worksheets and templates that we'll be referring to throughout this chapter. Take the time to download these now and save them in your SEO Idea Bank:

- Keywords Worksheet
- Site Assessment Worksheet
- Rank Tracking Worksheet
- Task Journal Worksheet
- Competition Worksheet
- SEO Growth Worksheet

And don't forget to copy your Goals Worksheet from Chapter 1, "Clarify Your Goals," into your SEO Idea Bank as well. From time to time throughout the rest of this book, we'll send you to the website to fetch some more helpful documents for your SEO Idea Bank.

Step 3: Start an SEO Task Journal. Your SEO Task Journal is a place to document what you've done, what questions have cropped up, and what you need to do in the future. Your Task Journal will prevent you from duplicating your efforts and help you keep track of what you were thinking last week and the week before. It's also a convenient holding pen for ideas and random thoughts that come up while you are working on Your SEO Plan.

One of the fun things about SEO is wandering down whatever path your explorations take you. But if you only have an hour and you actually want to accomplish something, you're going to need to keep yourself on track. Rather than going off on every tangent that is thrown your way, file those thoughts away in your Task Journal for later.

If the Task Journal isn't your cup of tea, use whatever organizational method works for you. You may be happy using a simple Microsoft Word document and changing the font to ~~strikethrough~~ when the topic is resolved. But feel free to get fancy. Consider experimenting with an online database in your own personal Yahoo! Group at groups.yahoo.com, or an online to-do list through a service such as tadalist.com.

With your SEO Idea Bank in place, you're ready for the fun stuff: choosing keywords!

Week 1: Keywords

Ask any SEO pro what the single most important part of an SEO campaign is, and we bet you'll get this answer: "Keyword choice!" Here's why: The keywords you choose *this week* will be the focus of your entire optimization process. Keywords (also referred to as keyword phrases, keyphrases, and keyterms) are the short, descriptive phrases that you want to be found with on the search engines. If you put the time into choosing powerful keywords now, you are likely to be rewarded not only with higher ranks, but also with these benefits:

- A well-optimized site, because your writers and other content producers will feel more comfortable working with well-chosen keywords as they add new site text
- More click-throughs once searchers see your listing, because your keywords will be highly relevant to your site's content
- More conversions once your visitors come to your site, because the right keywords will help you attract a more targeted audience

As SEO expert Jill Whalen told us, "There is more than one way to skin the SEO cat.… There is no special formula that will work for every site all the time." And this applies to your keyword targeting strategy. We suggest that by the end of this week you have 10 target keyword phrases in hand. We believe that this is a reasonable level for an hour-a-day project. But you may be more comfortable with 2 or 20 keywords. We welcome you to adjust according to your individual needs.

Here are your daily assignments for this week:

Monday: Your Keyword Gut Check

Tuesday: Resources to Expand and Enhance the Keyword List

Wednesday: Keyword Data Tools

Thursday: Keyword Data Gathering

Friday: Your Short List

Your Name Here

Recently, we were chatting with our friend Mark Armstrong, an auto mechanic in San Francisco. Hearing that we were working on an SEO book, he shared a common frustration: "All I want to do," he said, "is find the official website for this supplier out in Chicago. I know the name of the company, but even when I enter their name in the search engines, their website is nowhere to be found. Now that is just ridiculous! There should be some system where companies always come up first for their own name." We couldn't agree more, but due to the dynamic nature of competition and the innate complexities of search semantics, there's no guarantee that your site will come up first when someone searches for your organization's name. That's why we always recommend including it on your list of top target keywords.

Monday: Your Keyword Gut Check

Today you're going to do a brain dump of possible target keywords for your organization. You'll need two documents from your SEO Idea Bank: the Keywords Worksheet and your Goals Worksheet.

Now: Go to your SEO Idea Bank and open up the Keywords Worksheet and your Goals Worksheet.

In the Keywords Worksheet, you'll find columns with the headings Keyword, Search Popularity, Relevance, Competition, and Landing Page. Today you're only worried about the first column: Keyword.

Now, take a look at the list of conversions that you came up with on your Goals Worksheet in Chapter 1. You'll use these as jumping-off points for your keyword brainstorming session.

We met Jason back in Chapter 1 when he was thinking through his target audiences and the goals of his SEO campaign. Jason's company, Babyfuzzkin, sells unique, high-end baby clothes. We're going to follow him through his keyword week.

For now, you'll jot down whatever comes to mind, and save the fine-tuning for later. Here are a few ideas to get you started:

Be the searcher. For each conversion you wrote on your Goals Worksheet, take a few minutes to put yourself in the mind of each target audience that you listed. Imagine that you are this person, sitting in front of a search engine. What do you type in the search box?

Name who you are and what you offer. No keyword list is complete without your organization's name and the products, services, or information you offer. Be sure to think about generic *and* proprietary descriptions. Jason may jot down more generic words like "baby shower gifts" and "baby clothes," but he should also include trade-marked names like "Babyfuzzkin" and a list of the brand names he's selling. Likewise, if it's equally accurate to describe the products for sale on your website with the terms "spray bottles" or "X7 MistMaker Series," add both to your list.

Name the need you fill. It's not just what you offer, it's the itch that your product or service scratches. So Jason might write down "baby shower gift ideas" or "baby clothes free shipping." If you sold home alarm systems on your site, you might want to list terms that describe your customers' needs, such as "protect my home" and "prevent burglary."

Think seasonal. Does your product or service vary from season to season? Do you offer special services for special events? Think through your whole calendar year. Jason at Babyfuzzkin may want to list words like "baby swimsuits" and "Size 2T Santa Sweaters." A spa resort may want to list things like "Mother's Day Getaway Ideas" and "Tax Time Stress Relief."

Embrace misspellings, alternate spellings, and slang. Here's something you probably know better than any SEO expert: Alternate spellings and regional variations on your keywords. Jason bristles when he gets mail addressed to "Baby Fuzzkin" or "Babyfuss-ing," but he knows his company name is easy to get wrong, so he'll add those to his list. On a regional note, a company selling soft drink vending machines had better remember to add both "soda" and "pop." You do *not* need to consider variations in capitalization because search engines are not sensitive to caps (besides, the vast majority of searches are lowercase). However, you should include singular and plural forms on your list for further evaluation, and be sure to consider variations in punctuation, too: "tattle tale," "tattletale," and "tattle-tale" are not necessarily the same words to a search engine.

Locate yourself. In Chapter 2, "Customize Your Approach," we suggested that brick-and-mortar organizations include variations on their company name and location in the keywords list. If your company does business only in Michigan, you really don't want to waste your SEO efforts on a searcher in Nevada. And did we mention that search engines sometimes aren't all that smart? They do not necessarily know that "OH" and "Ohio" are the same thing. So be sure to include every variation you can think of.

Self-packaged
yellow tropical
fruit snack

Now that you've got an idea of what you're looking for, you can choose to brainstorm your list alone, or, better yet, brainstorm with members of your PR, sales, marketing, and writing teams. This can work well as an e-mail exercise, too; just shoot out a request for your colleagues to send you their own ideas for keywords.

When Homographs Attack

Homographs are words that have the same spelling but different meanings. For example, invalid means both "not valid" and "a person who can't get out of bed." Search engines have struggled with homographs since their inception.

As mothers to young children, we have a strong interest in making sure our homes are lead free. So naturally, we use the search engines to learn how. Unfortunately, the word "lead," meaning "a soft, heavy, toxic, malleable metallic element," happens to have a homograph: "lead," meaning "travel in front of." The environmental-lead-testing search results are crowded out by pages with information on leadership! In order to get the information we need, we have to lengthen our search phrases: "lead abatement," "lead contamination," and "lead poisoning."

Acronyms are particularly susceptible to this problem. One site we know (we've changed the name and identifying details to prevent embarrassment), Massive Media, Inc., has spent years targeting the term "AMC," which is an acronym for one of its products. But just in the top 10 Google results, this term is represented by the following entities:

- AMC Theatres
- The AMC network movie channel
- The Appalachian Mountain Club
- Albany Medical Center
- Australian Maritime College
- American Mathematics Competitions
- Applied Microsystems Corporation

None of these has anything to do with what Massive Media was trying to promote! Clearly, in targeting this acronym, it was navigating the wrong waters. It doesn't make sense to spend your energy competing with such a broad field.

If you are unfortunate enough to be promoting a company or product with a name that shares spelling with a common word or acronym, you will need to brainstorm on what secondary terms your target audience is likely to add and combine words to find a more appropriate term to target. Possibilities are the geographical location of your company, the generic term for the product, names of well-known executives, or the term "company" or "inc." And as a general rule, don't target acronyms shorter than four letters long.

Once you start spitting out your list, don't overedit yourself; you'll have time for editing later. For now, we just want you to get all of your keyword ideas in writing. By the end of tomorrow's task, you should have a big, hearty list—say, at least 50 keyword ideas for a list that will be trimmed down to about 10 by the end of this week.

Now: Go to the Keywords Worksheet and start your list under the Keyword column.

Tuesday: Resources to Expand and Enhance the List

On your Keywords Worksheet, you already have a nice long list of possible target phrases. But are there any you missed? Today, you'll troll on- and offline for additional keyword ideas. We've listed some of the places that additional keyword phrase ideas could pop up. There are more ideas here than you can use in just one hour, so pick and choose based on what's available to you and what feels most appropriate to your situation:

Your Coworkers If you didn't get your team involved in keyword brainstorming yesterday, be sure that they jump on board today. It will help your campaign in two ways: First, they'll provide valuable new perspectives and ideas for keywords, and second, they'll feel involved and empowered as participants in the plan.

Your Website Have you looked through your website to find all variations of your possible keyword phrases? Terms that are already used on your site are great choices for target keywords because they will be easier to incorporate into your content.

Industry Media If there are any magazines or websites devoted to your trade, take a look and see what terminology they are using to describe your product or service. Remember, now is not the time to edit your terms! So if the words are in use out there, be sure to include them on this list.

Your Website Statistics If you have access to a program that shows traffic statistics on your website—that is, a web analytics tool—review it to see what search terms are currently sending traffic and conversions your way. Terms that are already working well for you can be great choices for target keywords. We'll walk you through choosing and reviewing analytics tools in Week 4 later in this chapter.

Your Customers If you (or anyone on your SEO team) have the ability to check in with customers about what phrases they use to describe your products or services, now is the time to get in touch with them and find out! Your salespeople might also take this opportunity to confess: "Oh yeah, it's called Closure Management Technology on the website, but when we talk with customers, we always just call it *zippers*."

Your Internal Search Engine If your website has a search box on it, it's time to get sneaky! You can use its usage information for your SEO campaign. Talk to your webmaster about collecting the following information about site visitors who use your internal search engine:

- What terms do they search for?
- What results are they shown?
- What pages do they choose to click on (if any)?

Keep a running list of top terms your site visitors are searching for; these are likely to be good target keywords for your SEO campaign.

There's plenty more that an internal search engine can do for you. Visit Chapter 10, "Extra Credit and Guilt-Free Slacking," for more information.

xtra cred

"Related" Terms on Search Engines Many search engines offer suggestions for related terms after you perform a search. For example, Ask has "Narrow Your Search" and "Expand Your Search" columns along the left-hand side of the search results that show a variety of terms related to your search (see Figure 6.1). These related terms can be good additional keyword choices.

Friends, Neighbors, and the Unexpected One major problem we have observed with keyword choice is that businesses tend to become too caught up in the insider terminology they use to describe themselves. If your target audience goes beyond industry insiders, be sure to seek out input from unexpected sources. Your friends and neighbors or even the neighbor's kid can provide surprisingly helpful ideas.

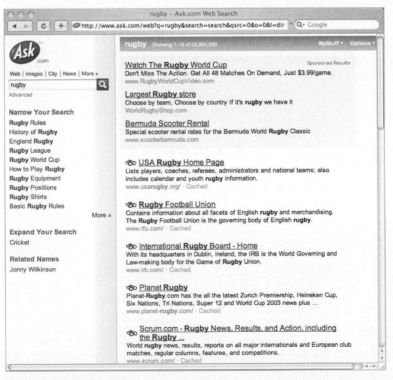

Figure 6.1 Related terms on Ask

Competitors' Websites Later this month, we'll have you digging through your competitors' websites like a hungry raccoon in a Dumpster. For the moment, try breaking up keyword writer's block by browsing your competitors' sites to see what terms they are using to describe themselves.

Now: Go to the Keywords Worksheet and add your new ideas to the list in the Keyword column.

Wednesday: Keyword Data Tools

You've got a nice long list of keywords. But the list doesn't mean much to you until you find out which of these keywords are actually being used by searchers. You're also going to want a sense of how competitive the SEO field is for a keyword so you can get a handle on just how hard you might have to fight to rank well for it.

Fortunately, there are keyword analysis tools available to help you suss out this important information. And also fortunately, there are *not so many* different high-quality options to choose from, so the decision is far from overwhelming. We'll discuss the top three here:

- Wordtracker
- Keyword Discovery
- Google AdWords Keyword Tool

Today is a "study hall" day. You're going to find these tools and get your feet wet using them.

Wordtracker

Wordtracker is the keyword research tool of choice for many professional SEOs. In a nutshell, it tells you how many people are searching for the terms you may want to use on your site. It does this by monitoring and recording searches on meta search engines throughout the Web. You can use it to get an estimate of how many searches will be performed for a given term, and it is also an excellent source of related terms and common misspellings (see Figure 6.2).

Wordtracker doesn't give an up-to-the-minute snapshot—its data reflects searches that took place a few months before you retrieve it. Wordtracker is available at www.wordtracker.com for a fee.

If you decide to go this route, you can use Wordtracker today and tomorrow as the primary tool for whittling down your long keyword list into something meaningful. If you need to be frugal, Wordtracker makes it easy for you: You can purchase low-cost subscriptions in one-week or one-month increments. They also offer a free version of their tool at http://freekeywords.wordtracker.com. Although this version lacks some features of the full version, it's a very useful reference tool.

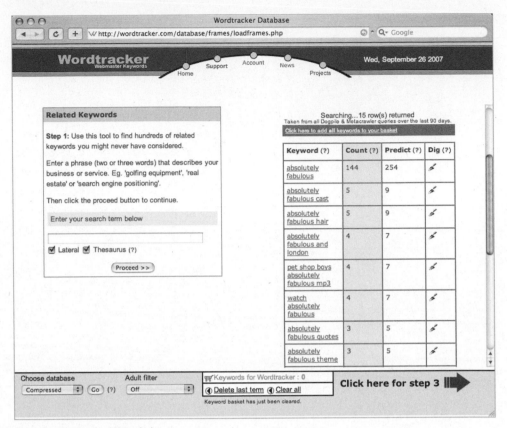

Figure 6.2 Wordtracker keywords data

Wordtracker isn't hard to use, so we'll leave the step-by-step instructions, if you need them, to the folks who made the tool. You can download their user guide once you have logged into the system. There is also a FAQ and other resources on their website. Be sure to read up on the different databases (Comprehensive, Compressed, etc.) available within the system so you can choose the best one for your needs.

Keyword Discovery

Keyword Discovery is pricier than Wordtracker. It is a feature-rich tool that has fast become the darling of many hard-core search professionals. Keyword Discovery's data comes from over 200 search engines worldwide, and the data displayed in the main search results are from a historical period of 12 months. Data is updated monthly (like Wordtracker, this data is not an up-to-the-minute snapshot). Keyword Discovery is available at www.keyworddiscovery.com. A limited free trial is available and easy to use.

Keyword Discovery claims that its "Global Premium" database is free from data skew caused by automated agents such as rank or bid checkers. What that means is that it attempts to deliver data derived only from human searchers, not robots or other software. We have our doubts that Keyword Discovery is significantly less "skewy" than Wordtracker, so don't let that be your deciding factor.

Even as professional SEO's, we find it hard to make full use of the feature set available here, but you might find some of their options irresistible. For example, Keyword Discovery allows you to review search popularity in some very specific databases, such as eBay, News, and Shopping, not to mention several international databases. These are great fun when you're doing an exhaustive, multitiered keyword research sweep for your site. But based on the data we've seen, we don't recommend these niche databases as a first-line tool for your research. We recommend sticking with the general databases and then graduating yourself to some deeper digging once you're familiar with broader trends.

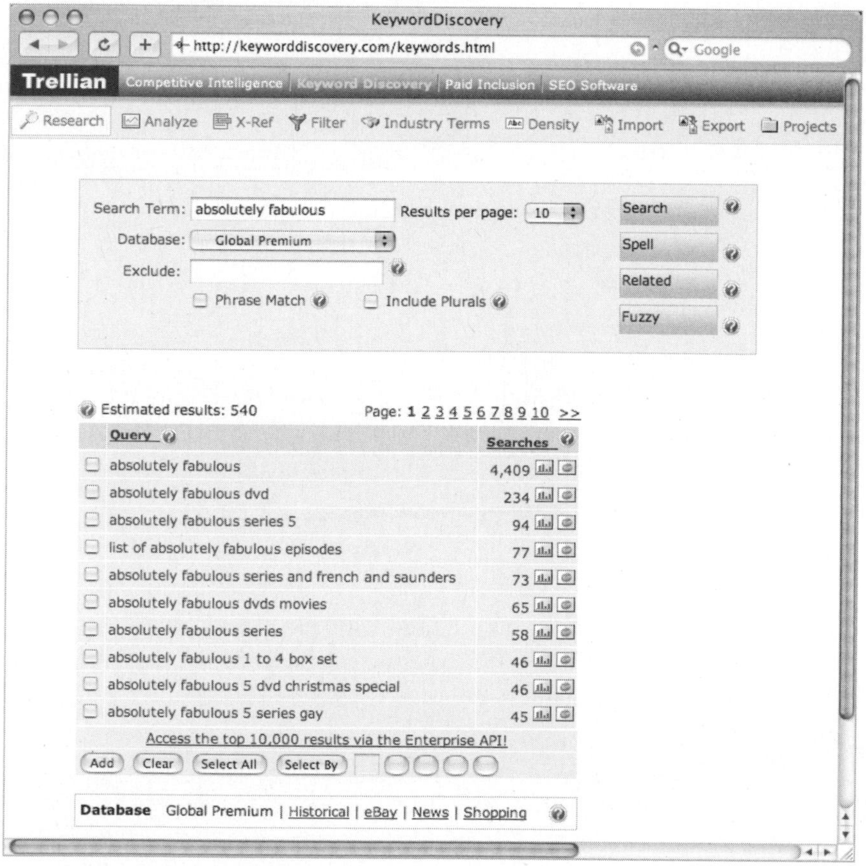

Figure 6.3 Keyword Discovery data

Google AdWords Keyword Tool

If you have absolutely no budget—or if spending a day without using a Google product makes you twitchy—take a look at the free Google AdWords Keyword Tool at https://adwords.google.com/select/KeywordToolExternal. Google isn't exactly tripping over itself to help you understand the data, or even where it's coming from (Organic traffic? Paid traffic? Their lips are sealed.) But it does show recent data, and it's a fine place to start if you want to identify search trends, or if you want to verify a trend you think you're seeing elsewhere.

This tool is primarily targeted to advertisers who want to tune up their Google AdWords paid search campaigns, but you can glean solid keyword ideas and popularity trends no matter what your end goal.

Notice that we keep saying "trends," not "numbers"? The Google AdWords Keyword Tool doesn't give you actual numbers—just bar charts to indicate popularity. But it also gives you at-a-glance competitor information (for paid competitors only), which can be quite enlightening as you pick through your keyword possibilities. See Figure 6.4 for details.

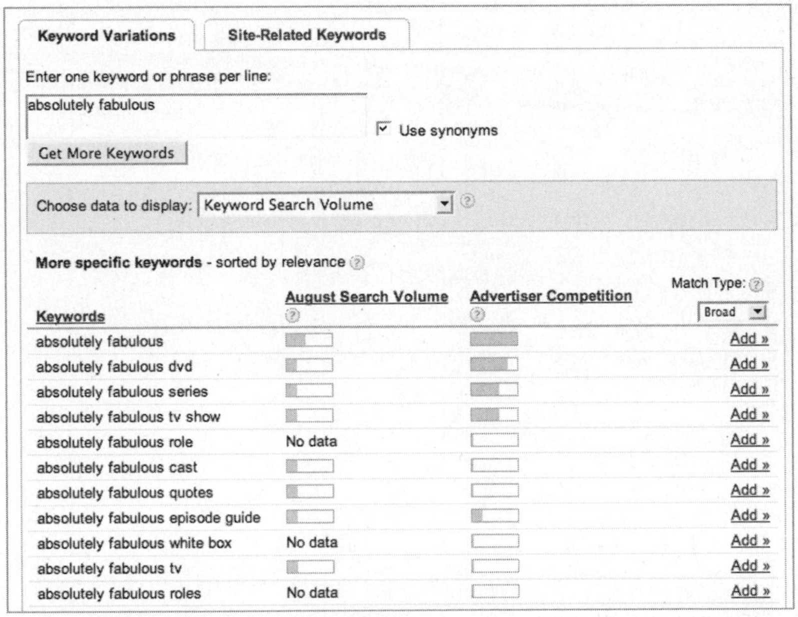

Figure 6.4 Google AdWords Keyword Tool data

There are lots of reasons you may want to use the Google AdWords Keyword Tool: It can be a real help if you can't drop the 30 bucks or so for a monthly subscription to Wordtracker. Or you may find the "Googleness" of it appealing—you love Google's users, so why not go straight to the source for keyword data? We find the lack of numerical data frustrating, but you may wish to be relieved of the burden of math. Even if you use a different research tool, the AdWords Keyword tool can still help you verify trends you're seeing elsewhere.

No keyword research tool is perfect, and you should always double-check the data you get with your gut instincts. We feel that Wordtracker, with its simpler interface and great customer support, is a better choice for small businesses that are taking the first step in keyword research. Keyword Discovery is more robust and expensive, and may be just the thing for experienced marketers who need to gather data over several different regions or target audiences. The Google AdWords Keyword tools is fine if you have no budget for a paid option. Your finances and preferences will dictate which one(s) you use.

Now: Go to each of the keyword research options listed earlier and test-drive them with some of the keywords from your list.

Thursday: Keyword Data Gathering

Congratulations—you're over the hump in your first week of SEO! You have a long list of possible keywords and tools in hand to help you analyze them. Today you will fill in those all-important columns on your Keywords Worksheet:

Search Popularity How many people are actually searching for a given term

Relevance How well a keyword connects with your site and conversion goals

Competition How many, and how well, other sites are targeting a given keyword

Finalizing your top target keywords will require a balancing act between all three of these factors. We'll look a little more closely at each of them here.

Search Popularity

Wordtracker, Keyword Discovery, and the Google AdWords Keyword tool provide values for keyword popularity (see Figures 6.2, 6.3, and 6.4). Today you're going to gather these values from your keyword research tool of choice.

It can be time-consuming pulling up the search popularity values for every term on your long list, but if you're using Wordtracker or the AdWords Keyword Tool, you can save time by copying and pasting several words at a time—or your whole list—into the search popularity tool. If you're good with Microsoft Excel, you can even export the search results from any of these tools for easy import into your Keywords Worksheet!

Jason at Babyfuzzkin used Wordtracker to determine the search popularity of his long list. We've selected a few of his results to show in Table 6.1.

▶ **Table 6.1** Search Popularity for Babyfuzzkin's Keywords

Keyword	Search Popularity
baby clothes	2125
unique baby clothes	134
infants	747
infant	376
designer baby clothing	65
designer baby clothes	438
baby gift	588
baby gifts	1629
baby shower gifts	614
unique baby shower gifts	667
cool baby clothes	236
layette	66

Don't pay too much attention to the absolute values of the numbers here. Search popularity values provided by these services do not give you the total number of searches throughout the entire Internet, so you should only use them for comparing the *relative* search popularity between two terms. If you're using the Google AdWords Keyword Tool for your research, you can just substitute AdWords' assessment (low, average, high, very high, etc.) for search popularity numbers. However, keep in mind that Google's search volume graphics are normalized—scaled up or down based on the popularity of the most popular term on the list. Be sure that you gather all of your keyword data at one time so they're all being compared fairly.

 Pearl of Wisdom: If you export the Google AdWords Keyword Tool data into a spreadsheet, the bar charts are translated into the numbers 0–5, which might be a little easier to work with.

You may notice while you gather your popularity numbers that you find other tempting keywords that you hadn't previously considered. Add them to the list! You'll begin slicing and dicing this list very soon, but for now, it won't hurt to add more promising ideas.

With these values in black and white, you'll have a much stronger command of which terms are going to be good performers for you.

Relevance

Relevance is in many ways a judgment call. How would a searcher feel if they searched for this term and found your site? Would your site answer their question or resolve their need? Does a good landing page for this term currently exist on your site, or could one be built? We are going to ask you to classify relevance on a scale from *Very Poor* to *Excellent*. Your relevance values should also incorporate the following perspectives:

Your Writers/Editors Ask yourself if the people who write content on your website will be comfortable using this term to describe your products and services. Better yet, go ask *them* the question.

Other Sites That Come Up in the Search Try entering the term into a search engine and see what other sites come up. Are the top-ranking websites from organizations that are similar to yours? Surprisingly, in SEO you often do want to be situated in the vicinity of your competitors. If a searcher enters a keyword and sees a page full of weird, seemingly unrelated results, they are likely to try again with a different search.

Value of the Conversion Your relevance level should also take into account the value of the conversion for a term. For example, if the two terms "ginger syrup" and "crystallized ginger" are equally well matched to your site, but you believe that people searching for "crystallized ginger" are going to be more valuable conversions (because it's a much more expensive delicacy!), then that keyword should get a boost. It's guesswork and intuition at this point, but after a few months, you'll have some tracking under your belt and a much clearer understanding of the conversion values for different terms.

Here's a detailed examination of a few of Jason's keywords. These examples should give you some guidance for thinking about your own keywords:

Keyword: *infants*, Relevance Rating: *Poor* Think about all the different things that someone might be looking for when entering the word "infants" into the search engine, ranging from gifts to medical advice. Yes, it's true that Babyfuzzkin's products do fall within this range, but so do millions of other sites. Here's a tip you can count on:

Look at any one-word keywords on your list. In what other context, other than your immediate conversion goal, could searchers be using them?

Keyword: *baby clothes*, **Relevance Rating:** *Good* We would rate this relevance level as *Good* because it uses two rather generic words to accurately describe the product that Babyfuzzkin sells. But it also encompasses lots of things that Babyfuzzkin doesn't sell. Searchers could use this term to look for used clothes and large chain stores in addition to boutique items like Jason is selling.

Keyword: *unique baby clothes*, **Relevance Rating:** *Excellent* This keyphrase uses a modifier—"unique"—to more clearly describe the product that Babyfuzzkin sells. You may be wondering, "Is a subjective word like 'unique' a good candidate for targeting?" It is, but only if you think it's accurate, and if you think people will use it to search for your product! So while "unique" may be appropriate for you to target, there's probably no point in targeting boastful terms like "best" or "finest." Sure, we know your offerings are the best, but is "best truck liners" really more relevant than something more specific on your list, like "heavy duty truck liners"?

Keyword: *cheap baby clothes*, **Relevance Rating:** *Very Poor* We would rate this relevance level as *Very Poor* because Babyfuzzkin is a high-end product and does not match the description "cheap." Although it may be tempting to target popular or appealing terms like "cheap," if it does not describe your product or service, it is going to be a wasted effort and a bust for conversions.

Keyword: *unique baby shower gifts*, **Relevance Rating:** *Excellent* This term describes Babyfuzzkin's products very specifically. As this example shows, highly relevant terms are often longer.

Keyword: *Babyfuzzkin*, **Relevance Rating:** *Excellent* You can't get a tighter match than the company name!

Now: Go to the Keywords Worksheet and use your own judgment to add your values to the Relevance column.

Competition Level

In SEO, you've got to choose your battles. Sure, we'd all love to have great ranks for the most popular terms: "real estate," "games," "golf," or "Angelina Jolie." But the time and money spent for good ranking on these terms can be prohibitive. That's why the Competition Level column of the Keywords Worksheet exists: so you can know what you're getting into and set your expectations accordingly.

There are lots of ways to assess the competition level for a keyword; see the sidebar "Sizing Up the Competition" for some of our favorite methods. We're going to ask you to rate your keyword competition level from *Very Low* to *Very High*. What's most important is that you use the same measuring stick for all of your terms.

Sizing Up the Competition

The Left Brain and Right Brain look at different perspectives on estimating competition levels for keywords on your long list:

The Right Brain says, "You know your business, so you know what aspects of your business have more, or stronger, competitors. If you work for a bank, you don't need the numbers to tell you that the term 'low mortgage rates' is going to be very competitive. But for terms that are less obvious, you can do a competition gut check by searching for that term and looking for the following indicators:

- "Do most of the sites in the top several pages of results appear to have the same conversion goals as you? Do you recognize some of your known competitors in there? Did you just find new competitors that you hadn't known about before? If you've got the same goals as the top-ranking sites, you're in a competitive space.

- "Are most of the sites in the top several pages of results trying to sell something related to the keyword you're assessing? Even SEO newbies can see that the vast majority of sites that show up for 'low mortgage rates' are trying to sell mortgages. But search for 'low literacy rates', and you can really see the difference—there's much less of a feeling that the site owners are jumping up and down, shouting, 'Over here!'

- "How many sponsored listings do you see for the term in question? Sites that are selling something are likely to spend more time and money optimizing, so terms with a lot of commercial results are likely to be more competitive."

The Left Brain says, "Industry insight is important, but quantitative values give you more solid ground to stand on. Anyone estimating competition levels for a keyword should research these numbers:

- "How many pages on the Web are already optimized for the term? To estimate this value, you can perform a specialized search on Google and find out how many sites have that keyword in their HTML page title tag. Just type **allintitle:** *"keyword"* into the search box (don't forget the quotes). For example, Jason would type **allintitle:** *"baby clothes"* to find out how many websites are using that term in their HTML title. (See our companion website at www .yourseoplan.com for other useful search tricks.)

- "As we showed you earlier, the Google AdWords Keyword Tool gives you an indication of the level of paid competition for a given keyword. However, if you have a Google AdWords account, you can go to the next level and review the top bid prices. This applies to other paid search services as well, not just Google. If you don't have a paid search account, we'll explain how to set up accounts and check these values in Part III."

Here are the competition levels, and the thinking behind them, for a selection of Jason's picks:

Keyword: *infants*, Competition Level: *Very High* On a gut level, most single-word searches are going to rate as very competitive; there are just too many sites in the world that contain this term. Quantitatively speaking, the allintitle search on Google shows that there are over 1.3 million websites with the term in their HTML titles.

Keyword: *baby clothes*, Competition Level: *Very High* This term is also rather competitive. Obviously, there are numerous companies, some very large, that sell this product online and that will be competing for this search traffic. You can click as far down as Yahoo!'s tenth search results page, and there's no end in sight to the companies selling baby clothes. Google shows over 300,000 pages with the term in their HTML titles.

Keyword: *unique baby clothes*, Competition Level: *Moderate* This one may not be so cut and dried. This is still a very competitive term at first glance: There's really not much difference in the "feel" of the competitor listings for this term as compared to the listings for "baby clothes"—they're very sales oriented. But with only roughly 300 pages showing on Google with this exact phrase in their HTML title, this term goes into the *Moderate* competition bracket.

Keyword: *unique baby shower gifts*, Competition Level: *High* There are only roughly 900 pages showing on Google with this exact phrase in their HTML titles. You might be tempted to call this one Moderate. But here's where the gut feeling comes in: *Unique* is a marketing word, making this term more commercial in nature. And take a look at the MSN search results in Figure 6.5. This is way down on page 15 of the search results, and you can still practically envision the websites trying to elbow each other out of the way to sell you their baby clothes. We would rate this term as *High* in competition.

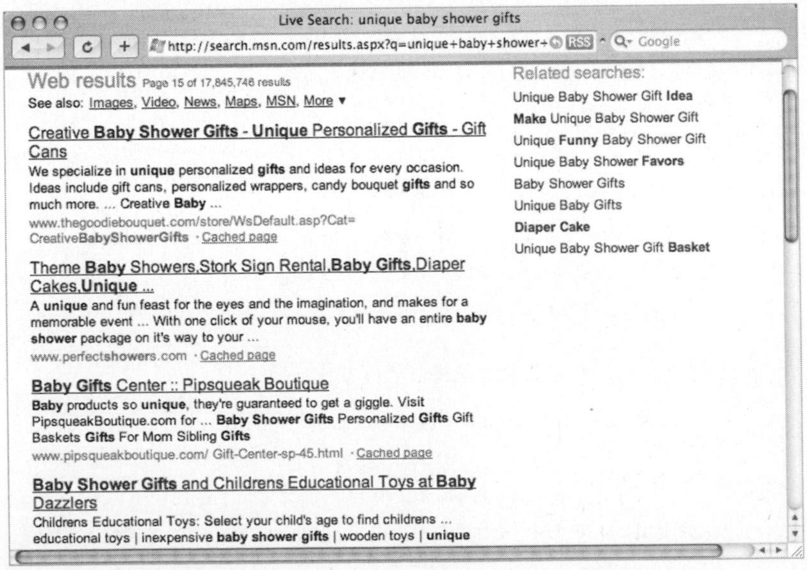

Figure 6.5 MSN search results for "unique baby shower gifts"

Keyword: *babyfuzzkin*, **Competition Level:** *Very Low* Actually, the competition level for this keyword is nonexistent. There are no sites ranking for it, and there don't appear to be any sites targeting it in their keywords.

Now: Go to the Keywords Worksheet and add your values to the Competition column.

Friday: Your Short List

Your Keywords Worksheet is full of useful information. Now it's time to whittle down your list into a manageable group of 10 or so top target keywords. Here are the steps to a nicely honed list:

- The Keyword Balancing Act
- Combining Keywords
- Matching Keywords and Landing Pages
- Finalizing Your Short List

The Keyword Balancing Act

The most useful keywords will strike a balance between popularity, relevance, and competition. We're going to ask you to identify some of these more balanced keywords. Here are some examples of a good balance:

Lower Popularity/Higher Relevance A low popularity/high relevance combination means that even if there are not so many people searching for the term, the ones who do come are more likely to click on your listing and ultimately convert on your site.

But don't go *too* low! Unless you have a reason to doubt the data, searches with zero popularity scores should probably not even be considered, except for your company name or a trademarked product name.

Higher Competitiveness/Higher Relevance If you are drawn to a competitive term, be sure that it is balanced out with a high degree of relevance.

Higher Popularity/Lower Competition/Higher Relevance This is the ideal balance. If you can find terms that are used heavily by searchers, are closely tied to your conversion goal, and are targeted by a reasonable number of competitors, you want them on your short list!

Consider Jason's keyword list. The term "baby clothes" is popular, but it's extremely competitive and does not balance that disadvantage with a high relevance level. Not a good choice. On the other hand, "unique baby shower gifts," while on the high side in competition, balances its disadvantage with a very high relevance. See Table 6.2; this term has great potential for Babyfuzzkin! Jason has flagged it using "highlight" formatting.

Keyword(s)	Search Popularity Wordtracker	Relevance	Competition Level	Landing Page URL
baby clothes	2125	good	very high	www.babyfuzzkin.com/clothes
infants	747	poor	very high	www.babyfuzzkin.com/clothes
unique baby shower gifts	667	excellent	high	www.babyfuzzkin.com/clothes

Now: Go to the Keywords Worksheet and highlight the terms that have the best balance between competition, relevance, and popularity.

Combining Keywords

Once you've flagged your preferred terms, look for terms that can be combined. For example, in Jason's case he can combine the terms "baby clothes" and "unique baby clothes" into just one term: "unique baby clothes." This is a great way to get double duty out of your SEO efforts, combining the search popularity of both terms.

If you are including geographical information with your keywords, now is the time to combine it with your other terms. For example, a manicure salon in Franklin, Missouri, may want to combine keywords to create the keyword phrases "manicure Franklin Missouri" and "salon Franklin Missouri."

Now: Go to the Keywords Worksheet and add combined terms to the list. Flag these as you go. They belong in your short list, too.

Matching Keywords and Landing Pages

For a keyword to perform well in the search engines, it needs to be matched to a landing page on your site that would be an excellent destination for someone searching for this term. A good landing page for a keyword will satisfy your visitors' needs, answer their questions, and direct them toward conversion if appropriate. Be sure the page contains information that is closely tied to the search term. And don't make the rookie mistake of only thinking about your home page:

Pearl of Wisdom: Your home page will likely be the best landing page choice for your company name but not for many of your other keywords.

Let's say you work for a toy store. For the search term "godzilla action figures," a good landing page is the page that contains the description of the Godzilla action figures you're selling and a link to purchase them. For the more generic term "action figures," a good landing page might contain a menu of all the action figures you're selling with links to learn more about each one. By the way, the landing pages you select today do not need to currently have your keyword of choice on them; they just need to be relevant to the keyword. We'll help you add keywords later, in Your SEO Plan. If you can't think of an existing page that is a good match for one of your keywords, you have two choices: Plan to build a new landing page, or drop the keyword out of your short list.

Now: One by one, step through your flagged keywords and assign a landing page to each one.

Finalizing Your Short List

You've researched, you've analyzed, you've combined, and you've assigned. Now, it's time to drop those last few not-ready-for-prime-time terms!

We're going to ask you to trim your flagged list to your top 10 or so. You probably already have a good idea of which ones are your favorites, but in case you're still on the fence, here are some ways to frame your thought process:

Am I being inclusive? While you were assigning landing pages, did you discover that you have flagged too many terms for one audience or that you left a conversion out in the cold? You didn't fill out your Goals Worksheet in Chapter 1 for nothing. Use it now to help choose keywords that reflect all your target audiences and conversions.

Does my keyword have a good home? If you love a keyword but you can't find an existing landing page for it, now is the time to examine your reasoning for flagging it in the first place. Does it represent a legitimate opportunity or goal for your organization? Do you have the resources to build a page around this term? Do a reality check now, because it doesn't make sense to build Your SEO Plan around terms you can't optimize for.

Am I overcrowding a landing page? For best optimization, each landing page can accommodate only a small number of search terms (one to three is a good rule of thumb). If you're noticing that you entered the same landing page over and over again for many of your terms, you should ask yourself whether this is a problem with your site (i.e., whether you have too many different topics on one page), whether you can drop some of the extra terms, or if you just need to use your noodle to identify some additional landing pages.

Will my colleagues agree? It's important that others in your organization feel comfortable—or better yet, enthusiastic—about your top keywords. Enlist the help of your colleagues if you can! Send out your list for review, or arrange a meeting with members of your team who hold an interest: writers, content creators, marketing managers, executives, and so on. With all the data you've gathered and the deep thinking you've put into your keyword choices this week, you're in great shape to sell your favorites to your team.

 Now: Select your top 10 or so keywords, and then copy and paste them at the top of your Keywords Worksheet under Top Keywords.

Pat yourself on the back. You've just gotten through the most important, and perhaps the hardest, week in the whole book!

Week 2: Baseline Assessment

Suppose you went on a diet but you forgot to weigh yourself at the beginning of it. A week of exercise and green leafy vegetables later, you step on a scale, and it reads 163 pounds. Is it great news or a great disappointment? You'll never know because you didn't establish your baseline. This week, you'll take care of the initial assessment for your SEO campaign so you'll always know whether it's time for a celebratory ice cream sundae.

Here are your daily task assignments:

Monday: Ranks

Tuesday: Indexed Pages

Wednesday: Inbound Links

Thursday: Historical Conversions

Friday: Site Optimization Assessment

Monday: Ranks

No matter how often we tell you not to obsess about ranks, we know you better than that. So if you're the one who spends your nights with visions of Googleplums dancing in your head, today is the day we'll let you give in to your passion!

Of course, conversions are more important than ranks, and your fundamental business goals are more important than search engine traffic. But great search engine ranks really do speak volumes, and checking your ranks can be an enlightening experience.

Rank Assessment in a Nutshell

To start your assessment, open the Rank Tracking Worksheet that you downloaded from yourseoplan.com. On this worksheet, you'll see spaces for each of your top 10 keywords. (Adjust the number if you wish, but don't increase it much beyond 10 if you want to keep this task manageable!)

Here's how you'll do it:

- Moving one by one through your short list, search for your top keywords on Google. (To save time, you can set your search engines to display 30 results per page using the Preferences screen.)

- Scroll through the top 30 ranks. If any page on your website shows up within these results, note the rank in the Rank Tracking Worksheet. If you don't see your site in the ranks, mark "none."

- We're recording ranks for organic Web results only! Local listings, videos, and images count. Sponsored Listings should not be tracked as part of your standard rank check.

- Repeat with MSN and Yahoo!.

Automated vs. Manual Rank Checking

There's no way around the fact that reviewing *all those* results on *all those* search engines for *all those* keywords can be a bit of a snoozer.

Some SEO professionals have dropped rank checking out of the equation altogether because it is less connected to your business goals than other metrics such as conversion tracking. Of SEOs that still perform rank checking, some use automated rank-checking software. Available programs include Advanced Web Ranking, Web-Position, and Digital Point Solutions.

But even with all of the available tools, we still perform manual rank checking for our clients, and we insist on it for you, too. Here's why:

- Manual rank checking is more accurate than automated checking. In the ever-changing search engine-results landscape, it often takes a human to determine whether your listings are surrounded by directory sites, partner sites, or even sponsored listings.

- Manual rank checking keeps you in close touch with the goings-on in the search engine ranks for your target keywords. We want you to drink in the details. Keep an eagle eye out for your competition and any interesting or unusual results. Who is ranking well, and are they doing well on more than one engine? Have you spotted any possible cheaters? Did an unexpected page of your site (or a

PDF or DOC file) show up? These are the kinds of things you can find if you take the time to look.

- Most search engines, including Google, frown upon automated rank-checking programs because they perform multiple queries that can create a burden on the search engine. Many of these tools actually violate the engines' terms of service.

If you absolutely *must* use an automated system (for example, your organization has a need to track a large number of keywords on a monthly basis), do everything you can to reduce the burden on the search engines. Most rank-checking tools offer a "be nice to search engines" mode, which will slow down your rank checks; be sure to use it. And you don't need to run a rank check every night—go with weekly or monthly.

Your automated tool, used sparingly and set to reduce the search engine's load, can at best be considered almost legal. Your site won't be penalized for automated rank-checking activity, but there is a chance that Google will get peeved and cut off your organization's use of the search engine.

The Scenic Route

As we touched upon earlier, your manual rank-checking task has fringe benefits: It provides a great opportunity to watch out for "uglies": bad snippets, broken links, or any other interesting, mysterious, or undesirable results your website is showing in the search engines. Be sure to make a detailed note (or even a screen shot) of anything out of the ordinary (use the Notes column in your Rank Tracking Worksheet, or enter it in your Task Journal) so that you can return to it later.

 Now: Go to your Rank Tracking Worksheet and fill in today's ranks. Write any interesting or unusual observations in your Notes column or Task Journal.

Feel free to break out your iPod for this work: Rank checking is one of the more tedious SEO tasks.

Tuesday: Indexed Pages

A very basic fact of SEO is this: Before your website can rank well on the search engines, it must be *indexed*, or present, in the search engines. Is your website there to be found? Today you are going to find out by answering these questions:

- How many of my site's pages are indexed?
- Are my top landing pages indexed?

In the next sections, we'll show how you'll do it.

Total Pages Indexed on Your Site

Follow these steps to find out the total number of pages within your domain that are present on the major search engines. Let's do Google and MSN first since they work the same way:

- Starting with Google, type **site:***yourdomain.com* (using your own site address in place of *yourdomain.com*) in the search box.

- Make a note of the number of pages returned. This is the total number of pages indexed from your domain. For example, in Figure 6.6, you can see that there are about 32,600 pages indexed within the domain mudcat.org.

- Repeat for MSN.

Pearl of Wisdom: This search can be tricky on some search engines. See our companion website at www.yourseoplan.com for an up-to-date list of search shortcuts and instructions.

site:www.mudcat.org – Google Search

http://www.google.com/search?hl=en&q=site%3Awww.mudcat.org&btn｜ Q▾ Google

Web   Images   Video   News   Maps   Gmail   more ▼   Sign in

Google   site:www.mudcat.org   Search   Advanced Search
                                                        Preferences
                                                   New! View and manage your web history

Web   Results 1 - 10 of about **32,600** from **www.mudcat.org**. (0.04 seconds)

The Mudcat Cafe
a magazine dedicated to blues and folk music; hosts Digital Tradition Folk Song Database.
www.mudcat.org/ - 14k - Cached - Similar pages

Mudcat for Kids
Learn how to make musical instruments from everyday materials.
www.mudcat.org/kids/ - 6k - Cached - Similar pages

The Alan Of Australia Web Page
"What is a Mudcatter? Find out at the Mudcat Cafe. Come in and join us. Also, check out the
Mudcat Songbook. If you have a MIDI file to post: ...
www.mudcat.org/alanofoz/ - 4k - Cached - Similar pages

Digitrad Keyword Search
Quick Links, Login, Log Out, Order Mudcat CDs! Product Request, Max's Blues Museum,
Song Origins & Info, Unanswered Requests, Member Photos & Info ...
www.mudcat.org/DTKeywords.cfm - 81k - Cached - Similar pages

Mudcat Pete Seeger
Biographical article covering the folk artist's life through 1997.
www.mudcat.org/pete.cfm - 10k - Cached - Similar pages

All Titles
Quick Links, Login, Log Out, Order Mudcat CDs! Product Request, Max's Blues Museum,
Song Origins & Info, Unanswered Requests, Member Photos & Info ...
www.mudcat.org/alltitles.cfm - 977k - Cached - Similar pages

Quick Links Login Log Out Order Mudcat CDs! Product Request Max's ...
Quick Links, Login, Log Out, Order Mudcat CDs! Product Request, Max's Blues Museum,
Song Origins & Info, Unanswered Requests, Member Photos & Info ...
www.mudcat.org/getnews.cfm - 51k - Cached - Similar pages

Figure 6.6 Google search results for the site www.mudcat.org

- Now, go to Yahoo!'s Site Explorer at http://siteexplorer.search.yahoo.com and type your domain into the search box.

- Make a note of the number of pages displayed. In Figure 6.7, you can see that Yahoo! has 271,228 pages indexed within the domain mudcat.org.

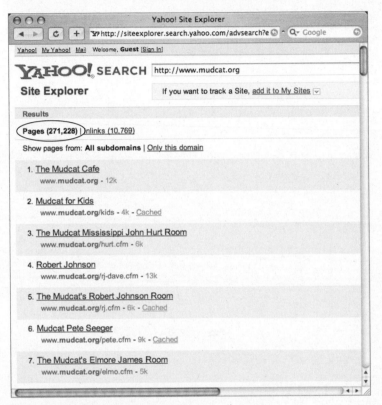

Figure 6.7 Yahoo! Site Explorer results for **www.mudcat.org**

 xtra cred

You will get more data from Yahoo! Site Explorer—and loads of information from Google Webmaster Tools—if you verify that you are the site owner. See Chapter 10 for details.

Keep in mind that there are limitations to this value. The total number of indexed pages may include broken links and old pages on your site. Think of it as a "big picture" number for watching trends or catching big drop-offs.

Now: Go to your Rank Tracking Worksheet and note the total number of pages indexed on each search engine.

Landing Pages Indexed

In addition to checking the total pages indexed, you'll want to determine whether each of your landing pages is indexed. After all, you wouldn't want to put a lot of time into optimizing a page that the robots can't see. Perform the following steps for each landing page:

- Enter the full URL of the landing page into Google's search box. If you get a listing for the exact page you were seeking, your page is indexed! See Figure 6.8 for an example.

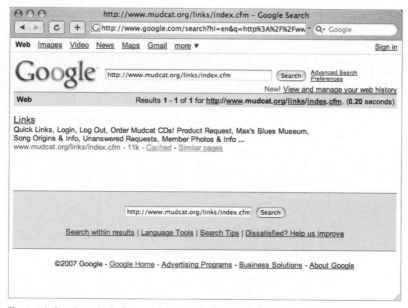

Figure 6.8 Search results for http://www.mudcat.org/links/index.cfm

- If the exact page you're looking for doesn't show up for the full URL, double-check to make sure it's not indexed. Find a unique string of HTML text on your page—one that is not likely to exist on another site—and search for it in quotes. Searching for a unique term like "Robert Johnson, King of the Delta Blues. Rumors and Tales swirl with the name" isn't likely to bring up anyone's site but the one you're looking for.

- Perform the same check in MSN.

- Go to the Yahoo! Site Explorer at http://siteexplorer.search.yahoo.com and type in the full URL for the page you are looking for. If the page doesn't show up at the top of the list, your page isn't indexed. (Do not try this search using the regular search interface at www.yahoo.com. It won't necessarily give you the results you're looking for.)

Now: Go to your Rank Tracking Worksheet and fill in Y or N for each of your landing pages in each of the four search engines.

My Site Doesn't Have Typical Landing Pages!

For most SEO campaigns, and especially for the SEO plan that an hour a day allows, it makes sense to focus your efforts on optimizing and tracking a small number of landing pages (no more than 10) on your site.

However, as we discussed in Chapter 2, there may be some of you who do not follow this system. For example, bloggers should consider every posting to be an equally important landing page. Large catalog sites may follow a long tail approach, with the expectation that users can enter the website via hundreds of product pages. And for some businesses, the choice of landing pages will shift with the season.

When your situation calls for a large or changing number of landing pages, you will have to adjust accordingly: You may wish to track more pages, or just your home page, or a select group of sample pages chosen from different areas of your site. You may wish to do separate SEO campaigns in sequence, or even scale up Your SEO Plan.

Yes, this SEO plan is scalable. Give it 10 hours a day, and you can multiply your number of landing pages accordingly. Just don't forget to do the other little things in life, like bathing yourself and feeding your dog.

Wednesday: Inbound Links

As you learned in Chapter 4, "How the Search Engines Work Right Now," the number of inbound links (other sites linking to your website, also known as *backlinks*) is an important part of the search ranking algorithm. Having plenty of inbound links will actually help your site in two important ways: indirectly, by improving your search engine ranking, and directly, by bringing visitors to your site through the link. In short, inbound links are valuable, and that's why Your SEO Plan will include some serious efforts in that arena.

Search engines are looking at not just the number of inbound links, but their quality, too. Does the hyperlinked text say, "Click here for Computer Equipment Deals" or "Click here for Overpriced Junk"? Are the links buried deep within a domain, among millions of other outbound links? Search engine algorithms take these things into account—and so do your potential customers. You'll learn how to fully assess link quality in Part III, when you start your link-building campaign. For now, you'll stick to gathering the numbers: How many links are pointing to your landing pages?

Finding the total number of other sites that are linking to your landing pages can be quite simple: Many search engines include search shortcuts that allow you to view a list of other sites that the search engine knows to be linking to specific pages within your domain. For example, on Google, you'll want to search for **link:http://*www.yourdomain.com/yourpage.html*** (using your own site address in place of *yourdomain.com/yourpage.html*) to find links to your page of choice. On Yahoo!, good old Site Explorer (http://siteexplorer.search.yahoo.com) will tell you painlessly how many inlinks are pointing to each page. See the companion website at www.yourseoplan.com for a current list of search shortcuts and instructions.

Social Search Status

If your website appeals to a consumer base, you might already be checking out the blogs, forums, and social networking sites to see who's talking about you. If you have a B2B site, you may think—erroneously—that social search has no relevance to your site. If you have any reason to network with people in the "real world," you have a reason to care about social search.

It's very helpful to learn which, if any, sites within the social Web are providing you with inlinks or bookmarks. Here are some starting points:

- To find out how many blogs are linking to your site, go to the blog search engine Technorati.com. Click on Advanced Search, and enter your URL under URL Search. You are in for a real treat if this is the first time you found out that people are blogging about you! We're not saying that *we* do this, but you will probably be unable to resist reading through the postings, punching the air victoriously at every positive mention, or bristling with indignity at every criticism. But we wouldn't know anything about that. Ahem.

- Find out who diggs you, and who thinks you're deli.cio.us. Socialmeter, at www.socialmeter.com, is a tool that quickly and easily shows how many tags or links your site has received on several social sites.

- Go down a social Web rabbit hole by doing the following: Go to www.omgili.com, a forum search engine, and type in your company name, your CEO's name, your trademarked product name, or anything else that is specific to your organization, and see who's talking about what in forums webwide.

- Set up the ultimate vanity search by going to Google Alerts (www.google.com/alerts) and making sure you get an email whenever your name (or other favorite search term) shows up in a blog posting.

You only need to find inbound links using one search engine, so we recommend Yahoo! Site Explorer for the most accurate results. Google has an annoying habit of underreporting inlinks. Regardless of the engine you use, these numbers are not exact. Just use them for trend spotting.

If you verify your site with Google Webmaster Tools, you will get that accurate inbound link reporting you crave. See Chapter 10 for details.

Now: Now, using the search engine of your choice, go to your Rank Tracking Worksheet and fill in the total number of inbound links to each of your landing pages.

Thursday: Historical Conversions

If you've got some form of conversion tracking in place, today is the day to document how many conversions your organization has had over the past three months.

If you haven't been tracking conversions, you may think you have nothing to document today. We disagree. Somewhere, somehow, there must be some information about how your website is performing for you. If there's a request-for-information form on the site, how many people have used it? If you suspect that people are researching your company online and then ordering over the phone, see if you can get a salesperson to back you up. Or just write down your suspicion. Even a guess is better than nothing here.

Now: In your Site Assessment worksheet, record your last three months' conversion numbers.

If you're pretty sure that the website hasn't given you any business, or recognition, or whatever it is you're looking for in the past three months, make a note of that, too. If you're starting from zero, congratulations! Your improvement will be easy to measure.

Friday: Site Optimization Assessment

Suppose you're a real estate investor looking for a good moneymaking opportunity. You see two homes, both the same size and price. One home has been totally renovated and looks pristine. It's got a few recent add-ons, and it fills up its lot nicely. The other home has some ugly carpeting over wood floors, chipped paint, and kitchen appliances that have seen better days. There's plenty of room for expansion on the lot. Clearly, you have a better chance of adding big bucks to the value of the second house after some investment of your time and money.

The same principle applies to your website. If your site is already well optimized, looking for big conversion increases from your SEO campaign may be a challenge. On the other hand, if your site is missing basic optimization, you can probably expect some good improvement in performance. This is why a site assessment is important: to identify areas in which your site is deficient, but also to set realistic expectations for results.

Take a look at the Site Assessment Worksheet you downloaded from www .yourseoplan.com. This worksheet provides a quick and easy way to get a handle on your site's current optimization level. Next, indicate yes or no for the following statements about each of your landing pages:

- This page has a unique HTML page title.
- The HTML page title contains my target keywords.
- This page contains 200 or more words of HTML text.
- HTML text on this page contains my exact target keywords.
- This page can be reached from the home page of the site by following HTML text links (not pull-downs, login screens, or pop-up windows).
- The HTML text links from other pages on my site to this page contain my target keywords.

We kept the worksheet short and sweet, but these quick answers provide a basic estimate of your current optimization level. And don't forget: Lower optimization just means more room to grow!

Now: Go to your Site Assessment Worksheet and fill in Y or N for each of your landing pages.

With your basic site assessment complete, you have a good picture of the current status of your website: current conversions, site ranks on the major search engines, inbound links, and your current site optimization level. This baseline assessment will serve you throughout your SEO campaign.

Week 3: Competition

Over the last couple of weeks, you've started to bulk up parts of your brain that are newly devoted to SEO. This week, we're going to use those portions of your brain to do something that you've been dying to do: snoop on your competitors. Here's how you've already gotten your feet wet in competitive analysis:

- You got a glimpse of your competitors' keyword preferences when you were selecting your own.
- You became acquainted with the top 30 players for all of your keywords during your rank check.

Now, we'll ask you to use your memory and your worksheets—and a couple of new tools and techniques—to dive all the way in:

Monday: Identify Your Top Five Competitors

Tuesday: Snooping Tools and Techniques

Wednesday: Assess On-Page Factors

Thursday: Assess Off-Page Factors

Friday: Paid Competition

Monday: Identify Your Top Five Competitors

Today you're going to choose which competitors to review in depth. To keep this week's tasks manageable, we recommend that you limit the number of top competitors you examine to five. This allows you to choose at least one from each of the three categories in the list that follows, and it leaves you with enough bandwidth to really dig in and dissect their strategies. If one of your biggest competitors doesn't have a website, then give them an honorary mention on your list. But for the purposes of this week, we want you to choose five competitors with at least some web presence.

Your review will be the most meaningful if you select your "Big Five" from the following categories:

Business Competition Even if you know who the major players in your field are, you should check with your sales and executive team members to get the backstory that you may not be aware of. For example, there may be different competitors for different products or target audiences. There may be a "new kid on the block" who's poised to enter a space that you're currently dominating. Or your company may have just lost a big job to someone in particular. Ask your colleagues to prioritize their competitors based on current issues, goals, and grudges.

Search Competition With last week's rank check fresh in your mind, you should have an excellent grasp of who's who in the top spots. Who did you see in the top ranks frequently enough to make you take notice? Whose listings were not only visible, but also well written? Whether these companies hold a candle to your organization in real life isn't relevant here. Even if they're just a blip on your business radar, if they're attracting the eyeballs that you want, you need to find out how they're doing it.

Paid Search Competition Even though sponsored ads and organic listings are different animals, they are displayed in direct competition to each other in the search engine results. So if there is a company out there who is showing up in the sponsored links for your targeted keywords, you may want to add it to your Big Five.

Search Results Competition

The Left Brain and Right Brain have different ideas about monitoring who is taking those coveted top spots in the search results.

The Right Brain says, "This is one of those SEO tasks that you can let flow over you. Search for your target keywords, browse the results, and you are likely to see some patterns emerging. Maybe there is a certain site that never shows at number one but has lots of results on the second and third pages of the search results. Maybe another site is consistently in the top five for several of your top terms. You would be right to include these among your Big Five search competition."

The Left Brain says, "When I used to grade papers in graduate school, I sometimes noticed my standards getting stricter and stricter as the hours passed. Pity those kids with tests at the bottom of the pile! The same thing can happen when you use a 'hunch' approach to choosing your competition: After an hour of reviewing search results, your opinions are likely to creep. That's why I think you should choose a simple numerical evaluation method: Your potential competitor gets a point for every time their site shows up in the top 30 for your keywords—and five points for every time in the top 10. Check your searches, add up the points, and there you have it: Your search competition rises to the top."

As you're going through your search and PPC competition, be on the lookout for "left field" competition. These are listings that are displayed for the same keywords that you're targeting but have no connection to your organization's focus. For example, the directors of the Green Acres Day Camp in Toronto are going head-to-head with trivia sites about the old *Green Acres* TV show. Whether you choose to review one of these sites is up to you. But if you're finding a lot more "left field" competitors than you expect, you may need to rethink your keyword choices.

Now: Use your own knowledge and your team's help to define your Big Five competitors. Add their names and home page URLs to the Competition Worksheet.

Tuesday: Snooping Tools and Techniques

Poking and peeking into other people's business is part of web culture and one of the more entertaining aspects of an SEO campaign. When you open a browser and look at a website, you're seeing just the content that developers intended for you to see. But there is a great deal more information available about a site, ranging from data on who owns the domain to the scripts used on the page. Here are a few tools and techniques that we have found most useful:

- The Google Toolbar
- Viewing page source
- Alexa data
- Firefox extensions

The following sections include the details you need to make these methods your own.

The Google Toolbar

This is a very popular tool with searchers and SEOs alike! If you already have it, you know how useful it is. If not, get ready for a treat.

The Google Toolbar, which can be downloaded from http://toolbar.google.com/, is a free add-on to your browser (Internet Explorer or Firefox) that contains several features to enhance your web surfing experience (see Figure 6.9).

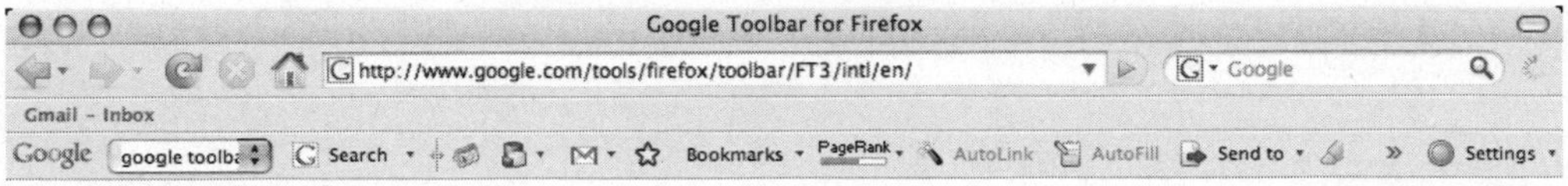

Figure 6.9 The Google Toolbar

The toolbar feature that we're most interested in using for our SEO efforts is a little green bar labeled PageRank. This bar displays the Google PageRank value for the web page being viewed. As you learned in Chapter 4, the PageRank value certainly has its limitations. However, viewing it in the toolbar can give you a quick estimate of how important Google thinks a certain page is. You can also use the "backwards links" feature to determine how many pages are pointing to a specific URL, but you should be aware that Google doesn't show all of the links that point to a page; some are omitted.

If you would rather not install the Google Toolbar, you can see PageRank information, and lots of other fascinating tidbits of data, at www.faganfinder.com/urlinfo/.

Now: Go to http://toolbar.google.com and download and install the Google Toolbar.

Viewing Page Source

Anyone who's put together a website already knows how to view page source. But if you never touch your site's code, this may be a new experience for you. Viewing page source is a simple way to see the inside workings of your competitors' (or anyone else's) website. *Source* is shorthand for *source code*, which is the HTML content that tells the browser what to show on the screen. In the source code, you can see all of the invisible text elements, such as meta tags and ALT tags (discussed in Chapter 3, "Eternal Truths of SEO.") You can also view the HTML title tag and other behind-the-scenes information on your competitor's page (see Figure 6.10).

```
Source of http://www.penzeys.com/cgi-bin/penzeys/shophome.html
<html>
<head>
<title>Penzeys Spices Home Page</title>
<meta http-equiv="Content-Type" content="text/html; charset=iso-8859-1">
<LINK REL="SHORTCUT ICON" HREF="/favicon.ico">
<META  NAME="description" CONTENT="Penzeys
        Spices has been in the business of selling top quality spices for more
        than ten years. We carry over 250 herbs, seasoning blends and spices from
        around the world.  Just open our catalog or step into our stores and you will see
almost every spice, herb and seasoning that you have ever imagined. ">
<META NAME="keywords" CONTENT=" spices, spice, herbs, herb, Penzeys, saffron,  pepper,
cinnamon, recipes,  retail stores, penzey, gift boxes, wedding, holidays, seasoning, BBQ,
grilling">
<meta name=target content="Penzeys Spices Home Page, Home Page, Index">
<script language="JavaScript">
<!--
<!--
function openWindowA(URL,Name) {

popupWin=window.open(URL,Name,'toolbar=no,location=no,status=no,menubar=no,scrollbars=yes,res
izable=yes,width=600,height=500');
}

//-->
```

Figure 6.10 Viewing HTML source code

It's easy to view source in major browsers. Here's how:

- In Internet Explorer, select View > Source from the Explorer menu.
- In Safari, select View > View Source from the Safari menu.
- In Firefox, select View > Page Source from the Firefox menu.

On Wednesday, we're going to ask you to view source to assess your competitors. But for now, take some time to get used to viewing source code on your own site.

Now: Practice viewing page source by opening up your own website and viewing the source code on a few pages.

Alexa Data

The Alexa database, located at www.alexa.com, provides interesting tidbits of info about websites: a screen shot of the home page, traffic data, inbound links, site owner contact information, related links, and even a link to old versions of the website on the

Internet Archive (a.k.a. the Wayback Machine). Most addictive of all, Alexa estimates your website's traffic rank among all sites on the Web.

Many in the SEO community have serious doubts about the accuracy of Alexa's numbers and believe that Alexa's stats are easy to manipulate, so take them with a grain of salt. But if you are looking for quick answers to general questions about a website (is this some crazy spammer or a legit business?), Alexa might be a good place to start.

To see a website's details, search for the full URL in Alexa's search box. If you fall in love with Alexa, you can even download an Alexa toolbar to add to your browser, similar to the Google Toolbar.

 Now: Go to www.alexa.com and search for your own website URL. See what comes up!

Firefox Extensions

If you use Firefox, you've probably already discovered the panoply of extensions that are available for free download online. If not, the fun starts at https://addons.mozilla.org.

We use a simple extension called Google PageRank Status, which displays a PageRank value at the bottom of every web page we browse. But if you're looking for more bells and whistles, there are plenty to be found. Here is a small sampling of extensions related to SEO:

SEOQuake This tool displays the Google PageRank for whatever web page you're browsing, as well as number of pages indexed on Google, number of inbound links, and many other values.

SEO for Firefox This extension, created by SEO expert and blogger Aaron Wall, displays a large number of factors, including the number of inbound links, inbound .edu links, blog links, and many others.

Web Developer This extension, designed for developers who are debugging web pages, allows you to quickly and easily turn Javascript or CSS on and off—which is a great way to see web pages the way search engines see them.

 Now: If Firefox extensions appeal to you, go to https://addons.mozilla.org and find some for your collection.

Wednesday: Assess On-Page Factors

Today, you're going to look inside your competitors' sites to determine whether there is any evidence of SEO. You'll be researching the following elements:

- Targeted keywords
- Basic optimization
- General characteristics of the site

In the following sections, we'll go into the finer points.

Targeted Keywords

First, try to determine what, if any, keywords your Big Five competitors are targeting.

Sometimes a competitor's targeted keywords will make themselves clear if you simply review the text on their site. It's a fair bet that your competitors are targeting many of the same keywords that you are, so you can glance through their page content and look for those terms or for similar terms that you may have considered for your own site.

But are they actually targeting these terms for SEO, or did their copywriter just get lucky with word choice? The quickest way to get a read on a competitor's SEO schemes is to view the meta keywords tag. You'll need to delve into the source code to do this. Inside the tag, your competitor's keyword list might include 500 words, it might be ridiculously un-optimized (formatted as a sentence or full of words like *a*, *an*, *the*, and *quality*), or it might seem to be a tightly focused, relevant list from which you can glean a hint of a strategy. While you're in the code, look for keywords in the HTML title and meta description, too.

By the way, if you've never stepped through someone else's HTML code, it can be a little disorienting. It can help to use your browser's find function (usually Ctrl+F or Edit > Find in the browser menu) to search for the words *meta* or *title*. These should land you in the general vicinity of the tags you're looking for.

For each of your Big Five competitors, open the home page and at least one other page on their site to scan the copy and view the tags. You aren't looking to record the top 50 terms here—just the ones that seem to be in direct competition with your own conversion goals.

Now: Open your Competition Worksheet and list targeted keywords of note for your Big Five competitors.

As you're sniffing around your competitors' page content and tags, you may find a keyword here or there that you hadn't thought of. You might want to highlight these terms in your Competition Worksheet; you can save them for future research.

Basic Optimization

Now, think back to the site assessment questions that you asked about your own landing pages last week. We'll have you look at a trimmed-down version of the list, which you can use to assess the home page, and at least one interior page, of each of your Big Five competitors' websites:

- Does the HTML page title for this page contain their target keywords?
- Does the HTML text on this page contain their target keywords?
- Can this page be reached from the home page of the site by following HTML text links (not pull-downs, login screens, or pop-up windows)?

Answer each of these questions to the best of your ability. If they get two or more yes answers, give them a yes for basic optimization on the Competition Worksheet.

We've also given you a "notes" column to assess general characteristics of your competitors' website, or to jot down things that are noticeably well done. This might be anything from "Simple, clean design," to "They're members of the International Palaeoentomological Society—wish we were!" You can learn from the things that they're doing well, and even consider folding some of their methods into your own strategy.

 Now: Fill in Y or N in the Basic Optimization column on your Competition Worksheet. Add any pertinent notes.

Thursday: Assess Off-Page Factors

Today you'll be looking at factors that are largely outside of the control of your competing site owners. Whether it's ranks, inbound links, or other algorithm-benders like Google PageRank, you want to know how the world at large is treating the sites you want to beat.

Ranks You already thought about your competitors' ranks when you named your Big Five. Maybe you singled out a competitor simply because they were ranking well, or maybe you chose one that has terrible ranks but has been stealing your "real-world" customers away. Now, summarize the overall ranking status of each of your Big Five competitors on your Competition Worksheet. This assessment doesn't need an exact value—it's enough to indicate whether they're dominant or barely there.

 Now: Open your Competition Worksheet and indicate the ranking status of your Big Five competitors.

Inbound Links Uncovering the number of competitors' inbound links can be a real eye-opener, especially if they seem to have good ranks without great site optimization.

Although you can't be sure that a large number of inbound links are directly influencing the ranks, it's a helpful piece of the puzzle.

Open the same search engine that you used to check your own inbound links in Week 2 so that you're comparing apples to apples. Using the specialized link search, determine how many links each of your Big Five competitors has pointing to their home page.

> **Now:** Fill in the number of inbound links to your Big Five competitors on your Competition Worksheet.

Google PageRanks Using the Google Toolbar or Firefox extension that you downloaded on Tuesday, determine the Google PageRank for your competitors' home page.

> **Now:** Enter the Google PageRank for your Big Five competitors on your Competition Worksheet.

While you're at it, take your Google Toolbar or Firefox extension for a test-drive through your own site today and find the Google PageRank for each of your landing pages.

> **Now:** Enter the Google PageRank for each of your landing pages on your Rank Tracking Worksheet.

Google PageRank is good to know, but it's not essential. If you're short on time, don't worry about gathering this data.

Red Flags and Opportunities

Through the course of your research over the last few days, you probably came across several red flags and opportunities for improvement. These are the isolated tidbits of information that make humans so much better at doing SEO work than any kind of automated system.

You've got worksheets for recording things like poor ranks and low inbound links, but we suggest you use your Task Journal to keep a log of other concerns that don't fit neatly into the worksheets.

Red flags are issues that may be detrimental to your overall SEO health, such as:

- I found several outdated listings for the following URLs available on Yahoo! and MSN....
- I found the term "X" instead of our current products in our listings.
- Much of the competition on search engines is coming from our own resellers.

Continues

Red Flags and Opportunities *(continued)*

Opportunities are untapped areas for possible SEO expansion. Here are some examples:

- Our CEO is interested in blogging, and there are a lot of relevant blogs out there where she could be sharing her expertise in comments.

- I found no reviews of our company on Citysearch, Google Local, Yahoo! Local, or any other similar sites.

- Our home page has fewer than half the inbound links compared to Competitor X.

Don't get bogged down in trying to figure out exactly how to handle these issues. Getting them documented and into your Task Journal will go a long way toward addressing them down the road.

Friday: Paid Competition

Now that you know which of your competitors appear to be putting an effort into SEO, you probably have a hunch about which ones are shelling out the dough for paid campaigns. Today you'll play "spot the PPC ad" to get a sense of your competitors' activities in the PPC arena.

It can be challenging to find competitors' pay-per-click ads. Even if you go looking for a particular ad, there's no guarantee that you'll find it. Some PPC services "rotate their inventory" so that you might not be able to view a certain company's ad if you happen to be looking at the wrong time of day. Or your competitor may have an ad with such a low bid that you'd have to spend too much time trying to unearth it from 20th-page results. And, of course, your competitors can turn their ads on or off at any time, so you may never know if there's *really* a PPC campaign with your competitor's name on it.

Regardless, it's worth it to look, because if you do find something, it can give you great insight into what matters most to your competitors. Here's how you'll do it:

- Moving one by one through your Big Five competitor list, perform a search for each competitor's company name on Google.

- Scroll through the top two or three pages of results. If you find an ad for your competitor, mark "yes" in the PPC column.

- If you don't find your competitor's ad, search for a specific product or service that they offer. If that turns up no ads, broaden your search to a general term related to what they offer. If you still don't find your competitor, you can feel comfortable marking "none found" in the PPC column.

- Repeat with Yahoo! and MSN.

Remember to look at sponsored listings only, not organic search results! If you do find something that looks like a competitor's ad, click on it to make sure it actually goes to your competitor's site. There are lots of PPC ads put out by affiliate sites and resellers, and if that's the case with the ads you find, then it's not really your competitor's ad. For example, do a search for any well-known brand-name medicine, like "Claritin" (or, if you don't mind your colleagues seeing what you've got on your monitor, "Viagra" or "Rogaine"). There are lots of ads displaying for that brand-name search, but only one is for the company that actually makes the product.

Now: Enter your assessment of the PPC sponsorships of your Big Five competitors on the Competition Worksheet.

If you have time, you can learn a lot about your competitors by checking to see if they have directory listings. See Chapter 10 to learn how.

You've worked hard filling your worksheets—and your brain—with data and observations about your standing on the Web. Next, in Week 4, you'll gather some important insight into your visitors' behavior!

Week 4: Analytics and Goals

You know the famous question about a tree falling in the forest? The same applies to your SEO campaign:

Pearl of Wisdom: No matter how hard you work and what you achieve, nobody will know about it unless it's documented.

And your job in SEO is to find out not just when the tree fell, but why, how, and is there as much fruit in those branches as we'd hoped for? That's why this week, you're going to get your web analytics groove on: You'll start by measuring what people are doing on your site, then use your newfound knowledge to set some reasonable goals for your SEO campaign, and finally wrap it all up in a brief report.

The quick reference report you compile at the end of this week will be the basis for your future SEO status reports, which will be your go-to documents for what you've accomplished, what's wrong, what's right, and where you need to go from here.

Monday: Web Analytics Study Hall

Tuesday: Tracking Online Conversions

Wednesday: Tracking Offline Conversions

Thursday: Benchmarks and Goals

Friday: Quick Reference Report

Monday: Web Analytics Study Hall

The area of web analytics, the measurement and analysis of online activity, is an exciting and rapidly changing industry. Today you'll learn the basics of web analytics and what metrics you need for your hour-a-day SEO campaign. This is a brief introduction to a large and fascinating area of study. If we leave you thirsting for more on the subject, consider dedicating another hour in your daily schedule to *Web Analytics: An Hour a Day* by Avinash Kaushik (Wiley, 2007).

Today you'll dig in with the following:

- Web Analytics Basics
- Going Metric—What to Watch and Why

Web Analytics Basics

You'd better believe it: You want to know what people are doing on your site. You want to know where they came from, what keywords they were searching for, and which visitors arrived at which outcomes. You want to know which parts of your site are being used and which are gathering dust. You won't find out exactly *why* all of this happens by using a web analytics program, but you'll get a whole lot closer than you would if you neglected the area. And here's the kicker: Now that Google Analytics—a robust and highly regarded web analytics tool—is free and readily available, there's simply no excuse for not using it.

How it Works

Web analytic programs come in two flavors: *tag-based tracking* (also called *hosted*, *client-side*, or *on-demand* tracking) and *server-side tracking*. Tag-based tracking generally works like this: You add a tiny piece of code or a tiny image to every page of your site. This little code (the "tag") communicates with a tracking system located on the analytics service provider's server. Information is gathered and used to build reports about activity on your site. Google Analytics is tag based. By contrast, server-side systems provide similar capabilities but stay on your own servers, are purchased like software, and must be set up by your IT team.

Web analytics programs are not just for IT geeks—they're popular with marketing and sales specialists, CEOs, and web developers alike. It takes only seconds to pop open the interface and view some serious trend-over-time reporting. In fact, you'll have so many different ways to see detailed site visitor information that you could easily overload and fall face-first into your computer screen. See Figure 6.11 for an example of a web analytics screen.

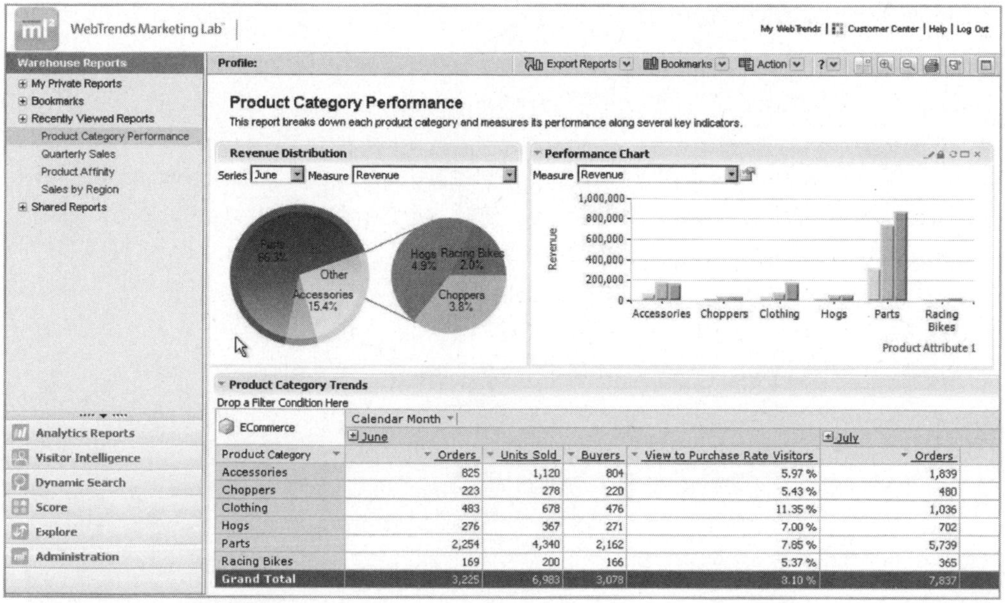

Figure 6.11 WebTrends data example

Service Options

Free or inexpensive web analytics options include Google Analytics, Clicky, ClickTracks Appetizer, and those ubiquitous stats packages, such as AWStats and Webalizer, that come bundled with many web hosting solutions. Additionally, paid search providers Google AdWords, Yahoo! Search Marketing, and MSN adCenter offer strong conversion-tracking capabilities, which do not take the place of a full-service analytics program, but are fabulously useful, and free with your advertising account.

For those with deeper pockets, major providers of advanced web analytics systems include Omniture, Visual Sciences, WebTrends, ClickTracks, and Coremetrics. Consult their websites for more information, or see our companion site at www .yourseoplan.com for links to reviews.

For a larger website, analytics can easily demand the attention of a full-time staff member. For a small business, this is something that you can visit about once a week, or more if you can't resist!

Feeling overwhelmed? We can save you some time:

Pearl of Wisdom: If you're a small organization, stop using the free stats package that comes with your hosting solution and start using Google Analytics.

Going Metric—What to Watch and Why

Setting up a web analytics program doesn't necessarily require tons of effort or expense, but we admit that it may very well involve some hoop-jumping and budget-bumping on your part. And perhaps you're wondering: Just what am I going to get out of all this? While there are thousands of reports, charts, data visualizations, and trend manifestations out there, you can go a long way with just a few simple pieces of information. These key metrics are:

Unique Visitors and Page Views Knowing the total traffic to your website doesn't tell you much. It won't tell you whether your visitors are the ones you targeted, what path they took through your website, whether they made a purchase, or how happy they were during their visit. Nevertheless, it's one of those little numbers that you. just. need. to. know. Your web analytics program will do its best to determine a total number of unique visitors based on IP addresses and any other info it can gather. Admittedly, the number is not perfectly accurate. But it's a good tool for tracking trends. After all, what does it really matter if you had 1,015 or 1,045 unique visitors this week? What matters most is whether you're up or down from last week.

And while you're at it, banish the word *hits* from your vocabulary. *Hits* describes the number of times a request is made to your server, and *page views* describes the number of times an entire page is called by a browser. So if there are dozens of images on a given page, there will be dozens of hits recorded for each page view. Depending on your conversion goal, you may want to focus on the number of page views or unique visitors, but never hits.

Referrers and Keywords After all your link-building efforts, wouldn't you love to know which sites are actually sending you traffic? After optimizing for the search engines, wouldn't you love to know which search terms your visitors used to find you? This is where your stats start to become truly useful to your SEO campaign. Your analytics program can tell you where your site visitors came from, and even more important, for those who came to your website from search engines, it can tell you the exact keywords they searched for. This can be a good source of ideas for new keywords to target. It is sure to tell you whether your paid directory listings are worth their cost. And it may even give you insights into what new content you should be developing for your site.

Keep in mind, referrer (also called *traffic source* or *acquisition source*) data is limited to folks who clicked to your site from another site on the Web. Users who typed your URL directly into their browsers, or clicked from a bookmark, or clicked from an e-mail, are harder to track.

Entry Pages Your SEO Plan focuses on a favorite set of landing pages, chosen by you. But your web analytics review may show you that people are entering your site on entirely different pages than you expected. Sure, you know people are coming to the home page, but would you be shocked to learn that a big chunk of visitors are entering somewhere else, like your Site Map page? And would that leave you scrambling to improve the messaging there? We love watching this metric because it reminds us to design *every* page on the site as a potential landing page. Top entry pages are the queen bee pages of your site. Once you identify them, you will give them the royal treatment: optimizing, monitoring, and protecting their integrity when a site redesign threatens to change them in any significant way.

Exit Pages and Bounces Site exits are often looked at as a sign that something's gone wrong on a web page, but remember: Everyone exits your site eventually. So unless you're looking at exits during a defined linear process, like right in the middle of a shopping cart purchase, site exits alone aren't going to tell you a whole lot about how to improve your user experience.

Since *exit pages* (the pages from which visitors leave your site) are a metric with limited usefulness, we suggest looking at *bounces* instead. A bounce is defined as a visitor leaving the site after viewing just one page. If a large percentage of your site visitors are bouncing out, either you're inviting the wrong crowd to your party or there's something very unappetizing greeting them at the door!

Here are a couple tricky points you should know about bounce rates:

- When looking at pages that bounce, don't be surprised if your home page is high on the list. It's common for people to arrive at your site and immediately realize it's not what they're looking for.

- Don't always assume that a page bounce is a failure. If you have a phone number on every page, for example, then a single page visit may be all your visitors needed to accomplish their goal.

- If you've got two different domains sharing the same analytics package or your store is on a different domain than your primary website, your bounce rates may be delivering faulty info. We've seen systems where every time someone clicks to the store, it looks like they're exiting the site. That means a store purchase will look like a bounce!

With these caveats in mind, we think you'll find bounce rates one of the more useful web analytics metrics. Combined with page views (which are really the same metric— a bounce rate is just a single page view), they can help you identify the best and worst keywords, referrers, and entry pages on your site.

Newbie Cheat Sheet: Setting Up Google Analytics

What does it mean to set up Google Analytics? Here's the deal, in ludicrously brief detail:

Step 1: Go to http://analytics.google.com. You'll need to set up an account and enter some basic information about your website.

Step 2: Follow the instructions so that Google can generate a tracking tag for your website. It might look like this:

```
<script src="http://www.google-analytics.com/urchin.js"
    type="text/javascript">
</script>
<script type="text/javascript">
_uacct = "UA-123456-7";
urchinTracker();
</script>
```

Step 3: Email this tag to your web developer, with instructions that they must be placed on every page of the site, in the <body> tag.

Time on Site In July of 2007, web traffic measurement firm Nielson/NetRatings began reporting time spent on a site as one of its markers of a site's performance. If your site contains a great deal of content that displays without refreshing the page (photo slide shows, online videos, or *Ajax* applications might fall into this category), then measuring the time your users spend on your site could be the best way for you to understand their level of engagement.

Errors Among other things, your server will log a *404 error* ("File not Found") every time a user tries to access a nonexistent URL. This can help you find inbound—or internal—links that are using incorrect or out-of-date URLs. Tag-based programs, including Google Analytics, may require a workaround to show you these errors.

The list of useful server stats could go on and on, but you have limited time, so we stuck with the basics.

If you already have access to your site stats through a web analytics program, congratulations! Today, you'll look through it for the information just listed.

Now: Open up your web analytics program (if it exists) and find the key information listed in this section. If you don't have a web analytics program or the one you're using can't provide the above metrics, read on.

If you don't have a web analytics program in place or you only have the package that was provided by the web hosting provider (these passed muster a few years ago, but you deserve better), we're going to give you some really simple advice: Do yourself a favor and set up Google Analytics. Consider it a pilot program: After six months with Google Analytics, you'll know loads more about your site and your organization's analytics needs, and you'll be fabulously prepared for your next analytics purchase, if needed.

Now: If you don't have a web analytics program in place, start the ball rolling on a Google Analytics setup.

With all the web analytics wisdom you gained today, you're perfectly positioned to start sorting out your online website conversion tracking tomorrow.

Tuesday: Tracking Online Conversions

Different organizations can have vastly different metrics, ranging from the number of people buying your product to how many third graders download your science report. Whether it's online sales, brand awareness, or just eyeballs you're after, you know what your conversions are because you defined them way back in Chapter 1.

Earlier in this chapter, we asked you to document the number of conversions on your site. Did you have a ball filling in the good news, or get depressed scribbling down some uncertain best guesses? Today and tomorrow, you'll develop a plan for tracking your conversion goals. Think "baby steps": You probably won't finalize your tracking plan, but you'll set the wheels in motion.

Online conversions, such as purchases, downloads, and form submittals, are relatively easy to track. Here's how the process works:

- Identify Your Conversion Pages

- Measure and React

Identify Your Conversion Pages

Web analytics programs typically define conversions (also called goals) in a simple way: When a certain page on your website is reached, the conversion has happened. You'll need to choose a page on your site that indicates a conversion has been completed. Very possibly, this will be your transaction completion page or confirmation page—it's wherever you say thank you to your customers for a purchase, download, registration, or form completion (You did remember to say thank you, didn't you?).

Let's agree and get it out of the way: A single-page conversion—the kind that's easy to set up and track with your analytics tool—isn't a perfect indication of success. It doesn't allow for exotic goals like "I want my visitors to visit at least three pages on my site," or "I want my visitors to stay on my site for more than two minutes." Don't let that stop you! There are ways to finesse even simple conversion tracking when you want to squeeze out a little extra insight:

- Your site can have more than one conversion goal. In addition to an actual purchase or form submittal, we often like to define conversions that describe a more modest level of success: perhaps a visit to the "Products" or "Contact" page. For B2Bs or other sites with a lower overall traffic level, getting more numbers into your conversion bucket gives you more useful information to work with.

- You can define unwanted conversions, too. This is particularly useful for paid search traffic. For example, if job seekers are not a valuable audience for you, you can define your "Employment" page as a conversion. You'll gain a better understanding of where those folks are coming from—and how much you're spending on that traffic.

- A dollar value can be assigned to online purchases. If you've got a good handle on their value, you can even assign dollar amounts to a non-purchase action, like a download or form submittal.

Now: Think about what page or pages on your site could be defined as conversion completion pages.

Measure and React

You may be thinking about your online conversions for the first time. But even for folks who have been doing it for years, it can be absurdly difficult to interpret in a meaningful way. Here are a few good ways to frame your thoughts around your conversion data:

Conversion Rates Tied to Paid Search Bids The quickest and most satisfying use of a conversion measurement is closing the loop with pay-per-click bids. With pay-per-click advertising, every sponsored keyword has a price tag associated with it. Knowing how many conversions you're getting for your money will tell you whether any current paid search efforts are on target. A good example is the "Employment" page we discussed previously. You'd probably be distressed to find that you're paying thousands of dollars to bring job seekers to your site.

Conversion Rates Inform Organic Search Targeting Here's a way to put your conversion tracking to good use. Using your web analytics or paid search program, discover which keywords are delivering the highest conversion rates. Are there any surprises on the list? Any that deserve their own landing pages? It's not too late to go back and add these keywords to your top-priority list. Remember that if you devote your energies to known success stories, even modest gains in traffic can mean large gains in conversion numbers.

Paths to Conversion Inform the Sales Process You may already know that more people are buying your cheaper products than your high-priced ones. But conversion tracking can tell you exactly what path your customers followed before they made the decision to buy. Did they go straight for the low-priced goods, or did they spend time considering your expensive products first? Did they read any reviews? Examining paths to conversion gives you meaningful insight into your customers' behavior, and may even help you figure out a new way to organize your products.

Even if you don't know what to do with this information, it's important to get comfortable with looking at it. Once your learning curve evens out, you may be surprised at how easily you can find real meaning in the data.

Conversion tracking: You know you want it! Now that you've digested the basics, you can use today to discuss it with your team. Then, it's decision time: Which system will you start with?

Now: Start the process of setting up online conversion tracking on your site. If you already have online conversion tracking in place, double-check the Historical Conversions you recorded in your Site Assessment Worksheet during week 2 and update that number if you have more accurate information at this time.

New software, new statistics, new jargon: These are the things that make tracking online conversions challenging to the uninitiated. Now, get ready for a whole new kind of challenge, because tracking offline conversions is practically an art form!

Wednesday: Tracking Offline Conversions

If you're having trouble tracking offline conversions, like phone calls or walk-in customers, you may find some comfort in knowing that you're not alone. This is a challenging situation that stumps even the biggest of bigwigs. And if your website is out there trying to convince someone to, say, vote for a certain school board representative, how are you ever going to measure the contribution that your SEO work made to the campaign?

To track your offline conversions, you'll need to be creative. Here are a few ideas for some of the more common scenarios:

Set up a special phone number. If a large percentage of your sales take place over the phone, it may be difficult to show that the website, much less your SEO campaign, had anything to do with them. But there is one way: Set up a unique phone number and display it on your website—and nowhere else. Then, have your sales team monitor and track how many calls come in to that line and how many of those calls turn into conversions.

For a greater level of detail, you can sign up with services (such as ClickPath or Who's Calling) that will generate unique 800 numbers and dynamically display them on your web pages, linking each call to a keyword and ad source.

Run campaigns on things nobody else is promoting. You can get an inkling of the effects of your SEO work by promoting a specific event or product that nobody else in your organization has taken the time to promote. For example, if you put your SEO efforts into promoting Tuesday Night Half-Price Pickles and there is no other marketing for it, you can relish the thought that most of the people who show up found out about the event as a result of your SEO work.

Include coupons or promotion codes on your website. How will you know if walk-in customers used your website to research your products or services? One way is to create coupons or promotion codes on your website that these customers can print out and bring into your store for a discount. Sure, it won't tell you whether they used a search engine to find your site, but at least you'll have something to link your "real-world" traffic to your online traffic.

Cultivate communication. If your site goals fall into the persuasion category, give your users an opportunity to tell their stories with "Post your success story here" or "Share your smoking cessation/parenting/SCUBA diving tips" links. An increase in the number of postings can indicate your SEO success.

Simply ask. When all else fails, simply ask your offline customers or clients how they found you. It's not the most accurate information, but it's better than nothing. Be sure that your traditional marketing, sales, and PR team put out the question in print, on the phone, or in person whenever they have the opportunity.

Now: Brainstorm with your team on options for tracking your offline conversions and finalize a plan.

Tracking the Intangible

Many organizations report that branding is a primary goal of their SEO campaigns. But how do you track these less-than-tangible factors? The Left Brain and Right Brain debate.

The Right Brain says, "Whether you call it Branding with a capital B or just 'keeping up appearances,' the image that your organization projects through the search engines is important. If the top-ranked website for your company name is a rant by a disgruntled former employee or if half of your inbound links mention an outdated product name, you've got an image problem that SEO can help fix.

"Branding improvements may be a fringe benefit of your SEO campaign, or they may be a central goal. Either way, you'll want to document outcomes like improved search engine listings; inbound link updates; cleanup of outdated, private, or inappropriate content; and mentions in other web media such as blogs or review sites. Keep a diary or log it in your Task Journal, and pull out these accomplishments when you need some good news in the analysis and interpretation sections of your SEO status reports! I think of these positive little pieces of information as 'exclamation point moments.'"

The Left Brain says, "Things like eliminating references to nonexistent products and services and monitoring blog references, media mentions, and hate sites are so important that they need quantitative measurement. When the effectiveness of an SEO campaign comes into question, you need more than an exclamation point; you need hard data!

"Try to quantify your brand-improvement accomplishments in some way. For example, 'Eight out of fourteen of our misspelled listings have now been corrected,' 'Our company name has been mentioned on 63 blogs this month, up from 24 mentions in the previous month,' or 'Our specially designed landing page now outranks the 'hate site' listing for the keywords 'I Hate ZappyCo,' a phrase that approximately 250 people per month search for.' Companies like Nielson Buzzmetrics offer products to measure online consumer gossip, reviews, and word of mouth, known collectively as *consumer-generated media* (CGM). Numbers will help provide a clear baseline and measurable change. You'll be glad to have facts and figures at the ready when you need to justify another round of SEO spending!"

Thursday: Benchmarks and Goals

Have you ever heard something like this from your auto mechanic: "Well, we can try to replace some parts, but we can't be exactly sure that it'll stop the rattling sound, and oh, by the way, it'll cost ya a bundle"?

SEO can be pretty similar. There are so many factors involved in SEO—some within your control (for example, page text and site structure) and some far, far outside of your control (for example, search engine ranking algorithms or partnerships)—that it is very hard to predict outcomes. But we know that in real life you need to have at least some inkling of what you can expect from your efforts. Mechanics offer estimates; SEO pros offer reasonable expectations. Let's create some reasonable expectations for your website today.

Here are some factors that can point to success for your SEO campaign: easy fixes, such as basic optimization factors that are missing from your current site; well-balanced keywords with low competition, high relevance, and high popularity; a poor current status; an enthusiastic team; a good budget for PPC; and competitors stuck in the Stone Age. How these factors combine and balance will affect your expectations. Let's look at some possible combinations and what you might conclude:

Poor Current Status/High Current Optimization/No Easy Fixes This is a difficult combination. Your current optimization level is already high, which means you don't have a lot of space for improvement. You should set your expectations low, perhaps focusing on fixing red flags and your least-competitive keywords.

Fair Current Status/Poor Optimization/An Enthusiastic Team You have room to grow and a team that can make it happen. It's reasonable to expect to bump up your Fair status. But will it go to Good, Very Good, or Excellent? That depends on the other factors: competitiveness, budget, easy fixes, and so on.

High Competition/An Unenthusiastic Team/A Healthy PPC Budget With two major factors working against you, you can't expect that your organic SEO campaign will show strong results. The PPC budget just might be able to pick up the slack.

We've created a worksheet to make today's goal-setting task a little easier.

 Now: Go to your SEO Idea Bank and open up the SEO Growth Worksheet.

First, assess your organization's SEO room to grow. Consider each factor below, and give yourself a "room to grow" point for everything below that is true about your website.

✔ Current search engine status is poor.

✔ Current optimization level is poor.

✔ I have compiled a list of well-matched, popular keywords.

✔ My SEO team is enthusiastic about making needed changes.

✔ I anticipate that it will be easy to make text changes to my website.

✔ I have the appropriate personnel available.

✔ I have the buy-in from the powers-that-be in my organization.

✔ I have a budget for paid search.

✔ My website faces a low level of competition.

✔ I have discovered untapped markets or SEO opportunities.

✔ My site is "buzzworthy," or my organization's activities are newsworthy.

Now: Fill in your SEO Growth Plan room-to-grow estimates.

With this list in your pocket, you'll know whether you can look for massive improvements or just a little upward bump. We've seen SEO campaigns that have brought in enormous improvements, along the lines of thousands of percent, but we've also seen campaigns that have worked hard to keep traffic steady through a stormy period such as a redesign or a company transition. If you have a lot of "room to grow" points, you can consider higher expectations for improvements.

Here are some ways SEO campaign goals can be structured:

• Increase unique visitors by X%.

• Double the traffic to the top X landing pages.

• X new leads in the next X months.

• Improve our listing quality in Google.

• Reduce the number of unqualified leads.

• Reduce the cost of our paid search campaign by X%.

Now: You can riff on an example from the list, or invent your own goal that best matches your organization's objectives. Finalize your campaign goals. Try to be specific, and realize that these goals can and should be revisited as you continue with Your SEO Plan.

We hope we've made it clear that there is a lot you can't predict in SEO. We've done our best to give you a general idea of what you might expect, but you should be very careful not to make any promises you can't keep. Remember, reputable SEOs never guarantee any particular rank on search engines.

Friday: Quick Reference Report

Anybody *can* look at your spreadsheets and notes to figure out how your site is doing now and where it might go if optimized—but probably less than half the people you encounter will *want to*. What's more, it's likely that the people who glaze over when they see a column of numbers will be the people you feel should know about them the most. So today you're going to boil all this info down into succinct, readable descriptions.

You spent four weeks researching and analyzing data about keywords, your competition, your site performance, and optimization, not to mention your business goals and conversions. But you want others to be able to "get it" in a five-minute read (or, let's be realistic, a two-minute skim). A Quick Reference should do the trick. Today's task is a writing exercise. We want you to open up a blank document and write a one-pager of major issues and goals. You might be tempted to skip this step, but please give it a try. The point of this effort is not just to document your work, but also to do the analysis and mental sifting that allows you to write about it intelligently. The way you tell your SEO story is what will ultimately separate you from the SEO hacks and newbies out there.

Build your Quick Reference document by answering the following questions:

What is this SEO campaign trying to accomplish? You may wish to copy and paste your Conversions table, including desired conversions and target audiences, from the Goals Worksheet you completed in Chapter 1.

What are the top keywords and landing pages? List your top keywords and the landing pages that you finalized in Week 1. We recommend that you break the keywords and landing pages into two separate lists for ease of reading.

Who are our top competitors? Copy the names of your Big Five competitors from your Competition Worksheet. Use your judgment to characterize the search engine competition as a whole on a scale of Not Competitive to Very Competitive.

What is our current site visibility? Rate the overall level of your site's current status on search engines: Poor, Fair, Good, Very Good, or Excellent. If you're finding mostly negative information in your links and status assessments, and lots of red flags, you're probably in the Poor slot. To get an Excellent grade, your site would need to have top page results for most or all of its target keywords, a lot of high-quality inbound links, and very few or no red flags.

What is our current site performance? This week, you had the opportunity to compile some nitty-gritty data about your website performance. If you have at least one month's worth of analytics data that you trust, you may wish to record any of the benchmarks we discussed previously. These include unique visitors, page views, top referrers and keywords, top entry pages, top exit pages, number of bounces, average time on site, and number of error pages visited. And write down your historical conversions here, too, whether you've got hard data or you're just using the "best guess" method we described in Week 2.

What is our current site optimization level? Rate your site's current optimization level on a scale of Poor to Excellent. Review your Site Optimization Worksheet. Do you see mostly yes answers? This means that your landing pages are in good optimization shape. A spattering of yeses and nos? Put your site in the Fair category. A whole lotta nothing? Rate your site Poor.

What are our major red flags and opportunities? Be honest about the problems you're seeing—write them down now even if you don't have a clear plan for fixing them. Whatever your SEO problems are, there's a good chance you'll be able to fix them by working through the rest of the book. Describe any exciting opportunities you'd like to explore.

What are the campaign goals? This is the place for the goals you figured out yesterday.

Now: Complete the "Quick Reference" document.

Now it's time to spread the news: Your SEO campaign is off and running! Deliver this report to anyone who has an interest or potential role in Your SEO Plan, and make yourself available to discuss it.

Your SEO Plan

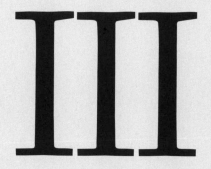

You've made it through the foundation and strategy phases, and finally it's time to implement Your SEO Plan! In this part, you'll follow three months of day-by-day steps to take advantage of your site's positive attributes and address its imperfections, and you'll establish daily habits to keep targeted traffic coming to your site.

Month One: Kick It into Gear

7

This month, you'll make a first pass at four important areas in your SEO campaign: basic organic optimization, site structure, link building, and social search. You'll spend a week making real headway on each activity, with daily tasks that we estimate will take an hour or less.

Chapter Contents

Week 1: Basic Site Optimization

In Chapter 3, "Eternal Truths of SEO," you learned that the text in your landing pages, tags, and titles is one of the most important and long-standing SEO factors. This week you're going to optimize them, with the goal of creating a better environment for your target audiences, not to mention positively influencing how search engines view and rank your website. You'll also tackle basic site-linking strategy to ensure that search engine robots have easy access to your landing pages. With these improvements in place, your site will have a basic level of optimization: nothing tricky or fancy, and no time wasted on tiny technicalities, just common-sense, best-practices solutions. Remember, there is no single silver bullet in SEO:

 Pearl of Wisdom: Site optimization usually includes many little efforts, which in combination bring better presence on search engines.

You'll keep track of all your changes in one document as you go, and on Friday you'll deliver this document to the folks in charge of making edits to your website. If you're the code-slinger on the project, wait until Friday to dive into your edits! Stay in the "optimization groove" Monday through Thursday, and you'll benefit from a more focused approach.

Here are your daily task assignments:

Monday: Page Titles

Tuesday: Meta Tags

Wednesday: Site Text

Thursday: Internal Links

Friday: Implementation

Monday: Page Titles

In Chapter 3, you learned that HTML page titles show up as the first line of clickable text in most search engine results. That fact, along with their considerable influence in search engine ranking algorithms, makes HTML page titles one of the most important optimization spots on your website.

Today, you're going to take a stab at writing unique and compelling page titles for each of your landing pages. We've created a document where you can keep track of these edits, called the Site Optimization Worksheet.

 Now: Go to www.yourseoplan.com and download the Site Optimization Worksheet.

You'll want the Quick Reference sheet you created last month handy to keep you in tune with your goals and keywords as you write. We've compiled some do's and don'ts to keep you on the right track:

DO keep it short. Like those old telephone answering machines that cut you off before you finish talking, most search engines display only 40 to 60 or so characters in the listing title. So to get your message across, include important keywords toward the beginning of the title, and make sure that the first 40 to 60 or so characters of your title form a complete thought.

DO include your keywords... Your HTML page title is important in the ranking algorithm, so it must include your target keywords! Since your space is limited, focus on the two to three keyterms that you previously matched with your landing page. Feeling a bit squeezed by the 40-to-60-character cutoff? Remember that you can combine keywords to save space.

...but DON'T overdo it! First and foremost, you want to connect with your intended audience. Excessive keyword repetition is a shortsighted strategy. Is this a marketing message or a synonym sandwich?

Bed **Linens**,Home **Linens**,Bedding,Quilts,Shams,Bed Skirts,Curtains,Duvet ...
Bed **Linens**, Home **Linens**, Interiors & Accessories, Fine Quality Bedding, **Pillow** Inserts, Linen Wash, Embroidered, **Linens**, Quilts, Shams, Curtains, Duvet Covers, Bed Skirts featuring ...
www.madaspenhome.com/products.html · Cached page

Remember to think of the big picture! Your approach to site optimization will affect more than just ranks... it will also affect your visitors' decision to part with their time and money.

DO include your name. Your organization's name will not only differentiate your listing from your competitors', it may also earn you more clicks. Maybe your name carries a good reputation with it, or maybe it provides important context, making your listing more attractive or relevant. Notice how the company names in the following listings provide crucial context for the search term "bass articles."

Harmony Central®: Hanging Ten On **Bass**
If you want to play **bass** fast, you need to use all your fingers - not just the ... If this sounds like where your at, then this **article** is for you. ...
www.harmony-central.com/**Bass**/**Articles**/Hanging_Ten - 16k - Cached

Bass Fishing Resource Guide® - Seasonal Fishing **Articles**
Hundreds of seasonal **bass** fishing **articles** by the pros about spinnerbaits, crankbaits, jigs, grubs and worms to techniques such as flipping, pitching, ...
www.bassresource.com/fishing/seasonal.html - 44k - Cached - Similar pages - Note this

DON'T assume your slogan does the job. Even if branding is your only objective, you need to think about whether your slogan contains your targeted keywords and, if so, whether you think it will encourage visits to your site. This listing shows a very catchy slogan:

Morton®Salt - when it rains it pours®
Provides information on consumer products of **Morton® Salt**.
www.mortonsalt.com/ - 13k - Cached - Similar pages

But is it really better for visibility and clicks than using targeted keywords such as "gourmet and specialty salts," "Ice Melter," or "meatloaf seasoning mix"?

DO write unique titles for each page. You've got enough competition out there. Don't add to it by pitting your landing pages against each other with identical page titles, like this site does:

Since each of your landing pages is already targeting a unique subset of your top-priority keywords, you can always find a different angle for each page title. Give each of your landing pages the chance to shine on its own merits.

DON'T duplicate site navigation in the title. Whether generated automatically or written by hand, page titles are often used as a place to mirror the navigational structure of a site. We won't say "Never" for this because, if your site sections are named well, it can be an effective way to display keywords. For example, a furniture store might have a landing page titled "Frank's Furniture – Patio Furniture – Wicker." This works—the navigation text is very brief and includes target keywords. But most sites aren't built this way, and you don't want words like "Index," "Main Page," or "Our Products" to take up space that's best reserved for your targeted marketing message.

DO think of formulas for larger sites or blogs. If your site contains a larger number of landing pages, you'll do well to write out a couple of formulas. Patterns like "Joe's Sauces: {Sauce Name}" can translate into zesty titles for large swaths of your website. Bloggers, a simpler formula for your titles could be: "{Blog Name} – {Post Title}."

DO use title case. In our experience, Titles With the First Letters Capitalized get clicked more.

> **Now:** Write optimized page titles for each of your landing pages, and add them to your Site Optimization Worksheet.

Tuesday: Meta Tags

In Chapter 3, you learned the basics of meta tags. Today you'll optimize two invisible text elements: the meta description tag and the meta keywords tag.

Meta Description Tag

We see London, we see France. We see… your site's meta description tag? Yes, not unlike your undies, your meta description tag is something that usually stays hidden but can be displayed to the world when you least expect it. For those rare times yours is exposed, you want to be proud of what people see (and here it's probably best to drop the undies metaphor). Many sites make the mistake of ignoring this tag. Today you'll make sure yours is not only present, but also written with your SEO goals in mind.

As you learned in Chapter 3, the search engines usually display snippets from your site text in their listings. Here are some possible scenarios in which your meta description tag might be displayed instead:

- When there is no HTML content on the page, such as in the case of an all-Flash or all-graphics site, or if the only content is a redirect to another page

- When someone searches for your site using your URL but no keywords
- When off-page factors make your site a relevant match for a search but no exact match is found in your site's text

Search engines often display 150 or more characters for the listing description, so you have a lot of space—relative to the page title, anyway—to convey your message. So if good writing comes naturally to you, you have a lot of opportunity to make this tag stand out. But if writing isn't your strong suit, this tag gives you a little more room to make mistakes. Bring in a proofreader if you need to; this is a bad spot for an embarrassing typo.

Here are some pointers for writing a great meta description tag:

Keep it informative. Think of the meta description tag as an "About Us" blurb, not a "Buy Now!" advertisement. It's your keyword-rich *elevator speech* (that's a marketing term for the description of yourself you might give in a 30-second elevator ride). It's not worth the upkeep to write this tag to promote special events or deals. And just as it's probably not helpful to scream words like "WORLD'S BEST!" elsewhere in your marketing message, the same holds true in your meta description tag.

Pair it with the page title. While you can't be sure exactly when or how people will see your meta description tag, it's a sure bet that when it is shown, it will be right under your optimized page title. So don't repeat your title text in your description tag.

Include your keywords... Although the meta description tag may not be a huge factor in influencing rank, it may have a big influence on the searcher who is lucky enough to view it. So include your target keywords because they'll be bolded in the search results. Notice how the bolding catches your eye:

> 1. South Metro **Jewish Congregation** - A Reform Jewish synagogue serving ...
> An inviting, spiritually rich **Reform Jewish Congregation** located just outside of **Portland**, **Oregon**, for Jews by Birth, Jews by Choice, and Jews at Heart.
> smjc.org - 3k - Cached

...but don't overdo it! Stuffing the meta description tag with a long keyword list isn't likely to help your ranks and will probably generate vast waves of indifference with searchers. Why not use this tag to give the searcher a reason to come to your site instead?

Make it unique. Like your HTML page title, your meta description tag should be custom-written for each landing page to match its specific content.

 Now: Using your newly optimized page titles and your landing page content as a guide, write optimized meta description tags for your landing pages in your Site Optimization Worksheet.

Here's some good news if you're interested in saving time: The combination of page title and meta description tag can be used as is, or with a little trimming or spinning, for any directories that you submit your site to later. And if you're looking for a keyword-rich tagline to add to the bottom of your page, your meta description tag can be a great starting point.

Some SEO strategists feel that with search engines doing such a good job of displaying text from your pages, you might as well leave off the meta description tag altogether. We're not in this camp—we try to take advantage of every smidgen of control we can get—but the slacker in you might embrace it. Here's one concession we *will* make: If you can't take the time to make this tag unique for each landing page, you're better off skipping it.

Meta Keywords Tag

As you already know, the meta keywords tag is not the most influential tag in SEO. But it won't harm you to optimize yours. Here's a quick-and-dirty method that you can use:

- Go to the Keywords Worksheet that you compiled in your Prep month, and look through your flagged keywords.

- For each landing page, decide which of the flagged keywords you think are relevant. Insert them into the Meta Keywords Tag column of the Site Optimization Worksheet.

- Add any keywords that didn't make the flagged list but that you think are appropriate and relevant.

- For each landing page, add your company name, location if applicable, and any common alternate spellings or misspellings you can think of.

    Don't overthink it. You're done.

 Now: Compile optimized meta keywords tags for your landing pages and place them in your Site Optimization Worksheet.

Hey slackers: What we said about the meta description tag holds true for this one, too. If you can't take the time to make this tag unique for each landing page, leave it out.

Wednesday: Site Text

Has there been something about your site's text that has been setting your teeth on edge since you started learning about SEO? Is there anything in the content that you know is working against your site's search engine visibility? Or are your keywords nowhere to be found? Now it's time to address these issues. Today is a momentous day because you're actually going to put your keyword research to good use on your site's visible text content.

First Impressions

Have you been wondering how people select which search results to click on—and how to make yours the one they choose? Search behavior research can help you understand and influence their click decisions:

- Research by search marketing firm Enquiro, Inc., on B2B search behavior found that 27 percent of searchers quickly scan the listings looking for words to jump out, while 15 percent read titles and descriptions carefully. But 57 percent start with a quick scan and then read the listings carefully if nothing jumps out at them first. Most searchers will click on the first appropriate-looking listing they find. (Source: Enquiro.com)

- Cornell eye-tracking research shows that searchers spend 30 percent of their time reading the listing title, 43 percent of the time reading the listing description, and 21 percent of their time reading the URL. The average total time before a click choice is made is 5.7 seconds. (Source: Cornell University Computer Science & Human-Computer Interaction)

- German researchers asked users how they chose what to click on. The winning factor was clear listing text. That means you should make sure your listings contain readable text, not keyword-stuffed garble. Other important factors were relevance of the listing to the search term, a clear and easy-to-understand description of the page content, and the inclusion of the website's name. (Source: Fittkau and Maaß on behalf of eProfessional GmbH)

Today you will comb through your landing pages for possible text improvements, documenting them as you go. You can approach documentation in a couple of ways: One way is to compile your desired changes in the Text/Content Edits section on the Site Optimization Worksheet. Or depending on the layout of your site and the extent of your changes, you may just want to print out your landing pages and mark your changes on the printout.

Your goal: Incorporate your two or three designated target keyterms onto each of your landing pages without going overboard and cooking up an unreadable keyword porridge. If you have any writers on your SEO team, get them on board for this session. Try these editorial strategies for making your text changes:

- Swap out a specific word for a top-priority keyword every time it appears.

- Swap out a graphic containing a keyword for text.

- Spell out an acronym (at least in its first appearance on the page).

- On a case-by-case basis, swap out less-effective generic terms for keywords.

- Make sure your company name exists in text form once on every page.

- Include keywords in links wherever possible.

- Add keyword-rich captions to photos.

- Add a keyword-rich tagline at the bottom of the page.
- Add keywords to page headers.
- Use bold text for keywords. This may provide some ranking benefit but has the potential for making your web copy look cluttered and confusing, so use with caution.

Figure 7.1 shows an example of the kind of edits you might want to make on your own site.

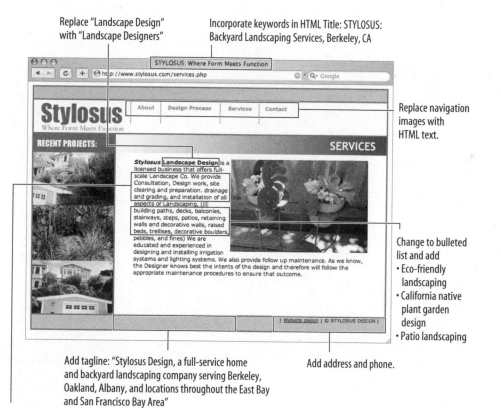

Figure 7.1 Text optimization suggestions for a sample page

Now: Go through your landing pages and compile your list of changes on your Site Optimization Worksheet or page printouts.

Thursday: Internal Links

As the search engines crawl through your site, they are doing more than just moving from one page to the next. They're looking for clues that tell them what the pages on your site are about. Links from page to page inside your site, and the text they contain, provide some of these clues. A well-planned internal linking structure might even help focus some link authority to your more important pages.

Are optimized internal links *the* answer to improved search engine ranks? Nope, they're not. This level of SEO detail is just one of the many little modifications you can make that will add up and make a difference.

From our experience, sites that pay attention to their internal linking text are usually a cut above their competitors.

Here are some things to watch out for in assessing your site's internal links:

Use every reasonable opportunity to link. If you want a search-friendly site, the robots need to be able to follow links throughout your site. Does your home page provide links to your landing pages? There may be some obvious opportunities for internal links that you aren't currently taking advantage of. Scan your page copy for product names, calls to action, or other opportunities to add robot-friendly HTML links within your site's text.

For example, we often see home page text that looks like this:

> We're proud of the great reputation our Popsicle Stands have earned. With JuniorPop Stands, SuperPop Stands, and high altitude stands available, you'll be blown away. You can find our products in many retail locations, or buy online.

But modify this text just a little bit, and look at the improvement:

> We're proud of the great reputation our Popsicle Stands have earned. With <u>JuniorPop Stands</u>, <u>SuperPop Stands</u>, and <u>high altitude stands</u> available, you'll be blown away. You can <u>find our products</u> in many retail locations, or <u>buy online</u>.

Why is this better? Because it provides clear, keyword-rich paths to each of your product pages, your store locator, and your online store, it provides a clue to the search engines that these are important pages on your site, and it's also much more useful to your site visitors.

Use meaningful text in your links. If you're serious about your site's usability and optimization, you should consider rewriting every "<u>click here</u>" on your site to something more meaningful. Imagine the contextual help you give to a search engine robot, and the favor you do for your website visitors, when you change:

> SuperPop Stands are famous for their compact yet sturdy construction. <u>Click here</u> to see why they're so popular.

To:

> Why are <u>SuperPop Stands</u> so popular? Because popsicle sellers love their compact yet sturdy construction.

Bloggers, you are guiltiest when it comes to lazy linking. How many times have you written a blog posting that looks like this: "I am the world's biggest Green Bay Packers fan, as you've seen here and here."

Oh, it's suave, it's carefree, it's ubercool. We get that. And it's fine by us when you're linking out to a YouTube video and you don't care what the search engines think of it. But when you use this linking style for your own internal pages, you've wasted an opportunity to give your link a little context, and your site a little optimization boost. And a link is a terrible thing to waste!

Another place we find lazy links in within a site's global navigation, a.k.a. the main menu. When you link to "Our Products" and "Our Services," what keywords are you missing out on? What if you linked to "Our Organization Tools" and "Our Time Saving Services" instead? Now, you don't want to overdo this one—the potential is there to make your page look keyword stuffed, and it might impact your site design. Work together with your designers or writers to see if you can come up with navigation text that looks great and includes keywords, too.

Play favorites: Link to landing pages. Maybe your most important landing pages exist alongside thousands of other pages in your site. Robots don't index every page from every site, so they may simply move on before they find the path to the pages you think are most important. This is a quick fix: Just be sure to add HTML links that place your landing pages no more than two clicks away from the home page.

Outbound Links

In the real world, nobody knows that you wrote in your pet gerbil for president. Online, it's another story. Outbound links pointing from your site to another website are considered votes, and they're traceable. Search engines, in particular, are keeping a close eye on outbound links on your site. If they catch you linking to a "bad neighborhood," your ranks could suffer. Here are some pages that shouldn't be getting links from your site:

- *Link farms*—pages that obviously buy, sell, or trade links

- Sites engaged in "black hat" SEO

- A large number of sites that have subject matter unrelated to your own

It's easy to find outbound links on your site—just search for **linkfromdomain:*yourdomain.com*** on the MSN search engine. Sites you linked to ages ago may have expired or been taken over by domain squatters, making them less-than-desirable outbound links, so make a habit of checking them once every few months, or anytime you see an unexpected drop in rankings.

An XML Sitemap is another way to steer search engines toward higher-priority pages. Read more about setting up XML Sitemaps in Chapter 10, "Extra Credit and Guilt-Free Slacking."

Now: Try to identify opportunities for improving links within your own site. Write down your findings in your Site Optimization Worksheet.

Friday: Implementation

All of your desired site edits are conveniently compiled in your Site Optimization Worksheet. Today, you'll send out these requests to your web team—or take the time to make the changes yourself.

If you've followed our advice, you've already done a little collaborating with the people who will be involved in implementation of these website changes. Here are some pointers for making this effort worthwhile:

Think in terms of a style guide. If your organization works from a style guide, now is the time to suggest which of your requested changes should be officially incorporated. Many of your site text edits from Thursday are perfect candidates for inclusion in a style guide.

Know your time frame. If you're not doing them yourself, these edits—and the buy-in they require—might take time. While you can move forward in this book without having all the changes in place, Your SEO Plan will work best with an optimized website. If you need to take a little time to get these important changes made, we won't rush you. We'll be here waiting for you when your site is ready to go!

Prioritize. If your team doesn't have the time to get all of these edits in place anytime soon, prioritize them in this order:

1. Edit HTML page titles.
2. Edit page text.
3. Edit internal links.
4. Edit meta tags.

Now: Distribute requests for edits to your web team—or get started making the changes yourself.

You should be proud—people charge a lot of money for the kind of SEO writing you've done this week! Now let's move on to making sure your site structure is robot-friendly.

Internal Link Structure

Want to know how link equity, link juice, page authority, link love, PageRank, or whatever you like to call that precious commodity so important in SEO is distributed through your site? Here's a visual: Champagne Pyramid. Just as the bubbly stuff flows merrily from glass to glass, your link juice flows through your site, following pathways created by internal links.

Inbound links from other sites bring power to your site, and *internal* links move it around. If your site is like most, the majority of inbound links are pointing to your home page. That means you need to share the wealth—using internal links—with other pages on your site. There's no single linking structure that maximizes link power for every site, but here are a few do's and don'ts that should help:

- DO point your main menu to key landing pages.

- Your site has a finite amount of overall equity. So DON'T link to low-priority pages unnecessarily. This is especially true for sitewide links such as copyright and legal.

- DO consider your site map page a landing page if it's linked from every page.

- DO amp up your deep-page-to-deep-page internal links. Related content links engage your users and increase the authority of the linked page.

- Subpages that have lots of inbound links carry link power. DO link from them to your top-priority landing pages.

- DON'T let any pages, especially top-priority ones, become "orphaned" (not linked from any page) or deeply buried more than five clicks away from your home page.

If you put some thought into your internal linking structure, we'll raise a glass to your SEO success!

Week 2: Site Structure Improvements

Last week, you took care of basic site optimization. Congratulations, your site is at a respectable baseline level! This week, you'll delve a little deeper into some techie decisions that can improve your site's optimization, indexing, and overall visibility success.

This week's tasks will involve some serious tech topics. It's a week when you will definitely want your team queued up and clued in to your needs and reasoning. Keep your meeting calendar handy as you review your daily assignments:

Monday: Robot Walk-through

Tuesday: The Spider's Eye View

Wednesday: Duplicate Content and Canonical Issues

Thursday: Flash and Ajax

Friday: Your Robots.txt File

Monday: Robot Walk-through

You're all dressed up, and the hors d'oeuvres are on the table. But is there a big Do Not Enter sign on your door? You know the basics of how the robots find your site, and you know whether or not your landing pages are indexed. Today you'll look for barriers that exist between the robots and your landing pages.

Take a look at your Rank Tracking Worksheet to determine whether any of your landing pages are not indexed. Here are several reasons a robot might not be reaching your landing page and possible ways to fix the problem:

Robots can't follow your links. This could be as simple as having no links from your home page or your main site navigation to one or all of your landing pages. Or maybe the links to your landing pages are created using hard-to-follow code, such as JavaScript pull-down menus or pop-up scripts. Often, this is an easy fix: Just add standard HTML text links from anywhere on your home page to your landing page. (You'll probably want a site map as well. We'll cover that next month.)

Your site asks too much from the visitor. If the queen came to visit, you wouldn't turn her away if she weren't wearing the right hat. Treat your spiders the same way! Some websites won't display to a viewer who doesn't have JavaScript. Guess who doesn't have JavaScript? The robots! Some websites require cookies. Guess who won't accept cookies? You get the point. You'll need to eliminate these requirements on your landing pages. If you're not sure what your site requires, you'll get a better sense of it when you look at the spider's eye view of your website tomorrow.

A server outage interrupted indexing. There's nothing like that warm and fuzzy feeling your customers get when they encounter... an error message?

Perhaps your pages are linked and structured properly, but the robot came crawling just at the moment your system administrator spilled his Red Bull on the server. Either the robot captured an error message, or found no site at all to index. There's nothing you can do in a situation like this but wait until the next indexing cycle. And if this seems to be a regular occurrence, look into a more reliable hosting situation. (By the way, for the perfect balance of caffeine and server protection, your sysadmin should switch to coffee with the little sippy lid.)

You told the robots to stay away. That wasn't very nice of you! Later this week, we'll get into the details of how you communicate with robots through a file on your site called robots.txt.

Your site is being penalized. It's possible, but unlikely, that you are violating a search engine's guidelines without knowing it. If none of the other problems are striking a chord and you are absolutely sure that your pages are not present in the index, and especially if you were ever engaged in questionable SEO practices in the past, this might be your situation. It's a tough one. Probably your best strategy is to work through the rest of this week, make sure your site is squeaky clean, and use the search engines' reinclusion requests. See yourseoplan.com for URLs.

Now: Try to identify the reasons your pages are not being indexed. Write down your findings, and determine whom you need to discuss them with in your organization.

Now that you know robots can access your landing pages, you're ready to put on your spider-vision goggles and see what they see when they get there.

What's Popping Up at the Exploratorium

Lowell Robinson of the Exploratorium, San Francisco's museum of science, art, and human perception, had a problem: how to display interactive video and Flash content on the museum's Science of Gardening website (www.exploratorium.edu/gardening). Most of this rich, interactive content was built within separate pop-up windows. Lowell and his team knew that this could wreak havoc on their search engine listings.

Their primary concern was not that the search engines would have trouble indexing the pages, but rather that the pages would be indexed and site visitors would click directly to the pop-up content—in a full browser window rather than a mini-pop-up window—without entering the Exploratorium website:

"After putting hundreds of hours into producing this rich content, we didn't want the search engines to index our pop-up windows as stand-alone web pages with no way to click to the parent website and none of our branding or credits displayed."

The Science of Gardening team came up with a clever solution: The web developer placed a piece of code on the pop-up page that identifies the referring URL. Now visitors who are already viewing the Science of Gardening website see the regular pop-up (see the left screen shot below), while

Continues

What's Popping Up at the Exploratorium *(Continued)*

surfers coming in from search engines or other links see the Flash or video content wrapped in a proper branding package, with easy access to the rest of the site (see the right screen capture below).

Although some less-than-ethical SEOs may use this method to trick the search engines and confuse site visitors (a technique called cloaking), this is one example of using the technique to help the audience rather than deceive them.

Lowell's team learned an important lesson: You can't always control how people arrive at your website! If you have a website with significant content displayed in pop-up windows or within frames, be sure to check how they look as stand-alone pages and make sure that you are comfortable with them being potential entry points into your site. If you aren't, follow the Exploratorium's lead and take steps to make those windows shine! (Full disclosure: Lowell is the beloved husband of one of the authors, and yeah, he got a little free advice on this project.)

Tuesday: The Spider's Eye View

Have you ever seen those photos that show what the world looks like to a dog? Or maybe you enjoyed the kaleidoscopic fly-cam scenes in the 1950s movie *The Fly*. Today you're going to learn how to take a search engine spider's eye view of your website. Viewer discretion is advised: What you are about to see might be surprisingly scary.

As you learned in Chapter 3, a search engine spider is simply software that goes through the Internet looking at web pages and sending information back to a central repository. It doesn't view content in the same way human site visitors do. Since spiders are an important—although by no means the most important—audience for your website, you want to know how your website appears to them. Today you will use a tool called a *spider emulator* to put on your spider's eye view glasses and do exactly that.

For example, here is a typical web page, as viewed through the browser.

And here is the same web page viewed through a spider emulator.

Are you scared yet? There are lots of spider emulators available on the Web. We use http://www.seo-browser.com often because we like its simplicity. Another of our favorites is http://tools.summitmedia.co.uk/spider/. You're going to view each of your landing pages through a spider emulator today.

Here's how to do it:

- Starting with your home page, go to www.seo-browser.com or the spider emulator of your choice and enter your page URL into the emulator.

- Once you see your page as it is seen by spiders, ask yourself some questions: Does this accurately represent the information I expected to see on my site? Is it readable and in the correct order? Are my target keywords present?

- For any noted problems, consider possible solutions. For example, if the well-crafted, keyword-rich content you added last month is not showing up, it may be that it's not rendering in standard HTML text. Print out this page and bring it with you to your web developer to track down the problem. Or are you seeing the same nonsensical image ALT tag (for example, ImgFile01) repeating multiple times on the page? Make a note to have it removed or revised with appropriate keyword-rich descriptions.

> **Now:** Perform your spider emulator check for all of your landing pages. Make a note of any problems and suggested solutions in your Task Journal.

Great news! With well-chosen keywords, basic page optimization in place, and landing pages that search engine spiders can access and read, you've made a real difference in SEO for your site!

Wednesday: Duplicate Content and Canonical Issues

Is it just us, or does "canonical issues" sound like it might have something to do with the pope? If the term gives your brain a rash, don't worry. Today we'll help you understand this mystifying issue and determine whether your site is at risk.

Duplicate Content

Picture this: You switch on your TV, and every channel is showing the same show, or nearly identical shows with slight costume variations. *BO-ring!* (And oh-so-painfully close to last Friday night's TV lineup!) *Duplicate content* is the same or very similar on-page elements showing up under more than one URL, and search engines don't like it. The rule of thumb is simple:

We're sorry to say that your site may—for perfectly innocent reasons—contain duplicate content. Here are some examples we've seen:

- Printer-friendly versions of pages
- Old versions of pages that exist at old URLs
- A *pointer domain*, also called a *masked domain*, which redirects site visitors but hides the fact that they have been redirected by keeping the original domain name in the browser address bar
- Several different URLs for the same product, generated by an e-commerce system
- Pages with various tracking tags (for example, &affiliate-id=3) tacked onto the URLs
- Articles or press releases that are reprinted from elsewhere on the Web

If any of these situations sound familiar, don't panic. We said search engines don't *like* duplicate content—we didn't say they *hate* it the way they hate spam tactics. Google, for example, is likely to choose its favorite page from among the clones and filter the rest out of its index. According to Google, link authority will be consolidated onto the favored version of the page. Don't count on that—we think your page authority could be diluted between all the multiple versions of your pages. Worst-case scenario: If search engines run into a large amount of duplicate content on your site, they may throw the remote control up in frustration and stop, or slow, your website indexing.

Here are several strategies for cleaning up or avoiding duplicate content on your website:

- If multiple pages on the site display materials that are identical or nearly identical, duplicates should be excluded from indexing using the robots.txt file or a robots meta tag (you'll learn how later this week), and only a single instance allowed into the search engines.
- Domain masking is not recommended. Instead, use a *301 redirect* (your webmaster or hosting company can help with this) from the secondary to the primary domain.
- Any page URLs with a tacked-on tag should be excluded from search engine indexing. And remove any unnecessary URL parameters.
- Each page should have a unique HTML title and meta description tag—if you can't make them unique, leave them off entirely.

If the extent of duplicate content on your site is a few pages here and there, you probably don't need to worry about it.

> **Now:** If duplicate content is a concern for your site, document the pages that need to be excluded or redirected.

Leave a sticky note for the person in charge of the website saying, "I'm coming for you."

Canonical Issues

If we tell you how to pronounce canonical, do you promise you won't use your knowledge to make other people feel dumb? All right then: it's pronounced can-ON-ical.

Canonical issues are a special case of duplicate content. Here's how: In the eyes of the search engines, the following four URLs are four different pages:

- http://www.yourdomain.com/
- http://www.yourdomain.com/default.asp
- http://yourdomain.com
- http://yourdomain.com/default.asp

Now, *you* know and *we* know that these are actually pointing to the same page, and we figure that soon enough the search engines will get it right. But for now, most search engines have what industry insiders call a *canonical URL* problem (*canonical* is a programmer's term for "standard," so a canonical URL would be the standard or preferred URL for your website) and it can have a significant effect on your SEO success:

> **Pearl of Wisdom:** If your web pages are displayed under more than one version of a URL, your ranks can suffer.

It's easy to determine if your site needs some fixing here. Open a browser and type in your home page URL with the "www" (http://www.yourdomain.com) and without the "www" (http://yourdomain.com). Do the URLs redirect to a single, favorite version, or do they just sit there looking guilty? Next, perform the same test with your site's standard file names such as /main.html, /index.php, or /default.asp.

> **Now:** Check if your home page displays with more than one URL.

Here's how to zap canonical issues:

- Ensure that all internal links within your site point to the same URL version. Choose a format and stick with it.

- Set up a 301 redirect that always points the variant URL(s) to your preferred URL. That will help search engines know which one is your preference. (By the way, this could be a tricky one for your webmaster, so don't suggest it without some sort of bribe in hand.)

- If there are inbound links from other websites pointing to the wrong URL format, write to them and ask for an update.

- Log into your Google Webmaster Tools and set up a preferred URL. Go to Chapter 10 to learn how to verify your site so that you can set this parameter.

Now: If you have determined that your site displays under multiple URLs, start tasking your team with the solutions we've just listed.

Thursday: Flash and Ajax

Oh, Flash, we love you. You always look so pulled together and professional. And, Ajax, you're so cute and modern: We're starting to have feelings for you, too. But… but… there's this one area of our relationship that just seems to be lacking. Why do you always fail us in the search engines?

Back in Chapter 1, we explained the importance of segmenting your site into landing pages that speak to your separate target audiences. Flash and Ajax share a primary SEO disadvantage: These technologies both typically display loads of content and interactivity on a *single HTML page*. See Figure 7.2 for an example. With Flash, you can view any number of topics and "pages" without leaving a single movie, and with Ajax, you can view a whole store's worth of products without visiting a new URL. And what you gain in 'zazz, you lose in search engine friendliness. Simpler sites have content that's displayed on a large number of separate URLs, each getting its very own morsel of search engine visibility.

Remember yesterday, when you learned that every URL should have its own content? There's more to that pearl of wisdom:

Pearl of Wisdom: If it feels like a page, it should have its own URL.

Another disadvantage, of course, is that Flash and Ajax code often prevents the search engines from reading the site text.

Figure 7.2 In this Ajax store example, no matter what you click on, the information will display in the same URL.

Too many categories of information in one page, and text information that's obscured or invisible to the search engines—this non-HTML territory is treacherous terrain for robots!

If your site contains a significant amount of Flash or Ajax, drum up some courage, a budget calculator, and maybe a licensed massage therapist, and see if any of the following strategies are feasible for your site:

Break up Flash or Ajax into separate HTML pages. Talk to your web developer about breaking up the Flash or Ajax so that each landing page has a separate URL. Flash and Ajax can be as-needed elements within HTML pages, rather than providing the entire navigation for the site. Your users will thank you for the browser Back/Forward button functionality and the ability to bookmark your pages, and the "linkerati" will be able to tag pages on social bookmarking sites and deep-link your site.

Provide alternate HTML content for Flash. Four out of five search engines agree: Standard HTML content tastes better. Providing alternative content in HTML is not only helpful to the search engines, it's also great for people without the Flash plug-in and for visually impaired site visitors. Just be sure that the HTML content exactly matches the content that would be visible to users with Flash—otherwise, you'll risk triggering spam penalties.

Create an HTML addendum. If you can't get your pages to show alternate HTML content, at least create some HTML pages in addition to the Flash or Ajax site. Beneath your Flash or Ajax content, add a standard HTML link or links to your most important content in HTML such as "Our Products," "About Us," and "Contact Us."

Focus on inbound links. If all else fails, optimize whatever HTML pages you have, and focus on getting inbound links.

Now: If Flash or Ajax is causing an SEO disadvantage for your website, explain the importance of individual landing pages and robot-readable HTML text to your web developer. Discuss which of our suggested work-arounds is possible.

Dynamic Site Smarts

Search engines are good at indexing dynamic sites, and the advice in this book applies just as well to ASP and PHP pages—and even pages with URLs containing a question mark—as it does to old-school HTML. If your site is of the dynamic variety, follow some basic guidelines to avoid common pitfalls:

- Be sure that search engines can follow standard links to every page on your site. Don't expect search engines to fill out a form or run a search to drill down to your most juicy content.

- You're trying to appeal to humans, so use human-friendly URLs. Would you rather click on this:

  http://www.yoursite.com/church-bells/discount/
  or this?

  http://www.yoursite.com/prod.php?id=23485&blt=234

- Limit the number of parameters in the URL to a maximum of two.

- Use the parameter ?id= only when in reference to a session ID.

- Be sure that your URLs function even if all dynamic parameters are removed.

- When linking internally, always link with parameters in the same order and format.

- Explore the idea of setting up an XML Sitemap if there is any reason to think that search engine robots aren't seeing all of your pages.

- Use robots.txt to exclude *stub pages* (autogenerated pages with no real content, such as empty directory categories and empty search results). Search engines want to index pages containing meaningful content, not empties generated by dynamic programs.

Your dynamic site has a lot to offer. And now you know how to help it reach its full search engine potential!

Friday: Your *Robots.txt* File

A robots.txt file is the first file that a search engine robot visits on your website. Like a snooty nightclub bouncer with a velvet rope, the robots.txt file decides which robots are welcome and which need to move on to that less-exclusive joint down the street. Robots.txt can admit or reject robots on a sitewide, directory-by-directory, or page-by-page basis.

SEO folks often feel a special affection for the robots.txt file because it provides a rare opportunity to communicate with a search engine robot. However, its capabilities are limited. Robots.txt files exist only to *exclude* indexing. Just as a bouncer can keep people out but can't force anyone to come in, the robots.txt file can't do anything to entice a robot to spend *more* time or visit *more* pages on your site. Also, compliance with your robots.txt file is voluntary, not mandatory. The major search engines will generally try to follow your instructions, but other, less-reputable types might not. This is why you should not rely on your robots.txt file to prevent spidering of sensitive, private, or inappropriate materials.

Do You Need a *Robots.txt* File?

You may not need a robots.txt file. Without one, all robots will have free access to non-password-protected pages on your site. To decide if you need a robots.txt file for your website, ask yourself these questions:

- Are there any pages or directories on my site that I do not want listed on the search engines, such as an intranet or internal phone list?

- Are there any specific search engines that I do not want to display my site?

- Do I know of any dynamic pages or programming features that might cause problems for spiders, like getting caught in a loop (infinitely bouncing between two pages)?

- Does my website contain pages with duplicate content?

- Are there directories on the site that contain programming scripts only, not viewable pages?

If the answers to these questions are no, then you do not need a robots.txt file. You've got the rest of the day off! If you have any yes answers, you'll prepare your robots.txt file today.

 Now: Determine whether you need a robots.txt file in your website.

Create Your *Robots.txt* File

Robots.txt files are very simple text files. To find a sample, go to www.yourseoplan.com/robots.txt and view ours, or go to just about any other site and look for the robots.txt file in the *root directory*.

The robots.txt file usually looks something like this:

```
User-agent: googlebot
Disallow: /private-files/
Disallow: /more-private-files/
User-agent: *
Disallow: /cgi-scripts/
```

In this example, Google's spider (called Googlebot) is excluded from indexing files within the two directories called private-files and more-private-files, and all robots (signified by a wild-card asterisk, *) are excluded from indexing the directory called cgi-scripts.

There are numerous websites that will walk you through building and saving your robots.txt file. A helpful robots.txt builder can be found here: www.clickability.co.uk/robotstxt.html. Answers to just about any question you could think of about robots are here: www.robotstxt.org.

Now: Create your robots.txt file and save it in the root directory of your website, or request that your webmaster do so.

If you are feeling any doubt about whether your robots.txt file is written properly, *don't* post it. The last thing you want to do is inadvertently shut out the search engines.

Here's a bonus: Robots.txt can also be used to tell search engines where to find your XML Sitemap. You can learn more about this in Chapter 10.

xtra cred

Robots Meta Tags

A robots meta tag serves a similar purpose as the robots.txt file, but it is placed within individual pages on your site rather than in your root directory. A robots meta tag affects only the page it resides on. Chances are you don't need to use this type of tag, but here's a quick overview in case you do.

You might choose to use a robots meta tag rather than a robots.txt file because it's easier for you to set up the exclusion using your web page template rather than the robots.txt file, or maybe you only want to do a brief, temporary exclusion. Another possible reason is that you do not have access to the root directory on your site.

To exclude the robots from a page using the robots meta tag, simply include the following code in the HTML head of the page:

```
<meta name="robots" content="noindex, nofollow">
```

This will prevent search engine robots from listing the page on which the tag resides.

Robot Exclusion for Google

If you plan to use robots exclusion to control the sharing of Google PageRank among pages on your website (for example, by excluding low-quality pages that you do not want hogging authority), you should know that Google handles the robots.txt and robots meta tag exclusions slightly differently:

- Pages excluded with either type of exclusion are allowed to accumulate PageRank authority.

- A page that is excluded with the robots.txt file may be listed in search results with a URL only, and no description. A page that is excluded with a robots meta tag will not be displayed in search results at all.

- A page that is excluded with the robots.txt file will not be crawled by Googlebot, and it will not pass PageRank to other pages to which it links.

- A page that is excluded with the robots meta tag may be crawled by Googlebot, and Google will follow links on the page. The PageRank that is accumulated by this page will be shared with pages to which it links.

Now: Add robots meta tags to pages on an as-needed basis.

Now, let's take a trip out of techie-ville, and get serious about building high-quality inbound links to your site.

Week 3: Link Building

You learned in Chapters 3 and 4 how important inbound links are for your website. Last month, you even dipped a toe into the ocean of link building when you used the search engines to find out how many other sites are linking to your landing pages.

Unless your site is truly wretched, there's bound to be somebody out there who is interested in linking to it. (And if you think your site is beyond linking, stay tuned! You'll get some content-building and linkability improvement lessons in Chapter 9, "Month Three: It's a Way of Life.") Put on your PR hat—or get your team's most talented communicator in the room—and get started on your SEO link-building campaign:

Monday: Your Existing Links

Tuesday: Submit to Directories

Wednesday: Surf for More Link Opportunities

Thursday: The Art of Link Letters

Friday: Submittals and E-mails

Surfing Is Not Slacking

Way back when, when we were SEO consultants working for a small web development firm, we were lucky to have an open-minded boss. On any given day, you might have seen five other workers knee-deep in HTML edits or up to their ears in database code, but what was on our monitors? Movie fan sites, Florida vacation sites, and sports nostalgia sites. We remember the day we had to send an e-mail around saying, "Don't worry: We're not looking for new jobs. We're just researching career sites for a client!" But it was all part of the SEO job, and an important one at that.

If you're in a corporate culture where personal e-mails and web surfing is frowned upon or prohibited, it is essential that you get the clearance you need to access the Web in the same way that your customers and competitors do. Likewise, if there are no actual restrictions on web surfing in your company but you just feel like a slacker when you're surfing the Web, just remember what surfing does for your company:

- Surfing helps you find and assess the quality of sites linking to you and locate new sites that may want to link to you.

- It helps you find new search products and opportunities that may be useful for promoting your organization.

- It helps you to think like a searcher, using a variety of techniques to find important information.

- And it helps you get familiar with the wide range of available search engine and directory listings.

Every SEO expert has a favorite generic search term to use for testing, one that's broad and popular enough to be represented by the full gamut of paid and unpaid listings, directory listings, and text snippets, not to mention official sites, unofficial sites, and misspellings. Ours continues to be "Britney Spears." Have fun finding yours!

Monday: Your Existing Links

Today, you will assess your website's existing listings and links with an eye toward improvement. We have created a worksheet to help you in your link-building efforts.

Now: Download the Link Tracking Worksheet from www.yourseoplan.com and save it in your SEO Idea Bank.

Last month, during your baseline site assessment, you determined the total number of sites linking into your landing pages. Now you will take a magnifying glass to these sites and document them in your Link Tracking Worksheet. Here are the steps you'll take:

- Document Inbound Links
- Assess Existing Link Quality

Document Inbound Links

On your Link Tracking Worksheet, you will see a section for existing inbound links. Today you'll identify the URLs of the first 10 or so sites that are linking to each of your landing pages. Ten should be plenty to work with for now.

Find the URLs using one of the following four methods:

- On the search engine of your choice, perform the special search you learned in Chapter 6 for finding inbound links. (We prefer using http://siteexplorer.search .yahoo.com because it's so easy to export the list and dump it into the worksheet.)

- If you have access to a website statistics program, review it for referring URLs.

- Use a backlink analysis tool, such as the one found at www.backlinkwatch.com. See Figure 7.3 for an example. This tool provides backlink URLs and also the text that the linking sites are using to link to you. Fun stuff!

- If you have verified your site with Google Webmaster Tools, you have access to a much more complete list of links than you'll get from the Google search engine.

xtra cred

No.	Backlink URL	Anchor Text	PR	OBL	Flag
1	http://en.wikipedia.org/wiki/Lucky_Charms	Lucky Charms official website	5	137	nofollow
2	http://www.freewebs.com/leprechaunworldthree/games.htm	Find Lucky - Find Lucky for us and make him pay!	NA	15	
3	http://www.worldleaderentertainment.com/production/con.....	Find Lucky - Find Lucky for us and make him pay!	NA	0	
4	http://samanthal.mhlearningnetwork.com/id19.html	click here to go to luckycharms.com	NA	79	
5	http://www.lexington.k12.il.us/teachers/jheuer/kinderga.....	www.luckycharms.com	NA	34	
6	http://guilds.camelotherald.com/guilds/guild.php?s=Gawa.....	http://www.luckycharms.com	NA	24	
7	http://www.prnewswire.com/cgi-bin/stories.pl?ACCT=104&S.....	http://www.luckycharms.com	NA	21	
8	http://www.prnewswire.com/cgi-bin/stories.pl?ACCT=109&S.....	http://www.luckycharms.com	NA	59	
9	http://www.marketingmag.ca/events/2006DMA_judging/dmaju.....	http://www.luckycharms.com	0	18	
10	http://www.marketingmag.ca/events/2006DMA_judging/dmaju.....	http://www.luckycharms.com	NA	18	
11	http://www.theboxheads.net/modules.php?name=Forums&file.....	http://www.luckycharms.com	NA	162	
12	http://en.wikipedia.org/wiki/Lucky_Charms_(cereal)	Lucky Charms official website	5	138	nofollow
13	http://fcsc.k12.in.us/TPage617.aspx	**http://www.luckycharms.com**	1	19	
14	http://www.bookrags.com/Lucky_Charms	Lucky Charms Official Website	NA	79	nofollow
15	http://www.taylorbode.com/favoritelinks.htm	www.luckycharms.com	0	12	
16	http://www.toolkitzone.com/community.php?user=13293	🖼	NA	43	
17	http://w4.nkcsd.k12.mo.us/~abarron/funlinks.htm		1	46	
18	http://www.italycharms.eu/keyword/lucky%20charms	Lucky Charms official website	NA	216	nofollow
19	http://guilds.camelotherald.com/guilds/guild.php?s=Gawa.....	http://www.luckycharms.com	NA	62	
20	http://www.worldleaderentertainment.com/production/wha.....	http://www.luckycharms.com	NA	0	
21	http://archive.lightspeedsystems.com/archive/Internet.a.....				
22	http://www.worldleaderentertainment.com/production/who.....	http://www.luckycharms.com	NA	4	

Figure 7.3 Inbound links for www.luckycharms.com shown on backlinkwatch.com

Perform this step for each of your landing pages, ignoring links coming from your own site. If your site has no incoming links from other sites, you can skip the rest of today's tasks!

Now: Open your Link Tracking Worksheet and fill in existing linking site URLs for each of your landing pages.

Assess Existing Link Quality

Search engines care about the quality as well as the quantity of inbound links. And *you* care, too, because a link is a direct pathway for potential customers to get to your site. Today you'll ask a few key questions about your linking sites that will help you determine if each link is going to help the right audience find the right page on your site. Later this week, we'll show you how to write to site owners to request changes to any problematic listings you discover.

The following key questions will help you assess the quality of your inbound links. It may seem like a lot to think about, but once you get a feel for it, you won't need the checklist. In fact, you'll probably be able to assess each link within 30 seconds of opening the page.

Starting with the first inbound link URL on your list, open up the page and think about the answers to these yes or no questions:

- Is this site related to the same general subject matter as mine?
- Does the linking page content speak to my target audience?
- Are my target keywords included in the text that links to my site?
- Are my target keywords included elsewhere on the page?
- Does the link work?
- Does the link go to the best landing page choice?
- Is the link up-to-date?
- Is the link flattering, or at least noncritical?

Although numerous factors can contribute to the quality of an inbound link, these are the most important. The more yes answers, the higher-quality link you have. If there are any no answers, flag this URL with a note of the problem. Obviously, some problems (like a link being from an irrelevant website) can't be fixed. And if a link is coming from inside a forum post or blog comment, it's good to know about, but there's no point trying to modify it. But others, especially links that don't work, are red flags that need to be addressed.

Get into the habit of asking these questions anytime you review a website, and it will serve you throughout your campaign—especially later this week when you are looking for new links.

Tuesday: Submit to Directories

Getting listed in human-edited directories is one of those incremental SEO tasks that can make a difference in the aggregate. It's relatively easy to find directories with categories that match your organization, and they represent a chance to build a link to your site using your own well-researched, well-targeted words. Think of a directory listing as just another inbound link with a slightly different link-request process (usually there's a submittal form to fill out, and specific editorial guidelines to follow, instead of a free-form e-mail correspondence). If you happen to have a nonprofit or noncommercial website, you have greatly increased potential for free links on directories.

Your directory requests will be accepted or rejected based on the judgment of human editors, and part of what they judge is whether your suggested title and description match your site's content. So if you have substantial optimization that needs to take place before this is the case, use today's task just to gather submittal information. You can perform the actual submittal when your site is ready.

Where to Submit

There are some big, well-established directories such as the Yahoo! Directory (http://dir.yahoo.com) and the Open Directory (www.dmoz.org), which survived extinction when the Age of Directories in the '90s made way for the Age of Algorithmic Search that came after. Submitting your site to Yahoo! and the Open Directory, while no longer crucial to a site's visibility, is a fine thing to do. They have specific categories that might describe your organization perfectly, such as Health: Alternative: Practitioners: Wellness Centers: North America: United States: Michigan. If the category fits, you may as well submit.

But the majority of today's directories, the ones you'll be spending most of your time on, are little guys with niche traffic. *Niche directories* are small, but they can be powerhouses for targeted traffic. You know your company, and you know your niche. Now it's time for you to find directories that speak to it. Here are ways you can go about it:

What are your competitors using? Check links to your competitors the same way you did in Chapter 6, but this time take some time to read through the listings. Are there any directories listed? Click them and see if this may be a good directory for you, too.

What offline opportunities do you already know about? Many publications, such as *Sweets* (http://sweets.construction.com) and *Thomson Local* (www.thomweb.co.uk) have online directory components. Check to see if your company is included in any such publication.

What comes up for your target keywords? Are there any directory pages among the top search results for your target keywords? (See Figure 7.4 for a visual.) You could benefit from their ranks by getting listed.

Figure 7.4 Directory in the top search results

Last but not least, be sure to search the search engines for relevant niche directories. For example, if your organization is a day spa located in Albuquerque, New Mexico, the search terms "day spa directory" and "Albuquerque directory" will both turn up many possible niche directories. But watch out for these pitfalls as you consider niche directories:

- Many of the directories that will come up in your searches will be repurposed versions of the Open Directory. Don't waste your time on a duplicate submittal.

- Don't believe the hype: If a niche directory wants a payment for your listing, you need to carefully check the link quality factors before you pull out your pocketbook. Websites are so easy to create that there are thousands of directory sites on the Web that aren't worth the virtual paper they're printed on. Unless you can get a several-month free trial, you should be cautious about paying for niche directory listings.

- While we've got you in a cynical mind-set, be sure to look closely at free directories as well. Don't fall for the idea that your website needs to be listed in every free-for-all general directory. If the directory categories are ridiculously generic, like "engineering" and "comic books," or if you don't actually need to select a category for your listing, the directory may not be trying to appeal to a human audience.

Your Best Listing

If you do decide to create your own directory listing, here are some tips on saving time and maximizing results:

Cluster with your competition. Search the directory for your top business competitors. If they're all in the same category, you want to be there, too.

Get specific. Browse the directory, starting from the biggest, top-level categories and working your way down to the one most specific to your organization. For example, if you provide tennis lessons, you don't want to be in a generic category like "Sports." You want to be in a more appropriate category like Shopping > Sports > Tennis > Training or a local category like Regional > North America > Canada > Ontario > Localities > T > Toronto > Recreation and Sports > Tennis.

Use category tiebreakers. If you are faced with two categories that seem to fit your site equally well, choose the better-quality category page based on the link-quality factors you assessed on Monday for inbound links in general.

Put some thought into your submittal. Most likely, you will want to submit your home page, but it's possible that a different landing page will also work. In rare cases, if your site has landing pages with unique content, directories may include multiple listings for your site. Use the HTML page title and meta description tag you prepared in Week 1 as a launching point to write your title and description. Be sure to consider what your competition is saying (or not saying) about themselves when you fine-tune your suggested listing.

 Now: Submit your site to directories that you've determined are worth your time.

Wednesday: Surf for More Link Opportunities

On Monday you began building the list of potential linking websites on your Link Tracking Worksheet. Today, you'll surf the Web to expand your list of sites. First, you need to know what makes a link worth chasing:

- Quality Links Defined
- Expand Your Link Requests List

Quality Links Defined

As you surf for potential linking sites today, you may be tempted to build the longest list you possibly can, with dozens or hundreds of sites. But every one of these link requests is going to take a five-minute chunk of time out of your life—why, that's only 12 per episode of *Battlestar Galactica*!—so you need to be choosy.

An Expert's Opinion: The Difference Between Success and Failure

If your only exposure to link building is spammy, reciprocal link request e-mails from pushy webmasters, you may be surprised to know that there is a very different way to build links.

"It's a very human process," says renowned link-building consultant Eric Ward. Eric is such an authority on the subject of successful linking campaigns that he has earned the nickname "Link Moses"—a bit of a misnomer given his fresh-faced good looks.

Eric feels that taking the time to carefully assess potential linking sites is critically important. "You can automate only so much of the process, and then it comes down to you and your browser window, making qualitative decisions about the target sites. Most people dread that part. I dig it. That's the difference between success and failure."

Over half of Eric's business involves teaching his clients how to do it themselves. According to Eric, "The most successful sites will take ownership of the link-building process and not depend solely on vendors."

So if it's better to do it yourself, how can you make sure you're spending your precious time on the highest-quality potential linking sites?

Eric offers advice on identifying quality sites: "The signs of value will vary depending on the subject matter, but one constant is the site's content will be high caliber and not coated with 10 or 20 pay-per-click ads. The site will not require a return link as a condition of giving you a link."

And how does he identify sites that aren't worth the effort? "If the majority of what I see on the page is advertisements instead of content, I'm immediately suspicious. If the site says 'Submit your link free!' it's likely to be of little value. If a page has never been crawled by any search engine (this can be verified), the page isn't likely to be of value."

Don't be intimidated if you're just getting started with link building. Eric advises, "Do a search on the phrase 'link building expert' and read all the articles you find. Those of us who do this for a living have shared many of the tips and tools we use."

Tell it, Moses! Eric shares his tips and tools on his website, www.ericward.com.

Between Eric Ward's factors to consider in the sidebar "An Expert's Opinion: The Difference Between Success and Failure" and the link quality factors you learned on Monday, you've got a lot of tools for analysis. But there's one more angle to consider: whether the site makes it possible for you to do your link-gathering job. Be sure to take these administrative issues into account:

- Is contact information available on the site? Without it, you can't request the link.

- Does the site appear to be regularly updated? Do a quick scan for the "last edited" date or other signs of life. If nobody is manning the store, there won't be anybody to add your link.

Now that you know *what* you're looking for in an inbound linking site, here are some ideas for *where* to look.

Expand Your Link Requests List

So far, you've only scratched the surface of your potential high-quality linking sites. Here are some places you can look for additional opportunities:

Sites Linking to Your Competitors By now, you're a seasoned pro at finding inbound links using the search engines. Do this now for your Big Five competitors. Who is linking to them? Can you get a link there, too?

Any Sites Doing Well for Your Top Keywords Go through the top listings for your target keywords—both organic results and sponsored results—with a fine-tooth comb. These would be great places to get links.

Your Clients/Customers/Fans Do you have a client base that is pleased with your service? Do they have websites that speak to a segment of your target audience? If so, they may be happy to provide a link to your site! Bonus points if they put your link alongside a glowing recommendation.

Your Service Providers/Vendors Are you a major client of any organization with a web presence that has a tie-in to your target audience? Maybe they would like to link to your site. Maybe they'd even like to list you as a "featured" client!

Your Partners Corporate partners are likely to include links on their websites. Check and see if there's one for you.

Sites That Already Include Your Company Name Perform a search for your company name in quotes. You may be surprised to find many websites that include your company information, maybe even a URL written in text, without making it a link! With a flick of the mouse, those could become inbound links for you.

Local and Regional Directories Any site that includes listings of local businesses will probably be happy to have their information updated—preferably with your organization's web listing!

Business Associations and Accreditations Most professional and trade associations include lists of their members. If your organization is accredited in any way, there may be a link in it for you.

Sites That Are "Related" to Yours In Chapter 6, you learned about the Alexa database of information. One of its tastier tidbits is Related Sites, other websites that draw the same audience as yours. Take a look at your related sites for linking potential.

Sympathetic Sites If your site has a religious, political, or philosophical theme, there is likely to be a large circle of similarly minded folks on the Web. These people will likely be enthusiastic about supporting one of their own. Ditto for specialized hobbies and enthusiasms.

As you surf, be open to wandering down unexpected paths—sometimes that's the best way to find new opportunities. And be sure to make a note of the site URL (location of potential link), name of site, and contact information in your Link Tracking Worksheet.

Now: Record additional potential linking URLs under "New Links/Requests" in your Link Tracking Worksheet.

Thursday: The Art of Link Letters

If you own a website, surely you've seen them: annoying requests for links. Usually they go something like this: "Dear Webmaster. I reviewed your site and feel that it would be appropriate for a link trade. Please add the following HTML code to your home page... after your link is added, we will add your link to our links page."

Most of the time, this type of letter goes straight into the Trash folder. Follow these dos and don'ts to craft link letters that *do* get results and *don't* annoy their recipients:

DO include key information. At a minimum, your letter must include the following: the URL from which you would like a link, your landing page URL, your landing page title, and your landing page description. Remember to choose the best landing page on your site, which, depending on the nature of the linking page, may not be your home page.

DO be straightforward. At the very least, it's going to take a few minutes for someone to add your link to their site. At most it might require a committee review and approval. You're writing to a total stranger and asking for a favor—don't pretend it's anything else.

DON'T offer a link trade. If your site is appropriate for a link, you should be able to get it without a reciprocal link agreement.

DO explain the benefits of the link... Website owners want to link to sites that their site audience will like. Specifically describe how your site relates to theirs.

...but DON'T write a novel. We're talkin' 25 words or less.

DO write from a company e-mail address. Webmasters want to know that you really come from the company that is requesting the link.

DON'T mass mail. Figure out the name of the person you're writing to, and use it. Then, sign with your own name and title.

And finally:

Pearl of Wisdom: DO say Thank You.

A Bulletproof Link Letter

Several years ago, we were doing some link-building efforts for a major media website that had just launched an innovative product. The product was interesting enough that we thought some of the industry thinkers with blogs might want to take a look, and maybe even write a review. So, like Little Red Riding Hood skipping into the forest, we sent out a bunch of our usual perky, polite link request letters.

Hoo boy, were we in for a surprise! Bloggers can be a little bit like sleepy dogs that wake up snapping their teeth. We received some less-than-polite responses: What were we doing pestering them? Who the heck would want this product? Why the heck did we send this e-mail?

Worse, at least one blog actually published the text of our e-mail, with our full name and e-mail address! That could have been more than a little embarrassing.

Luckily—or was it actually foresight on our part?—our letters were carefully written to avoid embarrassment to ourselves or our client. We were eminently polite and professional. We described the benefits of the product without resorting to heavy selling. And we took some time to review the blogs for relevance before sending out our e-mails. Our punishment took the form of exposure, and not worse.

Nowadays, there are blogs on every subject, from lost socks to lost souls, and surely there are some in your industry. At some point in your link-building campaign, you'll probably want to approach one. Keep these guidelines in mind when you do:

- Get to know the blog first. Read it for a while before you approach its owner.

- Remember, it's less about selling your site to the blogger and more about convincing them that your site would be interesting to the blog's readers.

- If you really want a blogger to review your product, you'll have better success if you send them a freebie. Likewise, if your product is on a page that requires a login, consider offering login information for the blogger's sole use. (But don't send out login information in your first correspondence!).

And, finally, imagine your e-mail posted on the blog for the whole world to see. Would this be embarrassing in any way to you or your organization? If so, you need a rewrite.

To make your life a little easier, we've written a sample link request letter for your use. Download it from our companion website at www.yourseoplan.com.

> **Now:** Open a new document and write your own general link request letter including your site's must-have information. Save it in your SEO Idea Bank.

Friday: Submittals and E-mails

You now have the two elements in place that you need for your link-building campaign: a list of quality sites that might be interested in linking to your site and a sample link request letter.

Today, step through the list on your Link Tracking Worksheet and, one by one, personalize and send out your link request e-mails. If you encounter a site with a Contact Us form, it's perfectly kosher to paste your link request e-mail into that as long as you dutifully enter your contact information into the proper fields. As you go, record the date that you requested the link, and who you e-mailed, in your worksheet. You will want this information later if you wish to send a follow-up request.

As the Internet moves away from static websites with links pages to a more dynamic and bloggy existence, you may be wondering if digging through websites and writing so many personalized letters is a feasible method for you. Link building can take a lot of time, and webmasters frequently ignore even the most carefully crafted approach.

We do want you to perform some link requests today, because this type of communication is essential to a well-rounded SEO skill set. But we know you're busy, so we'd like to offer you a few choices about how to move forward with link building for the long term:

Link Building, an Hour a Week In the Hour-a-Week approach, you systematically seek quality sites, make link requests, and document your efforts in your Link Tracking Worksheet. This is the nose-to-the-grindstone approach we have taken for years. It may be a good fit for you if you enjoy documentation, and is especially well-suited to you if you are hitting up an industry that still has a predominance of static websites containing links pages. Choose one day per week as your day to chip away at link building.

Catch-as-Catch-Can This approach is a reasonable alternative if your schedule does not accommodate an hour per week or more of link research and documentation. Not so much a process as a mind-set, the Catch-as-Catch-Can approach requires that you keep an eagle eye out for linking opportunities as you surf the Web and go about your daily business. For example, next time your CFO is quoted in a testimonial on a website, when you check to be sure her name is spelled correctly, you can also follow through on making sure the quote links back to your company's site.

Build It, and Links Will Come Following this approach, you build a useful and interesting website with linkability and social search in mind (as we will continue to coach you to do throughout the Plan) and hope for the best.

 Now: Step through your list of potential linking sites and send link requests to as many as you can. Decide which link-building approach is right for you for the long term.

With a week of link research and submittals under your belt, you're in perfect shape for your online social search debut next week.

Week 4: Social Search and Participation Marketing

There are two reactions we get when we tell our clients that it's time to think about social search. The B2B clients often become noticeably uncomfortable and try to change the subject, while the B2C clients are likely to want to dive right in. Want to know something funny? In most cases, these reactions hold true even when our B2B and B2C clients have no idea what we actually mean by social search. What we mean, by the way, are those Web 2.0 sites that compile human-fueled factors, such as votes, references, or recommendations to help you find sites. We're happy to tell you that—no matter what kind of site you have—there's probably some social search opportunity for you.

Let's demystify:

 Pearl of Wisdom: Social search "optimization" just means trying to get your organization included in online conversations that are taking place outside of your own website.

This week, you'll stop feeling uncomfortable when someone mentions the Social Web, and you'll also identify a participation plan that fits your website. By Friday, you'll be a fully qualified Web 2.0 ninja.

Your daily assignments for this week are as follows:

Monday: Study Hall: Surf the Social Sites

Tuesday: Create an SMO Feed Reader

Wednesday: "No Comment" Day

Thursday: Find Your Voice

Friday: Letting Others Spread the Love

Monday: Study Hall: Surf the Social Sites

Today you'll take some time to get familiar with the kinds of sites you'll come across on the Social Web.

Social Bookmarking Sites These are sites that allow users to give a virtual "thumbs up" to a web page, which in turn allows others to learn about it. Digg, Reddit, and del.icio.us are popular examples. As an online marketer, your goal on sites like these is to get votes for your content. Is your organization doing something fascinating enough, or does your website offer something so unique or so useful that a rising tide of voters will push your site to the top? The best way to get a quick read on these sites is to look at the most popular entries and then compare it to the slush in the "just added" section. Every site has its own special audience (Digg, for example, is popular with gamers and techies), so observing the successes will give you an idea of what content will be well received. You can contrast that with the no-vote entries, like the business owner who posted a press release about his company's great customer service. This should give you an idea of what kind of content is and isn't rewarded.

Blogs Your blog mission is either to get mentioned or to join in the commenting in a way that showcases your smarts and usefulness to your target audience. Niche B2Bs, yes, there is a blog that is at least loosely related to your industry, and yes, your target audience frequents them. Type your top 10 keywords into blogsearch.google.com and see for yourself. B2Cs, even though your keywords are mentioned all over the blog search engines, that doesn't mean that every blog audience has conversion value for you.

Forums The goal for forums is to join in the conversation, become a trusted voice, and keep your organization in that favorable top-of-mind position with your target audience.

Social Networking Sites Not a medium for the time-strapped, the goal for these sites is to make friends and communicate with them on a regular basis. Some examples of social networking sites are MySpace, Facebook, and LinkedIn. The marketing on these sites is mostly B2C (for example, you can be a MySpace friend with Rock Star Energy Drinks). These sites allow you to search profiles, which is handy for finding and communicating with members who have specific interests. They are excellent for plugging your videos or images or blogging about your activities. Not just for job-seekers or 14-year-olds with a band crush, these sites have plenty of potential for promoting events, causes, and all manner of expert consultants.

Interactive features on social sites tend to provide a head-spinning plethora of possibilities. For example, Digg combines bookmarking, video viewing, "making friends," and commenting. You do not need to be on top of every latest tweak to these sites' service offerings in order to make a difference in your organization. Just get in the habit of having a little study hall session prior to doing any actual interacting! That's a good rule of thumb no matter what social media site you're dealing with.

Now: Take a few social media sites for a spin. As a starting point, search for your top-priority keywords to find information that affects you. Pick a few sites that you think might apply to your organization's marketing goals.

Tuesday: Create an SMO Feed Reader

Yesterday you found your target audience and maybe your competitors on the Social Web. (Oh, and did you also find your college sweetheart? 'Cause we're pretty sure you looked!) Today you're going to create a feed reader so that you have updates from these sites in one convenient place.

A feed reader is a tool that receives updates about your favorite sites, and displays the newest content from these sites in a single page. Some feed readers actually download content so you can read it when you're not online, others require a web connection to view.

One of the easiest feed readers around is iGoogle. Easy to customize and simple to navigate, it's a newbie's dream come true. See Figure 7.5 for an example.

Figure 7.5 iGoogle Feed Reader

Other feed readers you might like include MyYahoo!, Sage (a browser add-on), Bloglines, and Rojo. These are all designed for use by normal folk, with easy-to-implement setups. Setting up a feed reader in a readily accessible spot (like your Google or Yahoo! home page) will help you stay current with your soon-to-be favorite blogs and social sites. Being greeted every day by your LinkedIn profile or the latest blog postings by your top competitor will go a long way toward keeping you engaged in the Social Web.

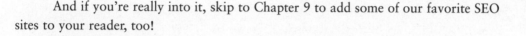

Now: Customize your feed reader with some of your new favorite sites.

And if you're really into it, skip to Chapter 9 to add some of our favorite SEO sites to your reader, too!

xtra
cred

Wednesday: "No Comment" Day

Etiquette is so important on the Social Web that we're devoting a whole day to keeping you from making a dope of yourself. The key is to take your time and read through as much as you can before you even think about clicking the Comment button. The penalty of breaking etiquette takes various forms, including being banned, ignored, or ridiculed. The surest path to this pain is to over-market yourself.

Let's say you're marketing your company's product, a foot massager, and you want to promote it on the Social Web. You used your Study Hall wisely on Monday and found the following four potential outlets:

- Foot Pain Forum
- The Gadget Review blog
- Shoeholic Cecile's blog
- Digg Health News

To the uninitiated, it might seem like a good idea to craft a cookie-cutter marketing spiel such as, "Our Toenado massager is the choice for millions of foot-pain sufferers. With patented 'heal the heel' technology, this massager will erase your pain. Don't pussyfoot around—come to www.toenado.com to buy now!" Then it might seem reasonable to start a new forum thread with this information, post it as a comment in the blogs, and submit your home page to Digg.

But that would be the wrong approach. The moderators of the Foot Pain Forum will delete your posting, you'll make no friends on the blogs, and Diggers won't know you exist.

Approach each venue with a plan:

- For the Foot Pain Forum, find a few folks who could really use some solid advice, and give it. "Oh, I know what you mean about how hard it is to walk the dog. Soaking in warm water is a great cure for this problem, but I also think you might need to contact a board-certified podiatrist about those jabbing sensations." Make sure your signature contains your company name and URL.

- For Shoeholic Cecile's Blog, you'll need to wait for a good reason to join the conversation. After a few weeks, she may complain about her feet hurting after a night on the dance floor. Then, give some nonpartisan advice about foot massagers, *without explicitly mentioning your product*. Again, make sure your signature contains your company name and URL.

- For the Gadget Review Blog, it's best to contact the blogger directly and tell them about your product. If it's valuable for their readers, they'll be interested in giving a review of your product.

- For the Digg category, unless you have something to contribute that's unique, interesting, and absolutely newsworthy, you probably shouldn't even bother. Either wait for some real news (Celebrity Says That Foot Massager Cured Her Migraines?), or put some serious effort into writing an article that sounds interesting and unique (Top 10 Reasons to Keep Your Foot Massager in the Refrigerator?). Another option: Comment on an existing article. Just be sure you follow hyper-strict comment etiquette.

Yep, it's a looong slow curve to the sale. But there is value in being the expert on a particular subject, and putting a personal face to your company can do worlds of good for your branding.

> **Now:** Choose a blog, forum, social bookmarking site, or social networking site and make your first contact: comment, posting, or message.

Thursday: Find Your Voice

One of the most common questions we're asked as SEO consultants is this: Should our company start a blog? The answer is a definite maybe. Not every organization needs a blog, but many organizations can benefit from having a voice on the Social Web. Today we'll help you find yours.

Blogging

Following are indicators that your organization has the capacity to create an excellent blog:

- You produce press releases on a regular basis—once a month or more.
- You currently post "What's New" or "Events" content on your website.
- You have products that change, update, or are released (as in comics, media, magazines, or books) often.

If You're Not the Expert

The exciting thing about the Social Web is that the barrier to entry is low. It's easy to participate and easy to operate, and it doesn't cost any money. But it does require a bit of reprogramming for the traditional marketer. Instead of promoting your company or products, often the venue is better suited to disseminating the thoughts or activities of a single individual in your organization. As an example, new product announcements in the Social Web are far outnumbered by musings, advice, and opinions of CEOs and consultants. Which participants rise to the top? Those with higher-than-average quotients of expertise and personality.

What this means for your organization is that your outreach on the Social Web will need to come from a person—or persons—who are willing to show their real face and use their real name on the Web. Whether posting in forums, writing their own blog, or commenting on another's, this person will need to know their stuff and have passable writing skills.

As the in-house SEO advocate, you may be a bit distressed to realize that the best candidate for Social Web outreach in your organization isn't you. It's possible, and preferable, for you to assist in the coordination of the Social Web outreach efforts, and you can certainly help write some of the blog postings or communications. That said, we believe it's best to keep it as real as possible. There's value in transparency.

Participating in the Social Web can be time-consuming, and ROI can be difficult to track. But it's certainly worth trying. What a wonderful idea, and rife with possibilities, to put a personal spin on your company's image! Perhaps you can nominate someone to fill this role today.

- There are experts or gurus within your organization who could participate in writing blog posts.
- Competitors in your industry tend to do a lot of blogging.

Do you have two or more "yes" answers to the above? You're probably ripe for starting a blog. Fewer than two? We are still convinced that you have something to offer. Read on for some other options.

Participation Marketing

If there's no blog in your future, you can still participate. Here are some indications that you should take the path of *participation marketing*—posting in forums or commenting on other peoples' blogs:

- Maybe you're not a recognized expert in your field, but you know your stuff and can discuss hot topics intelligently.
- You're already into the habit of surfing the same blogs and forums that your target audience frequents.

- You aren't looking for a quick return on investment, such as a lot of sales. Rather, you're content to build up positive branding for your organization, or yourself, over time.

- You have a good grip on forum or commenting etiquette, or you have the time to observe for a while before you post.

Social Networking

While blog creation and participation marketing are good choices for both companies and individuals, social networking sites can be better venues for individuals. Here are some ways to know if creating a profile on sites like Facebook or LinkedIn is a good direction for you:

- Your business goals benefit from keeping in close contact with a number of people, such as former clients or former coworkers. (Independent contractors would fit this description nicely.)

- Your list of accomplishments and work history, as they appear in your personal profile, make a good impression.

- You are a "joiner"—you belong to, or you'd feel comfortable participating in— hobby or professional groups.

- You have a good bit of time on your hands to keep your profile looking up-to-date and to respond to friends' messages so that nobody feels ignored or slighted.

 Now: Determine which, if any, of the social web marketing approaches are best for you and your organization. Dive in a little bit today.

Friday: Letting Others Spread the Love

Remember the story of how Tom Sawyer convinced his friends to whitewash his fence? He made it seem so appealing that everybody wanted to do the work for him. This is an approach you can try with social websites, in a way that's relatively easy to implement.

Here are ways to encourage your own site visitors to promote your website for you:

Social Bookmarking Buttons As easy as dropping a little piece of code on your page, you can add a "digg it" or "del.icio.us" button to your page. See Figure 7.6 for an example. These buttons allow your users to submit your page to these sites, or to give your page a vote.

As the dollar falters, travelers hunt for bargains

Updated 3h 6m ago | Comment ⊟ | Recommend ⬦

E-mail | Save | Print | Reprints & Permissions | **RSS**

By Kitty Bean Yancey, USA TODAY

With the dollar wimping out against the euro and pound — and tumbling to a 31-year low against the Canadian dollar this week — where's a value-minded international traveler supposed to go?

Here's some advice from budget-travel experts on foreign destinations where your dollar still goes far:

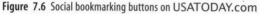
Mixx it
Other ways to share:
Digg
del.icio.us
Newsvine
Reddit
Facebook
What's this ?

⊕ Enlarge   By Omar Torres, AFP/Getty Images

Down Mexico way: The Merida town hall is one of the many architectural delights in the city, where hotels for less than $100 a night are common.

• **Cross the border to Mexico**, but avoid the tourist traps, say *Budget Travel* magazine editor Erik Torkells and Tim Leffel, author of *The World's Cheapest Destinations*.

Torkells found a vacation house on a beach south of Puerto Vallarta that sleeps eight for about $100 a night. "Mexico's still a good deal if you go off the tourism grid," he says.

Leffel recommends going to the interior, such as the architecturally rich city of Mérida, where it's easy to find a hotel under $100 a night and you can stay in "a lot of Colonial (Mexican) mansions that have been fixed up."

Figure 7.6 Social bookmarking buttons on USATODAY.com

Incentives to Top Commenters   If you have user-generated content such as a forum or blog on your website and you want to keep the party hopping, you can create incentives for people to increase their posting or commenting activity level. Forum users can receive a new label in their profile, say, moving from "Newbie" to "Forum Fanatic" as they reach milestones in their number of posts. Top commenters can be featured on the home page.

Photo or Widget Giveaways   Give, and ye shall receive. Give folks a badge, a photo, or a signature to display, and you're giving them a chance to spread the word about your organization. *Widgets*—as you learned in Chapter 4—are great giveaways, too, if you have the resources to develop them.

"E-mail This Page" Links   Just as easy as adding social media links are "e-mail this page" buttons. Welcome to the wide, wonderful world of online word-of-mouth marketing, which is a departure from SEO and might just deserve another hour in your day.

Our main goal for today is that you get creative and open your mind to the possibilities. Florists, make a "bouquet of the day" photo widget. Brick-and-mortar merchants, offer a discount to anyone who blogs about you and then prints out the page and carries it into the store. E-commerce sites, create a contest in which the contestant who posts the funniest product review on a shopping comparison site wins.

Now: Brainstorm ways to encourage your website visitors to spread information about your company.

Success in the Social Web depends on spontaneity, transparency, frequent communication, and being an authority on your subject matter. You could easily spend an hour a day on just social search. We wish we could generate hour-a-day tasks for you, but the Social Web is so dependent on your own offerings that you'll need to make it your own journey. If you want to go the extra mile in social search and participation marketing, follow these Web 2.0 gurus to keep you on the right path:

- Neil Patel's blog at www.pronetadvertising.com
- Dave Evans's articles on www.clickz.com
- www.mashable.com, a social networking blog

You've been at this SEO thing for a couple of months now, and maybe you've even taken a liking to it. Next month, you'll jump into paid search with both feet, get your site wonderfully entrenched in shopping and specialty search, and learn how to research SEO on the Web. Get ready to "establish the habit" of SEO!

Month Two: Establish the Habit

If it's true that it only takes 30 days to establish a daily habit, your SEO habit is now official!

Last month, you tidied up your website's optimization and structure, and started making some online connections. This month, you'll expand on your organic SEO gains with a starter paid search account. You'll take a refreshing dip into specialty and shopping search, and you'll spend a week honing your SEO research skills. It's all part of the clutter-clearing and routine-forming process that will keep your ongoing campaign cruising along.

Chapter Contents

Welcome to paid search with training wheels. This week you're going to develop good habits and a firm grasp of how the pay-per-click (PPC) system works, using a small-budget starter campaign. We can't tell you what "small" means, but whether you choose to invest less than $100 or more than $10,000 a month, we'll provide you with tips and pitfall-avoidance techniques that will help you spend your money wisely.

We recommend that you set up your paid search account and monitor it over the course of three months. This should give you enough time to judge cost-effectiveness, learn what you can expect to get for your money, and decide whether you have what it takes—both financially and administratively—to manage an ongoing paid search campaign.

Even if you're skeptical about the use of paid search in your long-term marketing plans, we still hope to nudge you into trying it for the short term:

Pearl of Wisdom: A paid search campaign can tell you a lot about your audience and your keywords in a relatively short period of time, which makes it an excellent research tool for your organic SEO efforts.

How Do I Choose My Paid Search Budget?

This is one of the hardest-to-pin-down factors of SEO, and one that has as many variables as a high school algebra fair. We'd love to put on our little green visors and help you arrive at the perfect number, but instead we'll have to give you some general guidelines and let you do the thinking:

Ask your boss (or whoever holds the purse strings). Whether you like it or not, somebody may already have a number that you'll have to roll with. Let's hope your paid search campaign pulls in enough conversions to convince them to up the budget when your trial period is over!

Look to your current cost per conversion. Perhaps you already have an idea of what a conversion costs your organization based on tracking for existing online or offline marketing programs. The preliminary research you do this week may help you make an educated guess about how much you'd need to spend on paid search to meet or beat your current cost per conversion.

Consider your competition. You already know whether or not you're in a highly competitive online space. This week, with the help of the paid search service of your choice, you're going to attach some dollar figures to your top-priority keywords. Will you need to spend $0.15 or $15.00 per click to wrestle into the top three paid listing ranks for most of your keywords? The answer will inform your budget-making process.

Think about your own level of enthusiasm. Even though it's likely that your paid search campaign will run smoothly, proper campaign management takes continued interest and effort. Campaigns with larger budgets often have more keywords and more ads, taking more effort than smaller campaigns. If you don't foresee yourself having the ability or time to keep up a large campaign, scale down your budget, along with your expectations for clicks and conversions.

Because it helps you tune into your most productive keywords, a relatively small investment of funds can increase the effectiveness of your organic SEO campaign enormously.

Here are your daily tasks for this week:

Monday: Study Hall
Tuesday: Prep Your Paid Search Keywords
Wednesday: Write Your Ad Text
Thursday: Turn On Your Campaign
Friday: Paid Search Quick Check

Monday: Study Hall

Getting familiar with a new interface, not to mention specialized terminology and guidelines, is an important part of a smoothly run campaign. Today, you'll do your homework and learn about the paid search service you want to use so that you can be a more effective advertiser in the long term.

As a paid search newbie, you may be confused by the many options that sprout up once you fire up the "start a campaign" page. For example, Google offers video ads, local ads, and even radio and newspaper ads through their AdWords service. But we advise you to stick with the basics: text ads displayed in the search engines...the ones that look like this:

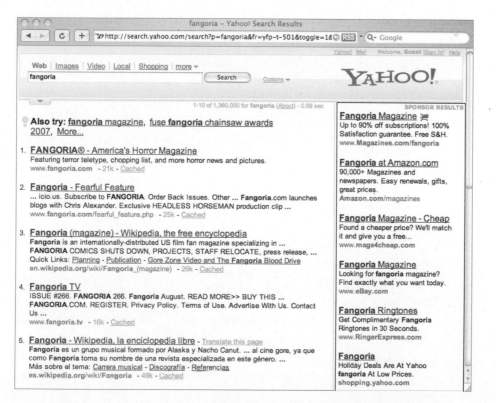

You can pay by the impression, by the click, or even by the conversion. We think you should start with a pay-per-click arrangement, which is likely to be the default setting for any service you choose.

If All Else Fails, Flip a Coin

Having a hard time choosing which paid search service is right for you? As we mentioned in Chapter 4, "How the Search Engines Work Right Now," there are bigger players and there are smaller ones in the search advertising arena. The current big guns in the U.S. market are Yahoo! Search Marketing (YSM) and Google AdWords, with Microsoft adCenter a strong third-place contender. We won't tell you which of the three to choose. We *can* say that unless you have a compelling reason to do otherwise, you should stick with one of these top three services for your starter campaign.

If you are the kind of person who needs to scrutinize the techie details before making a choice, put on your eyestrain glasses and check out the user documentation provided by the paid search services themselves. Yourseoplan.com has links to these and other resources that will help you compare the services. Use these resources to learn about YSM, Microsoft adCenter, and Google AdWords, and decide which is the best match to your needs. The key elements that you'll want to research are outlined in this section.

Now: Finalize your choice of a paid search engine and sign up for an account.

Spend the rest of your time today familiarizing yourself with the inner workings of your paid search service of choice. Next we'll describe the most important elements for you to understand as you attack your PPC learning curve.

Editorial Guidelines

Any respectable paid search service has a list of rules with which your ads must comply. Things like limiting obnoxious SHOUTING CAPITALIZATION or limiting the use of certain terms. In addition to style guidelines, there is a laundry list of products and services for which advertising is not permitted. (Google has a rather long list that includes many fascinating and confounding barred topics such as "e-gold" and "hacking and cracking." Entertaining stuff.) You should also know their editorial procedures: Do they publish your ad right away and review it later? Is there a waiting period before new ads can go online? Do they warn you before they take your advertisement offline, or do they just yank it for violating the guidelines?

Spending Requirements

This probably won't be a major issue if you are planning to use YSM, Microsoft adCenter, or Google AdWords; all three offer very low minimum spending levels. If you are considering another service, be sure that you are willing to cover their minimum spending or activation fee requirements.

Keyword Matching Options

If you love to micromanage, this section is for you. Paid search engines offer a variety of keyword matching controls:

Broad matching Causes your ad to display if searchers combine your keywords with other terms (for example, your ad for "wedding bands" will show when the term "platinum wedding bands" is searched). This may include plural forms of the term, misspellings, and synonyms.

Exact matching Causes your ad to display for the term you are sponsoring, with no changes to word order or plurals (for example, your ad for "wedding bands" will display when someone searches for "wedding bands" or "wedding bands in New Orleans," but not for "wedding band" or "bands for my wedding").

Keyword exclusion Allows you to exclude searchers who use certain words from viewing your ad (for example, if you're targeting "wedding bands," you can exclude people searching for "wedding bands jazz").

Ad Display Options

It's important to understand exactly where and when your ads will be displayed. If you're interested in a paid search service other than the Biggies, make sure they're up front about who they partner with for ad displays. You don't want to discover your ads unexpectedly displaying in annoying pop-up windows that may be detrimental to your branding. Many paid search services also offer these types of display controls:

Contextual vs. search engine display Contextual advertising displays your sponsored ads on a wide variety of websites, not just search engines. Your service should give you the choice of whether you want to include contextual displays. To keep things simple, we recommend turning off contextual advertising as you make your first foray into paid search.

Geotargeting Allows you to display your results to searchers in a particular location.

Dynamic keyword insertion Places the searcher's keywords directly into your ad. You'll learn more about this later when you write your ads.

Dayparting Allows you to specify the times of day your ads will display. A B2B consulting firm may want to display its ads only during the workweek, while the wee hours may be a better fit for sleeping pill manufacturers.

Bid and Position Management Options

Some bid and position management features vary among PPC services. Learn the answers to the following questions about yours:

Adjusting bid prices How do you change bid prices for individual keywords? What about for groups of keywords? Can you set parameters so that your bid automatically increases or decreases based on what your competition is bidding?

Budget caps Can you set daily or monthly budget caps? Can you set limits so that certain bidding or cost parameters are not exceeded?

Controlling position What kind of control do you have over your listing position? As you'll recall from Chapter 4, bid prices are not the only factors at play in determining the position of your PPC listings.

Tracking and Reporting Options

You will probably be pleased with the detail and flexibility of reports you can generate with whichever paid search engine you choose. Your role in paid search reporting will be less about compiling data and more about finessing the report parameters to get at the information you really want. Here are some things to look for: How recent is the data that is included in reports? Is conversion tracking an option? Is there at-a-glance information in your campaign management interface so you won't have to run a report to see how your paid search day is going?

Once your campaign is in full swing, at a minimum, you'll want to do a regular review of the following information:

- Top-performing terms
- Total campaign cost
- Average cost per click
- Total click-throughs
- Click-through rate
- Conversion rate
- Cost per conversion

Be sure you know how to find this information from your PPC service's reporting screen.

Account Services

Some PPC services will help you get up and running by offering setup assistance services for a fee. We generally don't recommend paying for such services, and anyway, you won't need them if you follow the procedures in this week's tasks. However, if you are destined to be a big spender with a PPC service (on the order of $10,000 or more per month), you may be able to get the free services of an account rep who can smooth over some of the bumps in the process.

Your PPC service may ask you to input your keywords and bids, and a starter ad, before you can complete the sign-up process. You can just enter your company name as a keyword for now.

Tuesday: Prep Your Paid Search Keywords

Today you'll compile a list of keywords for your PPC starter campaign. Your top 10 or so target keywords are a starting point, but any terms on your long list from Chapter 6, "Your One-Month Prep: Baseline and Keywords," are fair game.

Targeting the Long Tail

Perhaps you've heard of the "long tail" theory. It describes how our culture and commerce is moving away from a small number of very popular products (or movies or dances or even ideas) toward a very large number of niche products or activities. For example, not terribly long ago there were only three television networks that everybody watched (a short head). Now, there are hundreds of specialty networks, each with a much smaller audience (a long tail).

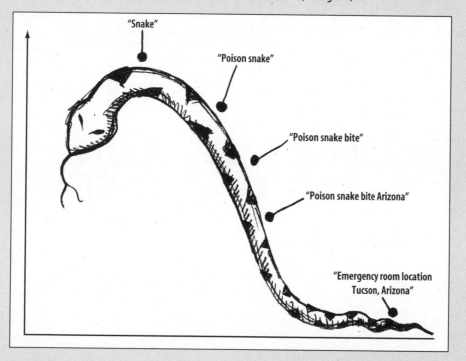

"Snake"

"Poison snake"

"Poison snake bite"

"Poison snake bite Arizona"

"Emergency room location Tucson, Arizona"

How does this apply to Your SEO Plan?

In SEO, a short-head search is something like "motel," while a long-tail search might be "baltimore pool motel airport." The short-head search is very broad and is used commonly, while the long-tail search is very specific and is used much less frequently.

Continues

Targeting the Long Tail *(Continued)*

Compared to organic optimization, paid search makes it much easier for you to target long-tail searchers. Here's why: In organic SEO, each keyphrase you target takes a certain minimum commitment of time and energy, so it wouldn't make sense to put hours of effort into rewriting your site for once-a-month, ultra-focused queries. In a pay-per-click advertising model, on the other hand, you can add your long-tail keywords to your account for free—and pay only when they receive clicks. Why sponsor long-tail searches? For one, they aren't likely to have much competition, which means lower costs per click. For another, by the time a searcher is using a long-tail term, they are probably closer to the end of the buying process. This makes long-tail searchers a very desirable group. Look again at the example: "motel" compared to "baltimore pool motel airport." Maybe you'd get 15,000 clicks for "motel" and only 100 clicks for "baltimore pool motel airport." But if you run a motel near the Baltimore/Washington International Airport with a pool, you're likely to get more reservations from those long-tail visitors.

Experiment with some long-tail terms in your paid search campaign, and you may discover some top performers that become candidates for future organic SEO efforts.

Paid search engines have their own tools to help you figure out which terms you want to add to your campaign and how much you want to spend on each. Today we'd like you to keep your campaign turned *off* while you use your paid search interface to select your keywords.

Choosing Keywords to Sponsor

Since you're starting small, you could easily sponsor just your top-priority keywords. But it won't hurt to include additional keywords you're interested in testing. Review your long list of keywords from Chapter 6. Were there any terms that caused a lot of debate but didn't make the cut? Were there two terms that seemed equally promising? Results of this test campaign will be a great tiebreaker.

How many keywords should you have in your PPC campaign? That depends on two things: your budget, and your desire to stay within the hour-a-day time frame. But we'll throw you a bone with this vague suggestion: somewhere between 10 and 50. For the purposes of this PPC trial period, it's best to keep your campaign smaller so that you can give proper attention to the details.

Assigning Landing Page URLs

Just as with organic keywords, your home page is not necessarily the best landing page for searchers arriving via your paid ads. You've done a lot of work segmenting your target audience, so make sure that your paid search campaign helps you continue this strategy. Match your keywords to the most appropriate landing pages.

Creating Ad Groups

An ad group is a subset of sponsored keywords that all trigger the same ad or ads. Think of ad groups as a simple categorization scheme for your paid search campaign. Since you've got an hour a day to work on campaign creation and maintenance, it would be reasonable to have from three to five ad groups. (Ad group names are not displayed to searchers. They are for administrative use only.) Even though more ad groups require more management and more ads, it's probably better to err on the side of too many categories than too few. Here are possible ways to group your keywords:

By landing page For example, an animal feed distributor may want to create an ad group for its Pet Care Tips page for terms like "overweight dogs" and another ad group for its Horse Care Tips page for terms like "preventing colic in horses."

By target audience For example, our animal feed distributor might create a category called Pet Products for terms like "dog food" and "cat food" and another category called Livestock Products for terms like "bovine feed supplement" and "equine grain mix."

By concept You can categorize based on the needs your product or service fills or the concerns behind the searches. For example, our animal feed distributor might create a category called Low Cost for terms like "cheap dog food" or a category called Pampering for terms like "dog treats" or "dog rewards."

Bidding for Position

If you can swing the bid price, try to land your ads in the top three. (Some studies show that these are the most effective positions.) This way, you'll improve your chance for click-throughs, and you'll be able to judge the performance of your paid search campaign in a more straightforward way.

Naturally, some keywords on your list will be more expensive than others. If it would take too big a bite out of your budget to bid into the top three positions for every one of your keywords, mix it up a little. Bid high on just one or two. You can always change it in a couple of weeks if you don't like the results. You can also consider adding modifiers to your keywords to see if a longer-tail approach is more feasible for your budget.

Estimating Click-Throughs

Predicting paid search click-throughs—especially when you're starting a campaign from scratch—is an inexact science. You can use the estimation tool that your paid search service offers, but don't trust it for more than a very rough ballpark figure. If your boss is breathing down your neck for a specific click-through rate estimate, we'd suggest that you just say no. You can't foretell how successful your campaign will be, but you *can* set up your campaign so that there will be few risks: Start with a low budget and bid price, and focus on fewer keywords. You can gradually increase these parameters until you're comfortable with the results.

Now: Enter your keywords and bid prices for your paid search campaign. Use placeholder ad text (we'll work on ad text tomorrow) and make sure your campaign isn't live yet.

How Pandora Partners, Inc., Miscalculated Cost per Click for Six Months!

We once worked for a client (the name and some identifying details have been changed to prevent embarrassment) who was very enthusiastic about pay-per-click (PPC) because his campaign provided valuable conversions in a very competitive market. We came on board several months after his PPC campaign was in full swing, and we were pleased to see that this client had made his own spreadsheet to track important trends over time.

After a few days on the job, we made an astonishing discovery: Due to an unfortunate spreadsheet error (we're going to be charitable here and call it a typo), this company was working on the assumption that they were paying an average of $3.80 per click as opposed to the actual value of $0.26! Can you imagine how that affected their advertising budget, not to mention their opinion of the value of their PPC campaign? Can you imagine the smoke that rose up from our speedy phone-dialing fingers when we realized what they had been doing wrong?

Even if you're like one of us (hint: not the one of us with a degree in engineering) and gave up math class at an embarrassingly early age, you need to know this simple equation:

Cost per click = (cost) ÷ (# of clicks)

As we've mentioned, any PPC engine provides this kind of data for you. But if you ever decide to create your own reports, you can save yourself a big headache if you take some time at the start to double-check your own formulas against your PPC engine's prefab reports.

Wednesday: Write Your Ad Text

Depending on your talent with words, today may be a fun little excursion into copywriting, or it may be as frustrating as trying to bait a fishing hook with mittens on. If you have writers on your team, this is a great time to include them.

For each of your keyword categories, you're going to create a succinct, compelling ad that is substantially more interesting than your competitors'. You may want to write two or three ads for each ad group if your PPC service rotates ads for you.

Your HTML title and meta description tag for each landing page are a good starting point, but you'll probably need to edit them substantially for PPC use, in part due to editorial guidelines and character limits. You can read your PPC service's guidelines for lots of advice on writing ads (after all, they make money on your click-throughs, so they have every interest in your success!).

Here are some additional tips that we think will help you:

DO use keywords in the text. Studies show that people are more likely to click on your ad if the exact keyword they searched for is incorporated into your ad text.

DO be true to your landing page. Make sure that you write each ad with its intended landing page(s) in mind. Does the ad mention a specific product or solution? The landing page had better contain a clear path to it. Does the ad set up a need? The landing page should tell your visitor exactly how to fulfill it.

DO snoop on your competitors. If you're stumped, and even if you aren't, enter your keywords into the search engines and see what you're up against in the paid search venue. If everyone's ads are mentioning a certain topic, such as their low, low prices, you might not want to ignore it in your own ad. Then again, if you notice that you're competing against a clutch of nearly identical ads, as seen in Figure 8.1, you may want to describe yourself using language that will help you stand out.

Figure 8.1 These sponsored ads for the term "wool cap" look awfully homogenous.

DO use dynamic keyword insertion if it's available... You researched on Monday whether your PPC service of choice allows you to automatically insert searched-for keywords into your title. If a searcher enters the term "halogen bulbs" or "chandeliers," you may want to format your ad to say, "Halogen bulbs and other lighting products" or "Chandeliers and other lighting products" to match the search. This can be a powerful way to attract the attention of your targeted audience.

...but DON'T insert the wrong keywords. If you've ever seen what appear to be inappropriate PPC ads, you can probably blame careless dynamic keyword insertion. It can create almost comical messages like "Tonsillitis: Buy Now at Shop-n-Ship.com."

Likewise, if you're sponsoring misspelled versions of your keywords, skip the dynamic insertion.

DO include a compelling message. What makes your audience tick? Is it price? Is it the hope of succeeding at something or the fear of failing at something? Is it convenience? A desire for quality? A need to fit in, or to stand out? Use your ad text to speak to this need.

 Now: Following your PPC service's guidelines, write your ads.

Thursday: Turn On Your Campaign

It's been three weeks since you sent out your basic site modification requests to your team or tasked yourself with making the changes. Is your site ready for its big debut? If you've finished optimizing your website, your landing pages will be clearly relevant to your paid search ads, and targeted users will be able to find what they need. Don't flip the switch until your site is ready. If your site content doesn't match your advertising campaign, it will confuse or annoy your visitors, and it may be removed by the PPC service for noncompliance of editorial guidelines.

Assuming your site is ready for the trick-or-treaters to come ringing the bell, let's get started. It's best to start this task early in the day so you can check that all is well before you go home for the night.

Here are things to watch out for:

No impressions Don't expect miracles, but do make sure you actually turned on the campaign.

Too many clicks If you're already close to blowing your budget after a few hours, something is out of whack. Either you underestimated the number of clicks your ad would receive (you could have worse problems!) or you entered your bid price incorrectly.

The wrong ad showing up for the wrong keyword It would be a fairly easy mistake to, say, place an ad meant for your Industrial Products category into your Home Products category. Enter some of your keywords into the search engine and view your ads to make sure you haven't made this kind of error.

We do not recommend micromanaging your ads on a daily basis; the PPC engines' bid management tools should make this unnecessary. Regardless, today is a good day to monitor them closely to make sure you haven't made any boneheaded mistakes. Also, seeing your PPC ads online is a moment for celebration in your SEO campaign!

 Now: Turn on your campaign. Check your account later today for errors and unexpected results.

Hey! Where'd Everybody Go?

We spoke with Anthony Severo, founder and managing partner of Vertical Spin, a business intelligence consulting company, to learn more about conversion tracking. One way that Anthony helps his clients is finding out where their site visitors are dropping out of the conversion process.

He explains: "Let's assume that I have a 1 percent overall conversion rate from the moment someone views the keyword on a search engine to the point at which the purchase is completed. That means that 99 percent of the visitors are not converting. This is great data, but you need to get to the next level of detail to take action and optimize the conversion rate. Where are the trouble spots:

- "Is the user not clicking through the ad [on a PPC sponsorship]?"

- "Is the user getting to the site and immediately exiting?"

- "Is the user engaged in the product description but not buying the product?"

- "Are they dropping off in the checkout process?"

Through further analysis and experimentation, Anthony works to discover exactly why users are leaving the site.

For example, "...let's say that 80 percent of the users exit when checking out. This clearly identifies an issue with the checkout process. You can conclude that the visitor is engaged, they found the product they were interested in purchasing, and were ready to buy, but somehow had a problem with the checkout process. This issue could be

- "The checkout process is too tedious and time-consuming.

- "The checkout process has a bug that prevents people from checking out (I experience this more often than you can believe).

- "The visitor continued shopping and somehow got distracted and never came back to check out."

The good news is, "If you can reduce this drop-off by even a few percent, it will greatly increase your conversion rate." Finally, a word of caution from someone in the know: "Tracking tools provide so much data, and you can easily spend hours per day viewing it." For a streamlined approach, focus on the highest-priority metrics:

- "Am I driving visitors to the site?

- "Are they converting?

- "What are my ad costs?

- "What are my revenues?"

Take Anthony's words to heart with a focus on identifying drop-off and tracking actionable data, and your SEO campaign will be sure to flourish.

Friday: Paid Search Quick Check

Every Friday from now until the end of Your SEO Plan, we're going to remind you to check in on your paid search campaign. This weekly Quick Check will ensure that your campaign doesn't go dramatically out of whack over the course of a month. We estimate that your Quick Check will take about 15 minutes.

Here are the steps to include in your paid search Quick Check:

1. Log in to your account.

2. Check your total campaign spending so far for this month. Is your campaign on track to spend your monthly budget on schedule? If you've set your daily budget appropriately, it's difficult to spend too much—but bugs on paid search services are not unheard of. You should also keep in mind that spending too little can be just as bad as spending too much; you want to be right on target. If your campaign is low, you may wish to add more keywords or increase some of your bids. If your campaign is high, reduce bids or remove or disable keywords.

3. For each keyword category, figure out how to sort the list of keywords by total amount spent. Some keywords are going to be naturally more popular and costly than others, so it's probably not realistic to expect that your spending will be distributed evenly among the keywords. If one or two keywords are using up too much of your budget and you don't think they're converting well enough, you may wish to temporarily disable them or lower their bids. Some keywords with extremely high click-through rates may need to be checked on a daily basis. If you've found a keyword that is gobbling up your entire budget, consider moving it into its own ad group so that you can watch and manage it more closely. If you are testing multiple ads for some keywords, review which are performing better.

Your paid search Quick Check will probably become second nature in time, but during Your SEO Plan, we'll remind you each Friday.

 Now: Add a weekly PPC Quick Check to your calendar. If you think you have enough data to review, perform a Quick Check now.

Now, with your site structure improvements in place and your paid search campaign purring, you've never been more ready to get serious about selling through search!

Week 6: Selling Through Search

If we had a nickel for every good company that settles for bad search visibility for their online store, well, we'd have a big shiny pile of nickels. And we'd spend those nickels buying stuff from an easy-to-find online store. This week we're going to push you to move your store beyond "good enough" and into the realm of thoughtful SEO strategy and solid optimization. This week applies to you whether your online store is a stand-alone entity or a component of your brick-and-mortar business. Don't have an online store? Skim through the week anyway. There are pointers here that might apply to you no matter how you're selling your product.

Monday: Store Visibility
Tuesday: The Site that Sells
Wednesday: Shopping Comparison Engines
Thursday: Consumer Reviews
Friday: Brand Busters

Monday: Store Visibility

The very nature of a good online store—rotating content, lots of dynamically generated pages—might be causing search visibility problems. Today you'll assess your store's presence on the major search engines and look for any rough spots that might need smoothing.

Your first stop on the road to a beautifully optimized online store is going to be the major search engines: Google, Yahoo!, and MSN. A quick visibility check will give you a sense of how well your store pages are doing there.

You can get a snapshot of your search engine visibility with a site: search. You first performed this search in Chapter 6 when you were assessing your website indexing. Today, this search will give an overview of your store's presence. If your store pages are on a particular section of the site, search only for that subdirectory. For example, you might perform a search for site:store.yourdomain.com or site:www.yourdomain.com/store/. An example of results is shown in Figure 8.2.

Review the search results for the following:

Number of pages indexed Are all of your product pages listed?

Listing quality gut check Do the listings describe the products in a compelling, click-able way?

Uniqueness of each listing Can you tell what you'll find on each page just by reading the listing?

Currency Are listings describing what's presently on a page, or what was on the page three months ago?

Now: On Google, Yahoo!, and MSN, perform a site: search for your online store pages and assess the indexing and listing quality.

Figure 8.2 Macy's catalog pages in Google

Today's assessment, combined with the rank check you performed in Chapter 6, tells you a lot about your store's search engine strengths and weaknesses. Tomorrow, you'll get to work on any fixes it may need.

Tuesday: The Site that Sells

If your store is underperforming, check to see if any of these common issues might be tripping you up:

Dynamic site pitfalls Many online stores are large, dynamic websites and are susceptible to a specific set of problems. In the case of your store, dynamic site issues can take the form of duplicate content, dynamic URLs with too many parameters, and a lack of unique page titles and meta descriptions. Go back and reread the sidebar titled "Dynamic Site Smarts" in Chapter 7, "Month One: Kick It into Gear," and identify any issues that may be handicapping your site's visibility in the search engines.

The product merry-go-round Are you constantly changing your products around on your home page? Do you regularly add new editorial content and new promotions? Good for you—you're keeping your home page fresh and encouraging repeat visits. But you also may be making your site vulnerable to shifts in rankings as your favorite keywords come and go with the new content. To counteract the effects of ever-changing product descriptions, make sure you've got at least one paragraph of permanent keyword-rich text on your home page, and make sure that the permanent navigation on your home page describes your products in keyword-rich, robot-readable text.

Tracking multiple domains If the e-commerce component of your website is hosted on a different domain from the rest of your website, be sure to tell your analytics program! You don't want your reporting to show that users have exited your site when they've actually entered your store. If this is happening in your stats, talk to your webmaster to determine how to track properly. It may be a bit of a hassle, but it's absolutely critical to maintain accurate tracking when your site shuttles customers from one domain to another.

Product pages = landing pages Ideally, every one of your product pages needs to be a landing page. At a minimum, this means that each page should have a search-friendly URL, unique HTML title and meta description tag, and a keyword-rich product description. Write your product pages for the prospective customer who entered directly from the search engines. This may mean describing your product and your business in more detail than you think you need.

Link wisely Let's say you're selling 1,000 products in a competitive market. You probably won't rank well for every one of those products, so why not concentrate your link authority to the products that have the best shot of breaking out of the pack? Five or so "top sellers" links from your home page might give your most promising pages a juicy boost.

Categorize with care Maybe your store divides your products into logical categories like blenders, frying pans, toasters, and so on. But rather than an inventory list of your products, why not create categories around your audience segments? "For Newlyweds," "For Him," "Gifts for Foodie Friends," and so forth. Each of these segments represents keyword-rich categories, and some very targeted messaging, that you can use to your advantage. Be warned, however, that if you display the same product in more than one category, your web development team may need to do some fancy footwork to avoid creating duplicate content pages.

Now: Identify problems that may be holding back your online store. Think through priorities and identify who you'll need to speak with in your organization to address them.

Spread Too Thin at Butterknife, Inc.

Butterknife, Inc. (the company name and identifying details have been changed), is a labor of love for its longtime hobby chef owner. The site, built using out-of-the-box storefront software, offers about 1,800 varieties of artisan knives and kitchen utensils. Each utensil has something special to offer, and product descriptions are detailed and well written.

Despite all it had going for it, this site had almost no traffic coming from search engines, especially Google. Ranks weren't great, and upwards of 80 percent of the site was in Google's holding pen for unloved web pages, the Supplemental Index. (This index no longer exists—Google combined its primary and supplemental indices in late 2007. We're almost sorry they did, because the pages that used to be in Supplemental were easy to identify as disadvantaged.)

We think that Butterknife, Inc., had such a large percentage of underachieving pages because the site's authority was spread too thin. With only a handful of inbound links, the amount of PageRank to go around simply couldn't support a site with many hundreds of pages. This, combined with the fact that many pages did not have unique HTML page titles, was enough to get the site snubbed by Google.

The best way to handle a spread-too-thin site is described by Google engineer Matt Cutts on his blog: "The approach I'd recommend in that case is to use solid white-hat SEO to get high-quality links (e.g., editorially given by other sites on the basis of merit)." We also recommend a sitewide cleanup of duplicated HTML titles and meta descriptions, and a little extra attention to internal link structure strategies described in Chapter 7.

Butterknife got serious about making positive changes, and after six months its numbers improved: About 40 percent of the supplemental pages were migrated into Google's standard index, and ranks rose significantly. Now that the company has a handle on page authority, they'll soon be a cut above their competitors!

Wednesday: Shopping Comparison Engines

Monday and Tuesday were dedicated to standard search results in the major search engines. Today we'll work on a more specialized family of search: shopping comparison engines. These search engines are primarily found in two different types: components of major search engines and independent shopping search sites. You're probably familiar with all of the big independents, which include BizRate, Shopping.com, Shopzilla, and NexTag. Yahoo!, MSN, and Google all have their own shopping engines as well. In case you're on a tight budget, take heed:

Pearl of Wisdom: Most shopping comparison engines operate on a pay-per-click basis.

Google Product Search at www.google.com/products is one very free exception.

Each of the major shopping engines requires you to submit a product feed. This feed may take the form of an XML document with your product information, such as product description, SKU, availability, and price. Creating a product feed can be a time-consuming process, so for your hour-a-day plan, we recommend starting with a short list—just 5 or 10 of your top sellers.

Shopping feeds have mandatory fields and optional fields. Just like anything else in SEO, the more time you spend optimizing your data feed, the better you'll look compared to your competitors.

Data feed optimization, which is the practice of optimizing and managing data feeds to get the best possible exposure in search results, is a natural complement to SEO. You can read more about it here: http://searchengineland.com/070328-150116.php.

xtra cred

If you don't have the time for full-fledged data feed optimization (if you're a glutton for acronyms, you can call it DFO), consider paying a few bucks a month to a service like SingleFeed (www.singlefeed.com) that will optimize and submit your feed for you.

Not sure whether shopping search is worth the bother? Here are some indicators that you may have success selling through a shopping comparison engine:

- Your prices are competitive. Many searchers use these sites primarily as price comparison engines. If you've got an appealing price (and this includes attractive shipping and handling costs), you might just get those customer click-throughs.

- You have attractive promotions that help your business stand out from the throng. Many shopping comparison engines allow you to enter messages such as "Free Returns!" along with your product information. Use this opportunity to tell the world why your store is better.

- Your website is attractive and professional. You're likely to be shown in the same results set as big-name competitors. If most people using shopping comparison engines have never heard of you, you will stand up to your competitors better if your site has a designer's touch and an air of credibility to it.

- Your product pages load quickly, and your shopping cart system works flawlessly. This may seem obvious, but you're paying for clicks even if shoppers give up on your slow-loading page or abandon your quirky cart.

- You have time to optimize your feed—or money to pay someone else to do it for you.

Now: Choose a shopping engine (why not start with Google Product Search? It's free!) and submit 5–10 products.

Be sure to track the results!

One Cheeky Yahoo! Store

We spoke with Dexter Chow, co-owner with his wife Anna of Cheeky Monkey Toys in Menlo Park, California, about their experiences running a website companion to a traditional brick-and-mortar store.

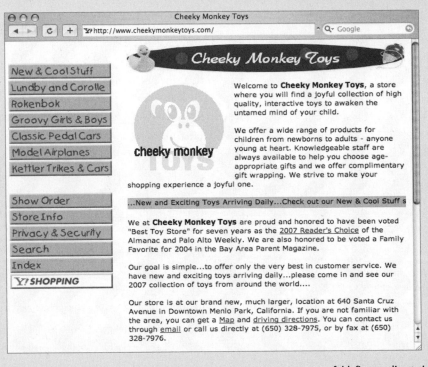

Their goals for the website, www.cheekymonkeytoys.com, are twofold: first, to direct visitors to their brick-and-mortar store with hours and location information, and second, to sell products directly online.

With the heavy demands of running the shop on a daily basis, Dexter simply doesn't have time to learn new web development technologies or search marketing strategies: "If there is a choice in where to spend time, the B&M side gets it." That's why he and Anna chose to use a Yahoo! Store for their website. The Yahoo! Store covers the HTML basics with a built-in editor that allows Dexter to easily maintain the store's product information online, includes e-commerce tools such as order processing, and—perhaps even more important—Cheeky Monkey listings are automatically integrated into Yahoo! Shopping results. Cheeky Monkey does well on Yahoo! Shopping searches "since we're hosted by Yahoo! and get indexed by them and pay money for Yahoo!'s searching indexing."

Many small businesses find the ease-of-use and search integration is worth the added cost of a Yahoo! Store. We think this can be a great choice if it suits your needs. But you don't have to stop there! Content on your Yahoo! Store site (and eBay stores, too) can also be integrated with Google Product Search listings. (For more information on optimizing your Yahoo! Store, read *Starting a Yahoo! Business for Dummies* by Rob Snell [Wiley, 2006].)

You already know that shoppers may leave your site and come back much later to make a purchase. You want to know if these buyers were originally paid shopping engine visitors, so do everything in your power to keep cookies tracking them as long as possible.

Thursday: Consumer Reviews

Online reviews have a lot of influence—a frowny icon or a short stack of stars can be all it takes for a potential customer to pass you by. When you think about it, a positive review is not the easiest thing in the world to attain. Most happy customers go their merry ways and keep their feelings of satisfaction to themselves. It's the disgruntled ones who always seem to find their way back to that "post a review" button. So you'll need to put some real effort into getting your customers to do you the very big favor of spending their precious time writing nice things about you.

Your Reviews: Good, Bad, or Ugly?

Major places to find online product reviews or ratings are Google (it displays its own Google Maps reviews, as well as some sourced on other review sites), Yahoo!, Yelp, NexTag, Epinions, Amazon, and Citysearch. Your business may also fall into a niche that has its own review sites; SnowBoard Reviews at www.boardreviews.com is an example.

Your first task is to find out how your business fares in the sharp-toothed world of online consumer reviews. Visit each of the sites listed in the previous paragraph and search for your business name and location, for example, "Zappy Construction Boston" or "Zappy Construction 02143." This search is likely to bring up your company listing if there is one (although we've seen misspelled business names, so take some time to dig if you don't find your business on your first pass). We don't *really* have to tell you the next step, because once you see a review of your business online, you'll have a hard time tearing yourself away.

> **Now:** Open up each of the review sites listed, find your company, and read the reviews.

If you didn't find a listing for your business, you can add one today—some sites have a free submittal, some do not. Figure 8.3 shows an "Add Your Business" link. See www.yourseoplan.com for a list of submittal links.

> **Now:** Add a listing for your business on any review sites where it's missing. You can skip Google Maps and Yahoo! Local for now—you'll be revisiting these next week during your Local Search optimization day.

Figure 8.3 Add a business on Yelp.

Accentuate the Positive

Here are some ideas for cultivating positive reviews:

Come right out and ask. If you have happy customers, a polite request for a positive review is not bad etiquette—it's good business sense. Send a follow-up e-mail after you've shipped your product. On your "thank you" page, mention how much you'd appreciate a review. Print a reminder on your packing slip. And while you're asking, make it easy to follow through! Provide your customers with a link to the reviewer page.

Send a freebie. If you've got a new product and you'd like to generate some reviews in the blogosphere, you might try sending freebies out to the bloggers whom you've been tracking as part of your social search efforts last month. As with any contact you make in the blogosphere, use great care when you stick your neck out: Only send your products to bloggers who have a reason to care about your product, and who you feel are likely to respond positively. While you can ask them to consider posting a review on their blog, don't make demands. Freebies should be sent with no strings attached.

Follow your reputation. Keeping an eye on your reviews is a fairly straightforward task. Bookmark some websites, search for your company name, and read what you find. You might even consider assigning this task to an intern or administrative assistant who can collect reviews from several sites and compile them into one document for you to read once a week. (For example: Sybex, the publisher of this book, generates a regular report called "What They're Saying on Amazon.") You'll benefit from knowing your online reputation, and you'll also benefit from knowing which locations on the Web might need a little extra effort on your part. For example, if your Epinions reviews are lukewarm, you can work extra hard to drive your happy customers to post positive reviews there.

Give a little guidance. Not everybody feels confident about their writing skills. You can help by politely providing "talking points" to your potential reviewers. We're not suggesting that you write your own reviews, but you can say, "We'd be honored if you'd consider mentioning our fast shipping when you review us on NexTag." And it never hurts to provide simple instructions on exactly how to create a review.

Write your own review. Really? Seriously? Yes, you read it correctly. It's OK to write yourself a review if, and *only* if, you clearly identify your relationship to the business. Introduce yourself and your business, and thank your customers in advance for helping you make your business better. Keep it simple, and you'll avoid any breach of etiquette or ethics that a self-review can tread perilously near.

Don't tempt fate if you don't have what it takes. Reviewers on the Web have a lot of power, and a vicious review can carry a lot of influence. That's why we recommend taking an objective look at your product, your customer service, your order fulfillment time—in short, any aspect of your e-commerce experience that could be commented on. If you're not ready—say you've just had a massive turnover in your customer service department or your supplier is causing a delay in shipping—don't put yourself out there with freebies and shopping search listings.

Stomach the negative. As the Yelp website states, "Negative reviews can feel like a punch in the gut." When you run across a particularly spiteful one, here are a few steps you can take to mitigate the situation:

- Step up your efforts to crowd it out with positive reviews. Here's a tip: If the offending review is displayed on Google Maps but is sourced from another site, a positive review posted *directly* on Google may be more prominent.

- Resist the urge to respond in your own defense—this only makes you look worse. If you must respond, stick to expressing your gratitude for the feedback.

- Check the review site's editorial guidelines to see if the review violates any. It probably won't (mean, nasty, and crazy talk is within bounds here), but if the review contains personal attacks, second-hand information, or bigotry, you have a chance of having the review removed.

Paying for Blog Reviews

Although it is clearly contemptible, no-good, sleazy, and slimy to pay for a positive review on a consumer-generated review site, there is some wiggle room in the area of paying for blogger reviews. Services such as PayPerPost, SponsoredReviews, and ReviewMe connect businesses with bloggers who are willing to write about their product—for a fee (ranging from roughly $50 to $200, last we looked). ReviewMe differs from other services of this sort in that it requires the blogger to disclose the paid relationship, which keeps it out of the ick zone. However, if you choose to go this route, be aware that the links in the reviewer post will probably be considered "paid links" in Google's ranking algorithm, so don't expect a ranking boost from them.

Whether you do all of the above or nothing at all, try not to dwell on the negative review or two you receive. There are always bound to be a few chuckleheads out there!

Now: Determine who in your company has the opportunity to politely ask for positive reviews. Determine which venues you will pursue and help craft the requests.

Friday: Brand Busters

Now: Before you get started on today's task, don't forget: It's Friday, time for your paid search Quick Check! See Friday of Week 5 in this chapter for instructions.

You might have a trademark on your product name, but that's no guarantee that your branding will hold up to your standards in the search engines. Today, you'll do something akin to looking at yourself in the dressing room mirror during swimsuit season—you'll scrutinize your search presence to find flaws in your branding. Squint if it makes you feel better—we're going in!

Affiliates and resellers If you're relying on other websites to help you sell your product, there's always the possibility that they can outrank you in the search engines. This is not necessarily a problem; however, you should check in periodically to make sure you're being represented in a good light. Take some time today to look through your affiliate listings, and make sure the wording in their listings matches your expectations (and any contractual agreement you might have in place). Another thing to look out for is algorithmically generated product matching features on your reseller sites. We once had a client whose high-end kitchen gadgets got mingled in an Amazon category with dog toys from another company with a similar name. This caused a lot of confusion with people who didn't know any better—even *we* thought they sold dog toys for a while!

Now: Find search engine listings for your affiliates and/or resellers. Review the accuracy of the text. Click through to make sure the product page looks as it should.

Your competitors There are a few ways your competitors might be trying to outrank you for your own brand name. One old trick is a product comparison page, in which your competitor creates a page chock-full of instances of your product name. The sneaky—but perfectly legitimate—goal is to rank well for your name, then draw people to their website, and convince your potential customers to buy their product instead. See Figure 8.4 for an example. Another thing they might do is sponsor your product name in a paid search campaign. Editorial guidelines may prevent them from displaying your product name in their ad, but they can still display a targeted message to your audience.

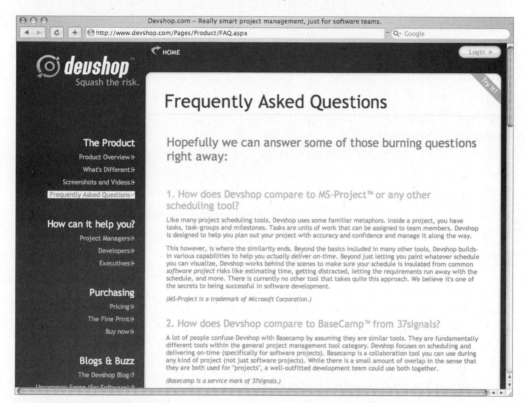

Figure 8.4 Devshop has optimized this page for its competitors' names, MS-Project and BaseCamp.

Now: Search "compare [your product name] and [your competitor's product name]." See if you can find a competitor's page optimized for your own product. Next, search for your product name and scan the paid search listings. Did a competitor's ad show up? They're sponsoring your name in their paid search campaign!

Your exes A web page can live well past its freshness date. This may be a problem if your product name, your distributor, or your feature set has changed over time but the pages describing it have stayed the same. Chances are good that an old page like this isn't going to outrank your vibrant, well-optimized, and well-linked website, but you should scour the top 20 or so search engine listings for your product name just to make sure nothing noticeably bad is happening.

What to do if you find something that made you wince? You have some options. Much of what you find will probably be unintentional, and probably nothing will be illegal, so you could try to approach the brand-busting sites and ask nicely for a deletion or a revision. For the intentional ones, you could try to beat them at their own game. Why not create a product comparison page or a pay-per-click ad, especially if you know your product will compare favorably to your competitor's? If neither of these options feels right to you, remember that living well is the best revenge. Create a well-optimized site, and make sure the listings you *do* control make you look good!

Week 7: Specialty Search

By now, you've got a good inkling of how your target audience behaves in its natural habitat. This week we'll help you develop an optimization plan that reaches those searchers who are looking beyond the standard text listings. Targeting special searchers like blog browsers and video junkies can grow to become a significant portion of your organic SEO efforts. Think of this week as a menu of new ideas—we hope you'll find some of them appealing enough to pursue.

Monday: Image Search
Tuesday: Local Search
Wednesday: Blog Search
Thursday: Video Search
Friday: Special Opportunities in Google

Monday: Image Search

Searches for images and photos comprise a modest portion of the overall search activity online. Optimizing for image search is not usually a critical element in an SEO campaign, but it's one of the many helpful activities that may push your site to the next level of optimization. Even if you don't think image optimization matters for your site, consider doing it anyway. Image search optimization can be so quick and easy that there's hardly a reason *not* to partake. Here are a few indicators that your site is a good candidate for an image optimization push:

- One of your site's differentiating factors is its images. Are they especially interesting, unique, or numerous? (Photographers, event planners, and talent agencies are some examples of businesses that should look seriously into image optimization.)

- Querying any of your target keywords brings up images at the top of the standard search results. See Figure 8.5 for an example.

Figure 8.5 Images in Yahoo! search results for "hot rod"

- Your business sells products that translate into compelling photographs.
- Bloggers and designers are among your target audiences.
- You have a strong interest in reputation management.

If any of these apply, don't overlook image search as a way to snag some targeted visitors.

We would be remiss if we didn't mention this important caveat:

Pearl of Wisdom: A portion of image searchers are only looking for pictures to decorate their blog posts or MySpace pages.

If you think your images are attracting this group, don't put too much effort into image search unless you feel that your site has a good chance of converting cut-and-paste photo scavengers into paying customers. Your analytics should show you whether folks referred by image search are a desirable lot.

Image Search Basics

Google, Yahoo!, and MSN each have pages that allow users to search strictly for images. Generally these are reached by selecting the "images" option from a navigation bar at the top of the search results page. See Figure 8.6 for an example.

| Web | Images | Video | News | Maps | MSN | More ▾ |

Live Search   [   ]   (Search Images)   Options ▾

Figure 8.6 Image Search Tab on MSN's Live Search

How many people are using image search? Last we checked, usage of Google's Image Search property was roughly 15 percent of its overall search. Sound paltry? Think of it this way: Fifteen percent of an enormous feast is no small potatoes.

More important, Google, Yahoo!, and MSN all mingle image search results into standard search results. That means your target audience may be seeing image search results, even without clicking on the "images" tab.

Now: Go to one of the major search engines and try some image searches for your top target keywords.

If what you see in the search results makes you eager for a way in, read on for image optimization tips.

Image Optimization

We all know that search engines can't read or understand images. So to rank images, they scout around for clues: text in critical locations tied to the image file and surrounding the picture on the page. To get the image search rankings you desire, be sure to include keywords in these important spots:

Image file name For example, if your image is a photo of an oscillating fan, the file name oscillating-fan.jpg says it all!

Captions directly beneath or above images For example, "Our 6-inch oscillating fan fits perfectly in a kitchen window" makes a clear and keyword-rich caption.

ALT and TITLE tags Use them both, and it's OK if you use an identical ALT and TITLE tag on the same image. Don't stuff them with keywords, though—one keyword is the max for these tags.

Text links pointing to the image For example, "<u>click for larger picture</u>" contains no keywords, but "<u>Oscillating Fan — View Larger Photo</u>" provides keyword-rich, and descriptive, clickable text.

Text on the same page as the image When a caption isn't enough, you can always add a longer description of the photo in the body of the page.

SEO with Flickr

Yahoo!-owned Flickr is a photo-sharing site and Web 2.0 phenomenon. This site allows anyone to create a profile and upload photos for sharing. Besides being a well-trafficked site, Flickr sometimes displays in standard search results—with particular prominence on Yahoo!, of course. We spoke with small-business SEO expert Matt McGee about strategies for business marketing on Flickr.

Commercial promotion on Flickr goes against its terms of service (here are the exact words on the website: "Flickr is for personal use only. If we find you selling products, services, or yourself through your photostream, we will terminate your account."), so just like other social media sites we've discussed, it's wise to tread carefully. "My advice is always to focus first on contributing to the community," says Matt, "and that applies to whatever social media you're using. Flickr obviously wants the community to grow, and if you're becoming a valued member of your groups, the other members will want you around, too."

Look to Flickr for a participation and engagement style of marketing, not a hard sell. Here are some of the ways to optimize your Flickr presence for search:

- Become an active participant in the Flickr community. Join groups, create favorites, and comment on photos. "There are groups for just about everything under the sun: boating enthusiasts, pet lovers, tech geeks, architecture mavens…you name it."

- Keep the sales text to a minimum: This is a place to share photos, and any marketing should be a fringe benefit. "Market without making it look like you're marketing, by focusing on giving to the community, not trying to get stuff from it."

- Tag your photos with target keywords, and use the Flickr geotag tool if your photos are location specific.

- Write a keyword-rich description for each photo. You may also wish to include links within your photo descriptions.

If this brand of participatory self-promotion sounds like your cup of tea, Flickr might be just the venue for you. You can find many more Flickr tips on Matt's website at www.smallbusinesssem.com.

Now: Look at the images on your top landing pages. Starting with the most promising ones, figure out where you can add keywords, and communicate your edits to the person who can make the changes.

Getting well-placed keywords around your images is a great start. Here are a few additional steps you can take to maximize your image search presence:

- Check and see how your images look when they're reduced to thumbnail size. Readable? If not, consider recropping or upping the contrast for a better presentation in image search results.

- Verify with your webmaster that your server settings allow image search engines to display your pics. And make sure that he or she didn't do something silly, like exclude the /images/ folder using the robots.txt file.

xtra cred • For those of you with a verified Google Webmaster Tools account, take an extra minute to check the "Yes" box under Tools > Enable enhanced image search. This will throw your site's images in the mix for tagging by actual humans. (Does labeling images sound like your idea of fun? Join the party—and see Google's ingenious game designed to improve its image search relevancy—at http://images.google.com/imagelabeler.)

Now: Consider additional image search optimization steps.

Your site has the primo images, and now you know how to flaunt them! Next stop, local search, where you can target a hometown audience for conversions.

Tuesday: Local Search

In Chapter 2, "Customize Your Approach," we talked a bit about the wonders of local search. Been waiting in line for coffee too long? Pull out your wireless PDA and search for another café in the vicinity. Sitting at home on a Saturday night? Order pizza and a video directly through the Web (and while you're there, join a local interest group on Facebook!). What's good for the searcher is even better for the search-savvy local business owner. Even if your organization doesn't have a brick-and-mortar component, if there's any local component to your business, you want to tackle local search today.

You'll focus today on the major search engines. Google, Yahoo!, and MSN all show local search results within standard listings for certain searches. For example, type **boston bakery** into Yahoo!, and at the top of the screen, you'll see prominently featured local results (see Figure 8.7).

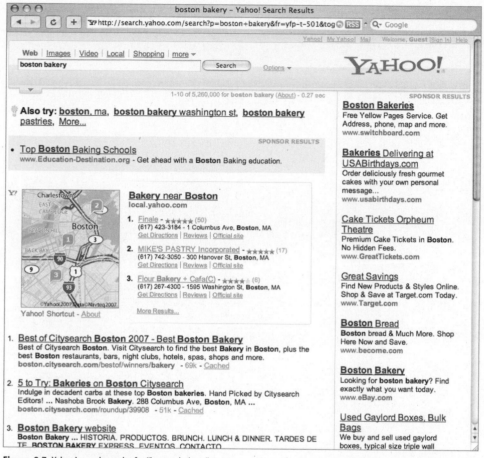

Figure 8.7 Yahoo! search results for "boston bakery"

Wouldn't it be nice to be listed there, maybe even with some sizzling five-star reviews next to your company name? Here's how to get started:

Make your own listing. Surf the major search engines' local sites—Yahoo! Local, Google Maps, and MSN Live Local—to see if your business already has a listing. If no listing exists, or yours needs an update, it's free for you to make the submittal. Check www.yourseoplan.com for submittal URLs.

We'd like to see you get the most bang for your buck, so to speak, on these free local search listings. Fill in all the extra information you can: hours of operation, languages spoken, and so on.

Beautify your listing. Your listing needs some bling! It's easy to upload photos on Google, Yahoo!, or MSN, so why not give your local search surfers one more reason to visit your business? (Square photos work best—upload one today!) Then, remind one of your adoring customers how much you'd love a review.

Integrate location info on your site. If your website's main job is to drive walk-in traffic, be sure to include your business address and phone number on all pages of the site. This is easy to accomplish using a footer or template, and sends the search engines a strong message about your whereabouts. Include variations of your locality keywords (such as "WA" and "Washington"), and don't forget the importance of neighborhood names. If your business operates out of several locations, create a separate landing page for each spot.

There is a special address format called hCard that might help search engines recognize your contact info. See Chapter 10, "Extra Credit and Guilt-Free Slacking," for details.

Explore localization in paid search. It's easy to test-drive a local paid search campaign. Just follow your paid search service's instructions for selecting your targeted geographical areas, and assign a budget for testing. Keep in mind, though, that if your local competitors include national retail chains, at least one PPC expert, Kevin Lee of the search marketing firm Didit, believes local PPC could be an uphill battle. When we asked Kevin what's coming up in local search, he shared these insights:

"My opinion is that for many sectors, the national players will be the dominant players in the local search marketplace. They have brand names, and this gives them an advantage in the hybrid PPC auctions. Dominos and Pizza Hut can coordinate locally targeted campaigns and have significant resources. The local pizza place may also advertise, but there is only room for half a dozen pizzerias in the search result. So, the number of local players involved in an area doesn't increase revenue to an engine. Kinkos, Sir Speedy, and AlphaGraphics can also coordinate aggressive localized campaigns, making it difficult for the local business owner to break into the results profitably.

"For professional services, there are not many national companies, so local players will be active. However, once again, there will only be two or three Atlanta divorce attorneys who pay enough to be at the top and get most of the clicks."

See yellow. According to an industry press release, online yellow pages usage is growing with each year. Better yet, the majority of yellow pages searchers are reported to actually follow through with an in-store visit! Most online yellow pages sites have some form of free business listing available. Here are some to try:

- YELLOWPAGES.COM
- Yellow Book
- Superpages
- R.H. Donnelley

Now: Update or create a local listing for your website on the local site of your choice.

Besides being bringers of targeted traffic, your local listings are recognized by search engines as inbound links. That's an all-around plus for your site's search presence!

Wednesday: Blog Search

Last month, you explored whether starting a blog would be a good idea for your organization. Blogs have their own special search engines—Technorati, BlogPulse, and Google Blog Search are the biggest players. Today, you'll learn how to plan and optimize your blog for success on these specialized sites.

Basics of Blog Optimization

The on-page optimization you've already implemented provides a strong start to your search engine presence. But your blog optimization needs to go a few steps further to take advantage of the increased opportunities in search that blogs offer.

Since every one of your blog postings can be considered an equally important landing page, optimization rules are best thought of as best practices that apply to every post. Here are a few touch-points. Try to follow as many of them as you can, as often as you can:

- Include keywords in your blog name. Many of your inbound links will use the name of your blog within the linking text, so this will provide a rankings boost.
- On your home page, include a tagline or other permanent text describing the blog. Since blog home page content is always changing, a basic description of your blog will provide consistent text for search engine robots to find.
- Write posting titles that describe the content of the post and form a complete thought. Often, these titles (rather than HTML titles) will be displayed on blog search engines as the clickable text. See Figure 8.8 for an example
- Include keywords in your posting title.
- Include a compelling teaser or summary of the post in the first line of each posting (100–200 characters). Often, this text will be used as the descriptive text in blog search engines or feed readers.

Now: Take a look at your most recent blog post. How many of the best practices listed here did you cover?

If you've discovered that your posts aren't making the grade, today's the day to set up your new standards for the future.

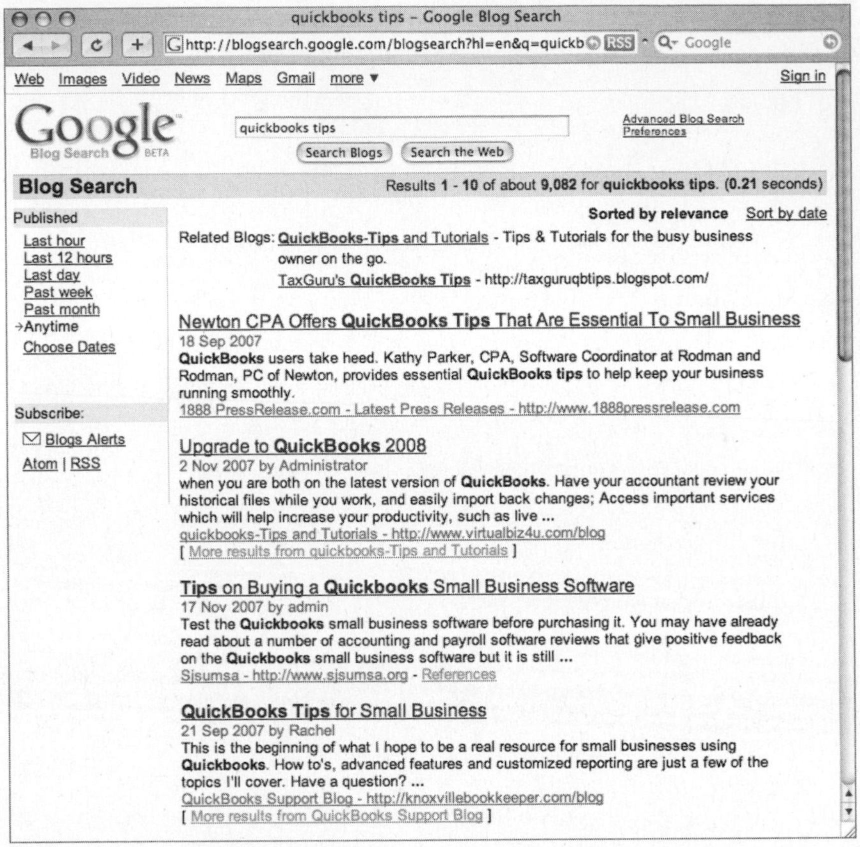

Figure 8.8 Google blog search for "Quickbooks tips." Keywords make the listings compelling.

Plug-in Power

Your blog post pages probably have a default HTML title and description built in. But you shouldn't settle for "default" optimization. We want you to dig deeper into SEO options.

If your authoring tool doesn't allow you to edit individual HTML titles, get a plug-in that makes it possible. In WordPress, a plug-in called "All-In-One SEO Pack" does the trick. Word on the street is that your HTML title should follow this pattern: {Post Title}:{Blog Title}. But we think it works just as well the other way around. Better yet, take the time to individually write titles and descriptions for each post. This applies to you especially if you tend to give your postings nondescriptive titles like "wow!" (But you should really stop doing that if you're going for high-quality search listings.)

 Now: If your blog authoring tool does not allow individual title tag edits, find a plug-in and set it up today.

With title tags squared away, explore more customization options. For example, if you use WordPress to write your blog, here is a sampling of what you can accomplish with free plug-ins:

- Edit each post's meta description.

- Automatically update your XML Sitemap and ping Google when you write a new post.

- Apply permalink redirection to give your posts search engine–friendly URLs.

- Add a tagging system to your posts. Tags are a snazzy spot for keywords!

- Display content related to the search queries that brought your audience to the blog. (For example, "Searching for 'wholesale green clay'? You might like this related post…")

Here are a few places to read up on available options for your blog:

- http://wordpress.org/extend/plugins/

- http://plugins.movabletype.org/

- http://community.livejournal.com/lj_design/

Now: Explore plug-in or customization potential for your blog.

Blog Promotion

Your blog promotion efforts can range far beyond on-page optimization. If you're ready to get even more bloggerific, here are a few promotion directions you should explore:

Reach Out. Like any site, your blog needs inbound links. *Unlike* other types of sites, blogs exist in the midst of a wildly link-happy environment.

Last month you learned about getting social in your online marketing efforts. For bloggers, this social element is mandatory.

Pearl of Wisdom: The best way to get your blog noticed is to actively participate in a community of bloggers.

Today, we want you to set a blog outreach goal that feels realistically within your capabilities. Can you join one conversation outside your own blog per week? How about writing one pithy comment a month? If even that sounds too hard, here's an easier assignment: Once a week, make a point of linking to another blog from one of your posts. Bloggers notice those links and are likely to reciprocate once in a while.

Submit. On www.yourseoplan.com, you'll find links to blog and podcast search engines to which you should submit your site. Luckily, these submittals are generally quick and easy. There are no titles and descriptions to craft, just a URL to submit.

Pay special attention to specialty lists. Your weekly sermons should be listed at Godcast.com, and your deep-sea fishing advice will fit right in at codcast.net. Just kidding...better try sportsblogs.org.

Make some news. If your blog contains regularly updated, unique, original content, it may qualify to be included on a news search engine such as Google News. Your site will be reviewed by an editor before inclusion, so don't waste your time or theirs with a submittal unless your content truly is news!

Blog your 'cast. Some podcasting tools include creation of a blog that goes along with your podcast. This is a great opportunity for you to write accompanying text for your podcast or videoblog files. An example is shown here:

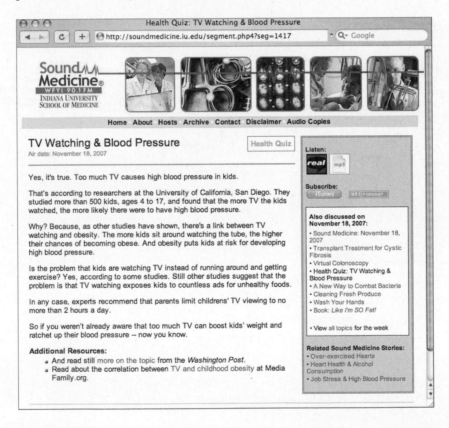

Potential subscribers will appreciate being able to read a description before downloading your podcast, and search engines will enjoy the tasty text treats you throw them in your synopses.

Account for yourself. We think all bloggers should set up accounts on major social media sites (del.icio.us, digg, StumbleUpon, Facebook, and so on), as well as any blog search engines that will let you. Take advantage of the opportunity to brand your profile with details about your blog and links to your blog posts. Technorati will even allow you to officially "claim" your blog and take some control over how your blog listings look in search results on the site.

Now: Determine if any of the expanded blog promotion ideas listed here are for you, and get started!

Feeding a Hungry Web

Most blogging tools will automatically create a *feed*, which is simply a text file listing information (title, description, permalink, and so on) about each of your posts. Originally developed for syndicating content, feeds are now a major distribution venue for all web content, with some savvy consumers ditching the surfing part of their web experience altogether and opting to let content come directly to them via a feed.

There are zillions of ways to optimize and promote your feed. Lucky for you, one website ties them all together: Google-owned FeedBurner.com. If you have a feed, set up an account at FeedBurner and follow their advice to the T.

Thursday: Video Search

If your website offers videos—whether they're local celebrity blooper reels or ultra-techie product demonstrations—you'll want to put some energy into video search optimization.

There are two broad categories in video search: video-sharing sites and video search engines. Generally speaking, video-sharing sites require you to upload your videos, while video search engines index the videos from your website but don't host them. Some video sites (such as YouTube) display results only from within their own database, while others (such as Google Video, Yahoo! Video, and Blinkx) display results from a variety of sources. See Figure 8.9 for an example of video search results.

Visit www.yourseoplan.com for a handy video search engine chart.

Video strategies can be boiled down to two approaches:

- Uploading your video for viewing on video-sharing sites.
- Optimizing your video for video search engine robots, and setting up a video feed. This approach means that videos can be viewed only on your website.

Here's some help figuring out which approach is right for you.

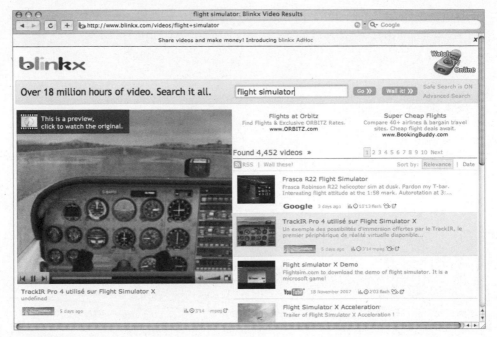

Figure 8.9 Video search results on Blinkx

To Upload or Not to Upload

Sometimes, we're amazed at all the original content people are just *giving* away to YouTube. Other times, we're shocked that a company *wouldn't* want to upload videos that could be useful in promoting their services. To decide whether video uploads are a good strategy for your organization, ask yourself these questions:

- Are these videos directly or indirectly promoting my business?
- Are these videos branded, and do they provide a clear identification of my organization and website?
- Would it be OK if these videos displayed on a total stranger's blog, with no link to my site or other identifying message?
- Am I completely comfortable with the terms of service of the upload site? (Yeah, we don't read those either. This time, you should.)
- Would I be happy if this video started showing up among standard search results, possibly even higher than my website?

If you answered "No" to any of these questions, then a video upload is probably not in your organization's best interest.

 Now: Decide whether your strategy will include video uploads, or keep videos on your site.

Spiders and Feeds

If your videos exist primarily to engage, inform, or entertain your website visitors, and not as stand-alone marketing entities, then you probably want viewers to always see them on your site. That means you'll need to forgo the upload option and stick to video search engine sites.

Here's an unpleasant truth:

Pearl of Wisdom: You can't trust search engines to come spider your videos.

All things considered, we think a well-crafted feed is your best bet for video submittals. Media RSS (MRSS) is the spec for syndicating videos. Start your journey—and view lots of helpful samples—at http://search.yahoo.com/mrss.

Google Video Sitemaps, introduced in late 2007, are another option for video submittals. Learn more about Video Sitemaps in Chapter 10, "Extra Credit and Guilt-Free Slacking."

Video Optimization

So, you're making a feed or hoping for a spider to come find your videos. Or, you're uploading and looking for some notice from the masses. Here are some places to include your nicely dressed, keyword-rich messaging (most of these tips apply both for videos on your site and for video uploads):

On-page text and links to the video   First and foremost, make sure all the videos on your site are presented on individual URLs. Text surrounding the video file, and links pointing to it, give contextual help to search engines, so include keywords there. If you're going the uploading route, you may not be able to control a great deal of the on-page text for uploaded videos, but you can certainly point keyword-rich links from your site to the pages containing your uploaded videos.

Video file name   Just like search-friendly URLs for HTML pages, video file names should contain descriptive terms, separated by dashes.

Video file metadata   Many video-production/encoding tools allow the input of metadata in the video file itself. This can include content-specific elements such as title, description, or even a text transcript, and can also include technical information such as format/encoding quality. If you have control over these elements, be sure to include keywords.

Media RSS enclosures   Naturally, this applies only if you're hosting videos on your site, not uploading. Of particular usefulness in SEO are the <title>, <description>, <keyword>, and <text> enclosures in your MRSS feed. We've already given you guidelines for title, description, and keywords tags for your web pages in Month One—that advice

xtra
cred

applies to tags that are describing your video content, too! Go back and reread Week 1 for a refresher course in writing good titles and descriptions if you need to. As for the <text> enclosure, that's a great opportunity to include a full-text transcript of your video, if you can.

Audio in the File

This may sound a bit *2001: Space Odyssey*, but some video search engines do use voice recognition as a part of their algorithm. While you probably don't want to alter your actual video content to include keywords, a voice slate containing target keywords may be a reasonable approach.

There's much more to learn when it comes to video promotion online. Here are a few of our favorite online resources:

- "Video Marketing on YouTube.com," at http://www.searchmarketingstandard.com/blog/2007/08/video-marketing-on-youtubecom.html
- "Promoting your video" in the YouTube FAQ, here: http://www.google.com/support/youtube/bin/topic.py?topic=10529
- "blinkx Video SEO White Paper" at http://www.blinkx.com/whitepapers

 Now: Look at your currently hosted or uploaded videos, and find opportunities for optimization improvement.

Friday: Special Opportunities in Google

 Now: Before you get started on today's task, don't forget: It's Friday, time for your paid search Quick Check! See Week 5 of this chapter for instructions.

We hear a lot of questions about special results within Google. That's why we decided you should spend a day wrapping your brain around some of the quips and quirks of the world's favorite search engine. Today, you'll learn about these features, find out how important they are to you, and arm yourself for future tectonic search-result shifts:

- Universal Search
- Google Base
- Google Sitelinks

Universal Search

There are lots of separate specialty search engines, a.k.a. verticals, within Google. Book search, blog search, image search, finance, patents, and so on, can all be accessed and enjoyed on their own happy home pages. But like that high school kid who hangs out with the jocks at lunch and the deadheads after school, Google just loves breaking paradigm. So Google blends its search results, a system that's modestly titled Universal Search.

As you saw earlier this week, Google often displays local, image, and video results within its standard search listings, and you've already gotten a great start on optimizing for each of these. Since Universal Search is highly subject to change, we can't tell you whether tomorrow will bring other results such as blogs, catalogs, and scholarly articles thrown in the mix. So today you'll search each of your top keywords using *any* vertical search that is relevant to your organization. Look for a list at www.google.com/options/. Even if blended results aren't currently showing up for your target keywords, good ranks within the vertical will have you well placed for any future display tweaks.

> **Now:** Check ranks for each of your target keywords on the Google specialty search vertical(s) of your choice. Make a note of status in your Rank Tracking Worksheet.

Google Base

Google Base is a free service that allows anyone to upload information such as lists of products, recipes, real estate listings, classified ads, and just about anything else. Google will display links to Google Base listings at the top of search results for certain queries, such as "{location} real estate" or "{type of food} recipe." See Figure 8.10 for an example.

Figure 8.10 Google search results for "New York Real Estate"

For sure, if one of your target keywords is displaying Google Base results, you should speed on over to http://base.google.com/ and set up an account. Even if you aren't seeing Google Base results now, be prepared to see them in the future.

Now: If you think Google Base is an option for your organization, go set up an account.

Google Sitelinks

Sitelinks is Google's name for those secondary links you sometimes see in search results. See Figure 8.11 for an example.

C&H Pure Cane Sugar
C&H Pure Cane Sugar, your partner in baking for over 99 years, brings you tips, tools, and delicious recipes to warm the hearts of family and friends.
www.chsugar.com/ - 15k - Cached - Similar pages

7 Varieties of Sugar	Careers
Contact Us	find out more
Tips & Tools	White Granulated
History	

More results from chsugar.com »

Figure 8.11 Google listing for C & H Sugar

Google can show as many as eight Sitelinks on a single listing, which is sweet by any measure! Not only do these additional links greatly increase the prominence and appeal of a listing, but they may very well help your visitors get one step closer to their goal by clicking directly to an internal page.

So, you want Sitelinks. Join the club! Unfortunately, Sitelinks are algorithmically generated—no human intervention here—and there is quite a bit of speculation in SEO circles as to exactly how Google chooses which sites qualify for Sitelinks on their listings. Our best guess is that it's based primarily on the volume of traffic to the pages. So your best chance at gaining Sitelinks, sadly, is to have a large amount of traffic to your site. In other words: Worry about something else for now.

If you're fortunate enough to already have Sitelinks on your listing, congratulations! You can maximize your benefits by doing the following:

- Keep tabs on your Sitelinks pages: Any page that's listed in Sitelinks should be considered a top landing page and designed accordingly.

- Use internal links to channel Sitelink visitors from those landing pages to your favorite conversion pages.

- Control which pages are listed, using the Sitelinks management tool within Google Webmaster Tools.

xtra
cred

As specialty search and standard search become more and more integrated, we think you'll be glad you took this week's trek to the cutting edge of search. Now you'll get into an R&D groove as Your SEO Plan enters its next week!

Week 8: Research and Development

You're more than halfway through Your SEO Plan, which means it won't be long before you're out in the SEO wilderness on your own. We want the transition to be a pleasant one, so this week, we'll focus on showing you the best ways to research SEO and develop your ongoing plan. The goal is for you to come away with an approach to use whenever you need to learn something new about search.

If you aren't yet confident in your advanced searching skills, or if you generally don't trust an answer unless you get it in writing from a paid expert, this week will help you stretch your abilities and save your money in the long run!

Monday: SEO News and Trends

Tuesday: Task Journal Investigation

Wednesday: International Search

Thursday: Rolling with the Hydroplaning Monkey

Friday: Analytics Meditation

Monday: SEO News and Trends

SEO moves fast! In the weeks since you started doing SEO, there have probably been a few changes (significant or not so significant) introduced by the big engines, a brand-new search engine launched in beta, and, oh, about 40 rancorous discussions about what's "right" or "wrong" in any number of SEO forums. It might seem that every time you go out for a cup of coffee, you come back to a whole new set of important players, rumors, and must-haves that weren't there before.

You're busy, so nobody expects you to keep up with every little twist and turn along the SEO highway. In fact, staying a month or so behind the times can prevent you from crowding your brain with unnecessary SEO rumors and speculation.

But we recommend keeping up at least a passing knowledge of SEO current events and stashing some solid SEO researching skills in your tool belt. When it comes time to do SEO on your own, you'll need them! Here's where to look:

SEO News Sources

One day soon you're going to need to learn something about SEO, something specific to your own site that we didn't cover in this book. The Web is the only way to keep up with the latest SEO news and trends. Unfortunately, not every site is reputable, so you'll need to wear your heavy-duty BS filters. You can't go wrong if you stick with articles on the following sites:

Search Engine Land, http://searchengineland.com Danny Sullivan and a team of industry leaders offer a blog bursting with updated search engine tips and insider information that nobody else comes close to. When we asked him what role the site plays in the SEO industry, he said, "We hope Search Engine Land is essential reading for the search marketer and anyone interested in search. Our job is to highlight the most important stories, tips, and advice from across the search marketing community, plus to help educate and inform with our lengthy features, news articles, and columns offering original content. It's easy to feel overwhelmed when you're new to search, and we think Search Engine Land makes it easy for anyone to do a daily check on what's happening and keep up on the essentials." Bravo, Danny!

HighRankings.com, www.highrankings.com Jill Whalen offers cheerful, no-nonsense, often low-tech advice that's perfect for do-it-yourself SEOs of all stripes.

ClickZ News, www.clickz.com The ClickZ network as a whole offers an impressive gamut of expert advice, news, and commentary on all avenues of interactive marketing, not just SEO.

Search Engine Watch, www.searchenginewatch.com Search Engine Watch, a respected source of SEO/SEM information with an active forum, is part of the ClickZ Network.

Information Overload

A thread on a search forum asked SEO professionals how they spend an average day on the job. Looking at the responses, you would think that SEOs are paid based on the number of search engine blogs they read, how many SEO podcasts are filling their libraries, and how many thousands of forum postings they've racked up. We won't bash this lifestyle, but we realized long ago that there's no need to live it.

Reading SEO info online can make even a seasoned Internet researcher hyperventilate. There are so many acronyms, rumors, and arguments (not to mention posturing…do these people really read 826 search blogs every day?), and so much conflicting advice that even if you understand what's

Continues

Information Overload *(Continued)*

being said, you probably shouldn't believe it at first blush. Follow these words of warning as you get your bearings in the overstimulating world of SEO news and advice:

- Always check an article's date before you read the article. This way you'll know whether you're reading something brand-new or a two-year-old history lesson from the archives.

- Beware articles posted on the websites of SEO firms. Many companies publish web articles and tips written by their in-house staff in an effort to improve their linkable noncommercial content and prove their worthiness in the SEO arena. These authors may be knowledgeable, or they may not be…it's very difficult to tell if you're new to the game. And these kinds of articles are often undated. Some of these authors may have moved on from the SEO company years ago! If you're inclined to follow the advice from an SEO firm, do a search for the author's name to help you determine if they are reputable in the larger SEO community.

- Lurk! There's no harm in checking out the SEO forum(s) of your choice, but don't post—or believe what you read—until you've gotten a feel for the competence of the regular posters and the moderators. Here are some indicators that the advice you're reading is reliable: Multiple people on multiple sites seem to be giving the same advice; you can corroborate this advice via an article written by a recognized SEO expert; or you can find your own evidence (using the "I wonder why that's happening" method) to back it up.

- Pace yourself. Unless you've got a life-or-death situation (and these are very infrequent in SEO), take in a little information at a time. SEO resources on the Web are great for researching specific questions on a need-to-know basis. Just do your best to tune out arcane details, like which Google search tab moved where or how many pages Yahoo! says it has in its index today.

In a short time, you'll have enough SEO expertise that you'll be able to choose a few sources that you trust and stick with them.

SEO Forums

In a conversation we had with Danny Sullivan, he cautioned, "Forums probably aren't the best place for beginners. They should do a lot of reading from more focused sites before diving in. As for advice, be wary of everything and always remember that nothing should be taken as fact." To begin your own SEO forum research, start with these tried-and-true sites:

- forums.searchenginewatch.com
- www.highrankings.com/forum/
- www.webmasterworld.com

- www.searchengineforums.com
- www.cre8asiteforums.com
- Or search several SEO forums here: www.seroundtable.com/forums.html

Jump in on the forums whenever you have a burning question that needs answering, but don't count on them for your regular SEO news fix.

Blogs and E-mail Newsletters

One of our favorite ways to keep up-to-date on SEO news is through blogs and e-mail newsletters. Here, seasoned and uncommonly generous SEO professionals distill the latest happenings into easy-to-read content. If you trust the source, you can trust the advice. Here are our favorite SEO blogs and newsletters:

- http://searchengineland.com
- www.mattcutts.com/blog (for Google-centric information)
- www.seomoz.org/blog
- www.problogger.net (for those with blogs)
- www.smallbusinesssem.com (for small businesses)
- Jill Whalen's High Rankings® Advisor Newsletter at www.highrankings.com
- Avinash Kaushik's web analytics blog, Occam's Razor, at www.kaushik.net/avinash/

As you continue surfing SEO sites, you'll probably see other premium content or regular e-mail updates; consider signing up for a subscription from sites you like. Then do what we do: Let them pile up in your inbox, and set aside a time once a week (you can even get away with once a month) to pour yourself a cup of coffee and browse the SEO news.

Bonus points if you can slip something interesting and *au courant* about SEO into your next conversation with your boss.

Tuesday: Task Journal Investigation

Your Task Journal is only as good as your ability to tackle the issues you add to it. Today is a freestyle day, set aside for you to look into, or take care of, one of your Task Journal issues.

If your Task Journal isn't yet filled with dozens of fascinating ruminations, look to Chapter 10 for some ideas to get you started.

Now: Go learn more about an issue of your choice from your Task Journal.

Don't be surprised if, in the process of knocking something off your task list, you add several additional items. That's the sign of a truly productive research session!

Wednesday: International Search

The Internet knows no borders, but unfortunately, your SEO campaign does. If your target audience includes an overseas component, you need to learn strategies for international SEO and put a focused effort into your international visibility. Ask yourself which country you are targeting. Is your international audience composed of English speakers? Which languages do you want to target? Answer these questions for your organization, and then start your research on international SEO with these general guidelines in mind:

International paid search marketing Google AdWords, Yahoo! Search Marketing, and Microsoft adCenter make it easy to add new campaigns and set them up for different countries and languages. If your international ads are in English, it's very simple to edit the targeting preferences on your current campaign to include additional countries.

You should custom-write your ads for non-U.S.-based site visitors, even if they are English speaking, to address their different terminology or needs. Separate sites or landing pages will also improve localization.

International organic optimization Let's say you want your chic boutique website to rank well for searchers in France searching for the French words "parapluie jaune."

One approach would be to choose this term as one of your top target keywords and optimize your landing page accordingly. Good start, but there's more you can do to optimize for the geographic audience you desire. Here are a few tips to help you sell more of those yellow umbrellas:

DO make sure your landing page is written in the language of the country you want to target. Your page titles and meta description tags should be in the target language, too. Even though there's an HTML meta tag that allows you to specify which language, your web page is written in, the search engine robots will probably ignore it and look at the web page text to make their own determination of language. Don't confuse the search engines by sticking substantial portions of several different languages on the same page.

DON'T use your home page for the sole purpose of selecting a language. If you are creating several subsites or site sections in different languages, don't waste precious home page real estate on choosing a language. Instead, include high-quality content in your most important language, with links to other language choices.

DO use a country-specific domain. Your site will get a lift if it has the appropriate country domain: This is a big clue to the search engines that the site should be shown to a searcher in your target country. And major search engines often allow their users to request only documents from their own country, so having the right domain will put you in the running.

DO consider building separate sites. Some sites redirect their international domains to their .com domain (for example, babyfuzzkin.co.uk and babyfuzzkin.de could both redirect to babyfuzzkin.com), and this is OK. Of course, it would be better—for your site and for your user—to create separate sites in separate languages (or in the various "flavors" of English), especially since key content like pricing and contact information may be different for each country.

DO seek inbound links from sites that are in your targeted countries. And be sure to request links in the appropriate language!

DO explore locally popular search sites. Google, Yahoo!, and MSN have a major presence worldwide, and if your site is in their indexes, it will also show up on the international versions of their search sites (for example, google.co.uk). So you could focus on those three search engines and let it go at that. But there may be smaller search sites that play an important role in your country of interest. For example, orange.fr is a major search engine in France. Your soggy Parisian seeking a "parapluie jaune" might look there rather than one of the Big Three.

You've probably figured out by now that a fully fledged international SEO campaign is outside the scope of your hour-a-day commitment. It may even involve a major web development effort, creating unique sites for each of your targeted countries. If international search is right for your site, here are the best places online to start reading up and develop your plan of attack:

- www.multilingual-search.com
- www.multilingual-seo.com (international SEO forums)
- http://searchengineland.com/lands/search-engines-outside-usa.php
- A helpful International Herald Tribune article here: www.iht.com/bin/print.php?id=3927066

Now: If international search is right for your site, start your research and determine your next steps.

¡Hola SEO!

According to the Selig Center for Economic Growth, the buying power of the Hispanic market in the United States is expected to reach $992 billion by 2009—that's 9 percent of the entire market! The Spanish-speaking population within the United States is growing, and with it grows an important sector of the search world. Many of the major search engines have created portals specifically for this audience—for example, AOL Latino, Yahoo! Telemundo, and MSN Latino. However, anecdotal evidence suggests that the U.S. Latino market searches extensively on the major English-based search engines using Spanish or English keyterms.

We won't claim to be experts in this domain. SEO for the Latino market is still relatively uncommon. But that also means it's a great opportunity to find untapped areas, maybe that top 10 Google spot you've been having such a hard time capturing! And, last we checked, PPC prices for terms in Spanish were much lower than their English counterparts.

Anyone ready to reach out to this audience may want to attend Search Engine Strategies Latino conferences (see www.jupiterevents.com for more info).

And remember, much of what you're doing in Your SEO Plan will aid your website in listings regardless of language. You're off to a great start already!

Thursday: Rolling with the Hydroplaning Monkey

In the first edition of this book, we wrote these fateful words: "You could easily gain some high ranks for, say, the term *hydroplaning monkey* because nobody else is optimizing for it…"

A few weeks later, mostly because of a hydroplaning-monkey sketch drawn in a Twizzler-induced haze, we posted a page at www.yourseoplan.com/hydroplaning-monkey.html, and in no time it was ranked #1 for the phrase on the major search engines (see

Figure 8.12). That's when the fun started! It wasn't long until someone else—an adoring fan, we hope—purchased the domain name hydroplaningmonkey.com and started to compete for the term. Over the intervening months, another domain, hydroplaning-monkey.com, appeared on the scene.

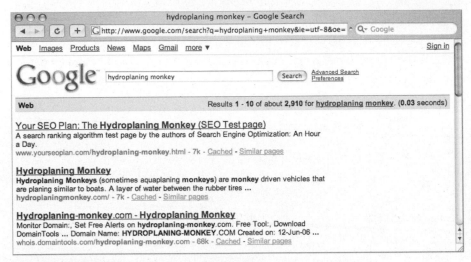

Figure 8.12 Google search results for "hydroplaning monkey"

We love the fun and have continued to use the page to test various on-page optimization theories. In fact, we've found it so helpful that we're giving you a Hydroplaning Monkey day: a day to develop your own experiments. You don't have to create a new page or use nonsense phrases. Just try something new and keep track of the results.

Today, think of an SEO question or mystery, something that you've been wondering about, and an experimental approach toward finding out what makes search engines tick. Here are a few ideas to get you started:

- Toss some alternate spellings, abbreviations, or misspellings into your meta keywords tags. Does it make a difference in your rank for these terms?

- Change some of your Google AdWords ads from title case to lowercase, or vice versa. Do you notice a change in click-throughs?

- Find a page on your site that isn't indexed in the search engines and add a link to it from your home page. Did that do the trick?

- Convert your global navigation from images to text on just one page of your site. Did that page receive a rankings boost? What about the pages that this page links to?

- Create a single press release containing your CEO's name, and post it to your site. Does searching for your CEO's name cause that press release to rank well?

Your experiments won't be truly scientific, of course, because you won't be working in a vacuum. Changes around the Web and on search engines will constantly interfere with what you learn. But we are quite certain that with a few of these tests under your belt, you'll have a whole new level of SEO confidence.

Prefer to leave your experiments behind in the eighth-grade biology lab? You can learn from the work of others by studying SEO contest results. These contests generally work like this: Someone well known in SEO announces a nonsense phrase, and anyone in the world can try to rank well for it. The top-ranking sites on a predetermined date win some prizes. Gloating, celebrations, and name-calling ensue! Learn more by doing one of the famous searches: "nigritude ultramarine" or "V7ndotcom elursrebmem."

slacker

Now: Think of an SEO experiment and get started!

Friday: Analytics Meditation

Now: Before you get started on today's task, don't forget: It's Friday, time for your paid search Quick Check! See Week 5 of this chapter for instructions.

During your Prep Month, we pushed hard for you to set up an analytics program of some sort. We hope our message hit home and that you're sitting atop several weeks of data. If you still don't have any analytics capabilities, skip today's assignment and spend the hour in a serious effort to get some!

Today you're going to enter your analytics program and just sift around the data, looking for jewels of insight. You are forbidden to focus on the same metrics that you've been gathering forever, the key indicators that your boss asked for, or the measure that you read about in an article once. Instead, keep an open mind and look for information in unexpected places. We'll guide you with a few sample sessions:

- Are there any keywords that are bringing a large number of people to your site but for which you aren't providing a solution? For example, we once knew a site getting a lot of traffic for the term "buy wine" that didn't actually *sell* wine. Would there be any way to help those visitors or leverage that traffic?

- Which keywords are sending an unusually high percentage of people to undesirable pages? Which referring sites? Are you paying any money for any of these clicks?

- Are there any entry pages on the site that surprise you? How many visitors are entering via the site map or Contact Us page? Are these pages designed appropriately for site entries?

- Look for patterns in navigation paths. For example, having a lot of people bouncing back and forth between two product pages may indicate that you need a comparison chart. Or, are lots of visitors starting at a higher-priced product page and then clicking to a cheaper product? Maybe you need to work on explaining the benefits of the high-end product.

- Look for keyword trends. Are more people converting when they search for "hair loss treatment" or "hair loss prevention"? Rather than looking at the exact phrases, look for trends by filtering for *all* searches containing the words "treatment" or "prevention."

- Review your site overlay if your analytics program offers this feature, which shows exactly where users are clicking from each page. Are a very large number of people going just one place from your home page? Should you consider displaying that content directly on the home page? See Figure 8.13 for an example of a site overlay screen.

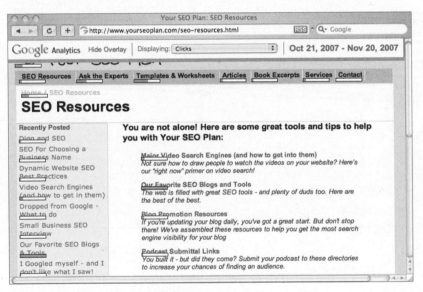

Figure 8.13 Google analytics site overlay feature

The purpose of today's exercise is to come away with an action, not just a report.

 Now: Look at your web analytics program and meditate on what you see, with an eye toward an action recommendation.

Now that you've socialized, specialized, and analyzed your way through so many different aspects of SEO, you're ready to move on to the third month of Your SEO Plan. Join us in the next chapter, where SEO becomes a way of life!

Month Three: It's a Way of Life

With so many SEO elements—organic, paid, on site, off site—in the works for your website now, you've built up a holistic approach to SEO that you can be proud of. But don't rest on your laurels yet. SEO is never done!

This month you'll find SEO-friendly solutions for expanding your site's content, and you'll learn how to get more out of your starter pay-per-click (PPC) campaign. You'll smooth out any rough edges on your website's visibility, and you'll take reporting a step further.

Chapter Contents

Week 9: Build Content

In Week 3 of Your SEO Plan, we encouraged you to search the Web for sites that may want to link to yours. Have you received the cold shoulder from most of these potential traffic sources? Or have you been slacking on link building because you think your site has no linkable content?

With more and better content, your search engine visibility will benefit in two ways: More people will want to link to it, and the search engines will find more unique pages to index. But building high-quality, linkable content is easier said than done.

This week, you'll uncover opportunities that you may never have realized existed and scrub out obstacles, all with the goal of bulking up your linkable and indexable content. Your daily assignments for this week are as follows:

Monday: Discover Content You Already Have

Tuesday: Develop New Content

Wednesday: Optimize Non-HTML Documents

Thursday: Content Thieves

Friday: Shape Up Your Site Map

Monday: Discover Content You Already Have

You know how great it feels to find a twenty in the pocket of a jacket you haven't worn in a while? Today is the day you'll look for linkworthy and search-engine-friendly content that you didn't know you already had.

Here are some likely hiding places:

On your website What could you already have on your site that's linkable? Here are some possibilities:

- Product comparisons
- Research reports
- Industry news
- Free downloads or clip art
- Case studies
- Games
- Photo galleries
- Forums

You may have content on your website that just needs a little tweaking—perhaps a reorganization or a minor rewrite—to become linkworthy.

What Makes Content Linkworthy?

Everyone is talking about getting inbound links. Some SEOs are even focusing on strategies specifically geared toward building linkable pages, called *linkbait*. For the best chance of gaining inbound links, content should be

- Original

- Unique

- Useful

- Noncommercial (or subtle in its sales pitch)

- Timely

- Accessible without a password or payment

And at the risk of stating the obvious, to be linkable, each page must be *linkable*—meaning it must have its own URL!

Perhaps you do have some of these elements on your site, but they're intertwined with your less linkable, commercial content. If so, your site may benefit from a simple reorganization of materials. You can cluster this content, or links to it, within a new section of your site, aptly named "Resources," "Fun," or something similar. And remember, your goal is conversions, not just inbound links, so be sure to provide a clear path from this new section to your landing pages.

Sometimes, even a simple title rewrite can dramatically change the linkability of a page. For example, one type of content that often draws inbound links is a product comparison. Perhaps your site has a page that compares features of your product with your competition's. The only thing stopping it from being linkworthy is the title "Why Choose Us?" which strikes a commercial chord. Give this page a new, industry-specific but neutral title like "Compare Medical Imaging Products," and suddenly the exact same chart becomes potential linkbait.

By the way, consider this:

Pearl of Wisdom: Pages requiring payment or registration to view are just plain not linkable. And—with rare exceptions—search engines will not index them.

So you should keep as much of your content outside the registration boundaries as possible.

Your sales and promotions Everybody loves a bargain, and next to "free stuff," a sale or promotion is a strong contender for links. Trouble is, most websites move their promotions around, showing them temporarily at whatever URL seems to suit the moment. Take the smart approach: If your site runs promotions, make *one specific URL* for all promo materials! That way, linking sites will have an easy time sending you their bargain-hungry traffic—and you'll gain inbound links. If your organization runs promotions but somehow doesn't manage to get that content up on the website in a timely manner, put linkability on the list of reasons to turn over a new leaf.

Tools, worksheets, and sample documents Are there any tools, worksheets, presentations, or documents that your organization is using in-house and might be willing to share? For example, countless SEO firms offer keyword assessment tools or other useful gadgets for free on their websites. Think they're doing it out of altruism? Nope. More likely, they're trying to attract links and repeat traffic.

Offline marketing materials You can add offline marketing materials, such as brochures and sales presentations, to your website in whatever format they were created in. However, from an SEO standpoint, HTML is still the best format for your web content. We'll talk more about optimizing non-HTML content later this week.

E-mail newsletters If you're already writing and sending out e-mail newsletters, why not add them to your site, too? What appeals to your customers or opt-in readers may also appeal to linking sites.

Press releases Press releases are excellent potential landing pages, naturally text based, keyword rich, and often linkworthy because they're news! In Chapter 5, "Get Your Team on Board," we discussed getting PR involved in optimizing press releases. If your organization hasn't been posting its press releases online, start now. But make sure the press release is linkable news before asking for links. New products fit the bill. New hires probably don't.

xtra cred Look to Chapter 10, "Extra Credit and Guilt-Free Slacking," for guidelines on optimizing press releases.

Now: Look for preexisting content within your organization that can be repurposed for your website, and make contact with the person who can help make the necessary changes to your site.

If you didn't have any luck finding usable content today, don't despair: Tomorrow you will work on easy strategies for creating *new* content.

Tuesday: Develop New Content

If yesterday's explorations didn't unearth any unique, linkworthy, and search-engine-friendly content for your website, you'll need to create some new content instead. Here are two approaches:

- Develop new content in-house.
- Use other people's content.

    You'll look into these options today.

Develop New Content In-House

Of course, you could hire a staff of professional writers and set them to work full-time building fascinating, linkworthy content for your website. If you've got the budget for that, set down this book and call HR today! For everybody else, here are some ideas for building out your website content with limited resources:

Monthly columns Is there anyone in your organization who might be interested in running a regular monthly (or weekly, but we won't hope for daily!) column on the website? Perhaps an "Ask the Expert" or "Helpful Hints" type of column, with no marketing agenda in mind. Once these columns build up steam, you might create an RSS feed for them to make it easier for your readers to find their way back. Or, you may want to share these columns with other websites through syndication or simply by contacting other site owners and requesting inclusion. Industry publications and e-mail newsletters are always looking for new content. But if you're going to be generous with your content, make sure you get as much SEO benefit as possible: Articles posted elsewhere should always link back to your website.

Blog Maybe you dismissed the idea of a blog as too much work after reading "Find Your Voice" in Chapter 7, "Month One: Kick It into Gear." But blogs may be your easiest option for keeping a fresh presence on the Internet—once the blog authoring tool is in place, you don't need to go through a webmaster or IT department to add new content. You can even spread out the workload by allowing contributions from several employees, or take it a step further and allow contributions from folks outside your company. At the very least, think of a blog as a convenient tool for posting press releases.

Compiled resources You know your business, so you know the kinds of things your customers always seem to need help finding or figuring out. Resources such as useful links, FAQs, reviews, and a reference table or glossary can be good draws for inbound links (not to mention bookmarks and repeat visits!).

Interviews Interviews with bigwigs in your industry, or anyone else who your target audience finds compelling, can be a great way to fill out your website. For example, if your company sells home furnishings, an interview with an interior designer could provide content of interest to your target audience while giving the designer a publicity boost. Look for experts or service providers in fields similar to your own, and try to pick someone with a strong reputation and an engaging personality.

Free tools and widgets If your company has the technical chops for it, there's nothing like a free online tool for drawing inbound links. Translate dollars into yen; calculate shoe size in the European standard; figure out how many tablespoons of ground coffee it takes to brew a pot. As long as it's potentially useful to your target audience, it's a great idea. As you learned in Chapter 4, widgets are fast becoming the fashionable way to spread your content webwide, so consider these as an option if your organization has a solid blend of creative ideas and programming skills.

Welcoming the Social Web to Your Site

You've started building some great new content on your website. Now you're hungry for a big hit on social bookmarking sites such as Digg, del.icio.us, or StumbleUpon!

We're not going to tell you the big secret of social media success—for that you'll have to buy our other book. Just kidding! Actually, *there is no big secret*. Just trial and error, and a lot of continued effort. Here are some basic guidelines that will help you get at least a fighting chance on the Social Web:

- Research the demographics of a social media site before you jump in. If your target audience is young, male, and techie, then by all means get your Digg shovel out! Slightly older? Stumble-Upon could have some potential. A nontechie, older, B2B audience? Yeah… we're still waiting for that social media site.

- Be sure all of your content is taggable. That means each and every page should have a separate URL.

- On each page of fresh content, include bookmarking buttons—icons linking to social book-marking sites. As you learned in Month One, "Letting Others Spread the Love," this makes it easy for folks to tag or bookmark your content.

- Recognize that you don't necessarily need a front-page blockbuster to be successful in social bookmarking. If you are regularly creating new content, the drip-drip-drip approach of a few tags here and there can accumulate into a significant number of links. Although these links are generally not followed by search engines and will not directly affect your ranks, they can lead to new traffic and indirect positive effects.

- Create a profile and work to become a valued member of any social media site that you would like to use as part of your promotion efforts. Otherwise, you risk overstepping eti-quette and having your site bashed, buried, or ignored.

> - *After* you internalize the previous bullet, start submitting or tagging your own website. Most people consider it acceptable to create a single self-submittal for content that is genuinely likely to interest the community. When you do this, be sure you optimize your tags. Use keywords, as well as terms that you see in common use on similar content. There's no reason to skimp on tags; you can typically use as many as you like!
>
> Building up social media kung-fu powers is largely a matter of participation and familiarity with the community you're trying to reach. If your target audience is using these sites, so should you!

Use Other People's Content

Whoa, there! We're not saying you should go out on the Web, find some great content, and cut and paste it onto your website. There's this little thing called "copyright infringement" you'll want to watch out for. But there are some ways to use other people's content on your website without the feds beating down your door. Here are a few ideas:

Articles featuring your company Does your PR department keep a record of articles that mention your organization or include interviews or quotes from company representatives? See if you can get permission to add all or part of these articles to your website. (It goes without saying that you should stick to the complimentary ones.)

Syndicated content It's quite easy to incorporate feeds onto your website—for example, industry news or blog posts. It's not unique content, but providing a group of topical links may add freshness and a sense that your site is up-to-date, thus increasing your linkability.

User-generated content One of our favorite ways to increase content is to let your users build it for you, with blog comments, posts in message boards, classified ads, or product reviews. This is content that constantly updates itself and can often be eminently linkable. But it also sets you up for abuse, such as people submitting meaningless content (a practice called *comment spam*), so be sure you have a moderator or other system in place to protect your site if you're thinking of offering these features.

Guest contributors Many talented writers and artists would love to have space on the Internet to display their work. This type of content can take the form of a post by a guest blogger, or an article stating expert advice or opinion. You could even assign a colleague to send a first-person account of a popular industry conference. And your contributors don't have to be professional writers. Many websites are nicely filled out with the free expressions of regular people, from birth stories to product success stories.

Copyright-free content Copyright-free articles on subjects ranging from wedding etiquette to tax advice can be added to your website, usually in exchange for a link or a courtesy notice. However, since this content is not unique, it's of little value for your search engine presence (and may even annoy your site visitors because they may have seen the same articles on other sites). So use it with caution, and only if you are certain it improves your site offerings.

An alternative to copyright-free content is Creative Commons (CC) content. The Creative Commons, at creativecommons.org, is an alternative type of copyright—you might call it a "some rights reserved" copyright. Explore CC content by searching for it using Yahoo!'s or Google's advanced search.

We've given you a nice long list of possible ways to add content to your website; not every one will suit your needs or abilities. Today, choose which technique you'll try first. Set a goal for yourself, perhaps adding one new page of unique content each week, and get started today.

Now: Set a content-building goal and get started.

Wednesday: Optimize Non-HTML Documents

There's no harm in posting documents on your website in non-HTML formats such as Word, Excel, PDF, or PowerPoint. All of these formats are indexed by the major search engines, and sometimes they rank well. However, good old HTML still has the upper hand in search. Non-HTML content can be a turnoff to searchers, for a couple reasons. Other websites might hesitate to link to non-HTML documents because viewing them may disable the "back" button. Also, many searchers will skip over links to non-HTML documents because they don't want to wait for a separate program to launch and they may not be in the mood for a long download.

Nevertheless, non-HTML content can be optimized and serve you well, especially for the long tail of search. For example, while your home page might rank well for "model cars," your product PDF could have a better chance of faring well for the term "die-cast model car assembly instructions." Today, you'll learn a little bit about what makes non-HTML content work on search engines. Then you'll make any needed changes to your own docs:

Metadata for Compelling Titles

Search results for non-HTML documents can be downright ugly, because the folks who wrote them never considered how these documents would be presented in the search engines. For example, here is a page of PDF search results.

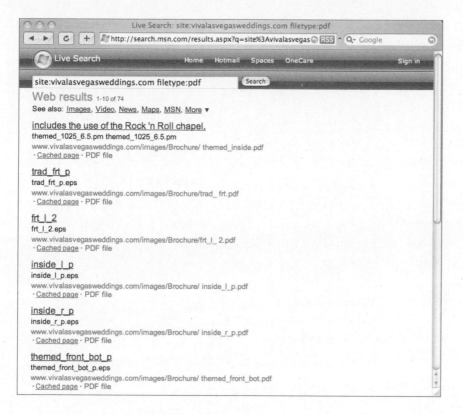

Look at listings number two and after: trad_frt_p? frt_1_2? What kind of page titles are those? That just isn't going to cut it in the split-second decision world of search results.

Here are possible places that search engines will look for a page title for your document:

- The document title as specified in *metadata*, which is extra information you write to describe the document (and is stored in a file's properties but is not visible in the body of the document)

- The first 60 or so characters of the document's text

- The file name

- Any text in the document that you happened to format in a larger font

Search engines will generally look for metadata first, so defining document metadata is the easiest way to improve your listings. In Adobe Acrobat and Microsoft Office applications, metadata such as Title, Author, and Keywords is very easy to define by selecting File > Properties or File > Document Properties. If you are using other programs to author your documents, look to their help pages for guidance.

Now: Open up one of your non-HTML documents and review the metadata. Insert an optimized page title if possible.

xtra
cred

You can also define a description in the document metadata, but the search engines will generally gather a snippet from the document content anyway.

Content Optimization

Non-HTML documents are basically thrown in the mix with all the other documents and websites in a search engine's index. So, in addition to inserting metadata as described in the preceding section, you should follow the same SEO guidelines for non-HTML documents as you would for your regular web pages: Include your target keywords in text, link to the document from other pages on your site, make sure URLs in the document are clickable so the search engine robots can follow them, and modify the content for improved snippets if desired.

slacker

We know it's not always realistic for non-HTML content to be edited based on SEO principles. And even if optimized, it's hard for non-HTML documents to rank well against HTML pages for competitive search terms. You may wish to skip optimizing the document content beyond basic metadata and hope for good results with the long tail of search.

Now: Make a determination about whether it's worth your time to attempt to optimize the visible content of your non-HTML files. If so, get started.

You can get a sense of how search engines see your non-HTML content by viewing the HTML alternate page created by Google.

Next to every search result for a non-HTML document, Google presents a "View as HTML" link. For example, here is the listing for a PowerPoint presentation.

> [PPT] The Multigenerational Workplace: Millennials enter the workforce
> File Format: Microsoft Powerpoint View as HTML
> Clockwatchers, drones, slackers, and suck-ups and how to get them all to leave you alone so
> you can get some work done. **Stewart Brower**, MLIS, AHIP ...
> notes.smbrower.com/The%20Multigenerational%20Workplace.ppt - Similar pages - Note this

Click on the listing title, and your browser will either display or download the PowerPoint file. But click on View as HTML, and you will see this page:

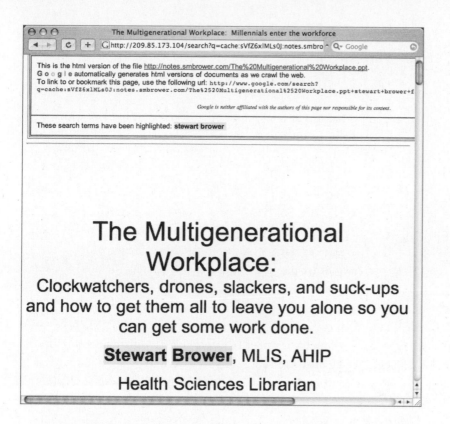

Viewing Yahoo!'s and MSN's cached version of non-HTML files is a similar experience.

Even if you choose not to spend time optimizing your non-HTML documents, we suggest you review this alternate version. Many of your potential site visitors will look here first before investing their time in a download. Nobody expects these pages to look perfect, but you don't want them to be an embarrassment to your organization.

When to Remove

You may be surprised to learn that keeping non-HTML documents—even if they rank well—can create disadvantages for your site. Consider the following:

* Files like PDFs and Microsoft Word documents are stand-alone entities, so they're not likely to be integrated into your site's navigation. If visitors click on one of these files directly from a search engine, they may never even look at the rest of your site. You should weigh whether making your non-HTML content available to the search engines is worth the potential loss of traffic to the rest of your site.

- Since non-HTML documents will often be downloaded onto searchers' hard drives, it's possible that your content could be used in ways you don't condone. If you're concerned about this, don't put them on your site. At the very least, be sure that every document is clearly marked with authorship information, copyright notice, and your web address.
- Non-HTML documents may contain confidential information hidden in the metadata that you don't wish to make public, including things like tracked changes, comments, and speaker notes. It's always a good idea from a security standpoint to review metadata for your documents before posting them in public view. Workshare's free software, TRACE!, available at www.workshare.com/products/trace/, can help you weed out potential problems.

> **Now:** If you feel it's for the best, remove non-HTML files from your website or exclude them from indexing using your robots.txt file.

With metadata in your pages and content rich with keywords, your non-HTML documents may turn out to be healthy sources of targeted traffic for your site!

Thursday: Content Thieves

You're starting to develop a lovely collection of content on your website, but is some outlaw mooching your message? Unfortunately, the Internet remains something of a Wild West for copyright law. Other websites might steal your content simply by cutting and pasting, or they may use *scraping*, a more sophisticated technique of automatically grabbing content from your web pages, to steal material from your site and put it up on theirs.

You want to be aware of content thieves, not just because they are using your content to compete with you for search engine visibility, but also because they may be damaging your brand. An employer of ours once discovered that another company had repurposed large chunks of our website's marketing content—but *hadn't even taken the time to change all of the instances of our company name!* If your content is stolen by a similarly pathetic character, unwitting users might actually think that they are visiting *your* website, and that's something you certainly don't want.

There are several ways to check if your material is being repurposed elsewhere on the Web. Here are a few:

Search for text. Using the search engine of your choice, search for a likely-to-be-unique text string (a sentence or two will do) from the body of your website, using quotes around the text. If the search engine finds sites other than your own, something fishy may be going on.

Use a page comparison site. Copyscape.com is a website specifically designed to help site owners find copies of their content online. A major limitation is that it searches only HTML content, not PDFs or other document formats.

Search for media. Stolen media such as images, audio, video, and Flash content is considerably harder to find than copies of your page text—for the very same reasons that search engines struggle with these formats in general. If media content is a significant portion of your site, you'll need to become an expert at using the video search engines and image search options discussed in Chapter 8, "Month Two: Establish the Habit," to help protect your rights online.

It's often easier to prevent media theft than react to it. If you're concerned about this, check in with your design team to make sure they're savvy to copy prevention options such as adding watermarks to images, building your Flash files in multiple pieces, or embedding your server information in media files.

Review your server logs. Other websites can display your media content such as images, audio, video, and Flash and make it look like it belongs to them. It's not uncommon for these nefarious nerds to point their links directly to your content on *your servers*. Not only does this practice, known as *hot linking*, infringe on your copyrights, it also puts an unfair burden on your servers, which are forced to serve up the content for someone else's site! Your server logs can help you find this sort of hijacking—yet another reason to make a habit of reviewing your analytics data.

Now you know how to look for misused materials on the Web. But what will you do if you find any? With any luck, a simple communication with the content thieves will clear things up. If not, you may need to contact the website host and request that the page be removed. Detailed advice and links to sample "cease-and-desist" letters can be found at www.plagiarismtoday.com/stock-letters.

Now: Choose one of the methods listed in this section and search for copies of your web content. Begin pursuing any that you find.

Friday: Shape Up Your Site Map

All this fabulous new content on your website might be a lot to navigate. If your site doesn't have a site map, today you'll consider creating one. If you already have one, you'll optimize it today.

Why Build a Site Map?

We think that just about every website can benefit from a site map. Most people know that site maps are good for the user experience: They orient your site visitors and help lost visitors find their way to the right page. But there's even more benefit when you consider SEO. A site map can improve the search engine visibility of your website in several ways:

- By providing search engine robots with links to navigate through your site
- By pointing search engine robots to dynamic or hard-to-reach pages that might not be accessible otherwise
- By acting as a possible landing page, optimized for search traffic
- By providing ready-to-use content for the File Not Found page where visitors are automatically taken if they try to go to a nonexistent URL within your domain

If your site is small enough that links to every page are included in your global navigation or absolutely every page on your site is available within two clicks from the home page, then you may not need a site map. But if your site is larger, and especially if it contains pages that may be hard for search engine robots to find, we highly recommend a site map.

Site Map Design 101

Simply put, a site map is a page that links to every major page on your website. If you're like many web surfers, you visit a site map as a last resort when you can't find what you need or if there's no in-site search function. You're happy to forget it as soon as you leave it. But if a robot visits your site map, it's not going to forget what it saw, and it will be pleased as Punch to come back on a regular basis. Here are a few pointers for treating both robots and human users well:

Include the most important pages. People will get lost if your site map contains too many links. That means, if your site has more than, say, 100 pages, you'll need to choose the most important pages. Here are our suggestions for pages to include:

- Product category pages
- Major product pages
- FAQ and Help pages
- Contact or Request Information pages
- All of the key pages on your *paths to conversion*, the pages that your visitors follow from landing page through conversion
- Your 10 most popular pages

Go easy on the autogeneration. Some content management systems will automatically generate a site map. As in so many other areas of SEO, we prefer the human touch. If you, or your tech teammates, are leaning in the automated direction, review the outcome carefully to be sure your site map has these characteristics:

- The layout is easy on the human eye.
- All links are standard HTML text that can be followed by spiders.
- The important pages (included in the preceding list) are easy to find.

Look at other sites for design inspiration. Don't waste time reinventing the wheel. There are zillions of site maps out there on the Web. Use one you like as a starting point.

Optimize your site map. We don't mean you should think of your site map as one of your top-priority landing pages. But if done tastefully, your site map can actually contain a fair number of your target keywords, not to mention compelling text. For example, instead of a link simply labeled "Fungicides," your site map could contain more keywords: "Organic Fungicides – Product details, how-to tips, and customer reviews of our Earth-friendly garden care products." Brief page descriptions can help your users find their way, as well as provide more text for search engines to read.

Link to your site map from every page. Users have come to expect a link to your site map in the footer of every page on the site, so make use of this spot. If your site has a search box, you may also wish to add a link to the site map near the search box, and make a link to the site map a fixture within the site search results page.

Now: Design your new site map or shape up your existing site map using the preceding guidelines. Deliver your requested changes to your web developer or make the changes yourself.

By the way, your site map isn't the same as your Google Sitemap. XML Sitemaps (A Google Sitemap is in this category) allow webmasters to submit URLs and additional page information directly to the search engines. See Chapter 10 for more information.

xtra cred

Week 10: PPC and ROI

Return on Investment (ROI) is one of those fancy terms for a simple concept: How much are you getting back compared to what you're putting in? Everyone wants a bigger, better ROI, and the best way to achieve one is to work within a framework that we like to call the *ROI loop*:

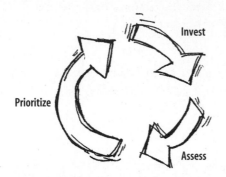

Over the past few weeks, you've invested both money and time in your PPC starter campaign. This week you'll move on to the next steps, Assess and Prioritize, and use what you learn to inform both your paid and organic SEO efforts. We'll get you started on some new endeavors even as you take stock of older ones:

Monday: Round Up Your Paid Search Data
Tuesday: Salvaging Poor Performers
Wednesday: Organic Opportunities
Thursday: Landing Page Optimization
Friday: Close the PPC ROI Loop

Monday: Round Up Your Paid Search Data

Paid search campaign management is a bit like exercising. You may start out with all sorts of good intentions and enthusiasm, but as time wears on, you might start to avoid it. And the longer you avoid it, the more unpleasant it is to get back into the groove. Today you'll line up your PPC data in preparation for shaking out some meaningful insights.

You have a lot of flexibility to create comprehensive, customized reports using your paid search service. Today, using your reporting interface, create a keyword report that includes the following data:

- Total number of click-throughs
- Click-through percentage
- Total cost
- Average total cost per click
- Total number of conversions
- Conversion percentage
- Conversion cost

We want you to review the list and identify your top-performing keywords. Every campaign has its own criteria. It's likely that you'll want to rank them based on click-through rate, conversion rate, conversion cost, total conversions, or some combination of these factors.

> **Now:** Use your PPC service to create a keyword report for your campaign so far, and sort the keywords from highest to lowest performers. It's best to export this report to an Excel file so that you can sort, filter, and search the data more easily.

Keep this data handy—you'll need it for tomorrow's task.

Tuesday: Salvaging Poor Performers

As you look through your paid search keyword performance data, you may find that there is a fairly even spread of clicks or conversions throughout your list of keywords. Or more likely, you may find a nice group of performers at the top and a steep dropoff thereafter. Perhaps you even have a disturbingly long list of zero-performers. But is it really time to prune your PPC campaign? Probably not. Before you give in to your slashing instinct, take the time to apply some solid analysis to your poor performers. Here are the most common performance failures and possible ways to improve them:

- Keywords with low click-through rates
- Keywords with low conversion rates
- Keywords with high conversion costs

Keywords with Low Click-Through Rates

As you learned in Chapter 4, "How the Search Engines Work Right Now," higher click-through rates will influence your rank on Google AdWords, Yahoo! Search Marketing (YSM), and Microsoft adCenter, so you may be tempted to start slicing and dicing keywords with low click-through rates. But while you may find these keywords bothersome, remember that as long as you're working in the standard search-targeted pay-per-click scenario that we advised you to set up, you're paying for clicks, not ad views, so they aren't costing you extra money. Ask yourself a few questions that may help you turn these low performers around:

Is my ad text doing its job? Take an honest look at your ad copy to make sure it addresses your low-performing keyword, and your audience, in a meaningful and compelling way. If the keyword doesn't have its own custom-written ad, perhaps it should. Consider inviting another writer on your team to give your ads a tune-up.

Does the term have enough impressions for me to make a judgment call? Make sure you're getting enough ad views to validate your doubts about the keyword. Sometimes, the number of impressions for an ad is so small that it's not getting a fair shot at success. This is especially true if the keyword is related to a seasonal or cyclical topic. Remember that terms on the long tail of search are naturally only going to get a few impressions.

Did I start out with realistic expectations? This is a great time to reassess your trust in your PPC service's traffic-prediction tool.

 Now: Review your keywords with low click-through rates and make changes for improvement if you determine it's necessary to do so.

Low Conversion Rate Keywords

Much more worrisome than the keyword that isn't bringing in traffic is the one that actually *is* bringing in traffic but not resulting in conversions. You're going to hold these terms to a much higher standard than the low-click-through performers because every one of these clicks is costing you cash. But you may wish to give these underachievers a second chance before you dump them. Here are some questions you should ask:

Is the landing page a good match for the keyword? You may be about to drop a keyword when you should instead be planning to add a new page to your website to better accommodate it. At the very least, consider pointing a keyword to a more appropriate landing page that already exists. Exploring different landing page options with a multivariate test (described later this week) may also be in order.

Did I get caught in a word-matching snafu? If you are using a broad matching option, is it possible there's a broad match to your term that's drawing in the wrong audience? You can fix this with a *negative match*, a type of matching that excludes words you specify so that your ad doesn't show up for those terms. For example, you may want to sponsor the term "shredder" for your snowboarding site, but you probably don't want to pay for clicks from people who are looking for those paper-eating office supplies. In this case, you'd want to exclude the words "paper" and "document" for this keyword.

Am I inadvertently using bait-and-switch tactics? If you owned a bike shop in Santa Cruz, California, you might think it's perfectly reasonable to sponsor the search terms "santa cruz bikes." Unfortunately, this is also the name of a popular brand of mountain bikes! Many of those click-throughs are going to be disappointed by your site. If you're in a situation like this, you'll need to review your ad text to eliminate ambiguity. Make sure your ads clearly represent your offering.

Review your keywords with low conversion rates and make changes for improvement.

Keywords with High Conversion Costs

Don't overlook the simple but important step of sorting your keywords by conversion cost. Keywords with high conversion costs can be easy to miss: They're not in the zero conversion pile, and they might not be in the low click-through pile. But there's nothing more depressing than seeing a $90 conversion cost for a keyword that you're using to sell a $45 product.

High conversion costs can be caused by any combination of the factors we listed for low click-through rates and low conversion rates. Although our suggested efforts earlier today will also help bring down the high-cost conversions, lowering your bid is the most direct fix for this problem. If you discover that more than a few of your keywords are running at an unacceptable conversion cost, it's time to pause those keywords until you figure out what's going wrong.

Now: Review your keywords with high conversion costs, and either try the changes listed previously for the other types of poor performers or lower the bids. Alternatively, pause those keywords if you feel it's necessary.

What's a Conversion Worth?

Determining the value of a conversion is anything but straightforward. The Left Brain and Right Brain share their perspectives.

The Left Brain says, "If you're paying for advertising, you need to have a way to determine if it's worth the cost. That means giving a numeric value to your conversions! For larger organizations, your marketing department probably already has a concept of the lifetime value of a new customer or client. For example, the PPC visitor who buys a digital camera online today may come back in a year for spare parts, and then recommend you to a business partner for a large purchase three years down the road."

The Right Brain says, "If your type of conversion is less tangible—for example, a visit to your Map and Directions page or downloading a white paper—you'll probably be hard-pressed to place a numerical value on it. This may be a case of 'I know it when I see it'—your gut will tell you that $10 per conversion feels like too much but $5 feels OK. If you can't place an exact value on your conversion, the best approach is to manage your campaign diligently so that you stay within your paid search budget and strive for the lowest cost per conversion possible."

Wednesday: Organic Opportunities

Yesterday, you worked on improving low-performing keywords in paid search. Were any of your top targeted organic keywords on the list? Today, you'll use your paid search campaign data to judge the organic keyword choices you made at the outset of your Prep Month. PPC data can reveal interesting trends, as well as over- and under-performing keywords that may need to be reprioritized.

This kind of analysis *could* take hours and hours of your time. No worries—we're going to coach you through a relatively simple approach. We're going to go out on a limb here and say you don't have an analytics analyst on staff, so let's do this the DIY way.

20/20 Hindsight

Your first task is to use your paid search campaign to find broad-brush keyword insights.

Using the same paid search performance data you looked at yesterday, highlight the keywords that are on your organic top-priority list (the ones you've already optimized your site for). Take a quick scan of the keywords that are on both your organic and paid search lists. Put yourself to the task of reviewing for the following insights:

- Your original keyword research led you to believe that a term is popular with searchers…but is it really? The number of PPC impressions it gets can help you confirm your suspicions.

- A keyphrase seemed targeted when you first assessed it…but is it? The number of click-throughs/conversions a term receives can give you a clearer understanding.

- If you've got your site analytics data tied to your paid search data (for example, Google AdWords links up with Google Analytics in a delightfully useful way), you can see the bounce rate, number of page views, and average amount of time a user spends on your site after arriving via your paid keywords. A lot of bounces for a given keyword indicates that you're wasting money on click-throughs, while a nice fat average visit time indicates good targeting.

- Now take a look at the paid keywords that aren't on your organic top-priority list. If a term is a standout PPC success, you may have underestimated its organic potential.

Now: Make a list of promising new keywords from your paid search campaign or existing organic ones whose paid performance was below your expectations.

xtra
cred

Consider the promising new keywords for your next round of organic SEO. Does a place exist for these new terms on your site right now? Maybe they're already well matched with a landing page, and it's just a matter of inserting them into the text and meta tags. As you incorporate new keywords into your organic efforts, you may want to drop underperformers from optimization and tracking.

slacker

Did you launch a paid search campaign without first doing the organic keyword research we assigned to you in Chapter 6? That's not good for your site (but your competitors say "thanks!"). Go back now and do the research, but use your PPC performance data as a cheat sheet. You can use this data to gain some solid insight into keyword popularity and the quality of targeting.

Cherry Picking at Cheeryland

Cheeryland (the company name and identifying details have been changed) is an amusement park. They have two primary target audiences: members of the public who may be interested in coming to visit, and sponsors who want to pay to have their name on the next big roller coaster.

That's two very different types of customers, one rare and valuable, and the other dime-a-dozen. The sponsors are the primo target audience—obviously, there aren't a whole lot of them out there, and landing this type of contract is quite a coup! Imagine the pay-per-click implications: Without careful planning, Cheeryland's paid search budget could be eaten up by the less desirable audience. When Cheeryland set up their first pay-per-click campaign, they wanted to attract their precious big-dollar target audience, and made the bold decision to try to eliminate PPC click-throughs from the general public.

Cheeryland's plan of attack? First, some organic optimization. They segmented their site into separate sections for the two audiences, each with its own custom-crafted landing pages. Careful keyword research helped them single out terms that only the more desirable audience would use. Then they launched a small paid search campaign, carefully focused on the sponsor audience. Careful monitoring of the PPC audience behavior ensures this budget is spent *only* on the high-end visitors.

Does it work? Cheeryland's careful steps are paying off. Their traffic is up across the board, but more importantly, a few of those coveted sponsor leads have surfaced. Although it may seem contradictory to expend a lot of time and effort on a trickle of targeted traffic, in the long run it paid off for Cheeryland because they weren't spending lots of money on clicks that they can easily gain for free using organic optimization.

Three cheers for Cheeryland's careful targeting!

Keyword Trends and Variations

Maybe you're using broad matching on your PPC campaigns, and visitors are arriving at your site using several variations of a particular keyword. Which is the most popular variation? Is it the one that you optimized your site for organically?

 Now: Using your site analytics tool, export the full list of paid search keywords that brought traffic to your site.

If you can't figure this out with your current analytics, here's a workaround: Turn off broad matching in your PPC account and add every variation of the keyword phrase you can think of to your account using exact matching. Then, after your campaign has run in this configuration for a while, you'll be able to use the PPC service to get an approximation of the report.

Scan the list with an eye for keyword trends:

- Is there any particular modifier that's delivering a lot of traffic? This might be a good term to add to your organic list. For example, if you sponsored the term "quilting supplies" and a lot of your broad matching traffic consists of people who searched for "quilting supplies wholesale," this might be a good phrase for you to target organically.

- Are there keyword variations (spacing and punctuation, misspelling, plural versions, synonyms) that are bringing in unexpected traffic through your paid search sponsorships? These can be a nice opportunity for organic targeting.

 Now: Look for PPC keyword trends that can inform your organic optimization choices.

A couple of month's worth of PPC data can be a treasure trove for an organic optimization campaign. Use it wisely, and you'll find PPC and organic SEO are a profitable partnership.

 ### Analysis Paralysis

Closing the ROI loop on your PPC campaign can range from an art form to a purely automated process. The Left Brain and Right Brain describe differing approaches.

The Right Brain says, "A little knowledge is a wonderful thing. But a limitless supply of raw data—which PPC services are very good at delivering—is difficult to wrap your mind around. An average do-it-yourself SEO may have a very hard time tackling this data, much less arriving at a meaningful take-away.

"So don't expect perfection, either in your campaign or in your ability to assess it! It's all about evolving toward a better ROI. Start simple, with the broad-brush, trust-your-gut-instinct ways that help determine if your SEO campaign is on the right track. If you're not comfortable with your method of assessment, keep your budget small until you find the method that's manageable for you and that offers data you feel you can trust. Remember, the ROI loop is a circle, not a straight line."

The Left Brain says, "I agree that some degree of instinct-based approach is needed for difficult-to-track conversions. But for more straightforward e-commerce sites, or anyone with a clear method of measuring profit per conversion, PPC offers the opportunity to be more empirical in your approach. You know what your conversions are worth, so you can set your bids as high as possible while still delivering a comfortable profit margin.

"Of course, bids are not the only factor in PPC ranking, and they may not even be the most important one. After all, even a top-ranked ad is worthless to you if your ad copy is no good. Ongoing testing can help you improve both your ads and your ROI. And there are even automated PPC campaign management solutions, such as Atlas Search or Efficient Frontier, that will help track and analyze your PPC campaign for you. They're pricey, but if you're ready to invest in closing the loop in a more sophisticated way, these solutions might be a good match for you."

Thursday: Landing Page Optimization

Picture this: You're sitting in the conference room working out the last details of your landing page content. The web designer wants the call-to-action link to be "Get started now!" and the chief copywriter thinks it should be "Contact Sales." Everyone has an opinion, but nobody has any evidence to back it up. Landing page optimization can give you some real data on which to base these decisions.

The most common types of page optimization testing are *A/B testing* and *multivariate testing*. These are jargon for two very simple ideas: A/B testing (also called an A/B split) compares the performance of two page designs, and multivariate testing compares the performance of a larger number of page designs by swapping out content in several sections of the page at once.

Even if you have strong convictions about what you think your page content should be, we recommend letting a page optimization test provide more clues. Many website owners report being shocked by what their tests ultimately show to be the most effective content.

Both multivariate testing and A/B testing are available via a tool within the Google AdWords management interface called Website Optimizer. You will need a Google AdWords account to access Website Optimizer, but it does not need to be actively running ads. Other companies offering multivariate testing tools (for a fee) include Offermatica, Optimost, and Memetrics. You might as well start with the free Google option. You can always move up to the paid services after you've fallen in love with page optimization testing.

Today, we're going to get you started on a page test of your own.

Your Multivariate Test

Ready to get started? We recommend performing multivariate testing rather than an A/B split for the simple reason that we think it's more fun. Here's how multivariate testing works:

- You designate a few sections of your web page that you would like to test. For example, you might specify the headline, the first paragraph of text, and an accompanying photograph as your three sections. See Figure 9.1 for an illustration from Google's Overview.

- For each section, you create two or more versions of its content.

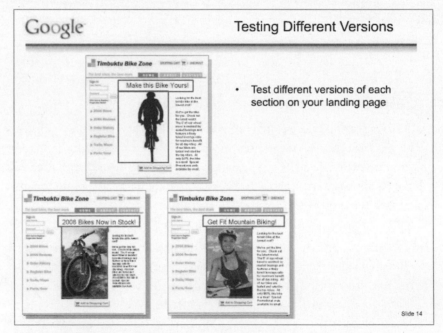

Figure 9.1 Google Website Optimizer

- The multivariate testing system plays mix-and-match with your variations, showing a random combination to each of your website visitors.

- After the test has run for some time, the combination with the highest conversion rate wins! The most sophisticated testing systems can find the best combinations based on statistics, even when those exact combinations haven't been tested. Some test results are shown in Figure 9.2.

Combinations	Page Sections				
Analysis for: Dec 3, 2007 11:34:42 AM PT - Dec 15, 2007 8:04:55 PM PT					
View: ⦿ Best 3 Combinations ○ Worst 3 Combinations			Download: [T] 🖼 📊	🖨 Print	🖼 Preview		
Combination	Estimated Conversion Rate Range [?]	Chance to Beat Orig. [?]	Chance to Beat All [?]	Observed Improvement [?]	Conversions / Visitors [?]
Original	17.8% ± 3.2%	—	10.5%	—	73 / 411
Combination 1	19.7% ± 3.3%	76.1%	43.8%	10.8%	85 / 432
Combination 2	19.0% ± 3.2%	67.6%	27.3%	6.87%	82 / 432
Combination 3	18.4% ± 3.2%	60.0%	18.3%	3.82%	78 / 423

Figure 9.2 Google Website Optimizer test results

Now: Either sign up for a new Google AdWords account, or log into your existing account. Find the Website Optimizer link and dive in.

Blue Willow Dog Coats—Barking Up the Right Tree

Blue Willow Dog Coats sells custom-made dog coats through its website at www.bwdogcoats .com. Blue Willow's owner is Sharon Couzin—but one of us calls her "Mom"! Lucky for her, Sharon has access to some of the best SEO opinions a person could hope for. Nope, not ours—we're talking about the opinions of her own site users! When Sharon had some tough questions about content, she turned to Google Website Optimizer for answers.

Blue Willow specializes in coats for Sighthounds (those of us not in the dog show set know these dogs as Whippets, Greyhounds, and Italian Greyhounds). But they can be custom made for any breed. Sharon wondered: "What should I say on the home page headline? Should I focus on the fact that I make coats for those hard-to-fit Sighthound breeds? Or should I focus on the customization?" A further review showed that some great content was being pushed below the fold by a long introductory paragraph. A shorter intro would help, but "will people be interested in clicking to learn more?" asked Sharon.

Continues

Blue Willow Dog Coats—Barking Up the Right Tree *(continued)*

Sharon, who already had a Google AdWords account, set up a Google Website Optimizer experiment to find the answers. She wrote two headlines: her original: "Extra Warm, Durable, Washable Winter Coats for Greyhounds, Iggys, Whippets and Dogs of all Shapes and Sizes," and a simplified revision: "Finally, a warm dog coat that really fits! Custom-made coats for dogs of all shapes."

Then, she wrote two versions of the intro paragraph: a long version that she liked, and one that felt painfully short. (In multivariate testing it's good to go outside your comfort zone.) Here are two examples of the resulting four versions of the page that Google Website Optimizer displayed for the test:

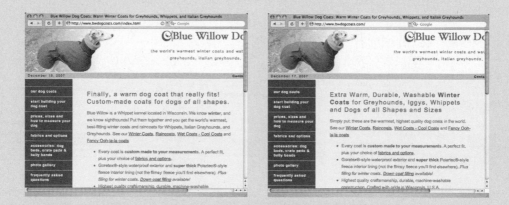

Sharon set up an easy-to-reach conversion goal: a visit to the purchase page. After a few weeks, she checked her conversion stats within Google Website Optimizer. The best performer? Her original headline, combined with the ultra-short intro paragraph.

The users had spoken, and the site was changed accordingly. A little reality testing can take your website to a better place, and Google Website Optimizer is a great option—regardless of whether you have an SEO expert at your Thanksgiving table every year.

Website Optimizer will walk you through the steps to creating your own test. You will need the ability to add JavaScript to your HTML pages, so if you're not the person who edits the site, walk over to his or her cubicle and see if you can get a few minutes of assistance today. Here are a few tips to keep in mind, in addition to Google's instructions:

- If you have a low-traffic site (say, under 200 visitors per day), you can speed up your results by testing your most trafficked pages and using a high-volume conversion definition. For example, rather than defining a conversion as an actual online *purchase*, you can define it as a visit to a product page. With more conversions, you'll have more data to compare your different page designs.

- Keep in mind that all of your page variations are going to be on display to your site audience—and your visitors have no idea that they're in the middle of a page optimization test. Use the preview feature to be sure that the content makes sense in all of the assembled combinations.

- Landing page testing is not just for paid search, nor is it only for e-commerce sites. You can apply these tests to any of your pages, and any type of online conversion goal.

- Take a chance and test some content that goes outside your comfort zone. We're not saying you should make statements that aren't accurate, but what about some zippier language or brighter colors? A true test needs to include some far-out options to be sure you're capturing the entire spectrum of possibilities.

Now: Go to Google Website Optimizer and set up your first test.

If you've got JavaScript expertise, you can stray from the standard instructions, and the system will still work. For example, putting the conversion tag on multiple pages will make them *all* count as conversions; similarly, you can copy your test content sections onto multiple pages or multiple spots on a page, and Website Optimizer will swap them *all* out. Find more details at www.prusak.com.

xtra cred

Alternatives to Landing Page Optimization

Maybe there are forces beyond your control that make it impossible for you to pursue a landing page optimization test. We've seen it before: tech departments that won't abide new JavaScript tags or marketing teams that aren't open to wild text experiments. Here are some workarounds that you can use to incorporate at least a bit of content testing into Your SEO Plan:

- If you're using one of the major PPC providers, A/B testing for PPC ads is easy! Just write one or two additional ads for each of your ad groups. As clicks come in, your PPC service automatically judges which ad is more effective and will increase its prominence for you automatically.

- Run a time-based test, in which you display one page version for a week or month, and then switch to another page version. Though seriously unscientific (was it really the page design change that caused traffic to rise, or was it the holiday season?), this approach is still better than nothing.

- If your organization performs usability testing, ask to have content variations incorporated into the tests.

Does page optimization have its limitations? Of course it does. You may figure out that one page is doing better than another, but unless you interview your target audience, you'll never know exactly *why*. Plus, your tests are limited to your ideas for edits, so unless you're a master at thinking outside the box, there may be big improvements that you miss. Nevertheless, landing page testing is one of the few ways of getting real data on the persuasiveness of your site's message.

Friday: Close the PPC ROI Loop

Today you're going to start a new "invest" cycle in your PPC ROI loop. You'll drop the duds—unsalvageable, low-performing keywords—from your PPC campaign. And you'll line up some promising new PPC keyterms and adjust bids based on performance data so far.

Sponsor New Keywords

Adding a few new keyphrases to your PPC account is a fairly flexible process. You can do this in any number of ways:

- Use your PPC service's keyword tool to suggest additional terms.
- Grab some more terms from your preliminary organic keyword list that didn't make the cut for top-priority optimization.
- Go for the "long tail" and add some longer, highly focused versions of existing terms.

 Now: Brainstorm more ideas for keywords in your PPC campaign. If your budget allows, add them to your account.

Adjust Bids Based on Performance

If you've been doing weekly PPC Quick Checks as we advised in Month Two, you've been adjusting your PPC bids to keep your spending balanced and on schedule. Today, adjust bids based on keyword performance.

On Tuesday, we suggested lowering bids for high conversion cost keywords. Today, take a look at the keywords that aren't on the red flag list. Can you make a good thing even better? For example:

- Consider raising bids on keywords with high conversion rates but low ranks and/or low conversion costs. This might increase your total number of conversions, with only a modest increase in conversion cost.

- Consider lowering bids on keywords with high conversion rates, but for which you are also ranking very well organically. This may help you wean your budget from clicks that you don't need to be paying for in the first place.

- Consider raising bids across the board if you're happy with your conversion rates and conversion costs but click-through rates are low due to low ranks.

Now: Adjust bids for improved performance.

Drop the Duds

On Monday, you got a good sense of which keywords are pulling their weight in your paid search campaign. You also know which ones may deserve a second chance. Now you'll drop any that are working against you. Here are the keywords we call "duds":

- Low- or zero-click-through-rate terms that are costing you more in administrative work than you think they're worth (tasks that eat up time include appealing an editorial decision, closely monitoring a very expensive term, or just performing routine management on a campaign that has grown too large over time).

- Terms for which you're paying more per conversion than your estimated conversion value.

- Terms that don't accurately represent your offerings.

- Terms that are already delivering great organic traffic because they rank consistently well in search listings and have compelling listings. Why pay for the PPC cow when you might be able to get organic milk for free?

If any of these factors are true, then go ahead and slash. You can always add them back later if you regret your choice.

Now: Comb through your low-performing keywords and delete those that are having a negative impact on your campaign.

Now that you've spent a week pruning and feeding your paid search campaign and planting the seeds for a healthier ROI, it's time to dig your site out of some common SEO challenges.

Week 11: What's Your Problem?

You're nearing the end of Your SEO Plan, so this week we'll give you a chance to tie up loose ends and chase down any remaining trouble spots in your search engine presence:

Monday: New Site, New Problems

Tuesday: Copywriting to Improve Your Search Results Snippets

Wednesday: Catch Up with Your Team

Thursday: Fun Tools for Site Assessment

Friday: Clean Up Ugly Listings

Monday: New Site, New Problems

It happens all the time, for big reasons or little ones, and it's one of the greatest challenges to an SEO campaign: a website redesign in which all or most of the URLs on the site change. Suddenly, every inbound link to your site is outdated. Bookmarks lead to broken links. Traffic plummets. Your search engine ranks drop off the map! And these problems can linger long after the revamp.

If your site was recently redesigned, or you're still working through repercussions from a long-ago revamp, or even if you're planning your site's next incarnation, here are some ideas for handling the sticky situations that crop up:

Page redirects Do all your outdated pages redirect to appropriate new ones? Don't just redirect them to the home page. Ideally, each old page would redirect to a new page with similar subject matter. If this is not the case with your site, your task for today is to create a list of old URLs that are still getting traffic and the new URLs that they should be redirecting to. Then send it to your IT team member, who can help set things right using a server setting called a *301 redirect*.

File Not Found page Do you have a kinder, gentler File Not Found (*404 error*) page? The page should, first and foremost, apologize to your patient readers for not being the page they're looking for. Next, it should *help them find the page they're looking for!* This could be by providing a site map, search box, or suggested links. And don't forget to include the global navigation on this page, just like on any other page of your site. If your File Not Found page is not helpful, your task is to propose new traffic-friendly content for the page and either implement it or deliver it to the person who can do so.

Inbound links Do you still have a multitude of links pointing to your old pages? If so, your task is to sweep the Web for links to your old URLs and request updates. We showed you how to find links that point to a specific page in Chapter 6, "Your One-Month Prep: Baseline and Keywords."

Internal links Did you clean up the links in your old navigation? You'll never know until you check. Run a *link validator*, a program that checks your website for broken links internally. Here's one to try: www.dead-links.com.

Massive site revamps have been known to cause more harm than good. So we would be remiss if we didn't tell you this:

Pearl of Wisdom: Sometimes it's best to follow the old maxim, "If it ain't broke, don't fix it."

Before you think about a site redo just to "keep things fresh," take stock of whether you're satisfied with your rankings, whether you have a good number of inbound links, and most important, whether your site satisfies the overall goals of your organization. Maybe, just maybe, you don't want to tempt fate with a redesign.

Prevent Link Rot

Next time you redesign your site, use URLs that you won't need to change—ever. Put some serious thought into file-naming conventions that will grow and expand with your website. Here are some rules of thumb:

- Don't name files with words like new, old, draft, current, latest, or any other status markers in the file name. This status will surely change as "new" files become "old" and "draft" files become "final." (It's a common problem! Last we checked, there were 771 listings in Google containing the preposterous file name final2.html—for shame!—and 520 listings for final3.html.)

- Name nested folders by year, and possibly month, for press releases or other dated materials (for example, www.zappyco.com/press/2005/august/newproduct.html). Put files in their final location as soon as they are launched rather than starting them out in a folder called "current" and moving them later.

- Leave out any information that may change in the future. For example, you don't want to include the name of a current copywriter in the file name. This URL will feel outdated and awkward three years from now when that individual no longer works at the company. Names of servers, the city where you're headquartered, or any other contemporary information should also be left off file names.

Follow these guidelines, and your search engine presence may survive the next site redesign without a hitch!

Now: Choose from the "new site, new problems" tasks listed in this section, and get started on the one that most applies to you.

Tuesday: Copywriting to Improve Your Search Results Snippets

You've already learned that searchers choose which result to click in a matter of seconds. Of course, you want your site to have the best possible representation in the search results—and that means you need a snippet that's on your side!

For example, which of the following search results would you be more likely to click? This one?

> **Mizuho** Securities **Asia** Limited
> shadow. shadow, shadow. **Mizuho Logo**. shadow, shadow. **Mizuho** Securities **Asia** Limited.
> ... **Mizuho** Securities USA Inc. **Mizuho** Bank (Schweiz) AG ...
> www.mizuho-sc.com/hk/ - 30k - Cached - Similar pages - Note this

Or this one?

> **Mizuho** Financial Group : Overview of **Mizuho Trust** & Banking
> **Mizuho Trust** & Banking Co., Ltd. provides products and services both for individuals and ...
> A variety of **trust** schemes focusing on the value of **assets** ...
> www.mizuho-fg.co.jp/english/ company/about/group/mizuho_tb.html - 15k -
> Cached - Similar pages

Both of these examples show snippets from websites that are divisions of the same corporation. Why does one snippet look deliciously clickable while the other looks more like a Dadaist poem? Stay tuned!

How Snippets Work

A snippet is text taken from a web page and shown when that page is listed in the search results. All of the major search engines currently use snippets for many (but not all) search results. The most important thing to understand about search result snippets is that they are different depending on what keyword has been searched. For example, a Google search for the term "animal cloning" returns this snippet:

> animal cloning
> As far as **animal cloning** is concerned, all **cloning** for research or medical purposes in the
> UK must be approved by the Home Office under the strict controls ...
> www.rds-online.org.uk/pages/ page.asp?i_ToolbarID=5&i_PageID=162 - 49k -
> Cached - Similar pages

A search for the term "animal cloning dolly" returns a different snippet for the same web page:

animal cloning
Dolly the sheep may have been the world's most famous clone, but she was not the first.
Cloning creates a genetically identical copy of an **animal** or plant. ...
www.rds-online.org.uk/pages/ page.asp?i_ToolbarID=5&i_PageID=162 - 49k -
Cached - Similar pages

Notice how each snippet includes the keywords that were searched? That means a search for your company name will return a much different snippet than a search for another of your target keywords will, even if both results point to your home page!

The specifics of how snippets are chosen vary for each search engine, but here are the basic rules:

- In general, the search engine finds the first instance of the searched keyphrase in the visible text on the page and displays it along with roughly 50 to 150 characters of surrounding text.

- The snippet often excludes titles and navigational elements.

- If the landing page doesn't include the exact phrase searched, the snippet will show sentences that include the individual words in the phrase.

- Searched terms will be bolded in the snippet, while stemmed and plural versions of the words (clon**ed**, clon**ing**, clon**es**) may or may not be bolded as well.

Check Your Snippets

The first step toward optimizing your snippets is reviewing them! To check your snippets, simply open the search engine of your choice and search for your target keywords. Scroll to your search result and see what you find.

> **Now:** Search for your target keywords on Google, Yahoo!, and MSN. Review any snippets that you find for your website. Make a note of any that you wish to improve in your Task Journal.

If your website is not ranking in the top 30 for a target keyword, you can skip the snippet improvement for now.

There may be other keywords you want to check as well. If you know phrases outside of your top-priority terms that are bringing traffic to your website, take a look and see if those snippets could use a makeover, too.

Your Snippet Makeover

If you came across some snippets that you would like to improve, here are some possible approaches:

Add text. Sometimes, improving a snippet is as simple as adding one keyword-rich introductory sentence to the beginning of your page copy. Be sure that it is formatted the same as the rest of the page copy—titles and headers may not show up in snippets. And use your good copywriting skills so it doesn't seem jarring or "tacked on."

Remove ALT tags. One of the less-appealing items in many snippets is repetitive image ALT tags. A graphic button displaying the words "Free Delivery in February!" should have an ALT tag containing matching text. But a tiny graphic that is used to create a corner on a button does not need an ALT tag stating "white button corner." The page will be just fine without it. (Yep, that's what caused the poetic, but completely ineffective, "shadow, shadow, shadow" listing for Mizuho Securities Company that we showed you earlier.)

Change your error messages. Search engine robots come calling at your website without any of the plug-ins, cookies, or JavaScript enabling that your site may require. If you're not careful, your search engine snippet might end up looking like this:

> **USGS (US Geological Survey) EROS**, Sioux Falls, SD
> Your browser does not support script. Your browser does not support script. Your browser does not support script. About **EROS** ...
> **eros**.usgs.gov/archive/nslrsda/ - 8k - <u>Cached</u> - <u>Similar pages</u>

We've already shown you the best ways to avoid this kind of listing: Be a stickler for good robot-readable content. But if you still have the odd error message making its way into the search results, remember that these messages are usually written by programmers without a marketing once-over. You might want to get in the loop!

Restructure the page. If your page is built using Cascading Style Sheets (CSS), it may be a simple endeavor to move scripts around in the source code so that navigation or other less-optimized content is situated below the page copy. This won't make any difference to your users viewing the page in the browser, but to search engines it will make your page copy come first. This may be a good strategy if your snippets are getting bogged down in navigation text.

 Now: Assemble your suggested edits for snippet improvement. Deliver them to whomever needs to make the changes, or complete the edits yourself.

If your search engine listings are haunted by an ugly description from an Open Directory or Yahoo! Directory listing, there are special meta tags that can help with your snippet makeover. Learn about them at yourseoplan.com/meta-tags.html.

This is one of those rare opportunities for you to see rather sudden and dramatic changes in your listing quality. You may even notice the difference in just a few days, the next time your pages are spidered.

Wednesday: Catch Up with Your Team

You're well into the third month of Your SEO Plan now—how is your team holding up? Are you all working together like a well-oiled machine? Or is your "team" more like a collection of squeaky wheels, revolving doors, and bottlenecks?

In Chapter 5, we covered some strategies for encouraging members of your organization to join your SEO effort. Here are some good questions that may help you keep everyone on the same path:

Are my edits getting implemented? This is a biggie for many in-house SEOs: Just getting simple (or not-so-simple) edits made to the website may require jumping through design, IT, and even legal hoops. If your recommended edits aren't being taken care of, take time today and figure out why. Are you sending your requests to people who don't have authority or access to make the changes? Are your requests playing second fiddle to another department with more "pull"? Or, did enthusiasm wane after the first round of edits didn't turn out the hoped-for quick results? Get the inside scoop on the holdup so you can take steps to flush it out!

Is SEO integrated into our processes? For Your SEO Plan to succeed, it needs to be part of the web development process. That means an SEO review before, during, or (worst case) after changes are made to the website. It also means integration of SEO considerations into the website style guide, if your organization has one. If you're feeling like an outsider, or if you think SEO is being given short shrift, you need to work on ways to integrate SEO into company processes. This means you may have to take on the role of SEO evangelist: Write up the first draft of an SEO style guide and deliver it to your developers. Ask to be included in copywriting or design meetings. If you don't overdo it, you can even send articles or SEO tips to a team member who might benefit from this information.

How's that conversion tracking going? By now, we hope you have conversion tracking in place for your organization. If your tracking method requires participation by members of your team (for example, you need Sales to track calls from a special 800 number), revisit it today and see if it's working. Are you getting the information you need? If not, what needs to change?

Will the Real Home Page Please Stand Up?

You met search engine expert P.J. Fusco in Chapter 5, where she shared advice for getting your team on board. Here, P.J. tells a cautionary tale:

"We needed to optimize a handful of pages in a 4,000-page e-commerce site. One of the elements required was meta tags—unique title, description, and keyword attributes for eight different pages. . . .

"The project manager informed me this portion of the organic project was complete, so I audited the work. Everything looked good, except for one thing. Every single page of the site contained the meta tags for the home page. Can you imagine what a search engine spider thinks when it's trying to index 4,000 pages all proclaiming to be the official home page of the company?"

You've heard of Murphy's Law: If anything can possibly go wrong, it will. Add to that our sad little truth: If any project is going to get rushed through, glossed over, or ignored, it will be SEO. Nobody is going to look after SEO details the way you, the SEO team leader, will. So keep P.J.'s experience in mind, and be sure that you have a process in place to check your team's SEO-related edits, even when you're sure nothing can go wrong.

Who's in it for the long term? Which members of your team have the energy, talent, and mind-set for a sustained effort? By now, you have enough SEO experience that you can spot the personalities with a natural affinity for this work. Now it's your turn to be the squeaky wheel: Do what you can with your higher-ups to keep those people on your team for the long term.

Now: Ask yourself the preceding questions and start sending e-mails or setting up the needed meetings for improvement.

Since your SEO team is made up of people who, like you, are busy doing other things, it's natural that your team's interest and ability to focus will wax and wane. So don't be surprised if you need to do checkups as you did today on a regular basis.

Thursday: Fun Tools for Site Assessment

From time to time throughout Your SEO Plan, we've pointed you to helpful tools available on the Web. Today, we'll share a few more of our favorites! Every one of these can help your search engine visibility; read through the descriptions and spend your hour exploring the ones that interest you the most:

Link validator There are many free tools online to check your website for broken links on a page-by-page basis. (For example, LinkScan/QuickCheck at www.elsop.com/quick/ and several spider emulators do this.) However, it's much more useful to run link validators sitewide. One site that offers a deeper crawl is the one we mentioned on Monday: www.dead-links.com.

Slow page load checker Your site visitors and prospective customers aren't the only ones who grow weary of slow-loading pages; some SEOs believe that search engine spiders also give up and walk away (Google Webmaster Tools will report these timeouts, if there are any on your site). You can find a good online tool for checking page load time at www.websiteoptimization.com/services/analyze.

Link popularity comparison Use the tool at www.marketleap.com/publinkpop/ to compare your website's link popularity with that of your competitors.

Keyword density tools The site www.live-keyword-analysis.com offers a quick and easy way to check keyword density in any text you choose.

Your own browser Here's a tool we know you already have: a browser. In Chapter 6, you learned how to view page source using your browser. You can also use your browser as a makeshift spider emulator. Here's how: Select Preferences or Internet Options from your browser menu. Then, figure out how to turn off image display and disable JavaScript. You can choose to reject all cookies while you're at it. Voilà! Your browser is now a speed machine and a crude approximation of a search engine robot.

If you use Firefox, a must-have SEO extension is "Web Developer," available at this URL: https://addons.mozilla.org/en-US/firefox/addon/60.

Accessibility check One of the fringe benefits of Your SEO Plan is that it will improve your website's accessibility for the disabled. By the same token, a more accessible website will tend to be more robot friendly as well. Jan Schmidt of Collaborint Web Management Services, a web design and development firm specializing in web accessibility, explains that many SEO practices "not only make it more efficient for search engines to crawl a website and index the content, but can also improve the disabled user's experience by providing easy-to-navigate links and machine-readable page text."

Tools are available to check your page with everything from voice browsers to color-blindness simulators. We recommend you start with Cynthia Says, a free web-based tool located at www.cynthiasays.com. Links and descriptions of many more accessibility tools can be found here: www.w3.org/WAI/ER/tools/complete.

Redirects and more Rex Swain's HTTP Viewer (www.rexswain.com/httpview.html) is a rare gem because it shows what kind of redirect is in place on a given page. This can be useful to you if you're wondering what kind of redirects you have on your site but can't get a straight answer from your IT department (maybe because you don't *have* an IT department?).

xtra
cred

If you're the type to spend hours testing out gadgets and techno-goodies, here are a couple of SEO tool smorgasbords that you may enjoy: www.seomoz.org/tools and www.faganfinder.com/urlinfo/.

 Now: Explore your favorites from the list of tools in this section.

Warning: Heavy use of SEO tools may result in an increase in the size of your Task Journal. Embrace it! Good SEO means never running out of things to do!

Friday: Clean Up Ugly Listings

 Now: Before you get started on today's task, don't forget: It's Friday, time for your paid search Quick Check! See Week 5 of Chapter 8 for instructions.

During your site visibility assessments, you probably found at least one listing in the search results that made you cringe. A broken URL from your domain available to the searching public? An out-of-date press release announcing the hire of a long-gone CEO? Today you'll take steps to clean up some of these brand-busting uglies.

Here are some of the more common problems we've observed and how to deal with them. You probably won't face all of these problems, but we expect you'll see at least one:

Broken links The search engines don't want broken links in their results any more than you do. They will eventually figure out that a page doesn't exist and remove it from their indexes. But why let a perfectly good search engine ranking go to waste? Try one of the following approaches:

- Since the URL is already indexed and may already have some good rankings, inbound links, or bookmarked traffic, consider creating a new page and saving it at the missing URL. However, do this only if it makes sense to create a new page with similar content—it would be awkward if your cabinet hardware products were listed at a page called "floral-arrangements.html."

- Talk to your IT people about setting up a 301 redirect, which carries traffic on this page to another page of your choosing. But don't make the common mistake of pointing the redirect to your home page! Choose the page on your site that best matches the one that has gone missing.

- Sometimes, broken links linger in the search results because your server fails to mention that the page is missing. That's right; it's possible for a server to return a "Page Found" message even if a page is missing! It's a riddle wrapped in a conundrum, but luckily it's an easy fix for your IT folks.

Obsolete offerings You don't want your potential customers seeing outdated product descriptions, promotions that are no longer active, or last year's price list in the search results. The best and fastest approach to this problem is to update your site's content while keeping the file in the same location so that it doesn't lose its search engine status.

In some cases, a simple update may not be so simple. For example, suppose you have found a well-ranked search engine listing for your web page featuring the Snackmaster 2004, but your company no longer sells this older model. Your website now has a new page featuring the Snackmaster 2008. If you rewrite your 2004 page to describe your new product, your site will contain two pages with identical content, which is a search engine no-no as well as an administrative headache. Instead, it's best to edit the 2004 page content to include a notice that a new model is available and link to the 2008 model page. A 301 redirect would be another option, especially if there's no customer support or archival reasons to keep the old page live.

Spring Cleaning Your Website for Better Search

We usually advise our clients to *add* things to their website as part of their SEO strategies—keywords, landing pages, more text, more unique descriptions. But, if spring fever has you wanting to toss more than just the moldy contents of your office fridge, we have some ideas for your website.

Here are a few things that you should consider pruning from your site in order to improve your presence in the search engines:

Duplicate content There are two reasons to purge your website of duplicate content. First, the search engines don't like unnecessary duplication, and second, it's usually a symptom of a larger organizational problem with your site's navigation. If your site is displaying identical or near-identical content on two separate URLs, chances are you're doing so unnecessarily. Follow the strategies from Chapter 7 to dump the dupes.

Non-HTML documents that make poor landing pages Think of this scenario: Following a link from a search engine, a visitor enters your site by landing on your PDF product assembly instructions, or a blank financial spreadsheet template. As you learned earlier this month, non-HTML documents are often poor entry pages to a website. Sometimes, spring cleaning involves hiding things away from public view, maybe stashing them in a closet or storage bin. In this case, the offending files could be added to your robots.txt file so that they are hidden from search engine indexing. You might need these documents on your website, but you don't need to offer them as potential landing pages.

Continues

Spring Cleaning Your Website for Better Search *(continued)*

"Strategic" outlinks Maybe you followed someone's outdated advice and took part in a reciprocal linking scheme, or joined an "undetectable" link exchange network. You were only trying to help your website, we know, but these links can be damaging to your site's ranks, especially if they are pointing to websites that have nothing to do with your own site's topical focus. Deep-six that "link partners" page! Instead, collect your inlinks in a way that's more beneficial to your site—by creating great content and making sure other sites know about it!

Outdated content Almost every website has outdated content, ranging from little stuff (like old calendars) to big stuff (like obsolete product lines). The problem with outdated content is that it can make its way into your search engine listings—and that can cause confusion, frustration, or even a bad reputation for your company. Does your footer say, "ZappyCo: Copyright 2005?" You won't believe how many times copyright notices show up in search results. Are you displaying promotions that are no longer valid? Don't play bait-and-switch with your search traffic—chances are those visitors won't come back. Make it a priority, and make some time to update or redirect that dusty old content.

Whatever's causing your slow pages to load so slowly There are various opinions on how slow is too slow. Some say frustration kicks in for visitors after just one second of load time, and many agree that abandonment is likely after 5–10 seconds of loading. The faster your load time, the less chance that your search traffic will move down the listings to your competitor. There are page-load-time analysis tools like the one from www.websiteoptimization.com that can help you figure out what might be causing the problem. Toss out the heavy stuff, and streamline your site's load time.

Remember, it's not just the sheer number of pages you have indexed in Google—it's the lusciousness of your listings! Any time of year is a good time to banish the parts of your website that are detracting from your search listings.

Private or inappropriate material There it is, staring out at you from between listing #5 and listing #7: your company's holiday gift list, with addresses and phone numbers of all your best clients! You need to clean up your act, and fast. Here's how:

- Remove the page from your site. Or, leave the offending file live, but immediately remove the offending content.
- Then request removal from the search engines (see www.yourseoplan.com for links to removal URLs).

By leaving the file live but changing the content, you may benefit from a quicker update than if you took down the page altogether. However, you should be aware that a search engine's cached pages may retain a snapshot of the content for longer than you're comfortable with, and there are historical web archive sites that may display the content forever. If you have serious legal concerns—for example, if you posted a disclaimer that said, "All information on this site is medical advice" rather than "...*not* medical advice"—you can use a copyright search method such as http://copyscape.com to search for instances of your content throughout the Web and seek removal.

While these are all positive steps, in truth there's little you can do to prevent robots from indexing pages that are live and accessible. If you really do not want pages to be found, secure them behind a password!

Week 12: SEO Status Report

Just like the talk you may be planning (or planning to avoid) with your significant other, the SEO Status Report is the time to turn your attention to the long-term view. SEO and your website have been in a relationship for three months now, four if you count the Prep Month. What's it all about? Where are you going? Are you committed to your keyword choices? Do you think it's time to start playing the field and looking for additional landing pages? Do you have an itch to check out new competitors?

This week is not just about producing a report, although certainly that's important. It's really about the thinking, planning, reviewing, and analysis that you do while you are gathering the information for your report.

Pearl of Wisdom: Without a period of time for review, reflection, and prioritization for the future, your SEO campaign can go off track, or just get lost in the busy day-to-day shuffle of your workplace.

Whether you ultimately choose to create an SEO Status Report on a weekly, monthly, or quarterly basis is really a question of your organization's needs and your own tolerance for documentation workload. Regardless of how often you check in, a commitment to tracking and documentation will always separate the pack leaders from the also-rans. Open up the SEO Growth Plan Worksheet you started in Chapter 6 and get started on your tasks for this week:

Monday: Check Organic Status

Tuesday: Check Links

Wednesday: Conversions and Traffic

Thursday: Monitor Paid Search

Friday: Opportunities and Action Items

Monday: Check Organic Status

During your Prep Month, you established goals for your site's visibility on the major search engines. Today, you'll find out how your standings have changed. We'll ask you to check three values:

- Search engine rankings
- Indexed pages
- Listing quality

But first, you need a place to record your observations:

 Now: Open up a new document and title it "SEO Status Report."

Here are the topics that we'll coach you through this week. You might as well add these titles to your report right now:

- Site Visibility
- Link Building
- Google PageRank
- Conversions and Traffic
- Paid Search
- Opportunities and Action Items

We won't tell you exactly how to format your document, and we'll trust you to organize and present the information in a way that makes sense to you and your team. Some of you might like splashy colors or charts to compare the popularity of various keywords. Others might prefer a "just the facts, ma'am" approach. What's most important to us is that the information be written down for the record books.

Search Engine Rankings

For this task, you will perform a manual rankings check on the major search engines for all of your top target keywords. You learned how to do this back in Chapter 6.

 Now: Open your Rank Tracking Worksheet and fill in your website ranks for this month.

With your before-and-after ranks side by side, it's easy to see what changes have occurred. If you were starting from zero or you had some easy fixes in your optimization, you may have some exciting improvement in ranks. If you aren't seeing the improvements you've been hoping for, take heart. Read the sidebar "It's a Marathon, Not a Sprint" for thoughts on SEO timing.

In this section, summarize your current standings as compared to the Prep Month. Here are some examples:

- We gained top 30 listings on MSN for three of our target keywords.
- We have a new #2 listing for the term "novelty napkin holders" on Yahoo!.

Next, put on your thinking cap and flesh out these bare-bones facts with some juicy analysis. How do these changes compare with the goals you established in the Prep Month? What could be done to improve any less-than-pleasing situations? Possible analysis might look like this:

- We gained top 30 listings on MSN for three of our target keywords. Our text optimization probably had something to do with this.
- We have a new #2 listing for the term "novelty napkin holders" on Yahoo!. However, the listing contains unflattering text from our customer forum.

Stymied about what to say? Think about who will be reading this report and try to imagine what questions they'll have. For example, if this is primarily for your own edification, your analysis might take the form of questions or a to-do list, such as, "Is it possible to improve this listing? If not, I should look into excluding the customer forum using the robots.txt file." If this is for your boss who is dubious about your SEO efforts, your analysis might take the form of educational tidbits, such as, "Seeing the customer forum in the #2 position indicates that there are no problems with the search engines finding and indexing our deep pages. This is good news, but I will look into how to improve the quality of this listing." As your experience with reporting continues, you will become more and more adept at this sort of SEO rumination.

> **Now:** Add your rankings summary and analysis to the Site Visibility section of your SEO Status Report.

Indexed Pages

In addition to monitoring search engine ranks for your top keywords, we recommend checking the total number of pages indexed. You learned how to do this in Chapter 6 using the site: search shortcut.

Now: Check the total number of pages indexed on your site in Google, Yahoo!, and MSN. Record the value on your Rank Tracking Worksheet and in the Site Visibility section of your SEO Status Report.

Why record the total number of pages indexed on a regular basis? For one, if you previously had obstacles to robot indexing on your site, you're likely to see a great deal of improvement here once those obstacles are removed. Ditto if you've been adding lots of new content.

xtra cred

If you're watching page indexing closely, you may have a special interest in robot activity. With a little sleuthing, you can see which search engine robots have visited your site. See Chapter 10 for more information.

Listing Quality

Whenever we're called upon to get a very quick sense of a site's presence on search engines, we perform a site: search and assess the quality of the listings. You already know the total number of pages that are indexed on your site. Now, give them a once-over for quality. Are the listings compelling and clickable? Does each page have a unique listing? How is your branding? Your status report should call out any improvements or trouble spots.

Now: Assess the listing quality for your site's search engine listings on Google, Yahoo!, and MSN and document it in the Site Visibility section of your SEO Status report.

I Hate Paperwork!

Do you hear that? Our eye-rolling detector is beeping! Someone out there is about to complain that all this documentation is useless!

In our opinion, the SEO Status Report is a cornerstone of a well-balanced plan. Why? Because we firmly believe that data is useless unless it's interpreted in a meaningful way.

A seasoned SEO professional confesses, "One of my first SEO projects was when I worked at a web development firm, and SEO was an add-on to building a website. With SEO being a new service, we had no established system for documenting or reporting on this work. I diligently performed all the tasks for the initial discovery phase of the project: choosing keywords, assessing the site and its competitors, and making recommendations for next steps. With each of these tasks, I worked closely with our client and e-mailed him all of the related data.

"At the end of the project, my boss (who didn't know SEO but certainly knew business best practices!) suggested that I put together a final report. What did I do? I printed out my previous documents and data, stapled them all together, and slapped on a title page.

"What a disaster! The client had nothing to show his boss, nobody wanted to wade through the data, and I wasted more time re-explaining everything I had done than I would have spent writing up a summary in the first place. Worse, all of the added value from my work—the thought, research, discussion, and analysis that had gone into our choices—was lost!

"Luckily, the client was forgiving. But I learned a hard lesson with that project: Document what you do and write it with a close eye on your intended audience!"

Have you guessed yet that the SEO pro quoted here is one of the authors? Lucky for you, you can learn from our mistakes! The point of this week is not just to document your work, but also to do the analysis and mental sifting that allows you to write about it intelligently. The way you tell your SEO story is what will ultimately separate you from the SEO hacks and newbies out there. Your SEO Status Report is a team-builder, a boss-pleaser, and a mental reinforcement for your SEO learning curve, all wrapped in a sensible white-inkjet-bond-paper bow.

Tuesday: Check Links

Today, you'll follow up on the link-building campaign that you started a few weeks ago. You made a few link submittals in Chapter 6, but what happened next? Did you go for an hour-a-week campaign, or did you go for one of the less intensive options we described? Whatever your approach, it's important to keep track of your link-building activities and accomplishments in a summary report. You'll document the following in both words and numbers: link-building activities and Google PageRank.

Link-Building Activities

Most likely, you've already had some correspondence, possibly even several back-and-forth e-mail communications, with potential linking sites and blogs. You may have also made directory submittals or explored linking opportunities in the Social Web. Today, review your e-mails and your Link Tracking Worksheet, and briefly summarize these activities. Here are some examples of this kind of commentary:

- I contacted 14 bloggers to alert them to our new line of Madras napkins, e-mailed five website owners seeking new inbound links, and requested updated URLs from four sites pointing to our old product page. Of these, our site received two link updates and one new link.

- On (date), I submitted our website to the Napkin Mania Directory in the category:...

- Surfing the Web, I found a long list of blogs and other sites that may wish to comment on or link to our website. Links will be requested after our new landing pages are complete.
- Three site owners stated that they would not link to us because...

If you received useful feedback from any site owners, such as a rejection letter that stated specifically why you were turned down, consider quoting it in your report so that the idea doesn't get lost in your e-mail inbox forever.

 Now: Document your link building activity in the Link Building section of your SEO Status Report.

Google PageRank

Despite our misgivings about the usefulness of the Google PageRank value, we recommend that you track it for your landing pages. Why? It's an easy way to gather at-a-glance numbers that can help you see changes in your status over time.

You can see Google PageRank just by browsing to your landing pages and reviewing the Google Toolbar that you downloaded in Chapter 6.

 Now: Browse to each of your landing pages and record the Google PageRank on your Rank Tracking Worksheet. Document anything noteworthy in the Google PageRank section of your SEO Status Report.

slacker   Google PageRank is good to know, but it's not essential. If you're short on time, you can skip this step.

Wednesday: Conversions and Traffic

Have you fallen in love with your web analytics program yet? We sure hope so. Today, you'll look at some of the key measurements that can show the effects of Your SEO Plan and point you in the right direction for ongoing improvement.

Conversions

Conversions, especially if you've defined them properly so that they match the overall goals of your organization, are truly the bottom line of Your SEO Plan.

During your Prep Month, you established a baseline on conversions to the best of your ability, and recorded it in your Quick Reference Report. Maybe you've got plenty of cold, hard facts and were able to document something like "One percent of site visitors, and 7 percent of search engine–based visitors, completed an online purchase transaction." Or, perhaps you had to improvise a little: "According to the development department, very few of our catering customers have any awareness of the website's existence, and there is no evidence that any wedding orders this year resulted from web visits."

Now: Open up your analytics program and export this month's conversion data. Or, if you're using alternative methods of conversion tracking (such as a phone sales sheet), take whatever steps you need to gather that information.

Take a look at your current conversion data as compared to the data you compiled for your Quick Reference Report. If there are differences, what caused them? Separating out all of the different factors that contribute to your bottom line—SEO efforts, seasonal effects, even regular month-to-month fluctuations—is almost impossible. Your mission in this report is to separate out the effects of your SEO campaign as well as you can. If there are any results that you *can* attribute directly to your SEO efforts today, make a note of them in your report. Here are some examples:

- Listing our site in the Home Décor Directory has resulted in a branding boost and 700 visits.
- Since we succeeded in getting the "Tea Time" page indexed in all of the major search engines, we have seen a 27 percent increase in lace doily sales.
- Four hundred click-throughs on our PPC campaign resulted in 16 sales of monogrammed napkin sets.

Now: Write your conversion data and commentary in the Conversions and Traffic section of your SEO Status Report.

Traffic Stats

Your well-defined conversions are the most important measure of your SEO success, but they don't tell the full story on their own. After all, knowing that conversions went up is nice, but it doesn't give you insight into *why* they went up and what you can do to reinforce the trend. Here are some of the other measurements that we find useful:

- Search engine traffic as a percent of total traffic and as a percent of total new traffic. This is a good metric if you're dealing with skeptical higher-ups, because some nice increases may help justify your SEO campaign.

- Overall average bounce rate compared to bounce rate by referrer, entry page, or referring keywords. For example, "The overall average bounce rate was 56 percent. Bounce rate from search engine visitors was only 25 percent, while bounce rate from our top referrer, ExpensiveDirectory.com, was 87 percent. Of our top landing pages, our new Napkin Holders page had the lowest bounce rate at 22 percent." This information can tell you which audiences your website is serving best and which ones are disappointed by your offerings. It might provide ideas for new landing pages or keyword optimization choices.

- Top referring sites. This information helps you assess the value of your link building efforts.

- Keyword-by-keyword conversions and dollar values. This is a great way to assess your keyword choices, and determine whether you need to adjust your focus. For example: "'Tea cozies' had 16 conversions with a total value of $345. 'Wholesale linens' had 4 conversions with a total value of $6,500."

- Conversion rate broken down by audience. For example, "Users who entered the site via pages in the Restaurant section had a 5 percent conversion rage, while users who entered via the Home section had only a 0.5 percent conversion rate." You can segment your audience in any way that you find meaningful, as long as your analytics program will support it.

- Number of page views and/or time spent on site by keyword, landing page, referrer, or any other type of audience segmentation. Although a larger number of page views is not necessarily a plus (it could signal that people are having trouble finding what they need on your site!), for many sites it is a good indicator of audience engagement.

Your goal in this section is not just to document traffic—it's to come up with ideas for site improvement. If you discover a trend that you can't explain, dig deeper until you have at least a hypothesis as to why it happened. Grab the most creative thinker on your team and brainstorm how you might test your guesses.

 Now: Write your traffic data and commentary in the Conversions and Traffic section of your SEO Status Report. This may be the place to compare data with goals from your SEO Growth Plan.

By the way, if anyone ever wants to see your *key performance indicators*, print out this section of the report and hand it over—you just compiled them!

Thursday: Monitor Paid Search

Your SEO Status Report should include important information about your spending and accomplishments with your paid search campaigns. Today, touch on these points:

- Paid search performance data
- Top-performing keywords
- Changes to campaigns

Here are some guidelines for making the most of the data you get from your paid search service.

It's a Marathon, Not a Sprint

As you've learned throughout this book, organic SEO is not a quick-and-dirty operation. We believe that the best SEO is a set of standards, and a mind-set to be integrated into web development processes for long-term results. Clients rarely believe us when we tell them that it can take 3–6 months to see results from what we do—but we're not just saying that for our health!

Take a look at this screenshot:

Continues

> ### It's a Marathon, Not a Sprint *(continued)*
>
> Are you surprised to see that most of the SEO on this site took place in February and March? Yet traffic and conversions didn't start ramping up until August. During the interim period, several SEO factors were improving: Inbound links were accumulating and becoming "aged," the domain itself was aging, and (most importantly) development of new content on the site was moving forward with a focus on SEO best practices. We can't promise you results like this, but we *can* promise that organic SEO probably won't move as fast as you want it to.

Paid Search Performance Data

You just compiled performance data in Week 10—there's no reason you can't reuse that data here. If you haven't done it yet, here's a reminder—at a minimum, we want you to record:

- Total number of click-throughs
- Click-through percentage
- Total cost
- Average total cost per click
- Total number of conversions
- Conversion percentage
- Average total cost per conversion

> **Now:** Use your PPC service to generate a monthly campaign report. Enter the keyword performance data in the Paid Search section of your SEO Status Report.

Keep your PPC service's campaign report open; you'll need it to complete the next section.

Top-Performing Keywords

Looking through long lists of keyword data should be banned by OSHA! Whether it's a large PPC campaign with hundreds or thousands of keywords or a smaller one with a couple dozen, the people reading your report will appreciate an abbreviated version. That's why we like to pull out some of the top-performing keywords for an eye-pleasing review.

First, you need to decide what you will consider good performance for your keywords. Some options are highest number of click-throughs, highest total number of conversions, best conversion percentage, best click-through percentage, highest total dollar amount spent, highest profit (total conversion value minus cost), and even a combination of multiple factors.

Once you have chosen your preferred performance measure, browse through your PPC service's campaign report and pull out the top 10 or so keywords based on performance. You will list them, along with their performance values, in the SEO Status Report.

Now: Record your top-performing keywords in the Paid Search section of your SEO Status Report.

Changes to Campaigns

Here is the place to record any changes that took place in your paid search campaigns this month—things like keywords bumped up or down the totem pole or changes to ad copy.

This is also the place to make your recommendations or plans for future changes, such as, "Based on the success of our Wrinkle Free Napkin promotion, we will add a wrinkle free ad group starting next month" or "Thirteen keywords with high click-throughs but low conversion rates will be dropped from the campaign."

Now: Document any notable paid search campaign changes in the Paid Search section of your SEO Status Report.

With your paid search campaign monitoring complete, you're ready to finalize your SEO Status Report with some forward-thinking analysis and action items.

Friday: Opportunities and Action Items

Before you get started on today's task, don't forget: It's Friday, time for your paid search Quick Check! See Week 5 of Chapter 8 for instructions.

Here is the section that everybody on your team will turn to when they get this report. And even if you're working alone, this to-do list will be an indispensable reference as you move forward into the next month.

One of the challenges that we've faced time and time again in our SEO efforts is writing reports that are complete and meaningful, readable, and most important, *actionable*. Yes, actionable—it may be a made-up word, but it sure is an important idea in SEO.

Pearl of Wisdom: The best reports are not just repositories of information; they are also tools to guide your team through the next steps.

To assemble your action items, review each of the previous sections of the report. Here are some likely candidates for your action items list:

- Ongoing tasks that need continued attention, like link-building and content development
- Any unimplemented optimization recommendations from the first month of Your SEO Plan
- Untapped potential: new opportunities you've discovered, either during this reporting week, during your ROI reviews this month, or during your analytics meditations in Chapter 8
- Red flags: problems such as unindexed pages or bad-looking listings

You're a professional, so we're betting you've seen an action item list or two in your lifetime. We bet you're used to seeing the following columns: Action, Person Responsible, Target Completion Date. Now, here's a curveball for you: We want you to add a column called *Reason* to your action items list.

The Reason column will be the hardest one to write. This is where you must provide a concise explanation of what good this action is going to do for your company. It hearkens back to what you learned in Chapter 5: Educate your team for best results in SEO. Giving your team a quick explanation of the reasoning behind your requested change will eliminate the "Why in heaven's name am I being asked to do this extra work?" or "Why should I allot this extra budget?" reaction. And being forced to write a reason for every action item will help you keep your own ducks in a row as well.

Now: Write your action items, including the Reason column, in the Action Items section of your SEO Status Report.

With your first SEO Status Report resting comfortably in your e-mail outbox, your four-month journey is complete! But by now you know that SEO is never really done. Read on for the next steps.

Moving On: Forging Your Own SEO Path

Congratulations! Since you've opened this book, you've absorbed a tremendous amount of SEO knowledge, been promoted to SEO team leader, and become even more valuable to your organization. The "scripted" portion of Your SEO Plan is over, with the exception of some helpful ideas for extra credit and slacking in the next chapter.

You may have noticed that the further Your SEO Plan progressed, the less we held your hand and the more you had to create your own directions. That's because, as SEO expert Jill Whalen said, there really is no cookie-cutter solution. You have to go where your organization needs to go, where your competition forces you to go, and where your market allows you to go. As you move forward on your own, you have endless options, but here are some possible ways to proceed:

- Make every day a Task Journal day, with the exception of a day a week set aside for link building and PPC management, and a day a month set aside for analytics review.

- Start Your SEO Plan over again with a new audience or conversion goal in mind.

- Start Your SEO Plan over again with a new set of landing pages in mind.

- Start combing through your site, page by page or section by section, and optimize based on your current best practices.

- Ask your marketing team what short-term promotions are coming up. A contest? A seminar? A sale? Make sure you have a say in any promotional text that's going up on your site, and consider setting up your PPC campaign to promote it for the short term.

- Depending on what you've learned, you may want to drop PPC and go full bore on organic SEO. Or vice versa!

Intelligent Outsourcing

Maybe you've developed into a full-fledged SEO expert over the course of reading this book. But it's also possible that you've discovered that it's not your favorite pastime and you're ready to outsource. In the years that we've been in the SEO industry, we've seen growth in the number of high-quality SEO service providers. At the same time, we've seen at least 57 varieties of snake oil on the market! If you do choose to go the outsourcing route, keep the following caveats in mind:

- Watch out for any guarantee of a specific search engine rank. A legit search marketing service will not guarantee a rank that they don't have control over.

Continues

Intelligent Outsourcing *(continued)*

- Some companies direct your traffic through intermediate pages on their own hosted domains and then "turn off" your traffic when the contract is terminated. You need to have control over your own content and traffic, so don't agree to this type of business arrangement.

Snake oil

- There are only a small number of important search engines to rank well on, so anyone who is talking about rankings on "thousands of search engines" is probably best avoided.

- Good search marketing is time consuming, and there are no shortcuts. If a company is charging $79.99, you are not getting a legitimate full-service solution.

The best news is, now that you know so much about sensible, effective, and holistic SEO practices, you'll be able to make informed judgments about any SEO help for hire that crosses your path.

The world of search is ever changing, and Your SEO Plan will need to change with it. Technological advances in personalization, local search, demographic targeting, synonym recognition, keyword categorization, and so on will require constant adjustment on your part. Will social bookmarking systems and "human intelligence" replace search engine algorithms? Will organic SEO become obsolete as PPC dominates? Will search become integrated with television and search marketing replace TV ads? Whatever the future holds, we hope this book will help you enter it with great SEO habits in place and a strategy for continued learning. Continue to give SEO an hour a day, every day, and you'll be able to ride the waves of change with confidence.

Extra Credit and Guilt-Free Slacking

Since you're not a full-time SEO professional, sometimes other work obligations will get in the way, and you'll need to give your campaign a little less attention. Other times, your website's unique problems or your own curiosity will inspire you to dig deeper. In this chapter we'll help you sort it all out by defining a range of reasonable slacking and extra credit behavior.

Chapter Contents
The Slacking Spectrum
The Extra Credit Continuum
Extra Credit Tasks

The Slacking Spectrum

Be honest: Did you flip to this chapter before you even started your SEO campaign? Have you been planning to do the bare minimum from the get-go? If you expected us to disapprove, you're wrong. Let us reassure you:

 Pearl of Wisdom: Any amount of properly executed SEO that you can muster will bring about some positive effect.

And this is especially true if your competitors are doing absolutely nothing in the way of SEO.

Slacking, as we're using the word here, simply means taking an honest look at your time and abilities and determining whether you can put off, or even blow off, a task or a group of similar tasks. Slacking can be the result of a simple judgment call; for example, if a task we assigned in Your SEO Plan doesn't apply to your site, don't do it. Or slacking can be a path you're forced to take due to a lack of time, budget, or personnel.

Take heart: There's really nothing wrong with having a slacker mentality as long as you follow these important do's and don'ts about slacking and SEO:

DON'T beat yourself up. Periodic dips in SEO activity are to be expected for busy people in dynamic organizations. An occasional bout of inattentiveness to your campaign is common. Dropping the ball every once in a while is no reason to abandon your SEO efforts altogether.

DON'T slack if your competitors aren't. If you are in an extremely competitive market, there's probably no easy way to shirk. You will have to work harder on your SEO campaign to see changes for the better. Likewise, if one of your sleepy competitors wakes up to SEO, you'll need to step up your efforts accordingly or suffer the consequences.

DON'T blame it on the budget. Just as you don't need a big SEO budget to be an overachiever, you don't need to slow down on SEO just because you're low on funds. Site edits, link building, landing page A/B testing, and competitive analysis—to name just a few—are tasks that most organizations can do at no extra cost.

DO be realistic. If you anticipate that you *never* will be able to devote an hour a day to your SEO campaign, it's time to think about sharing the load with a coworker or hiring a consultant. (We gave some guidance on hiring SEO help in Chapter 9, "Month Three: It's a Way of Life.")

Ideas for Reducing Your SEO Workload

For many sites, an hour a day pretty much *is* the bare minimum you can get away with for an effective SEO campaign. If you're starting a new SEO campaign, following the plan as written from your Prep Month on through to the end of Week 12 will give your site the best shot at success.

Throughout the plan, we've pointed out tasks that we feel can be dropped without a major impact on your SEO outcome. But if you think you need to trim down your SEO campaign even further, you may be looking for guidance on how to do it.

Some Slacking Is Not Guilt Free

Priorities will vary from organization to organization, but there are a few tasks you should never slack on because they form the foundation of your entire SEO campaign:

- Defining your conversion goals
- Identifying your audience
- Researching your keywords

And there are also certain red flags that you should not ignore because they can cause all of your other efforts to be wasted:

- Problems, such as coding errors, that block the search engines from indexing your landing pages
- Problems, such as broken links, that dump your audience into dead ends instead of delivering them to your site

Here are some ideas for bringing Your SEO Plan in line with your own less-than-perfect reality, whether it's related to your time, your budget, or your team's willingness to help:

Cut out early. Consider going through the Prep Month and stopping after Month One of the plan. Choosing your keywords and getting them onto your site using sound SEO methods is a substantial step forward and may help you realize a positive change.

Cut out PPC activities. This is a no-brainer if you have no money to spend on it. Unlike PPC, organic SEO will continue to deliver improvements long after you've quit devoting time to it.

Cut out organic activities. Cutting organic SEO and focusing only on PPC may be a smart strategy if you are short on labor and have a healthy budget to work with. With

PPC, you can expect quicker success than with organic SEO alone. But proceed with extreme caution: If your site isn't optimized for your target audience, it may not be an effective destination for PPC visitors.

Cut reporting loose. If you seriously don't have the time, consider delegating your SEO status data gathering to someone else in your organization. Yes, this will handicap your ability to analyze and improve your campaign. But asking an administrative assistant to gather numbers for you is better than not tracking at all. After all, if nobody's collecting information about your site's performance, how do you know whether you're wasting what little time you *do* have to spend on SEO?

Do it all, but with a smaller scope. If you're low on time, do your slicing the way the SEO consultants do: by limiting your campaign to fewer conversion goals, audiences, or landing pages. For example, focus on only one product line or one landing page, whittle down your top-priority keywords to just a couple, or focus on only one segment of your potential audience. In this way, you're still working toward increasing your targeted traffic using a holistic approach to SEO.

Be a dedicated dud-dropper. You'll save time if you drop activities that aren't delivering desired results. We'd love to be able to list SEO tasks in order from the best to worst effort-to-results ratios, but these factors vary widely from organization to organization. You will need to track your own results and figure out which SEO tactics are working for you and which are wasting your time. Once you have some data under your belt, feel free to slash and burn.

You may have the big idea to strip down Your SEO Plan to just focus on Google ranks and nothing else. While this is a common sentiment expressed by clients we've come across, it really isn't a reasonable slacking mind-set. There are a couple of reasons you shouldn't act on this kind of Google-centric instinct. For one, achieving good ranks in Google for any meaningful keyphrase requires the opposite of slacking; it's hard work! And second,

 Pearl of Wisdom: Google does not exist in a vacuum.

In fact, a well-rounded approach to SEO is the *only* kind that will improve your website's ranks in Google. You can't really strip out all but the Google-related tasks and have less work to do.

Slacker Stories

Just like the rest of your campaign, your slacking plan will be customized. Here are a few fictional examples of well-constructed "slacker" efforts:

Focusing on PPC Jeanna works at a five-person B2B software development firm. As the only admin staffer, she is responsible for everything from payroll taxes to coffee filters. She had hoped to spend an hour a day on SEO, but other crises are always interfering with her plans. Still, her boss is looking for results. As she learned in Chapter 2, "Customize Your Approach," one of the advantages of a B2B business is a high conversion value. That means that even a small number of conversions can pay off big for her organization. Jeanna convinced her boss to invest in six months of highly targeted PPC. She devoted about one hour per week to managing the campaign and a half day each month to documentation. Who knows? Maybe the new accounts that can be attributed to the PPC campaign can be used to hire Jeanna an assistant!

Focusing on a single goal or audience Alonzo is in Development at a mid-size nonprofit. The organization is optimistic about using search to improve volunteer awareness as well as to increase online donations. However, with limited time and almost no knowledge about the volunteer side of the organization, Alonzo chooses to focus his SEO efforts on online donations first and move on to volunteer awareness later.

Lengthening the process Laura works in Marketing at a medium-size B2C selling school supplies. She took advantage of the traditionally slow spring season to get started on her SEO campaign—the Prep Month and Month One only. She'll be able to see some advances from the basic optimization and continue with the remainder of the plan when time allows.

The Extra Credit Continuum

Extra credit in SEO doesn't require as much soul-searching and premeditation as slacking. Usually extra credit is just a natural extension of what you're already doing with your site. SEO encompasses a wide variety of disciplines and activities, from creative writing to coding. You may just discover one aspect of it that grips you and run with it.

But, if you're extremely gung ho on SEO extra credit, we will wave this yellow flag:

Pearl of Wisdom: Don't go so deep in any one area of SEO that you ignore everything else.

If you're going full bore on the technology side of SEO, make sure it's balanced out with a fully developed approach to optimizing text, too. We've said it before: A holistic approach is best.

And one more thing: Keep your perspective. There is a difference between extra credit and wasting your time. Checking ranks every day, logging daily unique visits (unless you have a short-lived or time-sensitive campaign), and spending all your time trying to decipher Google's algorithm are not worth the effort. Turn your attention instead to more reasonable tasks, like researching new keywords and gleaning new ideas from competitors, or legitimate never-ending tasks like link building.

Extra Credit Tasks

As you went through your Prep Month and Your SEO Plan, we listed several options for extra credit for you to pursue if you've got the time and inclination. Each of these tasks is a spin-off of a task in Your SEO Plan, but even if you haven't completed the original task, you can benefit from the information that follows.

Internal Search Function

In Chapter 6, "Your One-Month Prep: Baseline and Keywords," we mentioned that the internal search on your website can teach you about your site visitors, giving insights into who they are and what they need. If you already have an internal search engine on your website, don't let its data go to waste! Data from your internal search engine can help you determine the following:

What are your site visitors searching for? If you sell shrimp deveiners and your internal search function is logging a lot of searches for "shrimp deveiners," that might be a good thing...or it may not. It's certainly nice that your visitors seem to want your product. But why do they need to search for it in the first place? Why can't they find it by navigating your site? Finding a large number of searches for your top-priority keywords in your internal search means that you need to make this content easier to find.

What's the (key)word on the street? When you were choosing keywords in the Prep Month, we advised you to try to get into the minds of your potential customers. The in-site search engine is a great tool for doing just that. Are they searching for "shrimp de-veiners," "shrimp deveiners," or something unexpected, like "shrimp cleaners"? Keep in mind, though, that this audience, having already decided to visit your site, may not behave the same as your general search engine audience.

Who's coming to your site? If most of your site's internal searches are related to finding a job in your organization or some other activity that has nothing to do with your intended conversion, it may be an indication that a substantial portion of your site visitors are not your target audience.

Are they getting where they need to go? Find the top 10 phrases entered by users of your internal search engine. Then, take each of them for a spin. What results came up? Were they your preferred landing pages or some crusty press releases? Depending on the technology behind your search function, you may be able to improve the results by taking advantage of the features provided by your internal search tool (you may be able to create specially formatted metadata or assign destination pages using an administrative interface).

For example, for your Clearance Products page, you can assign keywords like "discount" or "sale"—even if these words don't appear on the page—and your internal search will then be able to show your Clearance Products page to anyone searching for those terms. Of course, you should never manipulate your internal search results to be irrelevant; you don't want to display your Clearance page when someone is searching for "returns," for example. But it's *your* site, and assigning reasonable synonyms and related concepts to your search function's metadata may be helpful to both your visitors and your conversion goals.

One of the easiest ways to find out all this data, and more, is by using the internal site search capabilities of Google Analytics. If you do this kind of extra-credit analysis, your internal search will be much more than a helpful feature for your visitors...it will also be a marketing tool for *you*!

Webmaster Tools

In Chapters 6 and 7, we talked about some of the benefits of Google Webmaster Tools and Yahoo! Site Explorer (MSN Live Search has a Webmaster Tool, too, currently in beta). These are the search engines' own services, designed to assist website owners and marketers—in other words, everyone reading this book—with getting your site indexed and listed properly.

Here's an up-front caveat: webmaster tools won't directly help with ranks or indexing (there's no "Rank me higher!" button). However, they are marvelous tools for troubleshooting indexing errors and communicating your preferences to the search engines. Here are the features that we think are the most important:

- Indexing and links
- Preferred URL
- XML Sitemaps
- Video Sitemaps

Indexing and Links

Using webmaster tools accounts, you can review basic data about your website, including when your pages were last indexed, what (if any) errors were found, and what feeds or Sitemaps you have submitted. Google's tool is by far the richest; here you can even view PageRank summaries of your site's pages and get your hands on some other cool tools: page analysis, robots.txt info, and a full list of inbound links.

Sign up for webmaster tools at these three URLs:

- Google: www.google.com/webmasters
- Yahoo!: http://siteexplorer.search.yahoo.com/
- MSN Live Search: http://webmaster.live.com/

To access the full repertoire of options on Google, Yahoo!, or MSN, you'll need to prove that you're the site owner (you'll need access to the server to upload a file or edit a home page meta tag). If you're short on time, you can stick with Google, since it offers much more than the other two. Once you're authenticated, here is some of the information about your site that you can find on Google Webmaster Tools:

Site indexing As SEOs, we follow a careful policy of being kind to search engine robots. Google Webmaster Tools will tell if you've done anything to offend the all-important Googlebot. Just log into your Webmaster Tools account and click Diagnostics, then Web Crawl. You'll see if there are any broken links, errors, timeouts, or unreachable URLs. Once you've got a handle on what's wrong, task your team with making fixes.

Inbound links One of the most common questions people ask us is, "Why won't Google show all my inbound links when I perform a link: search?" We won't speculate about Google's motives, but we can tell you how to get Google's full report of inbound links to your website. Log in at www.google.com/webmasters, then click on the Links tab. Voilà! We've seen Google Webmaster Tools report 10 times the inbound links you can see using the link: operator in the main search results.

What can you do with this information? Lots! You can spot-check the links for outdated mentions of your products or company. You can identify complaints or unflattering mentions that point to your website. You can find those friendly bloggers who are talking about you.

One thing you shouldn't do, though, is assume that each of these links is transferring authority to your linked-to pages. Just because Google knows about the link and reports it back to you does not mean that the link has any worth in Google's opinion.

Preferred URL

In Chapter 7 you learned about a common SEO handicap—a canonical problem—that happens when your site is accessible via more than one version of your domain. The most common canonical problem occurs when your site is available at both http://www.yoursite.com and http://yoursite.com (without the "www"). If you have set up 301 server-side redirects from the alternate version(s) to your favorite version as we advised, it's time to tell Google which URL you prefer. This is as simple as logging into your verified Google Webmaster Tools account, clicking Tools and then Set Preferred Domain, and selecting your favorite URL from Google's list. Lest you think that this is a cure-all for your canonical problem, here's the not-so-surprising truth: Google does not promise to abide by your preference.

XML Sitemaps

An XML Sitemap is a specially formatted text file that lists your website's URLs for the search engines. A Sitemap might help a search engine find all of your pages if it would otherwise have a hard time indexing your site, for example, if your site has a very large number of pages, dynamically generated pages, Flash, or Ajax-based navigation. Here are the basics:

Do you need a Sitemap? SEO industry opinions on Sitemaps range from "Every site needs a Sitemap" to "If you need a Sitemap, something's wrong with your site navigation." We tend to agree that a Sitemap shouldn't be necessary for a small or medium-sized website. The majority of these websites should be navigable by search engine spiders without any help. And, since Sitemaps don't speed up indexing or improve ranks, their benefit is hard to identify.

We think that Sitemaps are best used for the exceptional situation: a site that uses in-site search as a primary mode of navigation, or a large and busy site that shuffles links and doesn't always show all its pages in the navigation. And, of course, they're good for the head-of-the-class marketer who wants to be sure they've done absolutely *everything* possible to advance a website's search position.

How to create a Sitemap The simplest Sitemap consists of a text file listing all of your site's URLs. You can supply more information if you wish, such as how often the page is updated and how important each page is to you. Everything you ever wanted to know about the *Sitemap protocol*—that's geek-speak for the rules and instructions for building a Sitemap—can be found at http://sitemaps.org.

Lucky for you, Google, Yahoo!, and MSN all abide by the same Sitemap format, so you can create one Sitemap file and use it for all three search engines. There are numerous free or cheap *Sitemap generators* out there that will help you create your Sitemap file and keep it up-to-date. A hefty list of providers can be found at http://code. google.com/sm_thirdparty.html. You'll want to automate the process if you have a site that adds or changes URLs regularly. If you run a blog, there's a good chance that your blog authoring tool already generates a Sitemap, or that a plug-in is available to do so. Similarly, a Yahoo! store will automatically generate a Sitemap if you enable the option in the management interface.

Sitemap Submittal Next, you need the search engines to notice your Sitemap. There are three ways to do this:

- Our recommended approach: Sign up for a webmaster tools account at each search engine and then submit the Sitemap location from within the interface.

- Can't be bothered to sign up for webmaster tools? List the Sitemap inside your robots.txt file, using the following format: Sitemap: http://www.*example. com/sitemap-file.xml* (where *example.com* and *sitemap-file.xml* represent your domain and file name). In a rare feat of cooperation, all of the major search engines have agreed to *autodiscover* your Sitemap file by looking at the URL you provide in robots.txt.

- Feeling lucky? You can inform search engines of your Sitemap location (and resubmit every time the Sitemap is modified) simply by typing specially formatted URLs into your browser window. This process is called a *Sitemap ping*. Every search engine has a different specification for this process—check yourseoplan.com/seo-sitemaps.html for links.

Using XML Sitemaps *won't* help you rank higher or increase your PageRank, and it doesn't guarantee that your pages will be indexed. But it can certainly give your deep or dynamic pages a fighting chance!

Video Sitemaps

One of the more promising ways to submit videos to Google is with a video Sitemap. Google Video Sitemaps (in beta as of this writing) are an extension of the XML Sitemap protocol discussed in the previous section. They allow a site owner to submit not only the URL where a video is located, but also the title, description, and thumbnail location—bonus information that Google might otherwise struggle to find.

With Video Sitemaps, Google is setting a new course—away from the media RSS feed format that has been accepted for years. But we all know that when Google shows up at a party sporting a new fashion, the whole school will be wearing it the next day. So be sure to include a Google Video Sitemap submittal in your video promotion efforts, and keep an eye out for similar offerings from the other search engines.

Checking Competitors' Directory Presence

In Chapter 6, you researched whether your competitors were sponsoring paid search campaigns. It may also be helpful to know whether your competitors have taken the time to create directory listings. Finding a directory listing, whether paid or unpaid, is an indication of how well your competitors are covering all their SEO bases.

Start by searching Yahoo!'s directory:

- Open your web browser and go to http://dir.yahoo.com. This page allows you to exclude search results other than Yahoo! Directory listings.

- Moving one by one through your Big Five competitors list, search for each competitor's name.

- Since this is such a specific search, there will probably be very few listings. Look for one belonging to your competitor.

- If you don't find your competitor's listing, search for a product or service that they offer. If this search turns up no listings, broaden your search to a general term related to what they offer. If you still don't find your competitor, you can feel comfortable that they probably don't have a listing in this directory.

You can do the same with niche directories that you think are appropriate for your own site. Whether the directory listing is fee based or free is actually not important here. What's important is knowing whether a competitor is aggressive and savvy enough to find a directory and get their site listed.

hCards

Microformats are ways to tag various types of content, such as resumes, events, or geographical coordinates, so that they can be easily understood and classified by computer programs. The hCard microformat is designed for contact information, either individual or corporate. Ever heard of a vCard? This is the same thing, formatted for display on a web page.

Most likely you have some contact information on your website. Let's suppose it looks something like this:

Joe Strongly
Strongly Built Products
123 Mission Way
Dallas, TX 75287
(214) 222-2222

Certainly a search engine with some smarts will be able to look at this text and figure out that it's an address. But with an hCard microformat, you can eliminate guesswork for the robot. Here's how Mr. Strongly's hCard code might look:

```
<div class="vcard">
 <span class="fn">Joe Strongly</span>
 <div class="org">Strongly Built Products</div>
 <div class="adr">
  <div class="street-address">123 Mission Way</div>
```

```
<span class="locality">Dallas</span>,
<span class="region">TX</span>
<span class="postal-code">75287</span>
</div>
<div class="tel">(214) 222-2222</div>
</div>
```

The hCard code will not change how your contact info displays on a web page, but it will make the information a lot more readable by search engines. Google Maps and Yahoo! Local support the hCard format, so if you use it for the contact information on your site, you may end up with a better-looking Google Maps listing. Another perk: Searchers with the right browser add-ons can add your contact from the browser to their Outlook program with a simple click of the mouse.

hCards have their proponents in the SEO industry, but we think the search-related benefits are currently minimal. Still, if you're an early adopter type, you can build yourself an hCard listing with the user-friendly hCard creator at this URL: http://microformats.org/code/hcard/creator.

Task Journal Investigation

In Chapter 8, "Month Two: Establish the Habit," we advised you to spend a day working on items in your Task Journal. If your Task Journal isn't yet filled with dozens of fascinating ruminations, here are some ideas to get you out there and investigating:

- Is there a site that offers an award for your organization's product or service? Can you get your site in the running? Try a search for "[your product] web award" or "[your industry] web award."

- Can you search for your site in a way that causes your meta description tag to show up on the search engine listings? Try searching with your URL only or with text that appears only in links to you but isn't on your site. Is your meta description tag showing up the way you expected? Do you see any funny characters? Did it get cut off earlier than you expected?

- Are you unintentionally spamming the search engines? Search for old pages on your site that are still live and displaying the same content as your new pages. Check to make sure your pages aren't doing something silly and spammy, like displaying text that's the same color as the background.

- One of our favorite mysteries to investigate: Exactly which page on your site does Google think is your "official" page? (You learned about a related topic—canonical URL problems—in the section "Week 2: Site Structure Improvements" in Chapter 7.) Search for your organization's name and check the URL that Google returns for this search. It may be your home page, or it may be an alternate domain, or it may be something else deep within your site. Are you surprised? Dismayed? What's the reason that this URL is displaying? Is it the number of pages linking to this page? Or could it be that your site's internal links are pointing to this URL?

- Do you know how to search like an expert? Try using advanced search operators on your favorite search engine. For example, Yahoo! allows you to build your own search shortcuts. You can define a shortcut so you can type a custom text string into the search box, and Yahoo! will automatically search with the parameters you define. Make your own shortcuts here: http://search.yahoo.com/osc/create. Or try one of the numerous built-in shortcuts listed here: http://tools.search.yahoo.com/newsearch/resources. Are there any that your target audience might be using?

- Are your competitors tracking their conversions using Google Analytics? Peek into their source code and look for the Google Analytics tracking tag. (Just search for the text string "google-analytics" in their code, and you'll see the script.)

- Are there any additional domains that your organization should own? For example, do you own a .org domain name but not the .com? If a searcher had to guess at your site's URL, what do you think it would be? And when is your current domain set to expire? Make sure you don't inadvertently let it run out.

- Howz yore spelleng? Search for misspellings of your product or service and see what comes up.

- Do a little volunteer work for the search engines by helping them clean spam out of their listings. Every major search engine allows you to report spammers; Google's spam reporting tool can be found at www.google.com/contact/spamreport.html.

Optimizing Press Releases

In Chapter 9, "Month Three: It's a Way of Life," we encouraged you to get your organization's press releases online. Follow these guidelines to maximize your press release visibility:

- Include keywords in press release titles and page copy, but don't go so overboard that you sacrifice good writing. There is no magic formula for the perfect keyword density. Find the same balance that you found for your landing page text.

- Be sure to include links to relevant locations on your website. However, since press releases generally will not be edited after they are distributed, pay close attention to choosing URLs that you do not expect to change in time (see the sidebar "Prevent Link Rot" in Chapter 9 for more information on URL file-naming conventions).

- Submit your press releases to free online wire services and consider a fee-based distribution service if your release is particularly newsworthy. PRWeb at www.prweb.com is one of the best-known online distribution services.

- Don't count on newswires alone to distribute your press release. Find on-topic publications, blogs, or journalists and send them a brief, personalized e-mail including a link to your press release.

- Feed, feed, feed—make an RSS or Atom feed for your press releases. This will help them get listed in news services and blog search engines. To simplify this process, you can use a blog creation tool to post your press releases.

Many in the media use search engines to find information on the Web. If you spend the time to optimize and distribute your press releases, you're making great strides in improving your search engine visibility and media presence.

Robots Visiting Your Site

In Chapter 9, we discussed search engine indexing of your landing pages. With a little sleuthing, you can determine which search engine robots have visited your site and when.

To scope out robot visits to your site, do the following:

- First, find the name of the robot that you are interested in monitoring. Table 10.1 lists the robot identifiers for Ask, Google, MSN, and Yahoo!, but be prepared for some variations.

▶ **Table 10.1** Some Common Search Engine Robots

Search Engine	Robot Name
Ask	Teoma
Google	Googlebot
MSN	MSNBot
Yahoo!	Slurp

- Then, review your website analytics program. Look for a section called "User Agents," "Robots," or "Browsers" (servers interpret a search engine robot as a type of browser). Here's a bit of a bummer: Tag-based analytics programs such as Google Analytics typically won't track robot visits.

- Depending on the sophistication of your analytics program, you may be able to specify a date range and view robot visits. You might even be able to see exactly which pages within your site were visited.

If this all feels a bit too tedious, you may wish to look into software that provides simple yet detailed reports on robot visits. One such program is Robot Manager, available here: www.websitemanagementtools.com.

Whether you've followed Your SEO Plan to a T, had to make some tough choices to cut out some tasks, or have earned yourself an A for extra-credit effort, be proud of yourself! You're well on your way to becoming an SEO pro!

Appendix

A

In this appendix, you'll see screen shots of the worksheets that are referenced throughout the book. You can download these documents from the Search Engine Optimization: An Hour a Day *companion website,* www.yourseoplan.com.

From Chapter 1, "Clarify Your Goals," you'll recall the Goals Worksheet, named GoalsWorksheet.doc, a Word document where you can record the specific goals of your organization. This worksheet will help you lay the foundation for your entire SEO campaign.

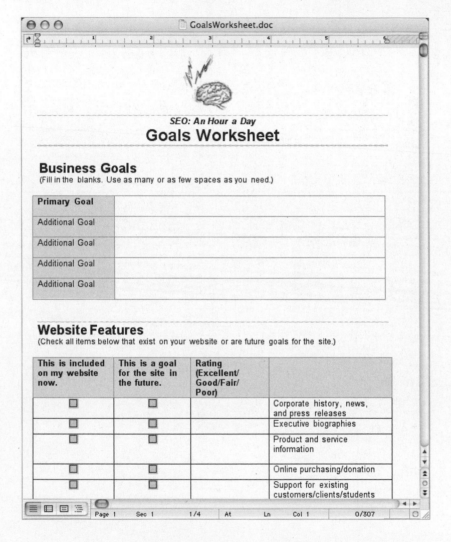

In Chapter 6, "Your One-Month Prep: Baseline and Keywords," we introduced several worksheets to help you organize Your SEO Plan. First off, there's the Keywords Worksheet (KeywordsWorksheet.xls), an Excel spreadsheet where you can list possible target keywords for your website along with important measures that will help you finalize your top picks.

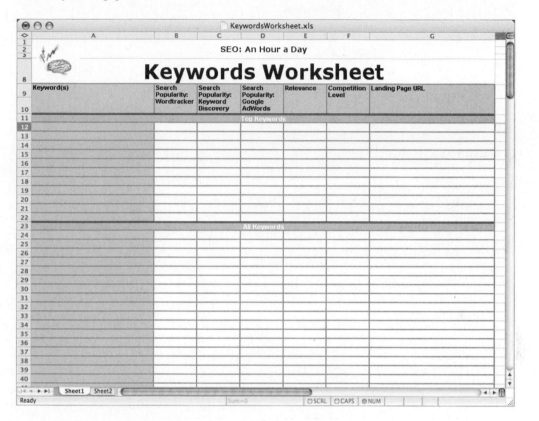

Next, the Site Assessment Worksheet (SiteAssessmentWorksheet.doc) provides a checklist of factors to quickly assess the current optimization level of your website's landing pages, and a place to record any conversion data you've been collecting.

SEO: An Hour a Day
Site Assessment Worksheet

Home Page URL:

Yes/No	
	This page has a unique HTML page title.
	The HTML page title contains my target keywords.
	This page contains 200 or more words of HTML text.
	HTML text on this page contains my exact target keywords.
	This page can be reached from the home page of the site by following HTML text links (not pull-downs, login screens, or pop-up windows).
	The HTML text links from other pages on my site to this page contain my target keywords.

Landing Page URL:

Yes/No	
	This page has a unique HTML page title.
	The HTML page title contains my target keywords.
	This page contains 200 or more words of HTML text.
	HTML text on this page contains my exact target keywords.
	This page can be reached from the home page of the site by following HTML text links (not pull-downs, login screens, or pop-up windows).
	The HTML text links from other pages on my site to this page contain my target keywords.

Landing Page URL:

Yes/No	
	This page has a unique HTML page title.
	The HTML page title contains my target keywords.
	This page contains 200 or more words of HTML text.
	HTML text on this page contains my exact target keywords.

The Rank Tracking Worksheet (RankTrackingWorksheet.xls) is an Excel spreadsheet that you can use to document your website rank and indexing status, both key indicators of your site's search engine visibility.

The Task Journal Worksheet (TaskJournal.doc) is a simple template that allows you to stay focused on Your SEO Plan by giving you a place to record outstanding questions, thoughts, and issues that come up as you work. Rather than constantly going off on tangents, you will revisit your Task Journal items when time allows.

You can use the Competition Worksheet (CompetitionWorksheet.xls) to document the basic site optimization and search engine presence of your major competitors.

Finally, the SEO Growth Worksheet (SEOGrowth.doc) helps you assess your website's potential—an important step on the way to determining reasonable expectations for your SEO campaign.

SEO: An Hour a Day
SEO Growth Worksheet

SEO Room to Grow:	
Yes/No	
	Current search engine status is poor.
	Current optimization level is poor.
	I have compiled a list of well-matched, popular keywords.
	My SEO team is enthusiastic about making needed changes.
	I anticipate that it will be easy to make text changes to my website.
	I have the appropriate personnel available.
	I have the buy-in from the powers-that-be in my organization.
	I have a budget for paid search.
	My website faces a low level of competition.
	I have discovered untapped markets or SEO opportunities.
	My site is "buzzworthy" or my organization's activities are newsworthy.
Campaign Goals	

Page 1   Sec 1   1/1   At   Ln   Col   0/107   ◯REC

In Chapter 7, "Month One: Kick It into Gear," you started Your SEO Plan in earnest with basic site optimization and link building. Two worksheets help with these efforts: First, the Site Optimization Worksheet (SiteOptimizationWorksheet.doc) provides a template for detailing the edits to be made on your website.

The Link Tracking Worksheet (LinkTrackingWorksheet.xls) is an Excel spreadsheet where you can document your ongoing link-building communications. Keeping this information organized will help you keep track of gains made and avoid embarrassing faux pas, such as resending a link request after it's already been accepted.

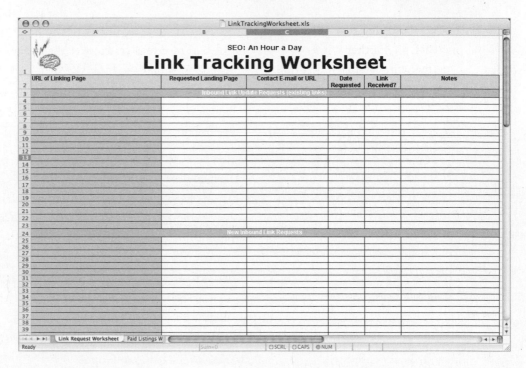

Glossary

301 redirect A server setting that redirects traffic from one URL to another while sending a 301, or "permanent," status code to the requesting client. Also called permanent redirect. See also *client*.

404 error The error returned by a web server when a requested file cannot be found. Also called File Not Found error.

A/B split A method of comparing the performance of two sponsored listings, landing pages, or other online content. Also called A/B testing.

A/B testing See *A/B split*.

acquisition source See *traffic source*.

Ajax Short for Asynchronous JavaScript and XML, a scripting technique that allows web applications to interact with the user and render changes to a web page, without reloading the page. With Ajax, the user may have an experience that feels like visiting several different pages, while the page URL remains the same throughout.

algoholic A person who obsessively follows search engine algorithm changes.

algorithm Any step-by-step procedure for solving a problem. In SEO, a search engine algorithm is the formula that search engines use to determine the ranking of websites on their results pages.

ALT tag An attribute included in the source code of an image to define alternative text for site visitors who cannot or do not wish to view graphics. The ALT tag may also be

displayed while an image is loading or when a user's mouse is rolled over the image. Also called ALT text or IMG ALT tag.

anchor text HTML text that links to another location on the Web. Also called linked text or linking text.

Atom A web feed format.

authority page A web page that search engines recognize as having an outstanding level of trust compared to other websites in a topical community. Inbound links are a significant contributor to a page's authority.

autodiscovery The process of a search engine or web browser software automatically finding an RSS or XML feed by following a link provided in a special tag on a web page.

backlinks See *inbound links*.

banned Removed from a search engine's index.

bid In pay-per-click advertising, the amount that an advertiser offers to pay when a visitor clicks on an ad.

black hat An SEO methodology that includes techniques not in compliance with the search engines' guidelines for webmasters. Also used to describe a person who engages in black hat techniques.

blog Shorthand for *weblog*, a regularly updated, journal-style web page that is generally presented in reverse chronological order (most recent entries at the top) and allows readers to post comments. Also used as a verb: *to blog*, meaning to write in a blog.

blogger A person who blogs.

blogosphere The entire community of blogs and bloggers.

bookmark search sites See *social bookmarking*.

bounce In web analytics, a site visitor who enters and exits on the same page, viewing a total of one page on the website. Depending on the analytics software, a bounce may also be defined as a visit lasting a very short amount of time, such as 10 seconds or less.

broad matching A pay-per-click keyword matching option in which an advertisement is displayed for all search queries that include a given keyword or phrase—in any order, with or without additional words. Variants, synonyms, and plural forms are generally also included in broad matching.

canonical URL The preferred, or primary, form of a URL. Many websites are displayed using more than one URL format, for example, http://www.yoursite.com and http://yoursite.com, and it can be difficult for search engines to determine which is the canonical form.

Cascading Style Sheets (CSS) A website coding method that allows developers to control the style (font, color, background, and more) and placement of content, often in files that remain separate from the content itself.

client A program or computer that requests information from another computer over a network. For example, when a web browser such as Internet Explorer requests a web page from a web server, that browser is the client in the client-server relationship.

client-side tracking A web analytics technique that includes adding small scripts or images to web pages and monitoring user activity via a third-party server. Also called on-demand, tag-based, or hosted tracking.

cloaking A deceptive technique of showing different content to search engine robots than would be seen by visitors accessing a web page via a standard browser. Also called IP delivery.

collaborative tagging A process that allows many people to assign their own keyword labels, called tags, to publicly available content, and to share these tags with others. See also *social bookmarking*.

comment spam See *spam comment*.

consumer-generated media (CGM) Online information, such as feedback, comments, and discussion threads, created by consumers and displayed in designated areas on an organization's website.

content management system (CMS) Software that allows site developers to add content to a website without the need to use sophisticated code.

contextual advertising Pay-per-click listings that appear on websites other than search engines. Such listings can be matched to the content of individual web pages through an automated matching algorithm, or the ad placement can be specified by the advertiser. Also called contextual placement.

contextual placement See *contextual advertising*.

conversion funnel A desired conversion path defined by a marketer or website owner. The conversion funnel is generally a linear, step-by-step process leading directly from site entry to conversion. It is conceptualized as a funnel shape because some users will depart from the path, leaving fewer users at the end than were at the beginning, while others will be "funneled" into completing a transaction. See also *conversion path* and *scenario*.

conversion (offline) An offline action taken by a website visitor that accomplishes the site owner's intended goal. Examples include telephone-based purchases and purchases made at brick-and-mortar locations.

conversion (online) An online action taken by a website visitor that accomplishes the site owner's goal. Examples include online purchases, downloads, and specific page views within a website.

conversion path The web pages that a site visitor passes through between entering a website and completing a conversion. See also *conversion funnel*.

conversion tracking The process of monitoring and measuring conversions.

cookie A piece of text placed on a user's hard drive by a website. The information it contains can be accessed by the site that originally placed the cookie but generally not by other sites.

crawl See *index*.

dayparting In online advertising, the distribution of an ad campaign so that it displays ads during specific segments of a day or week.

directory A categorized, descriptive list of links to web pages, usually created and maintained by human editors.

doorway page A web page, usually outside the parent website's navigational structure, designed to serve primarily as a destination for search engine traffic and immediately redirect that traffic to pages within the parent website. This term is generally applied to spammy pages that are used strictly for search engine traffic. See also *landing page*.

duplicate content A web page URL containing content that is identical or nearly identical to another page. Search engines try not to display duplicate content in search results, and may filter out these pages.

dynamic keyword insertion Automatic placement of keywords into pay-per-click ads to match the keywords entered by a search engine user. For example, the same ad may display the title "Save 30% on dog food" or the title "Save 30% on cat food," depending on whether the searcher used the query "dog food" or "cat food."

elevator speech Marketing slang for a brief but informative overview that one gives about oneself or one's business. So called because all of the important points should be delivered in approximately the duration of a 30-second elevator ride.

entry page See *landing page*.

eyeballs Slang for visitors to a web page.

exact matching A pay-per-click keyword matching option in which an advertisement is displayed only for search queries that match the exact order and format of a sponsored keyword or phrase. See also *broad matching* and *negative matching*.

exit page The last page viewed by a website user during a particular visit.

feed See *web feed*.

flamed Treated with extreme derision in comments or forum postings.

geotargeting A service that is offered by pay-per-click services and allows advertisers to specify the geographic region(s) for their ads to run.

ghost bloggers Persons who are paid to write blog postings, typically without attribution, on behalf of another person or company.

global navigation A set of links that are displayed on every page of a website, typically linking to the top priority pages of the site.

Googlebombing See *link bombing*.

graphical text Text that is contained in image files such as JPEGs or GIFs. This text generally cannot be read by search engines.

hit A communication made from a web browser to a website server requesting an element of a web page. When a web page is viewed, each item (such as a graphics or media file) on the page will log one hit to the server.

hosted tracking See *client-side tracking*.

hot linking On a website, displaying media content, such as images or video, that is hosted on the content owner's server rather than one's own server. Typically this is done without permission of the content owner, and is considered bandwidth and copyright theft.

HTML page title Code contained in an HTML document that briefly describes its contents. This text is usually displayed in a web browser's title window. In search engine results, the HTML page title is displayed as the first line of a listing. Also called the HTML title tag.

impression In online advertising, a single act of viewing a web page or advertisement.

inbound links Links pointing to a website from other sites. Also called backlinks and inlinks.

index A search engine's database of web page content. Also, the act by a search engine robot of following website links and gathering content. When a web page is included in a search engine's database, it is said to be indexed. Used as a synonym for *spider* and *crawl*.

invisible text Text on a website that is not visible to a site visitor using a standard browser.

key performance indicators A short list of metrics that indicate the level of a website's success, and that can be compared over time.

keyword A word or phrase describing an organization's product or service or other key content on its website. A word or phrase entered as a query in a search engine. Also called keyterm, keyphrase, and keyword phrase.

keyword density The number of times a keyword or phrase appears on a web page divided by the total number of words on the page. Usually expressed as a percentage.

keyword exclusion See *negative match*.

landing page A web page that is focused on a key audience or topic and that serves as a destination for search engine traffic. In this book, landing pages are the focus of optimization efforts. Also called entry page.

link bombing A coordinated effort to manipulate search engine results for a certain search query by linking to a website using specific keywords in the linking text. Also called Googlebombing.

link equity A search engine's measure of the value of a web page based on the quality and quantity of inbound links to the page. Much like a currency, link equity is passed between web pages through links. Also called link juice.

link farm A website that contains links to other websites, created without an editorial review, often using an automated form. Links from these types of sites are low quality and not likely to contribute to search engine ranks.

link juice See *link equity*.

link rot The gradual increase over time in the number of broken links on the Web or on an individual website. Also called linkrot.

link validator Software that checks the working status of links within a website.

linkability A web page's perceived potential for receiving inbound links.

linkbait Web content that has high linkability or that is specifically created to draw inbound links.

long tail Search queries that are significantly longer, more focused, and less frequently used by searchers than average search terms. Short, more generalized, and more popular search queries are sometimes referred to as "short head" in comparison. See also *short head*.

masked domain A website that redirects site visitors but hides the fact that they have been redirected by keeping the original domain name in the browser address bar. Also called pointer domain.

media RSS (MRSS) An RSS feed that lists media files along with specially formatted information about those files, including title, description, thumbnail location, author, and text transcript.

metadata Specially formatted information that describes characteristics of a document, such as its author, file structure, or keywords. Metadata can be used by search engines to help determine a web page's relevance and rank.

meta description tag Metadata contained in an HTML document that describes the content of a web page. Search engines may display the contents of this tag in their search results.

meta keywords tag Metadata contained in an HTML document that lists keywords related to the content of a web page. Search engines may use this tag to determine relevance.

meta search engines Search sites that display combined results from several search engines.

meta tag Code contained in an HTML document that holds metadata. See also *meta description tag* and *meta keywords tag*.

metrics Measurements or methods of evaluation.

mobile search Web search sites or tools designed to be accessed with mobile devices such as cell phones and PDAs.

multivariate testing A process of displaying several different variations of content elements on a web page and testing—or predicting—the performance of the resulting combinations.

natural SEO See *organic SEO*.

negative match A pay-per-click keyword matching option that prevents a sponsored ad from displaying if a particular keyword is used by a searcher. For example, a percussion website may want its ad to display for the term "drum" but not "eardrum." In this case, "ear" could be designated as a negative match. Also called keyword exclusion.

niche directories Directories that provide links to sites that focus on a similar theme or that relate to the same industry.

offline marketing Methods of marketing that do not involve the Internet. Examples include direct mail, billboards, and print advertising. Also called traditional advertising.

offline sales Sales that occur in person or over the phone.

off-page factors Optimization factors that are not contained in an organization's own web pages. Off-page factors, such as the number and quality of inbound links, cannot be directly edited by website owners and must be influenced indirectly.

on-demand tracking See *client-side tracking*.

one-way link An inbound link to a site, where the receiving site does not link back to the linking site. See also *reciprocal link*.

on-page factors Optimization factors that are contained on an organization's own web pages. On-page factors, such as HTML page title and text content, can be directly edited by website owners.

online marketing Methods of marketing that utilize the Internet. Examples include search engine optimization, direct e-mails, and banner advertising.

organic SEO Optimization efforts for areas of search that do not require payment. Also called natural SEO.

page authority See *link equity*.

PageRank Google's proprietary measurement of the importance of a web page. PageRank values vary from 0 to 10, with 10 being the highest level of importance. Often abbreviated as PR.

page view The group of hits that together make up a single viewing of a web page.

paid inclusion A service offered by some search engines that allows site owners to submit a list of URLs for the search engine to index and recrawl on a frequent basis. See also *trusted feed*.

paid link Links that are created on a seller's site, pointing to the purchaser's site, in order to improve search engine ranks for the purchaser. Also called text-link advertisement.

paid listing An advertisement displayed on a search engine or directory in response to a search query entered by a user. Fees for advertisers are typically charged on a pay-per-click basis.

paid search Search marketing efforts, such as pay-per-click or contextual advertising, that are typically brokered through a search engine and require money in exchange for ad views or click-throughs. The opposite of *Organic SEO*.

participation marketing Promoting oneself or one's organization through website participation, such as posting in forums or commenting on other people's blogs.

path to conversion See *conversion path*.

pay-per-call Similar to pay-per-click, this is a form of advertisement in which the advertiser sponsors keywords and runs ads; however, the ad displays a toll-free phone number rather than a website link, and the advertiser pays a fee to the search engine each time a listing results in a phone call.

pay-per-click (PPC) A form of advertisement in which an advertiser designates the specific keywords for which its listings will appear in the search results. The advertiser pays a fee to the search engine each time the listing is clicked. A subset of *paid search*.

personalized search Search results that vary based on the searcher's profile and past behavior.

ping In programmer's lingo, a way to check the validity of a link or connection between two computers by sending a small packet of data and waiting for a reply. In the blogosphere, a communication between a blog and a ping server indicating that the blog has been updated. In more general parlance, any type of contact between two parties that checks on the status of the communication, as in, "She hasn't RSVP'd yet. I'll ping her tomorrow."

ping server A service that receives notification (a ping) from a blog every time the blog is updated. Usually the blog owner sets up this communication with a ping server as a means of gaining additional distribution.

ping spam The practice of using pings to misrepresent content that is not genuine blog content or has not actually been recently updated.

pointer domain See *masked domain*.

reciprocal link An inbound link to a site, where the receiving site also links back to the linking site. Reciprocal links can occur naturally, but they are also often arranged based on mutual agreement. In the search engines' opinion, these links are likely to be less valuable than one-way links. See also *one-way links*.

robot Software used by search engines to travel the Web and send content from web pages back to the search engine for indexing. Also called spider and crawler.

robots.txt A text file containing code that can exclude certain pages or folders from being indexed in the search engines. It can also be used to block access for a particular robot. The robots.txt file must be located in the root directory of the website or the root of a subdomain.

root directory The top directory within the file structure of a website; it contains all other directories. Generally represented by a slash (/) after the domain name.

RSS Abbreviated form of Really Simple Syndication, a web feed format. It can stand for other terms as well, such as Rich Site Summary and RDF Site Summary.

scraping An automated technique of copying content from one website to another. Often used as a method of stealing content.

Search Engine Marketing (SEM) See *Search Marketing*. The term *SEM* may also refer only to paid search marketing efforts.

Search Engine Optimization (SEO) See *Search Marketing*. The term *SEO* may also refer only to organic SEO.

search engine optimizer (SEO) A person who performs search engine optimization.

Search Marketing A wide variety of tasks intended to improve a website's ranking and listing quality among both paid and unpaid results on search engines, with the ultimate goal of increasing targeted traffic to the website and achieving more conversions. Also called Search Engine Marketing (SEM), Search Engine Optimization (SEO), and SEO/SEM.

search popularity The frequency with which a keyword is used as a query on search engines.

search query The keywords entered into a search engine by users who are performing a search.

SERP Abbreviation for Search Engine Results Page.

server-side tracking A web analytics technique that includes setting up software directly on the server that hosts the website being tracked.

short head Search queries that are short, generalized, and frequently used by searchers. Longer, more focused, and less frequently used terms are sometimes referred to as "long tail" in comparison. See also *long tail*.

site map generator Software that automatically crawls a website and creates an XML Sitemap.

Sitemap ping A message that is sent to a search engine to indicate that an XML Sitemap has changed. See also *ping*, *ping spam*.

Sitemap protocol Documentation that defines the format, content, and usage for XML Sitemaps.

snippet Strings of text taken from a web page and combined for use as a summary or description of the page's content.

social bookmarking The use of shared lists of Internet bookmarks. Social bookmarking sites allow registered users to save and share bookmarks and classify them with user-defined keywords, called tags. See also *collaborative tagging*.

social networking In Internet terminology, creating person-to-person connections through participation in a website that facilitates social connections. Examples include dating sites, personal profile sites, and social bookmarking sites.

social search Any system that uses community-sourced information to determine search results.

source code In SEO, the HTML text and tags that define a web page.

spam Any of a wide variety of deceptive or abusive online practices, including sending unsolicited advertisements, misrepresenting a website to search engines, and posting nonsensical comments to blogs in an attempt to increase the visibility of a website. Can be a noun or verb (*to spam*).

spam comment A blog or forum comment that contains gibberish or irrelevant content and is intended only to promote the website of the person posting the comment.

spam weblog See *splog*.

spider See *robot*. May also be used as a verb, "to spider," in which case it is synonymous with "to index."

spider emulator Software that attempts to reproduce the way a search engine spider would see a web page. Also called spider simulator.

splog Shorthand for *spam blog*. A blog containing stolen or nonsense content, which exists only to promote affiliate sites or get page views for advertising.

sponsored listing See *paid listing*.

stemming Combining variant forms of a word for one stem, or root, word. For example, *listen*, *listens*, and *listening* all share the same stem word.

stub pages A web page that contains only a page heading and minimal, if any, content, but that may receive additional content over time. Often, stub pages are generated on dynamic sites. An example is a directory site with a category page containing no listings.

Supplemental Index In Google's terminology, a secondary database that was used to store less-desirable or unproven pages in Google's index. Google's Supplemental Index was eliminated in late 2007.

tag In social search, a label or category that a user assigns to a web page, often as a category for organizing bookmarks.

tag-based tracking See *client-side tracking*.

topical community A group of websites that share a common subject matter. Also called topical neighborhood.

traffic source In web analytics, the originator of a website visit. Often a search engine, referring website, or e-mail link. Also called acquisition source.

trusted feed A service offered by some search engines that allows website owners to specify a list of pages to be indexed. This is particularly helpful for websites that include content that would otherwise be hidden from search engines. Usually a paid service, trusted feed does not guarantee an improvement in ranks. See also *paid inclusion*.

unique visitors The number of different individuals who visited a website one or more times during a given period. This measure is based on available—but often incomplete—information. For example, two visits by the same person using two different computers may be logged as two unique visitors, while two different people using the same computer may be logged as a single unique visitor.

usability The elements of a website's design and copywriting that affect a site visitor's ease of use and navigation.

user-generated content (UGC) Content on a website, such as blog comments, consumer product reviews, and forum postings, that is created by the website users.

vertical search The conceptual grouping of search engine results into separate categories based on type of result or subject matter. Video, image, news, and local are examples of vertical search categories.

visible text Text on a website that is visible to a site visitor using a standard browser.

web analytics The measurement and analysis of online activity, especially page visits, conversions, and search queries used to find individual pages. See also *metrics*.

web feed A file that is created by a website owner and is intended to be retrieved and displayed by other websites. Generally includes summary information and a link to the primary content page. Web feeds are most often used for blog and news content. See also *web syndication*.

weblog See *blog*.

web log analyzer A software program that parses raw server log data and presents it in a more easy-to-read format along with filtering and sorting capabilities. Also called log file analysis software.

web syndication The practice of making content available to other sites through web feeds. Generally, a title and summary are displayed on the syndicating site with a link to the primary content page.

white hat An SEO methodology that includes only techniques that fall within the search engines' webmaster guidelines. Also used to describe a person who engages in white hat techniques.

widget Applications, such as news headlines or embedded media players, created for distribution across the Web and reuse on other websites. Usually distributed for free, widgets often serve as marketing tools by displaying the branding of the website that provided the widget.

XML Sitemap An XML file that lists URLs for a website along with additional information about each page (when it was last modified, how often it changes, and its relative importance on the site). An XML Sitemap can be submitted to search engines to help them crawl a website.

Index

Note to the Reader: Throughout this index **boldfaced** page numbers indicate primary discussions of a topic. *Italicized* page numbers indicate illustrations.

Make an impact with just An Hour a Day.

You'll be amazed at what you can do to enhance your online marketing efforts in just an hour a day with the expert advice and do-it-yourself techniques in our popular *An Hour a Day* guides. These practical books dispel common myths, help you avoid errors, and break down intimidating topics into approachable, step-by-step tasks.

978-0-470-13065-0
Available Now

978-0-470-34402-6
Available October 2008

SYBEX
An Imprint of WILEY

Available at sybex.com and wherever books are sold.